'A brilliant book that exposes the full horror and savagery of England's answer to Nero'

Frank McLynn, *Daily Express*

'Geoffrey Moorhouse offers us a new, vivid, and colourful account... This is history, not melodrama, with characters rather than heroes and villains. Moorhouse... tells a compelling story of conflicting interests and loyalties, of errors of judgment and messy compromises. He captures precisely the uncomfortable position of the gentry... Geoffrey Moorhouse has retrieved some of the voices of the Pilgrims from the interrogations and confessions which followed the collapse of their movement. In doing so, he has done us and them a service, showing that the history of the losers can be as fascinating as the history of the winners'

Richard Rex, *Sunday Telegraph*

'What Moorhouse makes clear in this thrilling piece of narrative history is just how close the revolt came to success' *Sunday Times*

'Geoffrey Moorhouse has written an engaging retelling of these momentous events, the great strength of which is its loving familiarity with the landscape and history of northern England... many people will enjoy and profit from this stylishly written and intelligent book'

Diarmaid McCulloch, *Guardian*

'... a rebellion known as the Pilgrimage of Grace, which has been superbly reconstructed by Geoffrey Moorhouse'

Andrew Roberts, *Evening Standard*

'Geoffrey Moorhouse restores both the drama and the personalities to a remarkable story' J. P. D. Cooper, *TLS*

'This book is a rare achievement. It manages to combine a scholarly appreciation of an immensely complex historical event with a passionate understanding which breathes new life into the past … It is quite clear that the author has been deeply touched by writing about this story. I defy the reader not to be equally moved'

Lucy Wooding, *The Tablet*

'Moorhouse has made a thorough study of the story … he presents a convincing picture. One senses from his narrative the deep anger which inspired so hazardous a defiance of royal authority, and the mob fury which sustained it … It is a tale of "old, unhappy, far-off things/And battles long ago", and Geoffrey Moorhouse tells it well'

J. W. M. Thompson, *Literary Review*

Geoffrey Moorhouse is 'one of the best writers of our time' (Byron Rogers, *The Times*), 'a brilliant historian' (Dirk Bogarde, *Daily Telegraph*) and 'a writer whose gifts are beyond category' (Jan Morris, *Independent on Sunday*). His *To the Frontier* (available in Phoenix paperback) won the Thomas Cook Award for the best travel book of the year in 1984. He is a Fellow of the Royal Society of Literature and for many years his home has been a hill village in North Yorkshire.

By Geoffrey Moorhouse

HISTORIES
The Missionaries
India Britannica
Hell's Foundations: a town, its myths and Gallipoli
The Pilgrimage of Grace:
The rebellion that shook Henry VIII's throne

JOURNEYS
The Other England
The Fearful Void
To the Frontier
Apples in the Snow
OM: an Indian Pilgrimage

PLACES
Calcutta
Imperial City: the rise and rise of New York
Sydney

SOCIETIES
Against All Reason
The Diplomats

NOVELS
The Boat and the Town
Sun Dancing

SPORTING PRINTS
The Best-loved Game
At the George

The Pilgrimage of Grace

The rebellion that shook Henry VIII's throne

GEOFFREY MOORHOUSE

PHOENIX

A PHOENIX PAPERBACK

First published in Great Britain in 2002
by Weidenfeld & Nicolson
This paperback edition published in 2003
by Phoenix,
an imprint of Orion Books Ltd,
Orion House, 5 Upper St Martin's Lane,
London WC2H 9EA

A CIP catalogue record for this book
is available from the British Library.

ISBN 1 84212 666 0

Typeset by Selwood Systems, Midsomer Norton

Printed and bound in Great Britain by
Clays Ltd, St Ives plc

In Memory of
JOHN ROSSELLI
Scholar and Writer
1927–2001

'Ye shall not enter into this our Pilgrimage of Grace for the Commonwealth, but only for the love that ye do bear unto Almighty God...'

The Oath of the Honourable Men, composed by Robert Aske

CONTENTS

ILLUSTRATIONS

The author and the publishers offer their thanks to the following for their kind permission to reproduce images:

1 Richard Whittern
2 The National Portrait Gallery, London
3 The Royal Collection (©2002, Her Majesty Queen Elizabeth II)
4 Historic Royal Palaces (Crown copyright)
5 The Baroness Herries
6 Wakefield Museums and Arts
7 Harris Museum and Art Gallery, Preston

All other photographs were taken by the author.

MAPS
(by John Gilkes)

FOREWORD

It was the great Barbara Tuchman who pointed out the capital difficulties of writing about the Middle Ages; and, although the purists insist that English medieval history ended in 1485, the same problems continue to occur in studies of the Tudor period, though maybe not as acutely as in earlier times. The chronology is very hard to pin down; contradictory facts are perpetually turning up in the sources; and there are frequent and frustrating gaps in the available information. The historian therefore needs to navigate with more than usual care from one piece of available evidence to another, needs to bear in mind that some of it may be unreliable and needs to employ a certain amount of informed guesswork, rather more than any scholar is really comfortable with. All this applies to a description of the great rebellion that broke out in October 1536 and threatened Henry VIII's throne – which is what this book is about – as much as to any other account of the six-teenth century. The uncertainties are made very obvious in my text by the recurrence of phrases such as 'it seems likely' or 'most probably' or 'perhaps', which go some distance beyond normally acceptable levels of doubt; but they are unavoidable. When no reason is given in any of the sources for Robert Aske's reluctance to take part in the negotiations with the Duke of Norfolk at Doncaster, though he was the chief captain of the rebel army and was with it at the time, one is left with no alternative but the use of imagination, while making it perfectly clear that nothing more substantial is on offer there.

Moreover, what we know about the Pilgrimage of Grace to a

large extent depends on documents which were screened by royal record keepers before they reached us. Many of these are the alleged testimonies of men who were being questioned on suspicion of treason and who may quite naturally have told stories that put them in the best possible light but were not strictly accurate accounts of their activities. It is also possible that officials doctored evidence that was passed on to the higher authority, or left out those parts of it which were deemed unacceptable. One senses that this was not a common occurrence, but the possibility must certainly be taken into consideration. It is, after all, held to be true that the history of conflict has always been written by the winners; which in this context means by Henry VIII and those most anxious to serve him loyally.

Some of the difficulties are more irritating than others. More than once I should have liked to check something in a parish register, but was unable to do so because nobody was obliged to keep such records until Thomas Cromwell ordered it to be done everywhere in 1538. Other impediments are trifling: the spelling of proper nouns, for example, which can vary from one document to another, depending on who has written it down; and in such cases one can do no better than choose the version that rings most true, that is most easily recognised by the reader, and be consistent thereafter. I have applied a similar criterion to my quotations from sixteenth-century sources, in the interests of intelligibility. The original text of the letter from the Lincolnshire rebels, begging the King's pardon, pleads that 'the comon voce and fame was that all the Jewells and goods of the Churches of the countrey shuld be taken from them and brought to your gracez councell and also that your seid lovyng and faithful subgets shulde be put of newe to enhaunsements and other importunate charges [*sic*]'. I have rendered this as 'the common voice and fame was that all the jewels and goods of the churches of the country should be taken from them and brought to your grace's Council, and also that your said loving and faithful subjects should be put off (i.e. excused) new enhancements and other importunate charges'. I don't believe that any important principle has been violated by this transliteration.

The same sort of judgement is required in the case of more serious textual contradictions, which are not at all uncommon in the sources. Thus, Henry's instruction to Norfolk on 22 February 1537, that he must vigorously punish insurgent monks, reads in the standard transcript of the King's official papers as follows: 'Finally, as these troubles have been promoted by the monks and canons of those parts, at your repair to Salleye, Hexam, Newminster, Leonarde Coste, St Agathe, and such other places as have made resistance since the appointment at Doncaster, you shall without pity or circumstance, now that our banner is displayed, cause the monks to be tied up without further delay or ceremony [sic]'. In the archival notes made a hundred years after the rebellion by Thomas Master, amanuensis of the seventeenth-century historian Lord Herbert, this becomes an injunction 'that all Religious persons, that (since the Appointment of Doncaster) have by any force kept theyr Houses (viz at Salley, Haxham etc) be while the Baner is displayed, hanged up because they have bin the Originall of these Comotions [sic]'. In a third version of Henry's order, also derived from the original state archives, the lengthier quotation above is repeated, but it ends differently – 'cause all the monks and chanons that be in any wise faultie to be tyed up without further delaye or ceremony to the terreble exemple of others [sic]'. The author has to make up his mind which of these to choose, bearing in mind that Henry, in fact, wanted the monks executed; which is not the meaning of 'tied up' to the modern ear.

The only way to confirm which of the above examples accurately copied Henry's order to the Duke of Norfolk would be to examine original documents in the Public Record Office but these, alas, are no longer available and their contents can only be studied on microfilm, which in some cases has made them scarcely legible. I confess that I gave up after a brief attempt to decipher some of this material and was subsequently much heartened to read one of the greatest authorities on the Pilgrimage of Grace, Dr Michael Bush, admit in the preface to a book on the post-pardon revolts of 1537 that – such are the problems these transcriptions have created for Tudor scholars – 'if this project had started under the new regime, it would have been quickly abandoned as an impossible task'. Instead of depending on the PRO, therefore, I have relied for much of the basic material on *Letters & Papers, Foreign & Domestic, of the Reign of Henry VIII*, which were published in twenty-one hefty volumes – forty books if you count the numerous two parts of separate volumes – between 1864 and 1932 under the direction of three different editors. The ones that most concerned me were the responsibility of a Scottish historian, James Gairdner, sometime Assistant Keeper of the Public Records. *Letters & Papers* were officially commissioned by the Master of the Rolls and are said to include about 100,000 documents, which are printed there either verbatim or in précis, and in translation where necessary. And this has been, after the manuscript documents themselves, the bedrock of all research into Henry's monarchy ever since the first volume appeared in the nineteenth century. No subsequent work has been done without acknowledging the author's indebtedness to this source material.

But the starting point of all compositions about the subject of my own book has been, since 1915, another tremendous work: *The Pilgrimage of Grace 1536–1537 and The Exeter Conspiracy 1538*, which appeared that year in two volumes from two Quaker sisters from County Durham, Madeleine Hope Dodds and Ruth Dodds. They cost 30s, which Ruth thought was so expensive that no one would be able to afford them. Almost every scholar since has found fault with Dodds, generally in its chronology and in some of its interpretations, especially in its (they feel) uncritical view of Robert Aske; and it is true that in her diary for 25 September 1909 Ruth is found lamenting, 'Oh Aske, Robert Aske, you are my patron saint... Oh if only I could write your story as it should be written.' This reveals an emotional attachment which some might think a handicap to a supposedly disinterested historian. My own particular quibble – and it is no more than a quibble – is that, considered principally as a narrative, the dense and convoluted detail of Dodds sometimes makes it a little difficult to see the wood for the trees. But no one has ever failed to admit – either openly or by implication in the incidence of quotations lifted from the sisters' text – that this is the great pathfinder, which opened up a trail that everyone since has been glad (and obliged) to follow before making his or her contribution to the subject. Nothing comparable has been produced since 1915, though there have been many learned papers and a number of books about aspects of the Pilgrimage and related topics, all of them written by academics, principally for the attention of their pupils, their colleagues and rivals. In his book about the raising of the Pilgrim armies, Dr Bush wrote in 1996: 'What is badly needed is a new narrative: one which incorporates the complexity of the regional revolts with an account of the successive stages of the uprising's development.' I had reached the same conclusion on first encountering the Dodds some years earlier.

This book is my attempt to satisfy that need. It has been written in the conviction that the very best histories for a general readership combine scholarship with what has been called the difficult art of literature. G. M. Trevelyan was the most celebrated advocate of this view in this country, and he is much despised for it today by certain academic historians who appear to believe that if a book sells 20,000 copies or more it is axiomatically inferior to one whose print run is only just in four figures and is unlikely to be found on many shelves outside the college library. I do not think their indictment is necessarily true, though sometimes it may be so. I am of the opinion that the choice and arrangement of words and the literary imagination of the writer are just as important as the accuracy of the information conveyed, and a penetrating insight into its significance. If a book is shapeless, pedestrian or otherwise ill-written, it doesn't do much for the spread of knowledge among those who are not already in the know.

Gairdner and the Dodds sisters are not the only ones to have provided the navigational aids that have made this particular piece of work possible. Everyone who publishes a new book or circulates another paper – academic historians and professional writers alike – does so only by standing on the shoulders of those who have studied and written about the subject before: that is what every bibliography tells and this work is certainly no exception to that rule. I am acutely conscious of how much I owe to the labours of Tudor specialists, from Elton to Bush, from Scarisbrick to Hoyle, from Reid to MacCulloch, from Dickens to Duffy, from Bowker to Haigh, from Knowles to James, and I'm most grateful for all that I have learned from them and from many others.

My gratitude must also go to a number of people who helped me in a different way. Most of all, perhaps, to Jacqueline

Whiteside and her colleagues at Lancaster University Library, where much of my research was done, especially into *Letters & Papers*, which saved me from many more journeys than in the end I needed to make to the British Library in London. Not far behind in my indebtedness are Elizabeth Heaps and her colleagues at the University of York, for allowing me access to the libraries on campus, at the Borthwick Institute, at the Minster and at King's Manor, and for assistance when I was working in these collections; and to Elizabeth Pridmore, the Minster's Archivist. Also to Susan Payne and the staff of the Lincolnshire Archives in Lincoln for their help, and to Val Ward and Lesley Willetts of the North Yorkshire County Library Service for a crucial piece of first aid when I had decided to embark on this enterprise. I'm grateful, too, for help I received from Jeremy Ashbee, Assistant Curator of Historic Buildings at the Tower of London, from Mr and Mrs G. R. Dickinson of Aughton Hall, East Yorkshire, from the Rev. Stephen Holdaway of Louth, the Rev. Michael Burson-Thomas of Horncastle, and Professor Stephan Kohl, of Würzburg, Germany.

Lastly, this work would have been much harder than it was without the encouragement of many people, most of all without that of Dr John Rosselli who, in the course of a long friendship and professional association, taught me much about the writing of history. My best thanks also go to my editor and publisher, Ion Trewin, for encouragement and unstinting help across three decades, which is most of my working life. And to my children, whose unfailing love and support have sustained me much more than they probably realise.

PRINCIPAL CHARACTERS

ap Rice, John Notary, Registrar of Salisbury Cathedral and one of Cromwell's commissioners in the preliminaries to the Dissolution of the Monasteries

Aske, Christopher Elder brother of Robert (see below) and Henry Clifford's receiver. Died 1539

Aske, John Eldest brother of Robert Aske and lord of the manor of Aughton. Died c.1542

Aske, Robert Lawyer and chief captain of the Pilgrimage of Grace. Executed at York, July 1537

Atkinson, John Rebel leader in Dentdale. Sent for trial April 1537. Fate unknown

Barton, Elizabeth The Holy Maid of Kent, visionary, prophet and Benedictine nun. Executed 1534 for treason

Bigod, Sir Francis Participant in the first siege of Scarborough and the key figure in the post-pardon revolts. Executed at Tyburn, June 1537

Boleyn, Anne Royal councillor's younger daughter and Henry VIII's second wife. Mother of the future Queen Elizabeth. Executed May 1536

Bolton, Thomas Cistercian Abbot of Sawley. Sent for trial in London, March 1537. Fate unknown

Bowes, Robert Lawyer and soldier, leader of the North-eastern rebels but by 1537 a member of the King's Council in the North. Knighted in 1539

Brandon, Charles Duke of Suffolk. Crony of Henry VIII when both were young men, and subsequently his brother-in-law. One of the King's commanders in 1536–7

Bulmer, Sir John   Pilgrim delegate at truce talks on Doncaster bridge who tried to raise the last of the post-pardon revolts. Executed at Tyburn, May 1537

Campeggio, Lorenzo   Bishop of Salisbury, Archbishop of Bologna and Cardinal Protector of England. Outwitted Thomas Wolsey in latter's attempts to secure Henry VIII a divorce from Catherine of Aragon

Catherine of Aragon   Daughter of Ferdinand of Aragon and Isabella of Castile, aunt of the Emperor Charles V and first wife of Henry VIII. Their marriage declared void by Archbishop Thomas Cranmer 1533

Chapuys, Eustace   Ambassador of the Emperor Charles V at the court of Henry VIII

Charles V   Descended from Aragonese Kings of Spain and Austrian Habsburgs. Holy Roman Emperor 1519–56

Cheyney, Margaret   Common-law wife of Sir John Bulmer and involved with him in a last futile attempt at rebellion. Burned at Smithfield, May 1537

Clement VII   Born Giulio de' Medici in Florence 1479, Pope from 1523 until 1534. Instigated first measures against Luther's teachings and excommunicated Henry VIII of England in a suspended sentence

Clifford, Henry   First Earl of Cumberland, occupant of Skipton Castle and principal lord in the Yorkshire Dales, in Cumberland and in Westmorland

Cobbler, Captain   Real name Nicholas Melton, shoemaker of Louth and ringleader of the local rebellion. Examined in Lincoln for his activities in October 1536 and never heard of again. Almost certainly executed

Constable, Sir John   Kinsman of Sir Robert (see below). Left in temporary charge of Hull after its surrender to Stapleton's host and after saying he would die rather than yield. Member of the royal commission which presided over the trial and execution of John Hallam and others at Hull, at the end of January/early February 1537

Constable, Sir Marmaduke   Another of Sir Robert's kinsmen, but always loyal to the Crown

Constable, Sir Robert   Friend of Sir Thomas Darcy who, like

Darcy, started as a loyal servant of the Crown but became a rebel leader. Executed at Hull, July 1537

Constable, Sir William   Brother of Sir Robert and another Pilgrim leader in 1536. Later sat on the commission responsible for executing Hallam and others in 1537

Courtenay, Henry   Marquis of Exeter. One of the royal commanders in 1536–7, subsequently accused of plotting against the King and executed in December 1538

Cranmer, Thomas   Archbishop of Canterbury 1533–56, who pronounced Henry VIII's marriage to Catherine of Aragon void. Largely responsible for the Anglican Book of Common Prayer (1552). Died at the stake when Mary Tudor restored Roman Catholicism in England

Cromwell, Richard   Nephew of Thomas Cromwell. Had a minor role in the military preparations for putting down the Lincolnshire Rising. Subsequently sidelined

Cromwell, Thomas   Born *c.*1485. Cardinal Wolsey's protégé and subsequent Lord Privy Seal. Principal agent in the Dissolution of the Monasteries. Accused of treason and beheaded in July 1540

Dacre, William, Lord   Member of a family whose power and influence was mostly in Cumberland, who were locked in enmity with the Cliffords. Out of favour with the King, but managed to avoid having anything to do with the Pilgrimage

Dakyn, Dr John   Cleric who advised the canons and monks of Cartmel, Conishead, Coverham and Easby to stand firm against the King's farmers. Sent to London for examination in March 1537, but never brought to trial

Darcy, Thomas, Lord   Steward of royal castle at Pontefract, who joined the rebels. Executed on Tower Hill, June 1537

Dymmoke, Sir Edward   Sheriff of Lincolnshire and a captain of the Lincolnshire rebels. Survived to become Champion of England at three coronations (Edward VI, Mary Tudor and Elizabeth) and Treasurer of Boulogne

Ellerker, Sir Ralph   Bitter enemy of Sir Robert Constable, though both joined the Pilgrimage under pressure. Was one of the emissaries sent to the King in 1536. Generally known as 'young Sir Ralph' to distinguish him from his father

Esch, Robert   The Friar of Knaresborough. Itinerant propagandist for the Pilgrimage. Examined in London with other rebels late in February 1537. Fate unknown

Hallam, John   East Riding farmer and ringleader in the Pilgrimage. Led fruitless attempt at a second revolt in Hull early in 1537. Executed in February that year

Hamerton, Sir Stephen   Rebel leader in Ribblesdale. Executed at Tyburn, May 1537

Hastings, Sir Brian   Sheriff of Yorkshire and steadfast in his loyalty to the King

Henry VII   Born Henry Tudor, scion of a Welsh family, who became King on wresting the throne from the Plantagenet Richard III at the Battle of Bosworth 1485

Henry VIII   Second son of the above, who inherited the Crown because his elder brother Arthur died as a sixteen-year-old, while their father was still king

Holgate, Robert   Prior of Watton and antagonist of John Hallam. Member of the Council in the North who eventually became Archbishop of York

Howard, Thomas, third Duke of Norfolk   One of Henry's principal commanders and sworn enemy of Thomas Cromwell. Subsequently fell from favour and spent six years in the Tower of London before being restored, under Mary Tudor, to all his dignities

Hudswell, George   Lincolnshire rebel who recruited Robert Aske to the cause. Executed at Tyburn, March 1537

Hussey, Lord John   Loyal to the King but compromised by his contact with the Lincolnshire rebels, who hoped he would lead them. Executed at Lincoln, July 1537

Kendall, Thomas   Vicar of Louth, whose sermon on 1 October 1536 initiated the Lincolnshire Rising. Executed at Tyburn, March 1537

Kyme, Guy   of Louth. Intermediary between Lincolnshire and Yorkshire rebels, and possible gun-runner. Executed at Lincoln, March 1537

Layton, Richard   Cleric, lawyer and one of Cromwell's commissioners in the process of assessing and dissolving the monasteries

Leache, William   One of the Horncastle rebels implicated in the death of Dr Rayne, he later turned up in Yorkshire and Westmorland. Escaped capture after being wanted in both Lincolnshire and the North, and never heard of again

Lee, Edward   Archbishop of York 1531–44. Almost made a vocation of dithering between allegiance to the Pilgrimage and the Crown, but survived in spite of that

Legh, Thomas   Lawyer and another of Cromwell's commissioners, who worked with Richard Layton in the northern visitations of 1535–6

Leo X   Born Giovanni de' Medici in Florence 1475, Pope from 1513 until 1521. Proclaimed Henry VIII Defender of the Faith, after the English King attacked Luther's position

Longland, John   Bishop of Lincoln 1521–47. Detested by the Lincolnshire rebels for his reforming tendencies

Luther, Martin   Augustinian theologian from Saxony, who challenged the primacy of the Popes and clerical corruption, and so gave the Reformation its first impulse

Mackerell, Matthew   Premonstratensian abbot of Barlings monastery, Lincolnshire. Had a passive and unwilling role in the Rising but was executed at Tyburn, March 1537

Mary Tudor   Henry's daughter by Catherine of Aragon. Effectively banished after the divorce of her parents. Succeeded Edward VI on the throne 1553–8

Maunsell, Thomas   Vicar of Brayton, near Selby, and self-appointed recruiting officer for the Pilgrimage

Middleton, Peter   Cumbrian landowner, besieged by rebels for four months on an island in Derwentwater

Miller, Thomas   Lancaster Herald and the King's principal fetcher and carrier of messages to and from the Pilgrims. Executed in 1538 for having abetted the Pilgrimage

Moigne, Thomas   Recorder of Lincoln and a leader of the Lincolnshire Rising after having been pressed into service by the rebels. Executed at Lincoln, March 1537

Morland, William   Former Cistercian monk who tried to have a moderating influence on the Lincolnshire Rising. Executed at Tyburn, March 1537

Musgrave, Nicholas   Rebel leader in Westmorland. Fate unknown

Nicholson, William   Husbandman (tenant farmer) who plotted the seizure of Hull with John Hallam in the first of the post-pardon revolts. Executed February 1537

Paslew, John Abbot of Whalley. Executed, probably at Lancaster, March 1537

Paul III Born Alessandro Farnese of the Roman nobility 1468, Pope from 1534 to 1549. Under him the Counter-Reformation began and Henry VIII's excommunication was ratified

Percy, Henry, sixth Earl of Northumberland Potential leader of the northern rebellion, he was a sick man who refused to have anything to do with it. Died June 1537

Percy, Sir Ingram Youngest of the Percy brothers. Took an inactive part in the rebellion but imprisoned in Tower of London, where he died

Percy, Sir Thomas Younger brother of Henry and rebel leader. Executed at Tyburn, June 1537

Pickering, Dr John Dominican friar in Bridlington and rebel songwriter. Executed at Tyburn, May 1537

Pickering, Fr John Chaplain to Sir Francis Bigod. Tried for treason in 1537 but acquitted

Pole, Reginald Protégé of Henry VIII, who turned against him and was made Cardinal by Pope Paul III. Potential leader of an invasion from the Continent

Pulleyn, Robert Minor Westmorland gentleman and rebel leader. Alienated from the people he had led after the agreement at Doncaster

Radcliffe, Robert First Earl of Sussex and member of the Privy Council. Led the commission which examined and punished rebels in North-west England

Rayne, John Bishop of Lincoln's chancellor, murdered by the Horncastle rebels, October 1536

Scrope, Henry, Lord Son-in-law of Henry Clifford. Played both sides at different times in the Pilgrimage but survived to retain his home at Bolton Castle in Wensleydale

Sedbar, Adam Cistercian Abbot of Jervaulx. Executed at Tyburn, June 1537

Seymour, Jane Lady-in-Waiting to Catherine of Aragon and Anne Boleyn, and third wife of Henry VIII. Died 1537 after only seventeen months of marriage. Mother of future King Edward VI

Stanley, Edward, third Earl of Derby One of the royal commanders and principal overlord in Lancashire and Cheshire

Stapleton, William Lawyer, friend of Robert Aske and captain of an East Riding host. Took no further part in the rebellion after Doncaster

Staveley, Ninian Yeoman of Masham and one of the first leaders of the rising in Wensleydale. In 1537 he operated in Westmorland, was later taken for questioning and released after testifying against Adam Sedbar and the monks of Jervaulx Abbey

Talbot, George, fourth Earl of Shrewsbury One of Henry's leading commanders

Tempest, Nicholas Rebel leader of Bowland. Executed at Tyburn, May 1537

Thompson, Robert Vicar of Brough and prominent rebel. Died in prison 1537

Tunstall, Cuthbert Bishop of Durham, whose home was wrecked by rebels when he fled to Norham Castle soon after the Pilgrimage began. Became President of Henry's Council in the North in 1537

Waters, Edward Cromwell's messenger captured aboard a ship sailing to relieve Scarborough Castle

Wharton, Sir Thomas Successfully evaded the rebels who came looking for him in October and in 1537 one of the King's most trusted lieutenants in Westmorland and Cumberland. Eventually Warden of the West March and first Baron Wharton

Whelpdale, Gilbert Rebel leader in Penrith, where he was known as Captain Poverty. Fate unknown

Wolsey, Thomas Cardinal Archbishop of York and Lord Chancellor of England. Born *c.*1472–4, died 1530 in disgrace

I

PROLOGUE

Royal scouts have been sizing up the rebel army for days and the prospect is intimidating. Something like 30,000 men have been advancing in extended order across Yorkshire towards Doncaster, where scarcely more than a token force is said to be deployed in time to obstruct their further progress south. Even when all the troops that Henry VIII has at his disposal are mustered together, they will be outnumbered by more than two to one – and they are not together: we hear that they are scattered across the Midlands almost haphazardly, the biggest and the nearest contingent consisting of no more than 6000 men. Unless something is done quickly, the rebels will have a walkover, picking off Henry's ill-equipped, unpaid and increasingly demoralised army in one isolated battalion after another. Then the way will be open to London; and in London they intend to confront the King, if he has not already fled in alarm. They will lay before him their grievances, which have been smouldering these past nine years and finally caused them to take up arms in what they are calling their Pilgrimage of Grace. And if he does not satisfy their demands, or at least make a compromise, then something terrible, perhaps unspeakable, may be done to their sovereign; also to Lord Privy Seal Thomas Cromwell – whom they appear to detest above all others – to Archbishop Cranmer and to all who might remain loyal to Henry till the end. This matter, this dispute between the King and his subjects, burst into flame in Lincolnshire some weeks ago and has spread across the North of England; and there is no telling how much further it will go, how far across a kingdom which is thought to be increasingly restive as a result of the new laws against the Church, as well as many other things, including Henry's dismissal of his wife.

Only a mile or two from Doncaster, the rebels in teeming rain made their last dispositions for the engagement that almost all of them crave. A company from Cleveland and the North-east led the advance beyond Pontefract, followed by Pilgrims from the East Riding, with the hard men from the Dales bringing up the rear. Reinforcements are expected to join this main army later, when they have finished laying siege to Skipton Castle and confronting the Earl of Derby on Lancashire's border with Yorkshire, and even these additions will not bring the number of insurgents up to their full potential strength. Fighting hosts from Cumberland and Westmorland are, even now, said to be moving towards Carlisle which, if it falls to them, will be a prize not much less important than Doncaster. But the chief captain of the Pilgrimage and his closest lieutenants have their eyes fixed steadfastly on the town guarding the River Don and what lies beyond. Take that, defeat two of Henry's greatest commanders in the process, and something unheard of in Tudor times will be well within their grasp. There is some talk of impending negotiations, but we have no confirmation of that; and certainly, to judge by appearances, one of the most important battles ever fought on English soil is not far away.

The rebel multitude yesterday reached the high ground overlooking the river and there they have this morning drawn themselves up in a highly disciplined battle formation. Company after company of them now stand waiting in close order, foot soldiers for the most part but with a useful leavening of cavalry. They flaunt their tokens of allegiance to impress and intimidate the enemy: the Banner of the Five Wounds, the crimson and silver banner of St Cuthbert, together with lesser pennants, all billowing in the wind; and with the badges of their overlords fastened to their coats – the crescent of the Percies, the cock of the Lumleys, the insignia of any house to which their local loyalties are pledged. Their commanders can be seen riding up and down the lines, encouraging, correcting, staying their men till the last order is given and the right moment comes; and priests are moving between the ranks, telling the Pilgrims that their cause is just, that to die in its defence is nothing to be afraid of, but will bring God's sure and certain blessing through all eternity. Full 30,000 of them there are and they have started singing their battle hymn, which is said to have been composed for them by a Cistercian monk; singing so lustily in such a mighty chorus that it alone will be enough to undermine the courage of their foe. And as the defenders of Doncaster look up and across the river and see what is ready and preparing to attack from the modest heights of Scawsby, so composed, so eager, so unified in aggressive certainty, some of the royal soldiers must be wondering how much longer they have to live. An hour or two at most, maybe, for to the detached onlooker it seems impossible that this thing can now be stopped...

II
A TURNING POINT

Henry VIII had been on the throne of England for eight years when, in 1517, Europe reached one of its great turning points. He had inherited the Crown only because his elder brother Arthur died as a sixteen-year-old while their father was still alive. Henry VII had secured the Tudor succession when he brought the Wars of the Roses to an end with his triumph at Bosworth Field, but a reign which had begun promisingly ended cautiously and the old King never inspired anyone very much except in that crucial engagement. He was a calculating man, a characteristic that he passed on to his second son, but the younger Henry was to develop a much more ample personality than that. The great Dutch humanist and priest, Desiderius Erasmus, who met the royal children when Henry was only eight, was impressed by his grace and, as the heir apparent approached maturity, everyone who encountered him found him an immensely attractive youth. He was tall, he had the body of an athlete and his face was so finely proportioned that it could have been feminine. A Venetian who was received at Henry's court shortly after he mounted the throne two months before his eighteenth birthday, reckoned that he was more handsome than any other monarch in Christendom.

He was in such good condition that he could stay in the saddle long enough to exhaust half a dozen horses, one after the other; he could hurl a heavy spear great distances and he could draw the longbow more impressively, it was said, than any other man in England. He liked to wrestle and go hawking, but his greatest delight was jousting and he was a formidable opponent in the lists, though this pastime nearly cost him his life when his friend – and subsequently his brother-in-law – Charles Brandon, Duke of Suffolk, almost smashed his face in because Henry had forgotten to close the visor on his helmet, allowing the lance to enter the aperture where luckily it splintered. An even more dangerous accident was to befall him when he was forty-four years old and still tilting: he was badly thrown and, while he lay on the ground, his horse, made heavier still by its own armour, landed on top of him and knocked him unconscious for a couple of hours.

But he possessed other attributes apart from those that belonged to this robust side of his nature. He was a gifted musician who amassed a large collection of instruments and himself played the lute exceptionally well, the organ and the virginals only a little less so. He could sight-read music as well as anyone and he had a very fine singing voice; and one of the most civilised and beneficial acts of his life was to provide the chapels royal with the best singers that could be found anywhere in the land. There was yet another side to him, and it was an extravagance of behaviour, a heartiness of appetites, that eventually produced the Henry that history would remember most, the bluff King Hal whose body became coarsened and unattractive through a gluttony that gave him the stomach for banquets lasting seven hours, who wore dazzling clothes that he made gaudier still with oversized baubles, and whose greatest pleasure in time was to be the irresistible centre of attraction in a great concourse of roistering courtiers. His finest biographer in modern times pictured him as 'a formidable, captivating man who wore regality with splendid conviction. But easily and unpredictably his great charm could turn to anger and shouting. And at such moments he could be exceedingly cruel.' On only his second day as King, he had two of his father's most loyal functionaries seized on hearsay evidence of extortion and, after they had been imprisoned for over a year on a trumped-up charge of treason, he had them executed. This was a disreputable way of earning yet more popularity at the outset of his reign, for the policies which the two men had supervised were the product of his father's own most reviled enactments. These were fiscal matters and had nothing to do with the religious issues in which the younger Henry would soon be embroiled.

The piety of England at his accession is almost inconceivable to the English mentality of our own day. For the Christian faith was not only held by every single body in the land, but it dominated their lives at every point.[1] The liturgical calendar was important not only because it kept track of the holy days and the seventy days in the year when people were expected to fast, but because it was often the only reference point for secular events as well: Michaelmas was when rents had to be paid, by which time the harvest should be in, and when a new law term began; Martinmas signalled the end of the farming year, when labourers found out whether they were to be retained or would need to offer themselves for hire by some other employer at a special fair. But a large proportion of everybody's time was passed in or about the parish church. Everyone was expected to attend services three times on Sundays and on feast days – of which there were many – and everyone was concerned, above all things, to ensure that their soul passed safely from this world into the next, with the minimum time spent between one state and the next in Purgatory. To this end they spent a great deal of their lives on earth and much of their resources. Every church had a recognised tariff of payments to be made in exchange for its spiritual assistance to an individual, and both the emoluments and the services rendered could be punishing. A Lancashire priest, Sir Piers Legh, stipulated that £20 must be spent when somebody died and expected something more than a number of prayers and a decent burial.[2] For this sum, within a month no fewer than 100 priests were to say mass simultaneously and these were to be subdivided into '20 masses of Jesus, 20 of the Five Wounds, 20 of Our Lady, 20 of the Holy Ghost, 10 of the Trinity and 10 requiem masses'.

The average parishioner not only paid tithes and other ecclesiastical dues, but also paid for and equipped the churches with a vast number of necessities for their various rituals: surplices and other clothes, altar frontals, banners, crosses, pyxes, chalices, platters, monstrances, censers, bells, candles, incense, organs, books

---

1 Jews had been expelled by Edward I in 1290 and were not allowed to return until Oliver Cromwell permitted it in 1656, after what some said was the best speech he had ever made.

2 Legh was not a knight. Tudor clergy who were not graduates were addressed as 'Sir —'.

of liturgy and books for chanting... the list was almost endless. The wealthy furnished their parish churches with sumptuous Easter Sepulchres, through which their memory would thereafter always be linked with that of Christ himself in his tomb. The poor left small sums to ensure that they would be included in the bede-rolls, their names read out and prayed for each week or, at the very least, on the anniversary of their deaths: this was known as the bidding of the bedes. Nor was all this devotion practised only in congregational worship, for the spread of literacy since Gutenberg's development of the printing press at Mainz in 1440 had produced an unprecedented hunger for reading about the faith. It has been estimated that there were more than 50,000 devotional Books of Hours circulating in England at this time and one volume, *The Kalendar of Shepherds*, which has been described as 'a delightful, well-illustrated but bizarre book... two-thirds astrological almanac, and one-third religious vademecum...' was the sixteenth century's equivalent of a modern best-seller.

Christian devotion was at its most concentrated and its most expressive in the parish church and its rituals. It was unthinkable that anyone should enter a church without dipping fingers in a stoup of holy water by the door and crossing themselves, then genuflecting as they first saw the altar. There were regular processions, at Rogationtide in order to drive evil spirits from the community and to reaffirm the boundaries of each parish, and at other times for witness to the faith and for various purposes. There were no ceremonials, however, to compare with those of Holy Week, the most venerated period in the Church's year. On Palm Sunday, at the start of the week leading up to Easter Day, the congregation circled the churchyard, to the singing of '*Gloria, Laus et Honor*' ('All glory, laud and honour, to Thee Redeemer King'), with people carrying flowers and branches which had been blessed by the priest to represent palm leaves, and with the Blessed Sacrament carried high in a special shrine under a silken canopy. Sometimes this also accommodated the church's holy relics – and they almost all had something, even if it was no more than a fragment of bone, which was said to have come from the knuckle of an obscure saint. On Maundy Thursday and Good Friday the tenebrae services were held, when scores of candles were progressively extinguished, the light diminishing as each of the Psalms came to an end, until the church was finally in darkness, to symbolise Christ's abandonment by his disciples. On Holy Saturday came the Easter Vigil, when the church would have a representation of the sepulchre even if it did not possess a permanent one in stone. On Sunday came the most sacred moment of all, when all was brilliant with light as the procession circumnavigated the church, with everything leading up to the moment when the Host would be elevated in the one communion service that everyone attended.[3]

It was thought so vital that everyone should be able to see the transcending act of consecration, even if they were on the wrong side of an obscuring pillar or wall, that apertures (called squints) were often made through the masonry and angled on the altar; and sometimes these pierced the church's outside walls as well so that lepers, who were not allowed into the building, could also take part. Everyone watched enraptured; the entire community; just as everyone took part in all the Church's rituals, from one end to the other of every year. For this was not only a matter of faith, something which sprang from that part of the human psyche which is instinctual rather than rational. It also appealed to the senses, playing on each one of them every time people worshipped together. Here was the smell of incense, with its symbolism of prayer rising to heaven. Here was the touch of the priest at the laying-on of hands and the feel of the water before the individual crossed himself. Here was the sight of gorgeous raiment in the vestments of the priests, and the glass and other vivid decorations of the church. Here was the taste of the wafer and of the wine which followed it to make sure that Christ's body was washed down. Here was the sound of bells and of voices from the choir, singing the music of Thomas Fayrfax, John Taverner and the up-and-coming Master Tallis. There was nothing at all in sixteenth-century English life that the Christian faith and its manifestations did not impinge upon.

And in this respect, at least, life on the island was in complete harmony with that everywhere else in Europe during those first eight years of Henry VIII's reign. That is not to say that

---

3 There were other communion services during the year, but relatively few people received the sacrament except at Easter.

Christendom in the West – Catholicism obedient to Rome, which had become separated by 1054 from the Eastern Orthodox of Byzantium – had remained harmoniously at ease with itself since the eleventh-century schism. The old autocratic rule of the Popes had gradually been eroded, and was no longer quite as truculently powerful as the pontificate of Innocent III had been between 1198 and 1216. It was Innocent who announced that he and his successors were the Vicars of Christ, who asserted the Vatican's overweening hold on almost all of Western Christendom, who excommunicated King John of England, who launched a ruthless crusade against the Albigensians, the Cathars, of southern France, and who once delivered himself of the brisk and anatomically accurate observation that '*Inter faeces et urinas nascimur*' – which may be roughly translated as 'We are all born between the piss and the shit'.

In 1303, after a dispute over money and the power it bought, troops belonging to the French King Philip IV had attacked the Pope's summer residence, manhandling and humiliating Boniface VIII so seriously that he returned to Rome a broken man and died within a month. This produced a split in the Catholic Church, whose loyalties were divided between its Francophiles and the rest, which culminated in the Great Schism of 1378 and resulted in two Popes ruling simultaneously, one in Rome and the other in Avignon, each with his own clientele of cardinals and secular rulers, both quite frequently appointing their own men to the same bishopric or as abbot of the same monastery. For four ludicrous years, in fact, there were three pontiffs and this bizarre state of affairs was not ended until a full Oecumenical Council (a gathering of prelates and theologians from every land, which was very rarely held) was summoned to Constance in 1414 and solved the problem by deposing two of the Popes, getting the third to abdicate and making a fresh start with a single new incumbent. But the damage had been done and although Constance is remembered most for its condemnation and incineration of the Bohemian reformer John Hus, and for its order that the radical English theologian John Wycliffe, who had been dead for thirty years, should be exhumed and reburied in unconsecrated ground, of more fundamental importance was its decree that 'This holy Council…has its authority immediately from Christ; and [declares] that all men, of every rank and condition, including the

Pope himself, is bound to obey it in matters concerning the Faith, the abolition of the Schism, and the reformation of the Church of God in its head and in its members.' After that, there could be no going back to the traditional form of papal autocracy. The time had come when Popes would need to make concordats with secular rulers in order to wield any authority at all outside the Papal States.

The old orthodoxies had been challenged across those centuries by others apart from Hus and Wycliffe. Some, like Thomas Aquinas and Duns Scotus, were theologians; others, like Francis of Assisi and Savonarola of Florence, were zealots with a different vision from the Vatican's of how the Christian life should be lived. None was more influential than Erasmus, whose *Enchiridion Militis Christiani* (*Handbook of the Christian Soldier*) proposed that the Church should return to the teachings of the early fathers and to Scripture, thus bypassing Roman authority altogether. From its publication at the beginning of the sixteenth century the *Enchiridion* was a best-seller and it laid the intellectual foundations of the Reformation. And everywhere, Bibles had become available in the vernacular since Gutenberg's invention, so that ordinary Christians no longer needed to depend on Latinised priests to discover what Christ had said and done, what the apostles had tried to carry on. The stage had been set for the entrance of Martin Luther. The great European turning point had come.

An Augustinian like Erasmus and the son of a miner, with some of the coarseness that came as part of his birthright, Luther had risen to a chair of theology at the Saxon university of Wittenberg, in the north-east of Germany. He was a scholar and a passionate man, who wanted no easy answers to the questions he asked, who desired above all things to be acceptable in his Maker's eyes but who was conscious, most of all, of his sins and of his absolute helplessness before God. From what would now be called his agony of conscience, he attempted to reach salvation by all the conventional methods advocated by Mother Church, by mortifications of one sort and another: by fasting, by self-inflicted discomfort and also by seeking pain. It wasn't until he fixed his attention on the instructions left by St Paul and on the works of St Augustine, that he began to see the glimmer of a solution that eventually took him back to the Gospels where, awaiting him, was the revelation that God above all was love; that this love promised the forgiveness of sins to all who truly believed; that such belief came through the grace that was in Jesus Christ; and that man could be saved by faith alone. This doctrine, of justification by faith, became the bedrock of the Reformation. Like Erasmus, whose writings helped to direct Luther's thinking, he had proposed a way of reaching God which did not require the mediation of a hierarchical Church. This is not to say that Luther wished to abandon the Church; but he did increasingly feel the need to reform it. A visit to Rome in 1510 had destroyed any illusions he might have had about the impeccable credentials of the Curia and since that time he had gradually been working his way to a belief that much of what the priesthood did merely obstructed humankind's endeavours to see God. He had also concluded, out of his own experience, that the more rigorous monastic disciplines were of no assistance at all. Eventually, he was to marry a Cistercian nun of like mind, in a union that endured happily for another twenty-odd years.

But first came the pregnant moment when Luther went to the Castle church in Wittenberg, on 31 October 1517, and nailed his ninety-five theses to its door. There was nothing exceptional in the act of making an announcement like this; scholars generally invited debate in this fashion and church doors had always served as a general parish notice board. But the content was unprecedented. The ninety-five propositions started mildly enough and some of what followed could scarcely be thought outrageous. But the twentieth Thesis begins to formulate the matter that most concerned Luther: 'The pope by his plenary remission of all penalties does not understand the remission of all penalties absolutely, but only of those imposed by himself.' Which is followed by '21 Therefore those preachers of indulgences are in error who allege that through the indulgences of the pope a man is freed from every penalty.' And by '43 Christians are to be taught that to give to the poor or to lend to the needy is a better work than the purchase of pardons…' In his final salvoes Luther exhorted Christians 'to endeavour to follow Christ, their head, through pains, deaths and hells', before reaching his final paragraph: '95 And so let them trust to enter heaven rather through many tribulations than through the false confidence of peace.'

He composed the theses in Latin but they were soon translated into German and spread by the printing press, which meant that they instantly became a matter for much more than rarefied academic debate. And while many of the faithful – and Luther's own immediate superiors – thanked God that someone had had the courage to say what most of them felt, the monolithic Church decided to hit back. Luther was attacked by a number of the Vatican's placemen, including the Dominican Johann Tetzel, a notorious peddler of Indulgences, and in 1520 he was summoned to a Diet, a congress, at Worms by the Holy Roman Emperor Charles V, the temporal guardian of the Church and the interests of the papacy. The untidy organism which he supervised had been created in 800 in order to fill a vacuum left when the old Roman Empire collapsed into the Dark Ages and no one was left to afford the Church the protection it had enjoyed ever since Constantine the Great ended the persecution of Christians in 313. Its first Emperor was Charlemagne, King of the Franks, who fought fifty-three wars against a variety of opponents in order to secure Europe for Catholicism. He made Aachen his capital, as did his immediate successors, but the imperial throne in time became associated with other cities, including Prague, Palermo and Vienna, as the Empire passed from Carolingian into other hands. And its boundaries were constantly changing, its vitality being most weakened by the rise of the national states in the fifteenth century. It only recovered its role as the great assurance of Christian survival after the Battle of Mohacs in 1526 made it conceivable that the whole of Europe might be colonised by Islam.

The Emperor who summoned Luther to Worms was a charmless and ungainly young man with little imagination, whose portrait by Titian emphasised a hugely jutting jaw. He was the grandson of Isabella of Castile and Ferdinand of Aragon, who had been dubbed the Catholic Kings of Spain by an Aragonese Pope and were responsible for unleashing the Inquisition. The Spanish connection was passed to him through his mother and their daughter Juana, who had married Philip of Burgundy, son of the Emperor Maximilian I. At the time of his accession Charles spoke no Spanish, only French and Flemish, but his immediate inheritance was the kingdom of Spain and its dominions, which included the Netherlands, where he was born, and the recent territorial acquisitions across the Atlantic in Mexico and Peru. Through his descent from Maximilian he had Austrian Habsburg blood, but he did not become Emperor by heredity, or even on the say-so of the Pope. Since 1356, the office had been in the hands of an electoral college, whose members were the Archbishops of Mainz, Cologne and Trier, together with the Count Palatine of the Rhine, the Duke of Saxony, the Margrave of Brandenburg and the King of Bohemia. These, in short, were the seven leading princes of Germany, who promoted him in 1519, though his anointing had to wait until 1530, when Clement VII crowned him in Bologna, the last time a Pope ever performed this function.

The reality of his position meant that Germany was where the Emperor derived much of his strength. The imperial apparatus was financed by the Fuggers of Augsburg, and many of the troops who tramped all over Europe at his behest were German *Landsnechts*. As a result, although Charles loathed Luther's teaching, many of the soldiers who marched to the beat of his drum were eventually staunch Lutherans. This was most disgracefully apparent when the imperial army, which had been locked in combat with the forces of Francis I of France in northern Italy, pushed on to Rome to consolidate its position and went on a rampage which didn't end until 4000 citizens had been killed amidst much pillage, rape and violation of Church property, including the Sistine Chapel. Clement VII fled to Castel Sant'Angelo, which was surrounded by troops bellowing Lutheran slogans; and one of them had already left Luther's name on a painting by Raphael in the Vatican. And there he remained, beleaguered, for the next six months. Europe was stunned by the Sack of Rome and yet, three years later, Clement went ahead with the coronation, because necessity dictated alliance.

At Worms, Luther was asked to recant and was allowed twenty-four hours in which to consider his position. And there, he left to posterity one of its great quotations: 'On this I take my stand; I can do no other; God help me; amen.' He had been given a safe conduct by the Emperor but, probably mindful that Hus, too, had been promised his life if he dutifully went to Constance, he secretly left Worms and headed for home. Before he reached Wittenberg, however, he was waylaid by men despatched by his patron, the Elector Frederick of Saxony, who never accepted all of Luther's ideas, but recognised his right to utter them. He was to be one of the six princes who, eight years later, at the second Diet of Speyer, signed the *Protestatio* (which gave us the word Protestant), affirming their belief that they should answer to God alone, not to the Emperor or the Pope, for the salvation of their souls. His more important act, though, was his benevolent kidnapping of Martin Luther, who was borne off to the Wartburg Castle, where he entered the most productive period of his life in anonymous safety, composing letters, sermons, lectures that were to be delivered *in absentia* by his friends in Wittenberg and elsewhere.

These writings played their part in fomenting a German insurrection, which occurred in August 1524 and would be remembered as the Peasants' War. It began in the Black Forest and by the time it was brutally put down the following May it had spread to the south, throughout central Germany and to parts of the north. Though its origins lay chiefly in agrarian grievances, Luther's courage in attacking authority clearly influenced the authors of the rebel manifesto, and one of their demands was for the right to appoint and remove their own pastors, another the abolition of all tithes but those administered by elected churchwardens. Rabble-rousers were responsible for much of the early bloodshed and a great deal of mindless vandalism, in which priceless works of art were destroyed, together with a number of castles and religious houses. No one, in fact, emerged with any credit, not even Luther, who was at first sympathetic to the peasants but turned against them as their violence got out of hand; he incited the princes and lordlings to 'Crush them, strangle them and pierce them, in secret places and in sight of men, he who can, even as one would strike dead a mad dog', which was much the same language used by Innocent III when he unleashed his terrible crusade against the Cathars. And this the German rulers had already started to do, with the kind of savagery that relishes hideous punishment and is indifferent to the scale of butchery. The horsemen of the Swabian League and its allies turned the final chaos into just another blood sport, as they rode down and chopped or speared to death all who fled before them. The death toll is uncertain, because medieval statistics are not always trust-worthy, but according to the most widely accepted estimate, 100,000 peasants were killed in the aftermath of their revolt. Never again would the German underclass dare to rebel against their masters.

Meanwhile, from the Wartburg, the momentum of the Reformation began to gather pace. And it spread. It spread unevenly but in every direction from *Mitteleuropa*, considerably helped by Germany's trade links with other countries. It travelled to Scandinavia by way of the Hanseatic ports and there it found a receptive audience almost everywhere, not only among the faithful at large, but with princes locked in power struggles who discovered the profit in adapting to this newly popular set of beliefs. It made little headway at first in France, where its enemies included the theological faculty of the University of Paris, the Sorbonne, which had always been a bastion of conservative thinking, so that Reform had to wait until the influence of John Calvin spread from Switzerland by way of French exiles to whom he preached in Strasbourg after his banishment by the Geneva city council in 1538.

Even less progress was made in Spain, where the Church had already undergone a self-determined renovation, if not outright reform, fifty years before Luther, and where the terrorism of the Inquisition, securely in the hands of extremely orthodox Dominicans, was more than enough to intimidate anyone who thought that the cleansing had not gone far enough. Italy proved more fruitful ground, though the Roman supremacy was never seriously threatened and, again, Calvin made more impact than Luther.

In eastern Europe, the Catholic and the Orthodox Churches rivalled each other in the strength of their grip on the imagination of Christians, and the increasing threat from the Ottoman Turks – whose highly professional army was by 1532 moving up the Danube towards Vienna for the second time in three years – tended to concentrate minds wonderfully on the potential safe-guards offered by the might of a well-established authority. But in Bohemia the Hussites were steadfast, Prague and Rome having reached an accommodation in this matter since the Council of Constance. Hungary proved to be the most susceptible of all the countries to the east of the Alps, not only among the descendants of German immigrants in Transylvania, but also, and more surprisingly, among the Magyars after most of their bishops were killed by the first Turkish invaders at the Battle of Mohacs.

Notably, however, there was one snub to the papacy which owed nothing at all to Luther's influence. This led to another uprising eleven years after the Peasants' War was put down and it took place in that idiosyncratic part of Europe which was separated from the continental landmass by the English Channel.

III

DEFENDER OF THE FAITH

It has been argued that Henry was not a deeply believing
Catholic, that he was more superstitious and conventional than
devoutly spiritual and enthralled by the numinous. He was certainly conventional enough to be regarded as a possible leader of
the Holy Roman Empire, before Charles V, always the more
likely candidate, secured the approval of the German electors. It
was said that not a day of his life went by without his hearing
more than one mass, sometimes several, and he made the great
English pilgrimage to the shrine of Our Lady at Walsingham in
Norfolk, walking barefoot all the way. He was enough of a tradi-
tionalist to bristle at any suggestion that orthodox teaching about
the Eucharist should be modified – he believed in transubstantia-
tion to his dying day – while at the same time he was willing to
see the cult of saints and the devotion to images somewhat
reduced. He had an amateur's taste for theology and wrote some
himself, most notably when Luther appeared on the scene. He
was, and remained, deeply hostile to the new propositions, publicly burning all Luther's books in 1531. But ten years earlier he
had earned great merit in the Vatican by writing (and presenting
to the Pope with a gold binding) *Assertio Septem Sacramentorum
Adversus Martinum Lutherum*, a tract which condemned Luther's
criticism of the sacraments so eloquently that Leo X promptly
dubbed him Defender of the Faith. Before his brother Arthur
died and opened the way to his enthronement, their father had
envisaged Henry as a future Archbishop of Canterbury.

Henry was to adduce the Bible in his great conflict with the

17

papacy over the matter of his marriage to Catherine of Aragon. This union had been formed once Prince Arthur's untimely death left her a teenage widow only five months after their matrimony was solemnised in St Paul's Cathedral. Dynastic alliances being the principal imperative of medieval diplomacy, Henry VII decided that his second son should inherit Catherine before he acquired the Crown, and a treaty to that effect was signed in 1503, when Henry was not yet twelve, Catherine only seventeen. The marriage was to take place when the boy reached the age of fourteen, by which time Catherine's Spanish parents would have deposited a second substantial dowry in the English Treasury. In fact, this matrimony was delayed until Henry was King for a variety of reasons. Because the marriage of a woman to her dead husband's brother transgressed canon law, a special dispensation had to be sought from the Vatican and this took several months to arrange. Henry VII may have had second thoughts about retaining Catherine as his daughter-in-law, but died himself before he could repudiate her; and, certainly not the least of the considerations, the Spanish dowry was seriously behind schedule in materialising. But married Henry and Catherine eventually were in the Franciscan church at Greenwich in June 1509, six weeks after his enthronement. The union began happily enough, in spite of the unusual age difference, but it was soon struggling, with the rumour of separation surfacing on the Continent after only a few years, though they stayed together long enough for Catherine to give birth to the Princess Mary, future queen of England, in 1516. But her hopes for further maternity were dashed by three miscarriages and two deaths a few weeks into infancy, two of the former being male foetuses, with one of the babies a boy. So Catherine had utterly failed to fulfil her first obligation as the King's wife: to provide him with a son who would ensure the Tudor succession. And Henry was acutely aware of this responsibility. He also had a roving eye, and probably had an affair within five years of his marriage, involving Elizabeth Blount, one of Catherine's ladies-in-waiting, who eventually bore him a son. He may subsequently have had another son with Mary Boleyn, married daughter of a royal councillor and diplomat. Then his eye fell on Mary's younger sister Anne and the course of English history began to change dramatically.

She too was part of the royal household, where she was wooed by a number of personable young men, for she was beautiful, though not uncommonly so, and she carried herself with the sort of grace that attracts and excites suitors. She was fifteen when she first came to court and it became obvious to everyone that Henry was interested when she was not much older, but what started as a casual dalliance had become something much more serious by 1525, when Anne was eighteen. She had, however, still refused to become the King's mistress (and no one has ever been sure whether that was virtue or cunning) as a result of which Henry became more and more besotted with her, though there were limits to his devotion: when London was ravaged by the sweating sickness and Anne became ill, he fled to Hunsdon House in Hertfordshire and salved his conscience by hearing three masses and making his confession every day.

Already he was getting ready to abandon Catherine, partly out of lust for Anne Boleyn, partly because of the dynastic imperative. By 1527, when the rumour of divorce had spread to England and all at court were simply waiting for it to happen, Henry was preparing to petition the Pope, who was now the vacillating Clement VII. He argued that his marriage to Catherine was invalid because she had earlier been married to Arthur and he quoted two passages from Leviticus in support of this: 'Thou shalt not uncover the nakedness of thy brother's wife: it is thy brother's nakedness' and 'If a man shall take his brother's wife, it is an impurity: he hath uncovered his brother's nakedness; they shall be childless.'[1] On the same grounds he claimed that the bull which Julius II had issued, enabling Henry and Catherine to marry, was also invalid. Unfortunately, there was a text in Deuteronomy which flatly contradicted the assertions of Leviticus, and not until Henry's theologians and canon lawyers had had a field day was the matter resolved, by pretending that the trickiest problem did not exist.[2] The submission to Rome was eventually based upon the premise that Henry had scriptural authority for the wrongness of his marriage, and that God's law could not be countermanded by the Church.

The petition was drawn up to this effect and was despatched to

1 Leviticus chapter 18, verse 16; and chapter 20, verse 21.
2 Deuteronomy chapter 25, verse 5.

the Vatican, heavily laden with the eighty-five seals and signatures of two archbishops, four bishops, twenty-five abbots, two dukes, forty other peers and a dozen courtiers below the ranks of the nobility. It respectfully begged Clement to 'declare by your authority, what so many learned men proclaim … as you not only can but, out of fatherly devotion, ought to do'. It also included a hint that Henry might have recourse to other unspecified measures if the Pope did not grant this boon. And by the time the document reached Rome with the officials who would argue the case further, Catherine's representatives were already there before them: she was not going to give up her share of the throne without a fight.

One of the most prominent signatures attached to the petition was that of the man to whom Henry had chiefly entrusted his hopes, Thomas Wolsey, Cardinal Archbishop of York and Lord Chancellor of England. The son of a butcher from Ipswich, Wolsey's climb to authority had been spectacular from the moment he was appointed Henry VII's chaplain and by now he was the most powerful man in the land apart from the monarch himself, and even that at times could be regarded as scarcely more than nominal; although Henry always had the last say when his interest was engaged, between 1515 and 1529 Wolsey was the effective ruler of England, directing all domestic policies and conducting the nation's foreign affairs. Arrogant by nature, he was also greedy for emoluments of one sort and another, a lucrative Church appointment here, the acquisition of property there. He built palaces, including Hampton Court, and in these he entertained extravagantly with an entourage which far outnumbered that of the Archbishop of Canterbury, who would attend royal pageants with seventy servants, whereas Wolsey always turned up with 300 or more. Like many another priest he fathered children and saw to it that his son was promoted to one valuable benefice after another, despite the fact that he was not even old enough to be ordained. On the other hand, mindful of his own background, he had much sympathy for the poor in any struggle they had with the rich (who regarded him as an upstart) and he appointed commissions to look into the vexatious matter of enclosures; though it did little good, because it did not address the real problems of rural poverty, he had illegally created hedges and walls pulled down and open fields restored. His greatest achievement at home was to overhaul the legal system and provide it with a sound bedrock on which later reforms could be built.

His excursions in diplomacy were little more successful, though they often captured the imagination more than his grinding progress through domestic affairs. He cobbled together the Treaty of London, which in 1518 brought the Pope, the Emperor, France, England and Spain into alliance against the threat from the Turks; but within three months it had fallen apart because Maximilian died and Charles V won the subsequent imperial election, thus seriously affronting Francis I of France, who had sprayed a great deal of money around Europe in the hope of becoming Emperor himself.

The diplomatic manoeuvrings continued, most spectacularly when Henry met Francis in the summer of 1520, in the extravaganza which became known as the Field of the Cloth of Gold. Henry and his Queen were accompanied by 5000 retainers from Dover to the Val d'Or, between Guines and Ardres, where 6000 craftsmen had preceded them many weeks earlier to build accommodation for the English party, taking the material for hundreds of tents and pavilions with them, together with vast quantities of plate, cutlery and glass, foodstuffs sufficient to fodder man and beast for three weeks and the tools to reshape the landscape a little, so that the monarchs and their retinues would meet on a level footing. The principal construction was a palace, with brick foundations and timbered walls, which included an enormous banqueting hall. There was serious business to discuss – the two were old rivals in European politics, after all – but most of the next fortnight was spent entirely on pleasure; in jousting, in wrestling (at which Francis tumbled Henry once) and in endless dancing and feasting. And all of it was masterminded by Wolsey, who was tireless in his attention to detail, whether it concerned the building works or the flocks of green geese and quails that should be mustered as a small part of the victualling. He also sang a Solemn High Mass at an open-air altar before the kings and their ambassadors, with an attendance of English and French choirs accompanied by their own organs. Then he preached a sermon on peace. It was a personal triumph for the Cardinal, whose greatest virtue, his ability to organise, was seen at its best. It was also a tribute to 'the competence of early Tudor administration'.

Wolsey's diplomatic skills were employed for two years in trying to get Henry his divorce from Catherine, but he was soon out of his depth in the swirls and eddies of Vatican politics, finding few allies among his fellow prelates and discovering that Clement was not always straightforward with him. There was also the considerable impediment that Catherine was Charles V's aunt, so that he could expect no assistance from that quarter. Breaking point came when he was outwitted by Cardinal Campeggio, who was Bishop of Salisbury and Archbishop of Bologna at one and the same time (also Protector of England in the Curia) and who had seemed to be an ally in Wolsey's efforts to obtain the papal bull that would give Henry what he sought.

Wolsey and Campeggio together were instructed to hear the arguments at a special legatine court, which was convened in London at the end of March 1529, and pass on their recommendations to the Vatican. But after proceedings there had dragged on for weeks, during which Catherine impressed everyone with her dignity and quiet resolve, Campeggio, with the connivance of Clement, had the matter adjourned until October for further hearings in Rome. This would have meant a Henry humiliated – and very angry indeed – by being ordered to attend cross-examination in the Vatican and it never happened. Instead, Henry dismissed Wolsey for his failure (the Cardinal died a year later in disgrace) and appointed Sir Thomas More – lawyer, diplomat, sometime Speaker of the House of Commons and latterly Chancellor of the Duchy of Lancaster – to succeed him as Lord Chancellor.

The King then spent the next three years applying a variety of his own pressures to make the Vatican compliant. He summoned Parliament, which hadn't met since 1523, and strong-armed the lower House of Commons into enactments against abuses in the Church, which alarmed the English bishops and made their support more likely than it had been when Wolsey was running the show alone. He sent people round the European universities to enlist their support for his cause, which was forthcoming from Oxford, Cambridge, the French and the northern Italian seats of learning. He attacked the English clergy as a whole for putting money in Wolsey's purse which, he claimed, rightly belonged to him and their convocations bought a royal pardon in return for £118,000, which was never paid in full. He then demanded that they should recognise him as the supreme head of the Church in England, at which – somewhat demoralised by now – they did not dissent. Still Rome would not budge and Henry appeared to be impotent. Then Thomas Cromwell stepped forward and, within sixteen months, Henry's union with Catherine had been declared void and he was married to Anne Boleyn.

Like Wolsey, Cromwell had emerged from the shopkeeping and lesser business class, his father a London fuller and blacksmith, who also kept a hostelry. He himself had a much more varied life than that before he entered the King's employment, as a soldier of fortune in Italy, a merchant in Antwerp, a lawyer back at home, where he sat in the House of Commons, and as someone who had dabbled in money-lending. He had married shortly after returning to England, but his wife died within a few years and, after that, Cromwell spent himself on nothing but his career, rarely taking holidays, but occasionally enjoying archery and hawking; he also had an aviary, and kept a small orchestra and a group of singers to entertain his guests. He was a short and heavily built man, a little clumsy in his movements, with the head of a well-fed mastiff, its brown eyes humourless and watchful, its mouth waiting for the next meal. But the face became animated if the conversation took a turn which interested him and Cromwell was well known for his sardonic wit. If he had any religious beliefs they were not strong ones but they were formed by the teachings of Erasmus more than Luther.

This background, and a fluency in several languages, gave him a much broader view of life than was usual in English court circles. But first he entered Wolsey's service as a counsellor who could be relied on for penetrating analysis and thereafter his rise was swift, notwithstanding his patron's fall from grace, in which he had no part, showing, indeed, a great deal of compassion in the last months of the Cardinal's life. Cromwell was a cold, often ruthless and, above all, calculating man with many faults, which became more and more apparent in his rise to power, but no one could ever accuse him of disloyalty to his old friends. He could be generous in other ways, too, and eyewitnesses have recorded that he provided food twice a day for scores of poor people, a regular clientele which gathered outside his London home for alms. His career might have foundered in the wake of Wolsey's downfall, but instead he came to the King's attention – how and why is not clear – and joined the royal bureaucracy early in 1530, having already learned a great deal about administration at this level from his previous employer. Two years later he was Master of the King's Jewels, a dignity which was followed, within another four years, by Clerk of the Hanaper, Chancellor of the Exchequer, Master of the Rolls and, finally, Lord Privy Seal. He was doing so well for himself that, although he was never in Wolsey's class for greed and accumulated wealth, by 1535 he was worth close on £4000 a year and he owned a number of properties.

Crucial to his ascendancy was some advice he gave his King, which resolved all Henry's difficulties; and before long he was enjoying and exercising even more power than Wolsey had had. Parliament, where there was as much resentment of clerical privilege as anywhere in Christendom, was encouraged to pass bills criticising the Church's independent legislation and attacking the practices of the ecclesiastical courts. With this support behind him, the King put his terms before the two convocations of Canterbury and York, and they were incisive. No further Church legislation was to be passed without Henry's assent, existing canon law was to be examined and revised by a commission appointed by the King, with half its members laymen, and nothing they proposed could be enacted without his approval. To browbeat convocation even further, Henry announced his dawning realisation that the English clergy 'be but half our subjects, yea and scarce our subjects', the other half of their allegiance being to the Pope, and he ordered the papal oath which English bishops made on their consecration to be read out in Parliament – what did the Commons think of that, eh?

The pressure worked. Finding the prospect of parliamentary meddling in their ordinances more than they could endure, the bishops in convocation accepted his demands without reservation, in a document known as the Submission of the Clergy; what they had merely not contradicted in 1531 they now, twelve months later, actively embraced. Henry VIII had become, in cold fact, the supreme legislator of the Church in England. Armed with this authority, he went on to the offensive against Rome by promoting a bill that would divert to the Crown the payments which all bishops made to the Pope after their appointment, the first fruits (the first year's total income) of their episcopate, but – and this was Cromwell's crafty suggestion – this bill of annates contained a clause which delayed enactment until the King chose to issue letters patent, thus giving Clement a last chance to comply with the monarch's petition before Henry took the earth-shaking decision to sever completely all English ties with the papacy.

The Pope remained immovable, and events now moved forward with even greater momentum, largely necessitated by Henry's discovery that Anne Boleyn was pregnant, and his awareness that if this resulted in the son and heir he craved, it was imperative that the birth should be legitimate. Cromwell drafted legislation, which has been described as his masterpiece and which became law as the Act in Restraint of Appeals of 1533. Its resounding preamble challenged Rome in the bluntest possible terms: 'Where by divers sundry old authentic histories and chronicles it is manifestly declared and expressed that this realm of England is an empire ... governed by one supreme head and king, having the dignity and royal estate of the imperial crown of the same'; as did its later provisions. It stipulated that 'all causes testamentary, causes of matrimony and divorce, rights of tithes, oblations and obventions ... shall be from henceforth heard, examined, discussed, clearly, finally and definitively adjudged and determined within the King's jurisdiction and authority, and not elsewhere ...' It threatened that if any subjects of the King 'do attempt, move, purchase or procure from or to the see of Rome, or from or to any other foreign court or courts out of this realm, any manner of foreign process, inhibitions, appeals, sentences, summons, citations, suspensions, interdictions, excommunications, restraints or judgements, of what nature, kind or quality soever they be' they would be arraigned on charges of *praemunire*: that is, lesser treason, which had carried penalties of imprisonment and forfeiture of goods since 1393.

The bill was enacted early in March, only a few weeks after

Henry married Anne secretly and after Thomas Cranmer, the Cambridge divine who had suggested canvassing the European universities, was made Archbishop of Canterbury. On 23 May, after hearing the King's submissions at his ecclesiastical court in Dunstable, Cranmer did what he had been appointed to do: he declared the marriage with Catherine over and done with. On the first day of June, Anne Boleyn was crowned Queen and, by September, Henry was irretrievably excommunicated.

More legislation followed in order to fortify the King's position at home and to ensure that the break with Rome would be permanent. The Act of Supremacy in 1534 ordered that 'the King our Sovereign Lord...shall be taken, accepted, and reputed the only Supreme Head on earth of the Church of England, called *Anglicana Ecclesia*...' Another act that year not only reinforced the earlier provisions concerning financial transactions, announcing that 'annates, first-fruits and every other sums of money...paid at the said see of Rome...shall utterly cease...' but introduced a new source of revenue for the Crown, which would henceforth take one-tenth of all clerical income. Then came the Ecclesiastical Licences Act, which assured the monarch that 'this your grace's realm recognising no superior under God's law but only your grace...is free from subjection to any man's laws, but only to such as have been devised...within this realm...' The Act of Succession, passed in the same session of Parliament, was designed to ensure that the throne would pass to any children Henry and Anne might have and, at the same time, it bastardised the Princess Mary. Much more ominously, another law made any criticism of the new marriage treasonable and also promised the ultimate penalty to anyone who suggested that the King was a heretic or in schism from the Church.

Cromwell's part in all this soon caused him to be the most hated man in England, though there were other reasons that some found just as persuasive. Most of the clergy disliked him not only for his religious convictions (or lack of them) but also because he derided them in order to lower their self-esteem. The nobility and the gentry had it in for him because he interfered with the course of justice, which was traditionally dispensed at a local level by the landowners, and he once enraged the citizens of York when he fined an entire jury for its verdict in a murder case which he thought wrong-headed. The higher reaches of society, of course, also found Cromwell an object of their contempt because he was a jumped-up commoner, like Wolsey, and he affected a pet leopard among other manifestations of his new estate. The populace in general increasingly vilified him as a heretic, who made use of magic rings – one, it was said, having belonged to King Solomon – in order to ingratiate himself with the King.

Apart from those who received his bounty, everyone loathed him because they were increasingly fearful of his power, and because many of his punitive measures were taken after information received from those who were maliciously motivated to injure somebody else, so that no one felt completely safe even from their neighbours, but his reputation as the head of a vast network of paid informers and spies was much overblown: he didn't need one when the baser human instincts served him so well. The really frightening thing was that Cromwell sooner or later had possession of all this gossip and other intelligence, and never shrank from acting upon it, whoever was involved. He 'was always busy investigating individuals'. One of them was a Cambridge vicar who, in his cups, denounced the King's clerical policies to a parishioner, who promptly reported him to the mayor, who passed on this treasonable talk to the higher authority.

Cromwell's power was wielded nowhere more spectacularly than in his attack on Church property, which was launched in order to subsidise a Treasury much drained by the cost of defending the realm against the possibility of Spanish attack, including fortifications in Dover and Calais (still, though not for very much longer, an English possession) and of maintaining the peace in Ireland, which was becoming increasingly rebellious as the English turned their backs upon Rome. There was also the costly and perennial problem of keeping the Scots at bay. A ponderous and sweeping clause in the Act of Supremacy had given the monarch 'full power and authority from time to time to visit, repress, reform, order, correct, restrain and amend all such errors, heresies, abuses, offences, contempts and enormities whatsoever they be'. Included in this comprehensive range of interference was the visitation of monasteries and other houses of religion, which traditionally had been conducted by bishops and their officials every three years, in order to ensure that both male and female religious were observing the rules of their orders, were not a source of scandal and were running their affairs with proper economy. Cromwell now proposed to send his own men in to make these assessments and, particularly, to draw up inventories of assets and incomes. He was mindful of the fact that the government had not much more than £100,000 a year to work with, and estimated that the income of the Church in rents, tithes, bequests and other sources could not be much less than £300,000 a year: milking it of tenths alone, with no allowance for first-fruits, would therefore bring £30,000 annually to the hard-pressed Treasury. And there was much else to plunder besides that: a total dissolution of the monasteries might yield undreamed-of sums, as well as critically damaging the standing and morale of the Catholic Church. It was reckoned that between them the religious houses owned about a third of all the land in the country.

On 15 January 1535 Henry formally became Supreme Head of the Church and Cromwell was given yet another hat to wear, as his vicar-general. By the end of that month he had drawn up commissions for each county, instructions to his officials on how to proceed and what to look for, as well as the necessary authority. The commissioners were to make their returns by the end of May and, even though some laggards failed to meet this deadline, a few not completing their work until September, they worked with remarkable speed and efficiency. There were, after all, 563 religious houses in England and Wales, populated by 7000 monks and 2000 nuns; also by 35,000 lay brethren, who were effectively the Marthas of the religious life, the toilers who did the manual labour while the choir monks played Mary and attended to more spiritual things.

At whatever level they functioned, their calling was neither as zealous, as popular, as influential nor as buoyant as it had been in the monastic heyday of the twelfth century when, with the Benedictine order already established here since 597, the Cistercians arrived from France and gave the religious life a fresh impetus, which was only increased by the subsequent settlement of Premonstratensian and Augustinian canons, Franciscan, Dominican and Carmelite friars and sisters, and other forms of the life. But only eight new houses of any obedience had been founded since 1400 and the entire monastic edifice had become enfeebled. Sometimes this was the result of scandal, more often because the old vitality and will were no longer there and everywhere there had been a conspicuous fall in vocations, which meant that communities began to dwindle, as the older members died and fewer postulants came forward to take their place; to some extent they had become secularised, their abbots as much businessmen as fathers in God, their premises useful locally as banks and convenient for the storage of parochial and other documents as well as for worship. In one form or another the religious life had lost its way. But it still had an important role in the wider community, though this had become much less the case in the south of England than in the shires north of the River Trent.

The monasteries as a whole might spend no more than five per cent of their income on charity, but in the North they were a great deal more generous, doubtless because the need was greater in an area where poverty was more widespread and very real. There, they still did much to relieve the poor and the sick, they provided shelter for the traveller, and they meant the difference between a full belly and starvation to considerable numbers of tenants, even if they were sometimes imperfect landlords. They made other substantial contributions to the local economy. The Benedictine foundation at Durham had long operated coal mines in the region and the Cistercians had introduced commercial sheep farming to England; the hills and pastures of Yorkshire in particular were dappled with the flocks belonging to their great abbeys of Fountains, Rievaulx, Jervaulx and Byland (though it should be remembered that Fountains, at least, also had two cows for every sheep it possessed). Like every other monastery, these were great places of pilgrimage, too, to significant proportions of the populace, guardians of sacred relics which were still piously venerated. It was known for several hundred pilgrims to converge on a shrine on a feast day, in order to do homage at the memento of a saint.

The assessments of wealth by Cromwell's commissioners were presently tabulated in the *Valor Ecclesiasticus*,[3] consisting of

3 Which can be translated as What the Church is Worth.

twenty-two volumes and six portfolios, which became popularly known as the King's Books, and was as comprehensive in its way, as important a source of basic information, as the Domesday Survey of 1086. Armed with the early volumes of the *Valor*, the commissioners began a somewhat different series of visitations in July, and soon the country was crawling with them, meticulously and thoroughly going about their task. They were working exactly within the law – and it is striking that neither Cromwell nor his master ever failed to do that, even if they had to pass a new law first in order to sanction their actions – armed with eighty-six articles of enquiry to be answered by each house they visited, and following twenty-five explicit injunctions, the purpose of which was to find out just how the monks conducted their lives.

But some of the commissioners became more notorious for their cavalier behaviour than others. Most arrogant, and soon to be detested above all others, were Richard Layton and Thomas Legh, the first of them a clergyman (sometime archdeacon of Buckinghamshire and eventually, as a reward for his services, dean of York) the second a lawyer. Layton came from Cumberland, where he was said to have thirty-two brothers and sisters, and he, too, had taken a law degree, at Cambridge, where he was also ordained. He had worked for Cromwell since 1533 and it was he who concocted the articles of enquiry, which were one of the tools of the commissioners. Legh belonged to a Cheshire family, another Cambridge man who had been to Eton first, and he became an advocate in 1531, shortly afterwards entering the royal service as ambassador to Denmark. He was later entrusted with diplomatic missions to the Low Countries and to Hamburg as well, after brief employment by his cousin, Rowland Lee, Bishop of Coventry and Lichfield.

These two men came together after Layton had written to Cromwell asking that they should be allowed to carry out the business in the northcountry, on the grounds that, between them, they knew it more thoroughly than anyone else in the royal service. It was an obsequious letter, in which Layton assured his employer 'that he will not find monk, canon, friar, prior, abbot, or any other, who will do the King such good service, nor be so trusty to him'. He informed Cromwell that they were already well acquainted with every religious house and its surrounding district, 'so that no knavery can be hid from them, nor can they suffer any injury. They know the fashion of the country and the readiness of the people. Their friends and kinsfolk are dispersed in every place ready to assist them, if any stubborn or sturdy carl proves rebellious.' First, though, Legh was despatched south in the company of John ap Rice, an Oxford-educated notary who one day would produce the first translations of the Lord's Prayer, the Creed and the Ten Commandments into Welsh, and who had lately been registrar of Salisbury Cathedral. These two made their first call in Worcester, and visited houses in thirteen other places, as far apart as Bruton in Somerset and Royston in Hertfordshire, before returning to London and compiling their reports. When that was done, Legh joined forces with Layton and headed north.

They set off just before Christmas 1535, starting in the diocese of Lincoln and working their way to the borders of Scotland through the north-eastern counties, before returning down the west. And it soon became apparent that they were bullying their way from one community to another, without the slightest regard for the people whom, in a way, they had claimed as their own. Layton, indeed, was downright contemptuous of the northcountry folk. 'There can be no better way,' he told Cromwell, 'to beat the King's authority into the heads of the rude people of the North than to show them that the King intends reformation and correction of religion. They are more superstitious than virtuous, long accustomed to frantic fantasies and ceremonies, which they regard more than either God or their prince, right far alienate from true religion.'

These two commissioners quickly earned a reputation for lining their own pockets as they carried out their legitimate occupation of investigating all aspects of the religious life. Legh had already made a considerable profit on his southern progress and complaints of his high-handedness were beginning to come in. One of his critics was none other than John ap Rice, who was scathing in a denunciation he sent to Cromwell:

1 He is too insolent and pompous; but as this was in London I thought you knew it. 2 Wherever he comes he handles the

fathers very roughly, many times for small causes, as for not meeting him at the door, where they had warning of his coming. More modesty, gravity and affability would purchase him more reverence than his satrapic countenance...He is also excessive in taking. At the election of the prior of Coventry, he took £15; at Bevall, the Charterhouse, £20 besides £6 costs; at Vale Royal £15 besides £6 costs and a reward...

and so on. This was not the first time Legh had earned the disapproval of someone in a position of consequence: Eustace Chapuys, the imperial ambassador to England, had informed Charles V, at the time of Legh's diplomatic appointments, that 'The King sends a doctor of low quality to the king of Denmark and Hamburg'.

Layton is open to the same charges, but in his case there was an additional offence. The man entered every house of religion with his nose twitching for the scent of carnal activity – an abbot keeping concubines here, a nun who had been impregnated there – and when he found it he clearly relished the opportunity to tell his salacious tales. Curiously, his reports switched into Latin when he came to the nature of the impropriety, though whether this was from a warped prudishness or because the matter became more titillating when it was put that way is far from clear.

Early in 1536 the King presented Parliament with a bill that swiftly passed into law as the Suppression of Religious Houses Act, which authorised punitive measures against the communities. Its preamble made much of the corruption found in amassing the data for the *Valor* and it stipulated that all houses with an income of less than £200 per annum should be closed down. The figure was chosen by Cromwell almost randomly and seems to have been based on the notional economy supporting a dozen or so religious. Some such choice was necessary if only to make the first assault on the monastic world manageable, but it may also have been dictated by a desire not to be seen at the outset in an act of monstrous obliteration: the time of the larger houses could, and surely would, come later; it arrived at the end of 1537, in fact.

According to the *Valor*, there were 372 houses in England, another twenty-seven in Wales, which immediately fell foul of the law and were now to be further harassed by Cromwell's agents after a full year of already being threatened with some unspecified but very imaginable fate. The despoliation began, but it is notable that the religious themselves were not ill-treated; were, in fact, given pensions or placed in secular benefices where they could not or would not transfer themselves to the larger houses of their orders, or abandon the religious life altogether: John Alanbrigg, Abbot of Byland, collected a pension of £50, while the monks of Rievaulx were given not less than £4 apiece. It was the stock and the stores, the buildings and the land that Cromwell had done his sums over and now began to pillage. Eventually, Henry's reign would have seen 1,593 allotments of monastic land disposed of, only a tiny proportion of them being handed over as royal gifts; the rest were sold to the highest bidders.

And so a nation already made uneasy by the treatment of its Queen and by the alienation of its Church from Rome began to stir with more discontent as the lesser monasteries were suppressed and their fabric was laid waste. Buildings which for centuries had been familiar landmarks throughout the country, as much a part of the panorama as hills, rivers and trees, and which had generally been regarded with at least some degree of affection – often with passionate devotion – were now being demolished, with everything that was in and around them, and marketable, seized. Lead was stripped from roofs and from stained-glass windows, bells were melted into ingots, stone was carted away after walls had been knocked down, woodlands were sold, objects made of precious metals or inlaid with jewels were confiscated. The commissioners even plundered the communities of their sacred relics. The visitations of Layton and Legh in Yorkshire had carefully noted what might be available there, when the first reckoning took place. '*Haltemprise* ... Rents £104. Here is a pilgrimage to Thomas Wake for fever and in veneration they have the arm of St George and part of the Holy Cross and the girdle of St Marie [*sic*] healthful for childbirth (as is thought) ... *Clementhorpe* ... Here also they have milk (as believed) of the Blessed Mary in veneration and here is made a pilgrimage to Saint Sitha. Rents £50 ... *Coverham* They have the girdle of Mary Nevell of iron, good for lying-in women (as is believed) ... Rents £140.' Also logged were the more substantial houses, for future reference: '*Jerivall* alias *Gerves*.[4] Here they have the girdle of St Mary (as is believed) safe for lying-in women. Rents £455 ... *Pontefract* Here they have in veneration Thomas, Duke of Lancaster, and his girdle which (as is believed) is safe for lying-in women and his hat for pain in the head. Rent £330. The house owes £20 ...'

For a while the English as a whole were muted in their response to all this: the definition of and the penalties attached to treasonable talk made sure of that. But too much official violence of one sort and another had occurred by the autumn of 1536 for the entire populace to remain quiescent indefinitely. Though she was not much lamented, Anne Boleyn had gone to the scaffold in May, having had a child who would become Queen Elizabeth, because she, too, had failed to produce a son and because Henry now wished to marry the skittish Jane Seymour, daughter of a Wiltshire knight and lady-in-waiting to both Catherine and Anne. Bishop John Fisher of Rochester (only just made a cardinal by the Pope) was beheaded in June for his opposition to the new policies and Sir Thomas More followed him in July. Since spring, six Carthusian monks and three other heads of religious houses had also been martyred. And people still remembered the fate of Elizabeth Barton, the Holy Maid of Kent.

She was a sixteen-year-old servant in the household of the archiepiscopal steward, not far from Canterbury, and she was prone to epileptic fits, which were accompanied by trances in which she made prophecies. She also announced one day that the Virgin Mary had appeared to her in a vision and promised that she would be cured on the Feast of the Assumption; and a ceremony duly took place on that day, before a large gathering of people, in a chapel which thereafter became an object of pilgrimage. She was investigated by a commission set up by Cranmer's predecessor, Archbishop Warham, and, as a result, entered a Benedictine convent, where she remained for the next eight years. The epilepsy and the trances continued, however,

4 i.e. Jervaulx.

and her reputation as a prophet who both comforted and admonished continued to grow. She made the mistake, however, of allowing her prescience to stray from the strictly spiritual into the secular world. When the King made his first moves against Catherine of Aragon, the Maid let it be known that she disapproved (but the Queen was cautious enough to refuse her the interview which Elizabeth sought) and in this she was only voicing the concern of many of Henry's subjects. The King actually summoned her to court so that he could inspect this daring woman himself and she was bold enough to repeat her now public reservations about his activities. Later she prophesied that he would cease to be King within a month of marrying Anne Boleyn, that he would die the death of a scoundrel. The remarkable thing is that, although she was now well beyond the threshold of dangerous territory, she was taken up by reputable figures who might have been expected to shun her, including the Archbishop's own chaplain. After she had been committed to the Tower of London and interrogated there remorselessly for several weeks, she was taken before a gathering of privy councillors, judges and the nobility, who found her guilty of treason. In April 1534 she, together with five of her principal supporters, was executed at Tyburn.

This was therefore still fresh in the collective memory, together with all the other bloodshed, to heighten the sense of indignation and resentment which was caused by the various attacks upon the Church. There were other reasons for the next episode in Henry VIII's turbulent reign. Since 1527 there had been a series of crop failures due to repeated bad weather and in 1535–6 wheat prices were eighty per cent higher than in the previous year, which had led to riots in Yorkshire in June 1535 and in Somerset the following April. The 1536 harvest was better, but it didn't have to be much good to be an improvement on that of twelve months earlier, which had been disastrous, and the price of oats was still all but prohibitive.

The enclosure of land was another difficulty for many, especially for small farmers and their labourers, whose rights and interests were rarely considered when common land was expropriated by wealthier individuals for reasons that could not possibly be regarded with sympathy by the underclass. A lord of the manor in Lincolnshire made no bones about the fact that he enclosed some land to increase his income in order to pay for expensive litigation. A number of pamphlets published in the sixteenth century (one of them composed by Sir Thomas More) attacked such agrarian practices, including the notorious tendency of large farmers to enclose more and more common land for sheep pasture so as to take advantage of the burgeoning market in wool. The government made some attempt to mitigate these problems with legislation, but it was never enough to relieve the burden on the peasantry.

There were grievances, too, about taxation, both direct and indirect, a feeling by 1536 that Henry had imposed upon his subjects too much for too long, that some of his revenues had been improperly spent: the extravagance at the Field of the Cloth of Gold doubtless still rankled with some, as did the fact that a high proportion of the King's perpetual debts – which were rarely settled out of his own pocket – was to creditors who supplied him with jewels and other luxuries. A number of aspirations were unrealistic in the extreme: Chapuys reported to the Emperor that some Englishmen felt 'especially that the king should not take money from his people except to make war on France and Scotland'. He was referring to the tax on lands and goods known as the subsidy, which had originally been raised specifically for the defence of the realm and which, since 1534, had been extended to provide for domestic purposes as well.

But even those who recognised the necessity of taxation for other than military reasons were increasingly hostile to the range of imposts placed upon the King's lay subjects, which were quite distinct from the revenues he collected from the Church. Such items as tenths and fifteenths, which had existed since the twelfth century and which were exacted on an individual's movable possessions – the first collected from urban inhabitants, the second from the rural populace – had become much more than a source of irritation by now: they were seen as a crushing imposition, as was the Poll Tax, which had been revived by Henry in 1513, after having not been applied since the fourteenth century. People had enough local burdens to bear without all this. In the countryside, tenants had to pay their lord cornage, a rent based on the number of horned cattle they owned, or avenage, which was payment in oats, or berbiage, which was demanded for the pasturing of sheep, as well as gressum, which was a fine paid by a tenant on first taking possession of his holding from the landlord; and townspeople were faced with comparable demands. These costs had been steadily rising for a number of years. A case which came to court in 1527 concerned a parcel of land in Northamptonshire, where the gressum had been raised from six shillings and threepence ha'penny to thirty shillings in one bound, and some commoners in Westmorland actually threatened their landlord with violence because he had increased his demands from four marks to forty pounds, about fifteen times as much.

On top of all this, rumour of new taxes began to circulate and there was also an alarming story going the rounds in 1536 that official debasement of the coinage was planned. This was the practice, which the royal mints had historically sometimes been authorised to carry out and sometimes not, of diluting the gold and silver content of coins with brass and other inferior substances in order to make the precious metals go further for the Crown (or simply for a particular mint).[5] Henry had no compunction at all about turning to this as a further source of revenue. He 'had taken over from his father the finest, the best executed, and the most handsome coinage in Europe. He left his son (Edward VI, Jane Seymour's child) the most disreputable-looking money that had been seen since the days of Stephen – the gold heavily alloyed, the so-called silver ill-struck and turning black or brown as the base metal came to the surface.' The alarm caused by the inflation of these times, which the threat of debasement turned into panic, was such that people began to hoard what they had of gold coins; like the Vicar of Halifax, Dr Robert Haldsworth, who kept a pot full, worth £800, under his stairs. The dangerous thing to the government was that, except in the case of the local impositions, hostility to taxation was felt by every one of Henry's subjects, irrespective of rank. Together with the anti-clerical policies, it was the topic that was capable of uniting the commons of both town and

5 Debasement did not include 'clipping', in which fragments of gold or silver were shorn from coins, to be melted down most profitably. This had become, in the sixteenth century, a capital offence.

country – the 'relatively poor, relatively powerless within their societies' – with the gentry and the nobility, as other matters could not.

Another complaint was made most vociferously in the North. People there felt remote from the government in London, which was a long, expensive and quite dangerous journey away, though the further from home you travelled the less likely were you to come to any harm, lawlessness in various forms being rather less prevalent in the South; on the other hand, there were said to be fewer people in the North who would betray their neighbours by informing on them to authority. What's more, the North wasn't represented nearly enough in Parliament, though this could not be laid at Henry's door, the plain fact being that many northern boroughs simply could not afford to send a member down to the capital. For the North on the whole was living much closer to the poverty line than other parts of the country, which was one reason why the monasteries still played a more important role there. Indeed, the counties of Northumberland, Cumberland and Westmorland, together with the Bishopric of Durham, paid comparatively little in the way of taxes, because the burden of raising troops to fight the troublesome Scots at frequent intervals was so heavy; one of the most demanding functions of the northern nobility was to discharge this responsibility, to keep an eye open for trouble on the Marches, on behalf of the King.[6] Northumberland alone could boast 113 castles, almost all in private hands, because the threat from the Scots and from other Border raiders was so very real and permanent. Meanwhile, all the royal fortresses in the North were in a sorry state, not having kept up with repairs for far too long, while the town walls of Berwick were falling down and Carlisle was thought to be virtually indefensible.

If all this was not bad enough, the northcountry folk felt deeply patronised by the southrons (as Richard Layton had patronised them), especially those who swarmed around the court, where it was commonly said that the North was 'the last place God made'. As a variant, the Earl of Sussex, unhappily finding himself in Lancashire on one occasion, told Cromwell

6 The Marches were the borders between England and Scotland (and also with Wales). The word is derived from the Old English *mearc*, which meant a boundary.

that he didn't believe fodder for man or beast could be so hard to get anywhere else in England. But Archbishop Cranmer (a Nottinghamshire man himself) was guilty of the most withering remark about the North. He wrote that this 'was a certain barbarous and savage people, who were ignorant of and turned away from farming and the good arts of peace, and who were so far utterly unacquainted with knowledge of sacred matters, that they could not bear to hear anything of culture and more gentle civilisation'. Lancashire was certainly one of the poorest shires in the land, with fewer parishes than anywhere else but Westmorland and Rutland; and, because it was thought to be one of the more benighted parts of England – among other things, it had 'a formidable reputation for theft, violence and sexual laxity' – it was generally served by an inferior and poorly paid clergy, whom the laity often regarded with hostility. It was not unknown for priests to be forcibly thrown out of their churches there and, in 1535, the Rector of Bury was twice assaulted in a dispute over a parochial appointment, once while he was taking part in a procession in the street, the day after when he was in church.

So the grudges had mounted in a nation which was painfully transforming itself from an utterly feudal way of life into something rather less primitive. At the beginning of the century the population of England and Wales had been something like two and a half million, and most of the English still dwelt in a countryside where the wolf had been a hazard within the lifetime of many people. London was home to slightly more than 61,000 citizens (a third of them were to die from the plague in 1563), but the only other places with more than 10,000 inhabitants were Birmingham, Bristol, Exeter, Newcastle, Norwich and York, and of these Norwich was by far the largest with 30,000 or so. The most fortunate could expect to live to between forty and forty-five years, but to do that they had to survive the horrors of medieval medicine, which still functioned according to principles laid down by Hippocrates, Aristotle and Galen, and had made few technical advances since classical times.

They were taught that illness sprang from an imbalance between the four humours (blood, phlegm, yellow bile and black bile). Diagnosis consisted in establishing which of these humours was out of line, and therapy in taking steps to restore the balance, either by blood-letting (by venesection, scarification or applying leeches) or by subjecting the patient to a course of purges and emetics... The patient's urine was taken to be the best guide to his condition, and there were some practitioners who even thought it enough to see the urine without the patient... Operations were largely confined to amputations, trepanning the skull, cutting for stone, bone-setting and incising abscesses...

All without anaesthetic, of course, which was why everyone was terrified of falling into the hands of the surgeon. At scarcely any point did the reality of the Middle Ages coincide with posterity's romantic regard for it, an exception perhaps being that most of its medicines – burdock and comfrey, foxglove and pennyroyal, and many other herbs – were indeed plucked from the hedgerows by every cottager. Burdock was thought to be an excellent antidote to the bite of serpents and mad dogs, comfrey would relieve the pain of bruises and sprains, pennyroyal soothed coughs and colds. Foxglove had to be approached with more caution than the others, because an overdose could be poisonous; but, carefully used, it worked wonders in a poultice for the alleviation of swellings and sores.

By September 1536 a tension had settled on the land and omens were being bandied about so much that Chapuys informed his master that he thought the English were a credulous people, very vulnerable to dangerous prophecies. Some of these were directed at the Crown, but many concerned Thomas Cromwell:

> Much ill cometh of a small note.
> As [a] Crum[b] well set in a man's throat
> That shall put many other to pain, God wote.

Most potent of all was the Mouldwarp prophecy, which had first been heard early in the fourteenth century, had surfaced again in the time of Henry IV and now reappeared in all its rambling strangeness. Its full title was 'Prophecy of the Six Kings to follow

King John' and its principal source was the Arthurian *Book of Merlin*. It began with the Lamb of Winchester (Henry III), a holy man beset by insurrections, who would be succeeded by the Dragon (Edward I), which would ravage Wales and conquer many other lands before giving way to the Goat (Edward II), whose reign was to be disastrous, after which came the Lion (Edward III), who would wear three crowns before he died; then would come an Ass (Richard II), with leaden feet, a steel head, a brass heart and an iron skin; and, finally, the Mole, or Mouldwarp, himself (Henry IV) would succeed to the throne. Unfortunately, his skin would be as rough as goat's hair and he would be cursed by God for his actions. He would be driven from the country and drown, after which his realm would be divided into three by conquerors, and his heirs and successors would lose for ever what was rightfully theirs. This piece of fantasy had been recycled during civil disturbances in the past – when Wat Tyler led the peasants' revolt in 1381 and again during Jack Cade's rebellion in Kent in 1450 – and now it was circulating again throughout Yorkshire, with Henry VIII cast as the Mouldwarp, in spite of the inconvenient fact that he was the twelfth sovereign after King John.

The word went round that something ominous was going to happen at Michaelmas, which traditionally signified the end of harvest time. Throughout the year, mendicant friars had been preaching sedition in all parts of the country; while the Prior of the Blackfriars in Newcastle gave a series of sermons in Lent attacking the Royal Supremacy, at the end of which he wisely disappeared in the direction of Scotland. So matters came to a head in October 1536, inspiring the nearest thing to a civil war that the Tudors ever had on their hands, which at one stage even threatened Henry's grip on the throne. The last straw may have been the Ten Articles of June that year, which introduced a number of Protestant attitudes to such matters as baptism, penance and the Eucharist (the only sacraments that Martin Luther esteemed) and to the doctrine of Purgatory – while Henry's own inbred feeling for the traditional ways of Catholicism permitted the continued veneration of images and the honouring of saints, and left largely unaltered the conduct of rites and ceremonies. But by this stage enough was enough and a further tampering with the old religion had become unendurable. For it was the religious grievances that pulled the idea of rebellion together more than any other issue, that united all the parties who had a number of other and often disparate complaints to put before the Crown. And when it came, the trouble first broke out in Lincolnshire, which the King would soon regard as 'one of the most brute and beastly (shires) in the whole realm'.

IV

THE LINCOLNSHIRE RISING

Two days after Michaelmas, on Sunday, 1 October 1536, godly
folk in the market town of Louth went to mass as usual in their
parish church of St James. Louth snuggles down in a hollow on
the edge of the Lincolnshire wolds, which sound deceptively
gentle but are, in fact, a series of quite steep, though not very
high, hills rolling down the north-eastern side of the county.
The town was not particularly large – it was home to something
approaching 400 families – but it was an extremely prosperous
market place for the surrounding agriculture and husbandry: it
had five times as many taxpayers as the flourishing Lincolnshire
port of Grimsby. Louth could be spotted several miles away
because the church was a very prominent feature of the landscape, which it had embellished for 300 years. As usual, the
building had taken place in instalments across these centuries,
and its most recent addition and greatest glory, the spire, had
only been added between 1501 and 1515. The churchwardens
and the other parishioners had had a vision of something that
would adequately bear witness to their deep devotion and
express their yearning for the divine, and to this end they had
borrowed money from their guilds and from the richer inhabitants, pledged their valuables and paid for much of the necessary
labour in kind. The masons who had most of the skill in this
enterprise, however, insisted on cash and one William Medylton
received three shillings for six days' work, while Rob Hareson
got sixpence for providing wood, five shillings for sand and fourteen pence for nails. When it was done, course upon course of

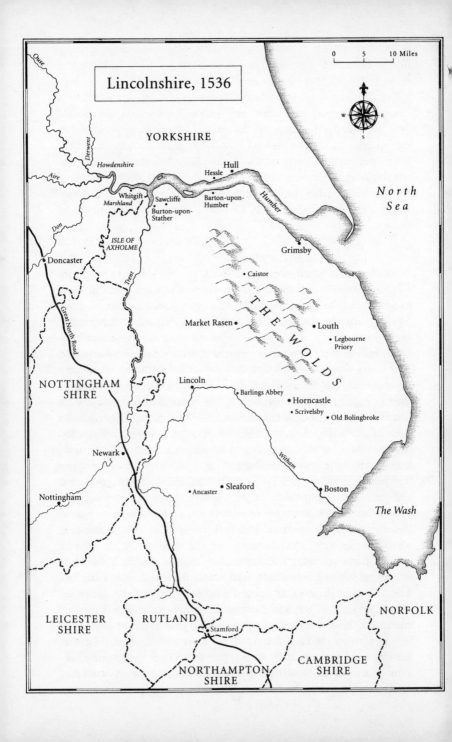

honey-coloured Ancaster stone which had been quarried at nearby Wilsford, delicately crocketed and upheld by flying buttresses from its base on the existing tower, it rose 295 feet above the street; so glorious a sight that, four centuries later, this would be acknowledged as 'one of the most majestic of English parish churches...', the spire having 'good claims to be considered the most perfect of Perpendicular steeples'. So joyful were the parishioners when the work was finished, that they celebrated this with a special mass, in which they sang the canticle '*Te Deum Laudamus*' ('We Praise Thee, O God') to an accompaniment of organs.

Though the Vicar of Louth in 1536 was a local man, he had not held the living when the spire was being built, having only been inducted two years before. He was Master Thomas Kendall, scholar of Balliol, University Preacher during Lent 1531, incumbent of an Essex parish before returning to Lincolnshire. It was while he was serving in Boxted that he had been asked by the Bishop of London to investigate some heretical opinions that had been expressed in Colchester, for he was an extremely orthodox and rigorous Oxford theologian. And now his most deeply held beliefs, his most tenacious loyalties, were being challenged and degraded by the King and by the apparatus of the state. On that sixteenth Sunday after Trinity, therefore, he decided that the time had come to counter-attack: his sermon was not only an indictment of the new religion that the Crown and its minions were propagating, against absolute devotion to the Virgin Mary and a wholesome awareness of Purgatory; it was even more pointedly directed against Cromwell's commissioners, who at that very moment were touring Lincolnshire, weighing up the wealth of a huge and prosperous diocese and seizing assets. More than 1700 parishes were spread across an area of 7265 square miles here, compared with York, which had only 698 parish churches in more than 8000 square miles; and, though Ely, Winchester and Canterbury were much wealthier, Lincoln's income in 1536 was close on two million pounds, which far exceeded the money coming into both York and Norwich.

There were, in fact, three different visitations going on at this time in the north of the county: apart from the one systematically working its way through the smaller monasteries to calculate their resources, another was assessing the second instalment of the parliamentary subsidy for that year, and yet another, also controlled by Cromwell but under the Bishop of Lincoln's immediate authority, was reporting on the moral state of the clergy and the way they practised their vocation generally.

At St James's the locals possessed quite a large number of valu-ables, acquired and passed on through many generations. There were 'thousands of ounces of silver vessels and ornaments, silver-gilt, enamels, jewels, amber, images, carvings; and an array of gorgeous vestments, hangings, banners, frontals, manuscripts and printed books...' Typical was a silver-gilt processional cross which had been bequeathed by a previous Vicar, Thomas Sudbery, to be used on major feast days, at certain funerals and when his own year's mind came round. And all of this was now in great danger of being taken away from Louth. So Thomas Kendall told his flock, at any rate: he informed them that 'next day they should have a visitation, and advised them to get together and look well upon such things as should be required of them in the said visitation'. Nobody in his congregation had any doubt what he meant, what he wanted them to do. Already, a neighbouring parish priest had told his people that their silver chalices were to be confiscated and replaced with tin ones, and everyone knew this for a fact, even though it had not happened yet. The sermon over, there was another battle cry in St James's that Sunday morning, just before the congregation formed up for a procession round the church. One of the singing-men in the choir, Thomas Foster, a yeoman who owned land worth £10, shouted, 'Masters, step forth and let us follow the crosses this day: God knows whether ever we shall follow them again.'

So a match was put to the touchpaper of some highly com-bustible material. Lincolnshire men who found themselves on business in adjacent counties had been dropping hints for weeks that, the moment the harvest was in, something special was going to happen where they came from. In Louth itself, on the feast of St Matthew, which was only nine days before their vicar's sermon, one of Cromwell's lesser officials had been silly (and brave) enough to announce that 'a silver dish with which they went about to beg for their church was more meeter for the King than for them'. At which a member of the congregation 'fashioned to draw his dagger, saying that Louth and Louthesk should make the King and his master such a breakfast as they never had'. Now rebellion was openly announced. After evening prayers that first day of October, a number of parishioners gathered at the choir door and relieved the churchwardens of the keys to St James's in order, so they said, to save the treasures inside. They then kept watch over the church until dawn, as they did night after night for the following week or so. Next morning, before the commissioner arrived for the visitation, about 100 people, most of them labourers and craftsmen, turned up and discussed whether they should ring the church bells as a sign that the action was about to begin.

Peals of bells had played an important part in the life of every community across England for at least 300 years and they had a secular as well as a religious purpose. Even the lowliest and most impecunious parish church had its common bell, which might be tolled on any occasion. There and elsewhere, a single passing bell was solemnly rung from church towers when someone was dying, so that all who heard it might pray for the repose of the departing soul and, at the funeral, every bell in the peal would be rung with each clapper encased in thick leather hemispheres in order to muffle the sound. But, as well as this, since the time of the Norman Conquest a curfew bell had been rung every night at eight o'clock and the habit still continued in many towns. The peculiarly English practice and pastime of change-ringing, which could go on for hours (depending on the number of bells in a tower) and produced endless permutations before a repetition occurred in the striking order, had been happening since the middle of the fourteenth century. Church bells were also rung at times of triumph and of national or local calamity. When trouble loomed, they were always rung backwards; that is, with the heaviest and deepest-sounding bell (the tenor) striking first and the rest following in an ascending sequence to the lightest and highest-pitched treble. This sound was to be heard very frequently across the towns and villages of Lincolnshire that October, and further north in the next three months.[1]

1 Handbells, of course, had been known from the earliest days of Celtic Christianity. The oldest known English bell in a church tower, at Claughton in Lancashire, is dated 1296, but there are thought to be others which are even older.

After gathering at St James's, the commons moved off to the town hall, where the annual election of the town officers was to take place, supervised by one of the Bishop of Lincoln's staff, John Henneage. The Bishop, John Longland, was a friend of Erasmus and was close enough to the King – he was Henry's confessor – to have been invited to the Field of the Cloth of Gold. He was a theologian and not all prelates were that, some having reached the bench of bishops from diplomacy or the law, with at least one of them a doctor of medicine. A humourless man, Longland was also extremely careful with his money and, although he was apt to be away from his diocese rather a lot because he was attending court instead, was extremely jealous and protective of what he deemed to be his episcopal rights and authority. His views on monasticism were rigorous long before Cromwell launched his suppressions, as a sermon he once preached to the Benedictines of Westminster had made plain: 'Let your frugal table, your hard bed, your mean clothing bear witness to your continual self-control. Let your shabby attire be the sign of a spotless mind, let food be simple and temperate and not fan the flames of lust…'

Longland was by this time widely disliked in Lincolnshire, because he subscribed to the new religious prescriptions without any sign of remorse and had also played his part in trying to get Henry a divorce from Catherine of Aragon: it was he who had presented Cardinals Wolsey and Campeggio with the papal commission instructing them to examine Henry's suit, and it was he who was sent to Oxford (where stones were thrown at him) to solicit the university's support. On top of all this he had, at the King's behest, informed his diocese at the beginning of September that saints' days were to be much reduced and that most patronal festivals would henceforth take place every year on 1 October, instead of being scattered throughout the calendar as the feast day of each church's patron saint came round. The legislation which ordered this revision started from the premise that feast days encouraged idleness and, in particular, that the harvest was neglected on account of superstitious practices. So all festivals between the beginning of July and Michaelmas had to go, likewise any that fell within the law terms; saving only the feasts of the Apostles, the Blessed Virgin and St George, Ascension

Day, the nativity of John the Baptist, All Saints' Day and Candlemas, which was celebrated in February and commemorated the purification of the Blessed Virgin Mary. The casualties thus included the festivals honouring St Mary Magdalene and St Swithin, St Augustine and St Alban, St Etheldreda and St Katherine, St Thomas Becket and St Edward the Confessor; also the feast of the Transfiguration and Holy Cross Day.

Some of the considerable hostility that Longland had attracted now rubbed off on to the unfortunate Henneage, who was seized by a mob carrying cudgels, pitchforks and scythes, and taken back to the church. Awaiting him there was Nicholas Melton, a shoemaker who was known locally as Captain Cobbler. It was he who had spread the story locally about the debasement of the currency, he who had told people that the church plate was soon to be confiscated and he may have been the source in Louth of a rumour that many churches were going to be closed down, leaving only one every seven miles to continue functioning. He was very close to the Vicar, who had promised him that he was doing Christ's work 'and in doing this you should lack neither gold nor silver'. Melton, in short, had become the paid ringleader of this disturbance in the life of the town, with a hard core of maybe twenty men ready and willing to do his bidding: among them, five others were shoemakers, two were weavers, two were sawyers, one was a blacksmith and three were labourers.

As leader, Melton had taken charge of the church keys the night before. He now made Henneage swear an oath to be true to the commons, on pain of death if he broke it. Oath-taking had a long history in England, especially in the administration of justice, where it was understood that perjury would surely incur the wrath of God. But it was also common in other areas of life and in various forms: in the past, oaths had frequently been taken over the tops of tombs (the ghost would arise and punish the offender if the oath was broken) and other objects, such as relics as well as Bibles, and many clerics found it a useful source of income to provide the wherewithal for such rituals.

Many oaths were to be taken in the next few months and the form was certainly not always the same. But one that was current in Lincolnshire at this time ran 'Ye shall swear to be true to

Almighty God, to Christ's Catholic Church, to our Sovereign Lord the King, and unto the Commons of this realm; so help you God and Holydam and by this book'. It is possible that this was the form used by Melton on Monday morning. That accomplished, the mob went over to the Saracen's Head where the Bishop's registrar, John Frankishe, had lodged the night before, because he was the official charged with conducting the episcopal visitation in Louth. They seized his books, including a New Testament in English, which was a particularly expressive symbol of the reformed Church's policies, and prepared to burn them. But first they made Frankishe climb the High Cross in the market place and he probably supposed they meant to hang him from it, but this was, in fact, simply intended as humiliation. At the nearby Corn Hill a fire was started and Frankishe was forced to burn all his papers, after which his books were pitched into the flames as well; all except one, which Captain Cobbler took possession of.

By this time the bells were ringing and pandemonium had broken out. Sixty parish priests had come to Louth that day in order to be examined in the visitation and these were now compelled to take the oath, too, as well as to promise that on their return home they would ring their own bells and stir up their own people. The town's elders were summoned from the municipal election and they, too, were sworn to loyalty. After that, some forty rebels headed for Legbourne and its Cistercian nunnery of St Mary, which stood in the low Marshland a couple of miles to the east of the town, a house which was so poorly off that some of its buildings were in ruins. That very day the commissioners had arrived and were beginning their business when the rebels also turned up. On their way they had seized one of Cromwell's servants and things began to turn ugly. At the nunnery the commissioners and their assistants were also taken prisoner and all were escorted back to Louth, being roughed up on the way while onlookers called for them to be put to death. Actually, prison and the stocks was the worst that befell them, but a very nasty tale was soon sweeping Lincolnshire, that one of them, a man named Bellow, had been blinded, sewn up in raw cowhide and baited to death with dogs. This was untrue, but the fact that it was thought to be conceivably true indicated the temper of the time in this place.

Someone now tried to stop what was happening, not because

he was against a rising in Lincolnshire, but because he thought it had started too soon, before it could be co-ordinated with a rebellion across the River Humber, where people were not yet fully prepared to join in. He was Guy Kyme of Louth, who had been in Grimsby through the weekend just past on some business to do with shipping, so he said, though many believed that he had actually been in touch with Yorkshire dissidents; and he certainly would, before long, be shuttling to and fro as a messenger between Lincolnshire and Beverley. Back home from the fishing port – or wherever he'd been – he tried to delay proceedings, with the support of one or two other townsfolk, but was ordered by a truculent Captain Cobbler to step aside, at which another man told Kyme they would kill him if he did not. Cobbler then announced from the High Cross that on the morrow, every able-bodied man between sixteen and sixty must assemble there for the next turn of events. Which, on Tuesday morning, was an advance on Caistor by no fewer than 3000 of the commons, some on horseback but most on foot. Not all of them were Cobbler's neighbours or customers, for since Sunday night the country round about had been in a fever of anticipating what might be in store for them. But conspicuously missing from this small army was the Vicar of Louth, who sent his curate instead.

Caistor is smaller than Louth, an old Roman settlement fifteen miles away to the north-west, and it is notable for a unique happening every Palm Sunday in its church of St Peter and St Paul, when the Gad Whip is cracked and then held over the vicar's head; a mystifying custom whose origins are so remote that no one knows when or why it first occurred. That Tuesday, the commissioners to settle the parliamentary subsidy were due to sit in the town, but they had heard the night before that trouble might soon be on the way, and so they had withdrawn to Caistor Hill to await and observe whatever happened next, leaving behind in Caistor itself many constables and the head men of the local wapentakes;[2]

2 An administrative division of a shire in that part of England occupied by the Danes in the ninth and tenth centuries; i.e. Derby, Leicester, Lincoln, Nottingham and York. Outside this Danelaw, the division was known as a hundred, possibly because it contained a hundred families or a hundred taxable hides of land, each of these being the area that could be ploughed in one year by one team of eight oxen.

also about 160 priests who had assembled for examination by the diocesan commissary court. Before ever the men of Louth appeared, however, armed citizens of Caistor began to assemble and the common bell was ringing, while an official told them to lay down their weapons, which they refused to do. Instead, they went to the church and asked the priests to join their cause, this being received so enthusiastically that the clergy promptly went out into the market place and there began burning their own books. A number of the commons had gathered round the commissioners, who told them that the subsidy was to be assessed by the citizens, not by the Crown, and that the tales about redundant churches and the confiscation of church property were false. But by now all the church bells were ringing and the sense of danger was mounting so much that, when the advance guard from Louth finally came into view, the commissioners lost their nerve and spurred their horses into flight.

The composition as well as the extent of the rising was expanding, as people who could not be described as cronies of Captain Cobbler and his like were recruited, not always willingly or wholeheartedly. An unusual addition was William Morland, who had been a monk of the newly suppressed abbey of St Mary, just outside Louth, and who had decided that he did not wish to transfer to a larger Cistercian house, as he was entitled to do, but would make some sort of new life for himself in the world outside the cloister. He had been given the task of distributing to people in a similar position the government permit (known as a 'capacity') which authorised them to become beneficed incumbents if they wished, on the same footing as the secular clergy. He was going about this errand on Monday morning when he seems to have blundered into the action by the High Cross from a mixture of curiosity and innocence, having got wind the night before of Thomas Kendall's inflammatory sermon. There he had given John Henneage a hand when the official was being menaced by the mob and was ordered by Cobbler to take the oath at the same time as the Bishop's man.

Now, on Tuesday, as a fully co-opted member of the Louth insurrection, he was riding with the advance guard to parley with the authorities in Caistor. He and about a dozen others rode up

Caistor Hill, which the commissioners had just left, and began to discuss matters with the commons, when one of them noticed that some twenty riders were galloping towards the home of Sir William Askew, one of the local commissioners. They set off in pursuit, caught up with the King's men and their attendants, and asked them to return and talk things over with the commons. Sir William, Sir Edward Madeson and a Mr Booth, effectively prisoners, did so, as did two others in the party, Sir Robert Tyrwhit and Thomas Portington, but a number of worthies got away, including Thomas Moigne, a lawyer from Wyfflingham and Recorder of Lincoln, Sir Thomas Missenden and Lord Burgh, who abandoned his servant Nicholas in his haste to put distance between himself and the pursuers. An appalled Morland then watched helplessly as this man was set upon and beaten so savagely that he later died from his injuries, after the ex-monk had confessed him and delivered him into the hands of surgeons.

The five captives were taken back into town, where they asked their escort and the people awaiting them, why the commons were making all this trouble. They were told very loudly by one John Porman, gentleman, that the commons did not at all mind the King making himself Supreme Head of the Church, that he should have the first-fruits and tenths of every benefice as well as the subsidy, as before, but that there must be no more suppressions and no further monies taken from the commons. They also wanted Cromwell handed over to them, together with the most prominently heretical prelates: their own Bishop Longland and Archbishop Cranmer, plus John Hilsey (Bishop of Rochester), Thomas Goodrich (Ely), Hugh Latimer (Worcester) and George Browne (Dublin). That evening, the prisoners and their escort returned to Louth, where the commissioners were instructed to compose a letter to the King. They did so, obviously under duress, assuring his majesty that

the common voice and fame was that all the jewels and goods of the churches of the country should be taken from them and brought to your grace's Council, and also that your said loving and faithful subjects should be put off new enhancements and other importunate charges. Which they were not able to bear by reason of extreme poverty and upon the same they did swear us first to be true to your grace and to take their parts in maintaining of the common wealth, and so conveyed us … to the town of Louth … where we as yet remain until they know further of your gracious pleasure, humbly beseeching your grace to be good and gracious both to them and to us to send us your gracious letters of general pardon or else we be in such danger that we be never like to see your grace nor our own houses, as this bearer can show, to whom we beseech your highness to give further credence. And further, your said subjects hath desired us to write to your grace that they be yours, bodies, lands and goods at all times where your grace shall command for the defence of your person or your realm.

The letter was signed by Robert Tyrwhit, Edward Madeson, Thomas Portington and William Ainscough. And that night, after it had been read to the assembled commons, it began its journey to London, which was normally two days of hard riding away, in the hands of Sir Edward and John Henneage.

Lord Burgh, meanwhile, sent off his own despatches: to the King, to the Earl of Shrewsbury (a privy councillor and royal commander) at Sheffield Park and to Lord Thomas Darcy (who had campaigned with the King in France) at his home near Selby. Thomas Moigne got in touch with Lord John Hussey, another of the King's trusties, who lived not far away at Sleaford, and Hussey passed on the warning to the mayor of Lincoln. Some hours later, on Wednesday morning of that week, Sir William Askew's two sons and one of Hussey's servants were taken to Louth by the commons, after the servant had been found in possession of two letters: one was from Hussey to Tyrwhit and Askew, offering his help to pacify the county, the other the mayor of Lincoln's reply to Hussey's communication. The seizure occurred near Market Rasen, where the bells had started to ring, and where the local commons grabbed Thomas Moigne as well, forced him to take the oath and bore him off to Louth with the other three. He had told the Askews and Hussey's man to hide the letters, which they failed to do, and when their contents were discovered, for a moment or two it seemed very likely that they would all be put to death by an angry crowd. In fact, they reached Louth just after mass and, when the letters were read to the assembled commons there, some people rushed into the church and began to ring the bells.

At this moment someone rode into town with news that Lord Burgh and 15,000 men were on their way to attack them. The rumour was incorrect but it roused the commons to further action, even though a number of the gentry who were by now involved in the rising counselled them to calm down a bit. Perhaps as a concession they also advised the insurgents to organise themselves properly against the moment when it might well be necessary to go out and fight. So they were divided into wapentakes and each was put under the command of whichever gentleman lived in that part of the county. Some of these men could not have accepted this role with much enthusiasm, but they probably felt that, in these parlous circumstances, they didn't have much choice.

Throughout the Lincolnshire rising, in fact, there was a constant tension between the commons and the gentry, even when they proceeded side by side and were nominally bound by the same oaths. Nor were the gentry themselves a homogeneous group, consisting as they did of old families who were socially closer to the nobility than to anybody else and the newly monied· class whose recent ancestors had given themselves a leg-up after commercial success. The commons felt that all the gentry, at both these levels, had an obligation to support whatever strategy they adopted, that terms should be dictated to the government from a position of strength; whereas the gentry, who doubtless felt that they had a great deal more to lose if things went badly for them (their property, for example) were much more cautious and conciliatory in their approaches to the Crown, urging the commons to present themselves as loyal supplicants rather than as a hostile body which the King had good reason to fear. William Morland and Guy Kyme, indeed, took it upon themselves to encourage as much harmony as possible between these two elements in the revolt, by acting as a bridge between them. Morland had helped both Henneage and Frankishe when the wrath of the commons looked as if it might get out of hand, before riding at the head of the rebels in the advance on Caistor, but he had also gone to the assistance of the man beaten to death. Kyme had entertained the captured commissioners to supper in his house, where they afterwards composed their letter to the King, but he was also instrumental in recruiting Yorkshire to the cause.

It was agreed that the following day they would all march on Lincoln itself as a united host. But that evening brought some desperate news from Horncastle, another town with Roman connections, fifteen miles to the south-west. The commons there had been agitated since Saturday, though no action was taken until Tuesday, when a parson named Nicholas Leache, and his brother William, a well-to-do yeoman, persuaded them to head for Scrivelsby Hall, a couple of miles away. This was the home of the locally influential Dymmoke family, who had been hereditary Champions of England[3] since the time of Richard II but had lately fallen from favour at court because they had become involved in a dispute about land and property with the family of Elizabeth Blount, who had been the mistress of Henry VIII before Anne Boleyn. In spite of this, one of Sir Robert Dymmoke's sons, Edward, was Sheriff of Lincolnshire and would one day be appointed Treasurer of Boulogne (which was captured by the Duke of Suffolk in 1544 and sold back to France six years later), an appointment which Dymmoke may be thought lucky to have obtained, given his conduct at home in October 1536. For, faced with some bullying by William Leache, he allowed himself to be sworn and then took charge of the Horncastle commons; after which, as its leader, he was party to the biggest blot on the rising throughout its course in Lincolnshire.

Some of the rebels had gone to Bolingbroke, where John Rayne, the Bishop of Lincoln's chancellor, had been conducting the commission of enquiry into the fitness of the clergy, most of whom he had deeply offended by his attitude; it is quite likely, too, that he was charged with promulgating the Ten Articles to the priests he examined and was scrutinising a little too carefully for their comfort such other matters as their financial affairs. He had a doctorate in law from Cambridge and had been one of the lawyers consulted by Henry when trying to obtain his divorce. Like Edward Legh and Richard Layton, he had become so

3 A purely ceremonial office, confined to a role in coronations.

thoroughly detested by almost everyone – though there has never been any reason to suppose that he much resembled those two in any other way – that when he was hauled before the commons of Horncastle, a great shout of vengeance went up and he was pulled down from his horse and done to death with staves, after pathetically trying to buy them off with twenty shillings for drink. Edward Dymmoke may not have laid a finger on the chancellor himself, but he certainly did nothing to stop the murder – nor did a number of priests who were watching and who urged on the mob – and he supervised the distribution of Rayne's money and clothes when the bloody work was done. It is possible that Captain Cobbler was in on this, too, for afterwards he was seen sporting a crimson cloak, which could have been Rayne's.

And this wasn't the only brutality of that day. One Thomas Wolsey, who was known to have been in the royal service, was pointed out by William Leache, accused of being a spy and hanged on the spot.

The effect of these murders was to spread the conflagration further, with people who had not yet done so taking up arms and preparing for the worst. Bells were ringing everywhere, beacons were lit along the south bank of the Humber and on Thursday morning the citizens of Beverley, on the other side of the water, awoke to the news that the whole of Lincolnshire had risen between the county town and Barton, where there was a ferry crossing of the river, which was almost a mile wide at that point. Messages were sent to the greater monasteries, so far untouched by Cromwell's men, where the monks were told bluntly that they had better join in, too, instead of leaving all the toil, the expense and the risks to the mass of commons and a parcel of gentlemen, these last shortly to be reinforced by others of their kind, so far uncommitted but now threatened with violence if they didn't also enlist.

At Cistercian Kirkstead Abbey, some distance outside Horncastle, a gang of men told the Abbot and his nineteen brethren that they should be in town by eleven o'clock the next day if they knew what was good for them. Matthew Mackerell, Abbot of the Premonstratensian monastery of Barlings, six miles north-east of Lincoln, had an even more unnerving experience when a party of commons led by a priest turned up and demanded bed and board for the night. Several men forced their way into the building and consumed the supper being prepared for the monks. Another group of horsemen appeared and said they were going to burn the place down, being dissuaded only because it was pointed out that some of their comrades were sleeping there. Instead, Mackerell was ordered to put on harness next day[4] and, when he protested that this was contrary to his calling, he was menaced so much that he agreed to go with them on the morrow. That night, he gave each of them a crown to buy more horses with and said a mass for them, but was so upset by everything that he repeatedly stumbled over the words. Mackerell wasn't the only religious superior who was coerced into funding the rebels, and it was subsequently reckoned that between 700 and 800 secular priests and monks became involved in the Lincolnshire rising, some much more gladly than others. A great deal of the incitement came from clergy like Thomas Kendall in Louth, who is said to have slapped the backs of his parishioners while telling them to get on with it. A number of them would pay for this with their lives.

The march on Lincoln was delayed for a couple of days while there was a great deal of to-ing and fro-ing across the north of the county, as one community after another threw its hat into the ring, too, and an attempt was made to organise a cohesive whole. On Thursday several of these hosts began to converge on Hambleton Hill just outside Market Rasen, where they were mustered in order to assess their strength and work out a concerted strategy. And a motley collection they were by now, both in their commanders and in their general composition. A Robert Tyrwhit (namesake and cousin of Sir Robert Tyrwhit, the commissioner) turned up at the head of a host from Yarborough and Thomas Moigne arrived with 200 men of his own. The monks of Kirkstead had accepted the inevitability of their fate, led by their cellarer and bursar, both of them mounted and carrying battleaxes, and they brought money which Edward Dymmoke took charge of. Walter Mackerell and his brethren joined the

---

4 In its fullest form this consisted of a leather jacket, armour for the arms and a helmet which protected the back of the neck as well as the head. Some version of it was worn by bowmen and billmen alike.

insurgents the following day, bearing beer, bread, cheese and six bullocks, then they asked leave to go home, but six of them were ordered to accompany the host, while Mackerell was given a special pass, so that he could tour the countryside collecting more victuals for what had become a considerable and hungry gathering of belligerent men.

The Louth and Horncastle contingents were also there, of course, the latter marching behind a silk banner of the Dymmokes, which had hung by custom in St Mary's church; and a man named Philip Trotter, a mercer, appeared wearing another Dymmoke heirloom that had been in the church's custody for well over a century, an old suit of armour, which would never be seen again after this week. All in all, it was estimated that some 10,000 rebels were mustered on Hambleton Hill, and they were ready and more than willing to head for the county town immediately. But Thomas Moigne counselled them only to send forth a small proportion of their number; the reason he gave was plausible, that much work needed to be done on the land at once, sowing the winter wheat and preparing the ground for next year. This advice was almost certainly not taken, because both the Louth and Horncastle hosts proceeded to Lincoln, as did many more.

Lincoln at this time was extremely run down, mostly because its prosperity had been based on the wool trade, which was now in decline owing to falling exports. Membership of the local craft guilds had fallen away, people were looking elsewhere for work, buildings that needed repair were neglected and projects that might have led to a revival – such as a proposal to link the city with the River Trent – had come to a standstill due to lack of money. Part of the trouble was a long-running dispute with the Earl of Rutland who, by kind permission of the Crown, had annexed the local fee-farm rents (a perpetual tax which amounted to at least a quarter of the value of land) and demanded that the hard-pressed corporation should pay its share, although this had been waived in the last half of the fifteenth century.

The newly arrived gentry of the mercantile class were as badly affected as anyone by all this; men such as Thomas Moigne, the city's Recorder, Robert Dighton, who was the son of a former mayor, and Vincent Grantham, alderman, former mayor and one of the city's sitting Members of Parliament. But they and their like had an additional reason for alienation from the government on top of the difficulties which they experienced in common with the rest of the populace. After five years of continuous pressure, Henry had at last succeeded in getting a Statute of Uses enacted by a very reluctant Parliament (whose members stood to lose a lot), and this had not only removed an individual's right on death to deploy his assets as and to whom he liked, but also asserted the Crown's feudal rights at the disposal of an estate: in short, it meant that the King got his cut as well. So important was this to the gentry that they had persuaded the Lincolnshire commons to accept a new clause in their list of grievances, which demanded the statute's repeal. For, as the gentlemen explained to them, 'Masters, there is a statute made whereby all persons be restrained to make their wills upon their lands, for now the eldest son must have all his father's lands, and no person to the payment of his debt, neither to the advancement of his daughters' marriages, can do nothing with their lands, nor cannot give his youngest son any lands.' It is very likely that this piece of legislation was crucial in the decision of men like Robert Tyrwhit and Thomas Moigne to throw in their lot with the rebels.

So the insurgents received a warm welcome when they reached Lincoln, the municipal officials instructing the shopkeepers and merchants there to provision the new arrivals at a fair price. The gentry lodged in the close of the Cathedral, whose towers and pinnacles dominated the city from the high ground above, and commandeered its Chapter House (where Edward I had called one of the earliest Parliaments in 1301) as a meeting place for the discussion of policy.[5] The building had ten heavily buttressed walls and its vaulted ceiling was supported by one tremendous central pillar, which swept upwards like a stone fountain; this was where the residentiary priests regularly met in chapter, sitting on a stone ledge which ran right round the inner wall, while they discussed all matters relating to the cathedral church of the Blessed Virgin Mary. While the gentry settled themselves in these atmospheric surroundings, the commons dossed down among the townspeople

5 The three towers were all topped with spires in 1536. One of these blew down in 1548, the other two being dismantled in the nineteenth century.

after venting their spleen on the episcopal palace – Bishop Longland fortunately being away – and all but wrecking it. They were now growing in confidence and this was partly, no doubt, because they acquired some artillery in the city, the first guns they had yet obtained. There is some reason to suppose that these had come from Grimsby, in which case they may very well have been ordered by Guy Kyme on his excursion to the fishing port. Morale was boosted even more by important news that came in from Yorkshire and from elsewhere in Lincolnshire. Letters arrived from Beverley and Halifax, informing them that they were now ready to follow the lead of Louth and Horncastle. Moreover, 2000 people of Boston had risen and were reinforced by more throughout Holland, that part of this sprawling county which incorporated its southern coastal lands and its portion of the fens. They were said to be converging on Ancaster Heath, some distance to the south of Lincoln, where they were all due to muster on Sunday, one week after Thomas Kendall had helped to provoke all this disorder with his sermon in Louth.

Meanwhile, the entire host of commons already in the city assembled and did two things. They abandoned the Dymmoke banner and in its place hoisted a piece of white cloth with an attached picture of the Trinity painted on parchment. Then, not yet having had a reply from the King to the letter sent to him on Tuesday night, they drafted a revised set of articles setting out their requirements. The King must impose no extra taxation except in time of war and the Statute of Uses must be repealed; the Church must have its ancient rights restored and no longer should tenths and first-fruits be taken by the Crown; no more abbeys should be suppressed and the land must be purged of heresy with heretical bishops punished and removed; the King should confine his Council to the nobility and surrender to the vengeance of the commons Cromwell, Legh, Layton and Sir Richard Riche (Chancellor of the Court of Augmentations, which had been created in 1535 to administer the lands, possessions and revenues of the dissolved houses). Finally, they asked that everyone involved in the rising should be pardoned. The commons wanted to despatch this document at once, but the gentlemen urged them to wait until the King's reply arrived. They had got wind of a royal reaction to the Lincolnshire rising and didn't want to make matters worse until they could be quite sure how things stood.

When Sir Edward Madeson and John Henneage had delivered their letter to the King, Henry summoned the Duke of Norfolk from his home at Kenninghall in the south of the county whose name he bore. Thomas Howard, a small and wiry man now in his early sixties, was the third Duke, and he had distinguished himself as second-in-command to his father (who was then Earl of Surrey) against the Scots at Flodden Field in 1513, subsequently commanding English naval operations against France and then, on returning to the North as Warden of the Marches, laying waste to the Borders as a punishment for Scottish overtures to the French. Howard was not known for his principles, had earned a reputation for bending them in any direction that might assist his advancement and increasingly had gained the ear of the King. He had been Earl Marshal of England for the past three years and might well by now have been Henry's most trusted adviser, had it not been for the fact that he loathed and did everything he could to bring down first Wolsey and then Cromwell – the first probably and the second certainly because he despised their origins – which didn't endear him to the throne. He was also comparatively second-rate as a politician, which Henry was astute enough to appreciate. There was, too, the puzzle of what Howard's religious beliefs were. Nobody was quite sure. It was said that, on hearing of the King's excommunication, he had fainted. On the other hand, he had been chief adviser to his niece, Anne Boleyn, and as such had helped her to supplant Catherine. This didn't, however, stop him from presiding over her trial for supposed adultery and arranging for her execution. Cromwell had then outmanoeuvred him so effectively that he had been obliged to retire to Kenninghall under something of a cloud. He was recalled now because he did have unquestionable military qualifications.

The King was so rattled by the news coming out of Lincolnshire that, while waiting for Howard to arrive from Norfolk, he set in train some arrangements himself. Courtiers were told to prepare to march on the rebels under Cromwell's nephew Richard and the Lord Mayor of London was instructed to obtain horses by any means he pleased – he did so by requisitioning animals belonging to everyone who could be roused, including foreign merchants in the capital, on the pretext that they were needed temporarily for a state occasion. Henry also thought it prudent to increase the garrison at the Tower, just in case he might need to take refuge there. But Howard was elated by this new turn of events, in which he saw his opportunity to regain the royal favour, possibly to engineer Cromwell's downfall at the same time. The Lord Privy Seal, meanwhile, had sent his own men north to find out more about what was going on up there. They reported back that there had been 10,000 rebels on Tuesday, but by Thursday night this figure was said to have doubled. Next day another estimate spoke of 40,000 or more, at least a quarter of them well harnessed, most of the others having some kind of equipment if not the whole kit.

Another figure now came on stage, the ailing sixty-eight-year-old George Talbot, fourth Earl of Shrewsbury, who had served Henry VII in wars at home and abroad before becoming an increasingly ineffective commander, an ambassador, a privy councillor and Lord Steward for Henry's son. A confirmed loyalist, he had nevertheless been slow to support the King's remarriage, had been a friend of Sir Thomas More, hostile – though not as much as Howard – to Wolsey and Cromwell, and only five months before had suffered an appreciable setback with the confiscation of his land and property in Ireland by an act of the Irish Parliament, which transferred them to the King. After he had been alerted to what was happening by Lord Burgh, following the latter's flight from Caistor, he had been trying to confirm and secure the allegiance of a strangely elusive Lord Hussey. Talbot was now in Nottingham and in a position to raise an army from the adjacent counties, but not at all sure that he could wisely commit troops to Lincolnshire when they might be needed more in Yorkshire, where similar events were beginning to take shape. This potential force by that weekend was but one of several options available to Henry.

He proposed moving his court to the royal palace at Ampthill in Bedfordshire, where Catherine had been confined during the divorce proceedings; and from there, he now said, he would lead an army against the rebels in person. Richard Cromwell, who had been busy pressing recruits in London and tapping the Tower arsenal for the small cannon known as falconets, was on his way, but slowly, because the roads were clogged with mud after recent heavy rain. On the edge of the fen country, at Huntingdon, Henry's friend Charles Brandon, Duke of Suffolk, was hoping to raise men, though he had not yet enough to be sure of overcoming what might await them further north. An even smaller force was strategically astride the Great North Road at Stamford but they, too, were regarded as inadequate to handle any crisis that might befall. As for Thomas Howard, the King still did not regard him favourably enough to give him what he might have expected, which was overall command; instead, the original orders were countermanded and he was instructed to remain in Norfolk to quash any rebellion that might break out there. Henry, in short, had become so alarmed by the way things were going and the further possibilities, that he had second thoughts about leading his army into battle in person. Brandon, he decided, would take control and Howard was told to send his son, the Earl of Surrey, to the new commander's assistance with whatever resources he could bring. Even when Richard Cromwell arrived with his contribution, however, the forces at Brandon's disposal might not have exceeded 3000 men.

But the sound of their coming was enough to frighten the rebellious gentlemen of Lincolnshire, the more so when Brandon sent them a message from the King which they anxiously debated in the Cathedral Chapter House on Tuesday, 10 October. It promised the most terrible vengeance if they did not submit forthwith, including the destruction of all their property by an army of 100,000 which was simply waiting to be unleashed upon Lincolnshire: a characteristic Henrician bluff. Their choice, though, was by no means a straightforward one. The royal forces, they correctly surmised, were badly organised, without the necessary funds to pay what were essentially mercenary troops and did not yet have any ordnance, which was still in transit along the Great North Road. The hosts that the rebels might put in the field were not essentially any different from these men insofar as both sides consisted of very ordinary civilians who were prepared to take up arms, and needed paying to keep themselves and their families alive. But they were very different indeed in one vital respect: the rebels had a cause which they now passionately believed in and for which they were more than ready to put their lives at risk.

For the soldiers of the King, who were mostly pressed men and certainly not professionals, often serving because they were required to do so in obedience to their local lord, who was under his own obligation to answer any summons that came from the Crown, this was at best a bread and butter job and nothing more. The chances were quite good that, with their higher morale and their numerical superiority (whatever that might actually be on the ground) the rebels would win an engagement between the two sides; and if that happened there was no telling how far across England the rising might spread. The commons, moreover, were becoming increasingly impatient with the delay, were demanding that the gentry should lead them into battle at once. But the gentry were haunted by the thought of what would happen to them if things went the wrong way. Execution, exile, loss of estates, impoverished descendants, their little dynasties effectively wiped out, would all be likelihoods after defeat. And if they won, it seemed to some of them, the best they could look forward to was another widespread civil war, like the awful conflict between the Plantagenets and the Tudors, which was thankfully now half a century in the past.

Lord Hussey's support was desperately important to them if they were to join the commons in their crusade, but that nobleman's position had become highly ambiguous since the day he tipped off the mayor of Lincoln about what was afoot. The rebels needed him on their side because he was easily the person more qualified than anyone else in Lincolnshire to turn this spontaneous rising into a serious political challenge to the government. Not only was he close to the Earl of Shrewsbury, Lord Darcy and others of the northern nobility, but as Sir John Hussey he had fought for Henry VII against the rebels supporting the pretender Lambert Simnel, and he had commanded the rearguard in Henry VIII's war with France in 1513, subsequently being employed on various diplomatic missions, most notably as envoy to the Emperor after the Field of the Cloth of Gold. In the wake of these appointments he was ennobled and made Chief Butler of England[6] and he had made representations to the Vatican in pursuit of Henry's divorce.

6 Another ceremonial role, fulfilled at coronation banquets, instituted by the Normans in exchange for manorial rights.

But then his relationship with the King had changed, though to what degree is far from clear. There is reason to suppose that he was not at all unsympathetic to Elizabeth Barton, the Holy Maid of Kent and, in the year of her execution (1534), Eustace Chapuys (not always an accurate reporter) informed the Emperor that Hussey appeared to be considering some kind of rebellion, which would only succeed if Charles V declared war on the English throne. If it was true, then this might well have had something to do with Hussey's regard for Henry's first daughter, Mary. He had been appointed her chamberlain in 1533 and his wife Anne had formed a deep attachment to the young woman, but made the mistake of referring to her as 'Princess', which was a forbidden word as far as Henry was concerned. For this, Lady Anne Hussey had been sent to the Tower and was only released a few weeks before the Lincolnshire rising began.

In whatever state of mind this put him, Hussey certainly behaved from the outset like someone who was not at all sure which side he proposed to back. His very first act, on being told what was happening, was simply to pass the message on to the mayor of Lincoln, when he might have been expected, as a liegeman of the King's, to put his retainers and tenants at Henry's disposal at once. The day the commons decided to march on Lincoln and murdered John Rayne in Horncastle, they wrote to Hussey, inviting him to join them; and he cautiously asked that a deputation be sent to Sleaford, where he would listen to them, though he had just promised that he would meet Lord Burgh in Lincoln with 300 of his men. By the time the deputation arrived, Hussey had discovered that his people could not by any means be relied on to serve the King, so his reply to the commons was a classic example of sitting on the fence. He said he would not be disloyal to his sovereign but, on the other hand, he would do nothing to injure the rebels. And when he received a summons from George Talbot to join him in Nottinghamshire, Hussey's reply was that he would like to help yet couldn't, as he was now watched closely by his people, but would try to escape when he could. It was at this stage that the gentlemen with the commons realised that Hussey was trying to manoeuvre them into putting their proposals to him in writing and a penny dropped that he just might be playing a double game. Talbot, too, was beginning to have his suspicions and, in replying to Hussey's message, rather heavily assured him that 'on my troth, all the King's subjects of the counties of Derby, Salop, Stafford, Worcester, Leicester and Northampton will be with me tomorrow to the number of 40,000 and I trust you will keep us company'.

The hosts in Lincoln sent a party of horsemen to bring Hussey in, but by the time they reached Sleaford on Saturday night he had fled, disguised as a priest, leaving behind Lady Anne to face whatever happened next. The first instinct of the rebels was to burn the house down, but Anne persuaded them to leave it alone after promising that she would retrieve her husband for them. She also gave them food – beer, bread and salt fish – both that evening and the next day, and offered money, which the leader of the party refused to take. And she kept to her side of the bargain (at least, she did her best to), setting off in search of her husband with one of their servants, eventually overtaking him on the outskirts of Nottingham. She begged him to return with her, but he angrily insisted that she should accompany him at once to the royalist camp. They reached the city on Monday morning and there received a frosty reception, Talbot having heard one rumour too many that Hussey had gone over to the rebels. Nor was he much impressed when Anne Hussey begged him to let them return to Sleaford, where their children were at some risk, which incurred yet more of her husband's wrath. Hers was a foolish expectation, in view of what had already transpired, and the Husseys were detained for the time being, while the Earl made further enquiries.

This was enough to shatter the resolve of the rebellious Lincolnshire gentry. Things seemed difficult enough to them, with the commons becoming daily more restive, more inclined to act insubordinately towards captains they had appointed themselves but who were, very often, gentlemen who had been coerced rather than coaxed into joining forces with them. What those gentlemen badly needed above all was someone of substance to lead them, with sufficient dedication to the cause and with enough authority to command the unquestioning obedience of the commons. They had supposed that Lord Hussey could be such a man, but Hussey had evidently decided that the leadership was not for him. Best get out now, they must have reasoned, while it might still be possible to retrace their steps from this act of treason – of insolence, at the very least – against the throne and survive. Their feelings of uncertainty were already plain to the commons, whose suspicions turned to outright hostility that Tuesday afternoon, when 300 men confronted the gentry in the Chapter House and insisted on the communication from Brandon being read aloud. Thomas Moigne was persuaded to do this but, halfway through, he left out a sentence which he thought would incense the commons further. Unfortunately, a priest was reading the document over his shoulder and blurted this out, whereupon there was bedlam in the chamber. Someone shouted that it was time to kill these turncoats and someone else threatened that if any harm befell the commons now, not one gentleman in Lincolnshire would be left alive. Only with some difficulty were the more belligerent protesters ejected into the cloisters and out into the street. The gentlemen were conducted by their servants to the safety of the Chancellor's house.

Next morning they and some of the commons they had learned to rely on, all in harness and prepared for more trouble, met the rest of the host in the fields below the Cathedral. They told them that they had written to Charles Brandon, asking him to speak to the King on behalf of all of them, and until a reply was received they intended to do nothing more. This so took the commons by surprise that instead of attacking their former commanders they began to drift away. That night, Lancaster Herald arrived in Lincoln from Nottingham and found everything in disarray. He had been sent by George Talbot to tell the rebels that if they did not disband forthwith, they would be attacked on Ancaster Heath. On Thursday, 12 October he met the insurgents in the Castle garth, on the hilltop which the fortress shared with the Cathedral, and delivered his message, which so undermined whatever zeal might still be left in the host assembled there that they heard him without protest. The gentlemen, indeed, took this opportunity to call it a day officially and turned their thoughts to how they should approach Brandon in order to make the best of a bad job. Apart from a stubborn rump, which persisted in its vision of corrected wrongs, other people began to slip off home, too. The Horncastle contingent returned with a new and complicated banner they had just devised and lodged it where all their most potent symbols had always been kept, in St Mary's church. The men of Louth went home with news that was not expected to make Thomas Kendall sleep easier at night. A messenger was sent over the ferry from Barton-on-Humber to Beverley, to nullify a letter that Guy Kyme had carried across the river on Monday morning, informing the Yorkshiremen of the situation in Lincoln and enclosing a copy of the new articles which were being sent to the King.

Meanwhile, Brandon, his army and his ordnance, were slowly advancing on Lincoln, with instructions to seize every piece of armament the rebels possessed. He was also to proclaim the King's acceptance of the surrender and his assurance that mercy would prevail. In fact, Henry had instructed his commander that four of the leaders from Louth, three from Horncastle and two from Caistor must be seized for trial and execution at once.

The rebels had been aware since Tuesday of the mood the King was in, having heard the reply Thomas Moigne read out, which was blazing with anger against 'the Traitors and Rebels in Lincolnshire'. Henry was openly contemptuous of the 'rude and ignorant common people ... the base commons of our realm!' He repeatedly insisted that many of the things the rebels complained about – the suppressions, the taxations, the Statute of Uses and so on – had been authorised by 'all the nobles, spiritual and temporal, of this our realm, and by all the commons of the same by Act of Parliament', that therefore 'how mad and unreasonable your demands be, both in that and the rest, and how unmeet it is for us, and dishonourable, to grant or assent unto, and less meet and decent for you, in such rebellious sort, to demand the same of your prince'. As for their presumptuous demand that they should have some say in the appointment of the King's councillors and the Church's prelates, they were not 'persons meet, or of ability, to discern and choose meet and sufficient councillors for a prince'. He deeply resented 'your ingratitudes, unnaturalness, and unkindness to us ... without any cause or occasion' and he reminded them of their obligations to him. 'Wherefore, sirs, remember your follies and traitorous demeanours, and shame not your native country of England, nor offend no more, so grievously, your undoubted king and natural prince, which always hath showed himself most loving unto you; and remember your duty of allegiance, and that you are bound to obey us, your king, both by God's commandment and law of nature.'

Then came the passage calculated to chill the blood of all who heard them proclaimed that bleak and hopeless day in Lincoln.

> For doubt ye not that we and our nobles can nor will suffer this injury at your hand unrevenged... And thus we pray unto Almighty God to give you grace to do your duties, and to use yourselves towards us like true and faithful subjects, so as we may have cause to order you thereafter; and rather obediently to consent amongst you to deliver into the hands of our lieutenant 100 persons, to be ordered according to their demerits at our will and pleasure...

Mercy was not going to be one of Henry's great priorities.

THE MAN WITH ONE EYE

Yorkshire was only a little slow off the mark. In its East Riding, people had been as exercised about Henry's attack on the old faith as the men of Lincolnshire, though the emphasis was slightly different in their case. On the south side of the Humber people had been angered both by the injury done to God's Church and by the economic effect that the transfer of religious wealth to the Crown would have on the county. If anything, the people living opposite them across the river were even more concerned about the enforced reduction in monastic help to those in greatest need of charitable assistance. They had seen four houses suppressed in the Riding in August alone, there was an expectation of more to come and there was the additional anxiety that, so rumour said, the parish churches were to be the next item in the royal campaign against the old order. This was therefore very fertile ground for the dissidence spreading so rapidly to the south and, although we do not know when Guy Kyme or anyone else from Lincolnshire first carried news across the river, we do know that, within four days of Thomas Kendall's sermon in Louth, beacons lit by the Lincolnshire men were clearly visible over the water and well understood in Beverley and its hinterland, and that by the end of that first week nobody could get across the Humber without a permit signed by the Lincolnshire men. It is even conceivable that, when the bells of Louth were rung backwards on the day after the sermon the sound might have carried as far as the Yorkshire shore, where they would have had little doubt what it meant. We also know that on Wednesday the 4th someone used the Barton ferry into Lincolnshire on a journey that was to transform the situation from a purely local rising into a rebellion that presently involved almost all of northern England. His name was Robert Aske and, soon, he and his activities would be common knowledge throughout Henry VIII's kingdom.

There may not be another significant figure in English history of whom we know so little. We know what he did every day of his life – sometimes every hour – for nine months of 1536–7 but otherwise it is almost a complete blank. We can guess that he was now in his early thirties, though the precise date of his birth is unrecorded, and we can suppose that he was physically a robust man: no one else could possibly have survived the life he led during those months, which included riding horses over long distances, day after day. But he had only one eye. This we know for sure because an acquaintance who was similarly afflicted said as much to Charles Brandon under interrogation ('we two have but two eyes; a mischief put out his other') yet we have no idea how he lost the missing one.[1] Before long, there was a reference to this in the version of the Mouldwarp prophecy that was going the rounds at this time:

> Foorth shall come a worme, an Aske with one eye,
> He shall be the chiefe of that meinye,
> He shall gather of chivalrie a full faire flocke,
> Half capon and half cocke,
> The chicken shall the capon slay,
> And after that there shall be no May

The Aske family were very typical Yorkshire gentry of a long and well-landed line, complete with coat of arms (*Or, three bars azure*). They were principally associated with estates in Swaledale, just outside Richmond in the North Riding, which they had secured some time after the Conquest, and where Conan de Aske was steward in 1183. A few years earlier Roger de Aske had founded the nearby Benedictine nunnery of

---

1 In her novel *The Man on a Donkey*, H. F. M. Prescott imagined that the eye had been poked out with a fishing rod during some adolescent horseplay with his brother Kit.

East of the Pennines, 1536

0   10   20 Miles

Newcastle-upon-Tyne

DURHAM

• Durham

• Brancepeth

• Bishop Auckland

Tees

Darlington

North Sea

• Wilton
• Guisborough
Mulgrave Castle •

Whitby

Cleveland Hills

Richmond
• East Cowton
Easby Abbey

• Mount Grace Priory

• Northallerton

NORTH RIDING

Jervaulx Abbey

Swale

• Bedale

YORKSHIRE

• Lastingham

• Rievaulx Abbey • Pickering

Scarborough

Masham
Ure

• Byland Abbey
Hinderskelfe Castle

Kirkby Malzeard •

• Newburgh Priory

Malton •

• Settrington

Flamborough •

Bridlington •

Ripon •

• Sheriff Hutton

Wolds

Knaresborough •

• Great Driffield

WEST RIDING

Wetherby •

York •

EAST RIDING

• Watton

Wharfe

• Wighill

Kexby •
Sutton upon Derwent

Market Weighton

Great Hatfield •

Tadcaster •

Cawood •

Derwent

Holme-on-Spalding-Moor

Beverley •

Burton Constable •

Selby •

Ouse

Aughton •

South Cave
Ellerker •

North Ferriby

Hull

Yorkshire

Hessle

Templehirst •

Howden •

Wakefield •

Aire

Pontefract •
Wentbridge •

Snaith •

Don

Hampole •

Hatfield •

Trent

Grimsby •

Doncaster •

LINCOLNSHIRE

Marrick Priory, which was destined to be suppressed by Henry VIII when there were only a prioress and a dozen nuns in residence, who had become so poverty-stricken that no guest was allowed to stay more than one night, their income being reduced by 1535 to £64 18s 9d, including twenty-four shillings per annum from the tithes of local lead mines.

But a branch of the family had at some stage before the fourteenth century moved away from this area to the far side of York, where these Askes settled in the Derwent valley of the East Riding, after marrying into the most powerful family in the district. Their seat was the manor of Aughton, which dominated a very small community of cottages that straggled along a byroad terminating in the moated house with its stained-glass windows and the adjacent church of All Saints, which the Normans had built. The Derwent was a tributary of the Ouse, which flowed into the wide expanse of the Humber, but it was nevertheless navigable where it passed below Aughton and was very prone to flooding across the adjacent low ground in winter, the water sometimes reaching the church walls. When this happened, the sodden countryside here became home to great flocks of wild geese and other waterfowl. This would have been the case in the late autumn of 1536, when October saw so much rain that the floods didn't begin to fall back to the Derwent until midway through the following month. In these surroundings, Robert Aske was brought up, the third son of Sir Robert Aske and related to the powerful Cliffords of Skipton Castle on his mother's side. By 1536, with their parents dead, Aske's eldest brother John was lord of the manor, while their sibling Christopher was mostly away from home in the household of the Cliffords at Skipton. They had four sisters: Margaret, Anne, Agnes and Dorothy, all married, the eldest of them to Thomas Portington, the commissioner who was captured by the Lincolnshire rebels at Caistor and who became, perforce, one of the signatories to the first document submitted to the King.

Unmarried himself and with his home still in Aughton when he wasn't away on business, or staying with other members of his widespread clan, Aske had been very briefly employed in 1527 by the sixth Earl of Northumberland, Henry Percy, who was his second cousin, but later that year he was admitted to Gray's Inn, one of the four ancient Inns of Court in London. These were sometimes collectively referred to as the Third University of England, because in them young men were not only trained for the law but were also taught history, Scripture, music, 'dancing and other Noblemen's pastimes'. The legal education was particularly rigorous, consisting as it did in the study of case histories going back to Magna Carta, and excruciatingly complex disputations designed to test the vocational skills of students in preparing intricate writs and pleadings. Anyone who graduated from this process and became an attorney was not only an individual of high intellectual ability; he had just found a well-connected way into all levels of government and could therefore become one of the country's most powerful elite, just as much as anyone emerging from Oxford or Cambridge. Gray's Inn certainly existed in 1355, though its origins may have been over half a century before that; and, like the other three Inns of Court,[2] it was a place where young men dwelt as well as studied during the law terms, the place that they could regard as a base for the rest of their professional lives. Robert Aske was just such an alumnus, and so was someone else he had almost certainly become familiar with in London, Thomas Moigne.

It was in order to get back to London for the start of the Michaelmas law term that Aske left Yorkshire on Wednesday, 4 October. He and his brothers had just spent some time with their sister Agnes and her husband, Thomas Ellerker, whose home was only a mile or two from Faxfleet Ness, where the Rivers Ouse and Trent combined to become the Humber. With three of his nephews, two of whom were also destined for the law, Aske rode to the ferry at Hessle[3] and, by the time they had reached the southern shore, the ferryman had told them of all the goings-on in Lincolnshire that week; though it would be surprising if Aske hadn't already heard something of the sort. From Barton the four set off again for Sawcliffe, en route to a crossing of the Trent, after which they would ride on to the Great North Road. The Portingtons lived at Sawcliffe and there the travellers would first spend the night. But before they had left Humberside the leader of the Caistor commons, George Hudswell, and some other

2 Lincoln's Inn, Inner Temple and Middle Temple.
3 Just downstream from today's great Humber bridge.

horsemen caught up with them and obliged them to take the oath to be true to God, the King and the commonwealth. The rebels allowed them to continue to Sawcliffe, but Aske then found that Portington had been detained with the other commissioners at Caistor, so he and the boys turned their horses for home. Once more they found their way blocked, so they returned to Sawcliffe for the night.

Before dawn, more rebels arrived from West Ancholme and demanded that the Yorkshiremen accompany them; and Aske, having persuaded them to let his nephews go, allowed himself to be escorted to a muster which was taking place a few miles away, before some 200 men marched to Hambleton Hill, on which a number of hosts were converging for their great strategic assembly that afternoon. At this rally Thomas Moigne besought the commons to let Aske speak. By this time Aske appears to have been pressed into service as leader of the West Ancholme rebels and, presumably because of this, they allowed his return to Sawcliffe. The following morning he made two more river crossings that he would become very familiar with in the next few days. One was at Burton-upon-Stather, where the Trent, only a little less majestic than the Humber now, flows beneath a thickly wooded cliff towards the confluence; the other over the Ouse at Whitgift, with marshes and reed beds spread widely on either bank. By the time he got home, on the day the Louth and Horncastle commons were entering Lincoln, Aske found that the wapentakes of Howdenshire and Marshland – the first in that part of the East Riding immediately to the north of the Ouse, the second just below the river, which meant that it belonged to the West Riding – were on the brink of rising, too; but almost at once he went back over the water, having heard that the authorities in Yorkshire had started looking for him.

Insurrection was particularly in the air in Beverley. The town was no longer the highly prosperous place it had been at the end of the fourteenth century, when it thrived on the wool trade and on its manufacture of a distinctive 'blue' cloth for export, because it had been been overtaken in commerce by the greater vitality of both York and Hull, whose energies had been augmented by their being on the banks of a river system which began far away in the Pennine hills and finished up where the

Humber, one of the mightiest English waterways, flowed into the North Sea. Unfortunately for Beverley, this priceless natural asset, which directly linked its two competitors with the continental markets, had bypassed the town, whose population declined from 5000 or so in its best days to fewer than 2000 in 1536. Nevertheless, it was still vigorous enough to sustain two weekly markets and four annual fairs. With its back to the Yorkshire wolds, it dominated the poorly drained wetlands which formed the landscape on its other three sides; it was itself a community whose streets wound along the banks of several small watercourses, and all of them metaphorically in the shadow of its Minster, though there were other churches in the town.

Beverley was, in fact, an ecclesiastical creation before ever it was a successful commercial centre, distinguished as such because it had become attached to an eighth-century bishop, an acquaintance of the Venerable Bede's, who was later canonised as St John of Beverley. His relics were enshrined in the great church and were an object of devotion by pilgrims from all over England. His legend associated him with a number of what may be regarded as fairly conventional miracles (restoring speech to the dumb and hearing to the deaf) but he was also credited with supernatural military powers, which enabled him to sway the course of battles in favour of his devotees. Not only pilgrims made for Beverley Minster from the world outside: this was also one of England's major sanctuaries, where fugitives could gain a respite for forty days, while the Minster's clergy negotiated with their pursuers. And there were a lot of clergy attached to the foundation, for this was a college of secular canons as well as a parish church. By one count there were upwards of fifty clergy here, including the chantry priests whose chief function was to say daily masses at the tombs of wealthy benefactors. Many of the canons, however, were absentees; including Thomas Winter, Provost since 1525, for whom Beverley represented an emolument and a promotion and nothing more, which had been arranged for him by Cardinal Wolsey, whose bastard son he was.

The citizens of Beverley still responded to this sanctified presence with great piety. As in the case of York, a regular cycle of Mystery Plays, in which all the local craft guilds participated, was one of the nation's most notable manifestations of Christian devotion. For nearly 200 years the guild of the Blessed Virgin Mary had enacted another performance of its own at Candlemas, when one of its members cradled a Christ doll in her arms and, followed by men representing Joseph and Simeon and other biblical bit parts, some of them carrying candles weighing half a pound, made a procession round the town and into the Minster, where the candles and coin were offered up, and a mass was said. The building housed sixteen (possibly more) subsidiary altars in addition to the principal one which was associated with St John, and each of these had become connected with the different craft guilds in the town, who maintained the expensive wax lights that burned perpetually there and also in front of the various images in the church. The creelers, the painters and the goldsmiths had thus attached themselves to the altar dedicated to St Christopher, the tailors to St Andrew's altar, the cooks to an image of St Katherine, the tilers and the dyers to a crucifix which hung just inside the north door. People asked to be buried in front of these ritual objects and they frequently bequeathed money and other valuables to specific shrines, as did Cecily Lepington, who left 6s 8d to St John's shrine and her best bed covering to the Minster's Easter Sepulchre 'as an ornament'. Although its income had fallen with the decline in Beverley's population, the Minster's accumulated resources still made it by far and away the richest outpost of the Church in the East Riding, and the third or fourth wealthiest in the whole of Yorkshire, including the mother church in York itself and all the major Cistercian monasteries like Fountains Abbey, whose great substance had also been founded on wool. It was very ripe for despoliation by the Crown, as the citizenry was well aware.

The mood of the East Riding in general may be gauged by what happened some miles to the north of Beverley on the Sunday before the feast of St Wilfrid; that is, one week after the sermon in Louth. A local farmer, John Hallam of Cawkeld, 'so cruel and fierce a man among his neighbours that no man durst disobey him', had for some time been in dispute with the Prior of Watton, Robert Holgate, who was one of the up and coming men in the Church of England, a friend of Thomas Cromwell's and one of the King's chaplains, a former university preacher in Cambridge and, latterly, Master of the Order of St Gilbert of

Sempringham, to which Watton Priory belonged; a mixed community of men and women which, though uncommon, was by no means unique. Holgate was generally disliked in the area because of his high-handedness and he had fallen foul of Hallam in particular because, after insisting that the tenant pay his tithe in cash rather than in kind, he had evicted Hallam from his farm.

The last straw for the farmer came on that Sunday when, in the priory church, before a congregation of lay parishioners as well as religious, Holgate did not mention that St Wilfrid's feast was approaching. This had always been especially honoured in the north-east of England because Wilfrid was one of their own, the man who led the Roman faction against the Celts at the Synod of Whitby in 664, which had secured the English Church's allegiance to the Vatican. Holgate's reason for the omission was very simple: he was following the King's instructions because this was one of the holy days that had been abrogated by Henry in his recent legislation. A wrathful Hallam at once leapt to his feet and challenged the priest on the grounds, as much as anything, that 'it was wont always to be a holiday here' and neither he nor the rest of the congregation was mollified when Holgate replied that the omission was sanctioned 'by the King's authority and the consent of the whole clergy in Convocation'. They threatened Holgate so seriously that eventually he announced the feast day, after which the service ended in uproar. So dominating a figure was Hallam, and so much was his protest to the general taste, that he emerged from that day as the ringleader of the commons everywhere between Beverley and Driffield. Later in October he returned to Watton with a company of armed men and deposed Holgate from his priory under threat of smashing the place up. He was to play an important role in all that happened in the East Riding in the next few months.

By the time of the Watton protest, matters in this part of Yorkshire had moved on from rumour and a stiffening of resolve to join the men of Lincolnshire, and were on the very edge of action. First there had been the sighting of the beacons along the Humber, then there had been a letter from the Archbishop of York, Edward Lee, to his receiver in Beverley, warning the official to beware of hotheads in the town and telling him that George

Talbot was preparing to move against the Lincolnshire rebels from his base in Nottingham. And bills had started to appear, nailed to church doors and elsewhere, warning that the government was planning yet more unspeakable impositions, including the suppression of parish churches and a variety of new taxes, one of them aimed at the sacraments. The bills were the work of Robert Esch, a Trinitarian friar, whose order had been founded in France at the end of the twelfth century for the express purpose of ransoming Christians held in captivity by the Saracens, if need be by substituting themselves in a prisoner exchange; but, this vocation being no longer in demand by the sixteenth century, the Trinitarians had become almost indistinguishable from Augustinians. Esch belonged to his order's house in Knaresborough, but he had been licensed to preach and to beg for alms in Beverley. He now appointed himself the propagandist of the East Riding protest movement, and soon he was dashing about the North and West Ridings as well, to spread the word and raise the alarm, but always returning to Beverley to replenish his purse with funds provided by the local commons.

On the day of the disrupted service in Watton Priory, two emissaries from Lincolnshire crossed from Barton to Hessle and rode straight to Beverley, where they let it be known that their rising was led by gentry, who would be obliged if the Yorkshiremen joined them. Later someone else arrived, bearing the articles composed in Lincoln. Word also went round that, just before his hasty retreat back across the Humber, Robert Aske had left instructions with one of Beverley's town governors on how to organise a rebellion, starting with bell-ringing, proceeding to oath-taking, followed by a general summons to muster. So stirred by all this were the locals that, in the market place later that Sunday, some people were even talking big about marching on London, and they mentioned plunder in the same breath. They had certainly come prepared for action, because many of them were already armed. The common bell was rung, the assembled throng was sworn in on the spot and everyone moved a little way out of town to muster on the gentle slope of Westwood Green.

There was then a small setback. A little to the south-west of Beverley was the Risby home of the Ellerkers, who were friends of the Askes and one of the most influential families in the East Riding; one of the Ellerker sons, as we know, was Robert Aske's brother-in-law. The commons had evidently decided that another son, young Sir Ralph (their father was old Sir Ralph), should be the gentleman to lead them, but he failed to answer the call to muster and instead sent a message that he was already sworn to the King and therefore could not take their oath; like the Archbishop of York's receiver he, too, had been warned by Edward Lee to be on his guard. So the commons turned to another landed family, the Stapletons of Wighill, near Tadcaster, and here they had better luck. Sir Christopher, his wife and son, together with his brother William, happened that weekend to be staying at the Beverley Greyfriars, the local house of Franciscans, which was on the edge of Westwood Green. Sir Christopher was in ill health, 'and lame both foot and hand', and the family had come to Beverley for a change of air, a regime they had followed for the past year or two. As the commons were arriving for the muster Lady Stapleton – who sounds as if she had a mind of her own, like Lady Hussey in Lincolnshire – called to them from the other side of a hedge 'God's blessing have ye, and speed ye well in your good purpose' and, when the commons asked where her menfolk were, answered that they were inside the house, that the commons should 'Go pull them out by the heads'.

Like Lord John Hussey, who didn't want to be compromised either, Sir Christopher was dismayed by this turn of events and asked his wife what on earth she thought she was doing; to which she replied that it was God's quarrel. Next day the insurgents returned and, probably because he feared the worst if these highly belligerent men were denied, one of the friars appeared and suggested that William Stapleton was their man, a notion that they received with great enthusiasm. 'Master William Stapleton shall be our captain!' they cried; and, given their mood, Stapleton doubtless felt he had no other choice, like many a pressed gentleman in Lincolnshire the week before. He had been trapped in more ways than one, for he was not only another attorney of Gray's Inn and another ex-employee of the Earl of Northumberland but, also like his friend Robert Aske, he had been prevented from going to London for the new law term by the disturbances across the River Humber. And

although, in the next few days, he tried more than once to relinquish the leadership that had been so unceremoniously thrust
upon him, he was stuck with it. With no military experience
whatsoever he had, willy-nilly, become captain of a host of 400
or 500 men. That night they fired a beacon at nearby High
Hunsley, on the edge of the wolds, which was guaranteed to be
visible right across the East Riding flatlands.

Stapleton did all he could to keep his men under control when he
realised that this was the best he could do in the circumstances, by
making sure that their now rampant ardour for the cause did not turn
to excess. He 'moved them to proceed in this quarrel as brothers and
not make spoil of any man's goods'. But they had lit the beacon
without his permission and, in response to its summons, people were
coming in from the countryside round about to sign up for a rebellion, itching for a fight, becoming very dangerous. Many of them
had been incited by the Friar of Knaresborough (as Robert Esch was
soon referred to), who had composed the announcement that they
must muster or take the consequences. Stapleton pandered to their
mood by appointing two petty captains from their own ranks, one a
yeoman farmer, the other the bailiff (the estate manager) of Beverley,
but this was his way of holding them in check, as was a letter which
he now wrote and intended to be read in Lincolnshire. This made a
ritual submission 'to God and our prince and his lawful acts and
demands' followed by an insistence that the antagonism of the
commons was directed against 'all them that be councillors, inventors
and procurers', whose base intention was 'utterly to undo... the
commonalty of the realm'. In other words, the object of their anger
was not Henry, but Cromwell and his like. It stressed that everywhere in England the commons were now restless and of one mind
as a result of bad government, but this was not a document announcing class warfare; it made plain the fact that Stapleton believed very
much in a society of orders, which bad government was now under-
mining, by tampering with the Church among other things. Next
day, Guy Kyme and two others from across the Humber arrived and,
at a great muster on Westwood Green which attracted 4000 from
Beverley and the surrounding countryside, gave a rousing account of
the doings in Lincolnshire, where there was now an army, Kyme
said, of 20,000 'which was like to come of the Holy Ghost... able to
give battle to any king christened'. He could not have known that

the Lincolnshire rising was within twenty-four hours of collapsing altogether.

By this time Robert Aske was back in Yorkshire and showing a great natural talent for leadership, having crossed to or from Lincolnshire no fewer than six times on one errand or another in the five days since 4 October. He very carefully kept control of the situation in Marshland and Howdenshire by instructing the locals on their bell-ringing strategy. He told the inhabitants of Howdenshire – his own people above all others, because this was where Aughton stood – that they should not start ringing until they had heard the bells of Marshland calling to them across the Ouse, and he gave the Marshlanders the same order in reverse; thus ensuring, he believed, that no bells would ring until he himself had given the signal to one or the other of them. At this stage he was unwilling to promote a rising in Yorkshire, or even to allow one to happen by accident, until he knew how the King had responded to the Lincolnshire petition; he saw rebellion, indeed, as a desperate last resort to remedy ills that pained him as much as anyone. If it could be avoided on this side of the Humber, if the events in Lincolnshire could persuade the government to modify its policies, then Robert Aske would be well content. But he was prepared to fight if there was no other way, which was more than could be said of his brothers. John and Christopher had only shared Robert's initial instinct to restrain the hotheads in their part of the East Riding, but the moment things looked as if they might be getting out of hand they wanted nothing more to do with dissidence there. Having managed to dodge all oath-taking, and mindful of the fact that Christopher was custodian of more than £100 in revenues from the East Riding estates of Henry Clifford, first Earl of Cumberland, they saddled up in Aughton in the middle of Monday night and fled to Skipton Castle, forty miles away to the west.

In the event, the bells of Howdenshire started ringing without Aske's authority, apparently prompted by the burning of the beacon at Hunsley the night before; another factor must have been an instruction from the Sheriff of Yorkshire to the local gentry, ordering them to raise men for the King and to take these to Nottingham. The bell-ringing, answered obediently from the steeples of Marshland, stopped any such recruitment in its tracks. Whereupon Aske accepted the full mantle of responsibility for what was now taking place and made his first proclamation of leadership. It told all towns to ring their bells forthwith, all commons to muster on St Wilfrid's Day at Skipwith Moor, a little to the west of Aughton, where they were to appoint captains. They were to 'make your proclamation, every man, to be true to the king's issue and the noble blood, and preserve the Church of God from spoiling; and to be true to the commons and their wealth'. It was signed 'by me, Robert Aske, chief captain of Marshland, the Isle and Howdenshire' and by six others, 'captains of the same', one of whom was his nephew Robert (the eldest of John Aske's five sons), another one of his brothers-in-law, William Monkton. The Isle he referred to was, interestingly, the Isle of Ancholme (or Axholme) in Lincolnshire, where he had been briefly pressed into captaining the local rebels.

The document makes plain something that Aske and his closest followers insisted on throughout the coming months, in all their various oaths and other statements; echoing William Stapleton, it insisted that their quarrel was not with the King or the nobility, but with the government of the realm, with Cromwell, Cranmer and others of their kind, who had crept close to the throne and were now manipulating it, in the rebels' view, for their own ends, profit and satisfaction. Like Stapleton again, Robert Aske never wavered in his belief that a just and well-ordered society was based upon a due recognition of rank and privilege, starting with that of their anointed prince, Henry VIII.

And things were happening elsewhere now. Henry Clifford was drawn into events, whether he liked it or not, by order of the King. It scarcely needed that when Clifford was devoted to his sovereign, and this dated back to his childhood when he had been brought up with the sons of Henry VII, his mother being one of Henry Tudor's cousins. His father had distinguished himself against the Scots at Flodden Field in 1513 (had, indeed, captured three pieces of James IV's ordnance and carried them home to Skipton) but the family had been climbing to its present powerful position since the end of the thirteenth century, as a result of marriages, alliances, inheritance and opportunism, which was the common currency of advancement at their level of society throughout Europe. The most recent of their successes had followed the sidelining of their greatest enemies, the Dacres, who had a long history of abducting (and once marrying) Clifford heiresses and profiting from the result, the control of Carlisle Castle being a big bone of contention between them: it belonged to the Crown but its command was delegated to one or other of the nobility, tenure offering obvious advantages in the pursuit of purely private interests.

Henry Clifford had been appointed Lord Warden of the Marches in 1525 but had lost the position two years later to Lord Dacre, only to recover it when Dacre was charged (on dubious grounds, with Cromwell's connivance) with treason in 1534. He was acquitted because the evidence was insufficient, but he was fined £10,000 instead of going to the block and was now in disgrace. The Cliffords were not responsible for his arraignment (though the jury was packed with Clifford clients) but their position was certainly strengthened as a result of the outcome. Henry Clifford had become indisputably one of the great northern magnates, the dominant figure in Cumberland, Westmorland and the Yorkshire Dales, just as his brother-in-law Henry Percy, sixth Earl of Northumberland, a sick man with not much longer to live, was the chief patron in Northumberland, Durham and the East Riding, and Edward Stanley, third Earl of Derby, was the principal power in Lancashire and Cheshire, his authority also stretching into Staffordshire.

Clifford had acquired a reputation for being the hardest landowner in the North, an avaricious man who put profit before the principles of good lordship. Thomas Howard, Duke of Norfolk, once said of him: 'He must be brought to change his conditions, that is to say, not to be so greedy of getting money of his tenants and others unto him.' Another verdict was that 'the Earl of Cumberland is in great danger of his life, for no man is worse beloved'. Certainly, a John Procter of Winterburn had no reason to love him, having been expelled from his farm in 1534 with fifty-nine years of his lease still to run. It has recently been argued that history may have been a bit hard on Henry Clifford; that, in Cumberland and Westmorland at least, he was seen more 'as an incompetent and absentee warden of the West March rather than as an extortionate lord'. Further south, the Craven district of the West Riding, which Skipton Castle dominated and which was therefore deeply under his influence, had seen a number of separate riots against enclosure in the summer of 1535; and nineteen men had gone to prison for that.

In one of the disturbances, at Giggleswick, 400 men had pulled down the local dykes and hedges, and similar upheavals had occurred just outside that village at Stackhouse, at Airton, a mile or two to the west, and somewhere else in the region, which has never been identified for certain, but which may have been close to the Clifford manor of Winterburn, or at Rylstone, whose commons had been offended by Clifford enclosures some years earlier. But Giggleswick was part of the enclave known as Percy Fee, whose lord was the Earl of Northumberland,[4] while the men of Stackhouse were tenants of Furness Abbey, and those of Airton had their quarrel with Henry Clifford's clerk of courts, John Lambert, who had enclosed part of the moor there for his own use. Clifford was nevertheless tainted by this enclosure because he had, after all, considerable influence in the area and therefore he could have stopped it had he been inclined to do so. Landholdings were often untidy in their patterns, they were not arranged straightforwardly, in the sixteenth century. There were, indeed, disputes involving Clifford as landlord of both commons and gentry that would tell against him in the next few months, but another cogent reason why he became something of a bogeyman at this time was that he remained steadfast in his devotion to the monarch and his government.

The King ordered Clifford to march on Hexham, far away to the north, where the Augustinian priory had somehow fallen foul of the commissioners, even though its income put it over the limit within which smaller houses of religion were to be immediately suppressed. When Cromwell's men arrived, it was to find the streets of the town full of men carrying billhooks and other weapons, bells ringing and the priory closed to visitors. Next day its gates were thrown open and out marched the twenty canons, all in harness, together with sixty armed men, at which the

4 Percy Fee also included Settle, Long Preston, Gisburn and other places in Ribblesdale, as well as upper Wharfedale, Littondale and Langstrothdale.

commissioners prudently withdrew, having been told by one of the religious that 'afore any either of our lands, goods or houses be taken from us we shall all die, and that is our full answer'. Clifford received this intelligence, together with his instructions from the King, in the second week of October but decided to ignore the order because trouble by then had broken out much closer to home, in the Dales.

As far back as 25 September – a full week, that is, before the inflammatory sermon in Louth – 500 men were reported to have taken oaths 'to certain unlawful articles' in upper Wensleydale, which was just over a Pennine spur from the town of Dent. Together with Sedbergh, a few miles away, Dent had been particularly restless ever since the Craven riots of the year before and one William Breyar had been roughed up there a few days after the oath-taking; he is an indistinct figure, but he was wearing clothes that gave him away as someone in the royal service. It was this which attracted the hostility of the Dent men, but they were not all of a like mind about whom they were hostile to. A blacksmith told Breyar, 'Thy master is a thief, for he pulleth down all our churches in the country.' But others shouted the smith down and someone yelled that 'It is not the King's deed, but the deed of Cromwell, and if we had him here we would crum him and crum him that he was never so crummed, and if thy master was here we would new crown him'. Whereupon Breyar fled and managed to get away to tell his tale. Which included his opinion that the fear of losing their churches – not only in Dent and Sedbergh, but also in nearby Garsdale – was the matter uppermost in his assailants' minds. This was an anxiety that may well have been shared by the people of Aysgarth, a huge parish, one of the biggest in England, which sprawled across the great sweeping expanses of upper Wensleydale and included, as well as the church in Aysgarth itself, a chapel of ease at Askrigg, with yet another in the much younger Hawes, right at the head of the dale, both these Christian outposts resulting from the distances between the communities there.

Clifford may or may not have been aware of these events, but shortly after Henry's instructions arrived, he certainly heard of the news that reached Ripon on 10 October and its immediate repercussions throughout the Dales. This ancient town, with a cathedral where St Wilfrid had once been a Benedictine abbot, was also notable for two other things. One was the custom of blowing the Wakeman's horn in the market place each day at sunset, in order to guide people safely home from the surrounding countryside; the other was the annual Minster horse fair, which straddled St Wilfrid's Day and attracted dealers from all over the North and even further afield. That year it was buzzing with the tidings from Lincolnshire, which were conveyed in a copy of the same letter that Archbishop Lee had simultaneously addressed to Beverley and York, and which also included the advice that a royal army would shortly be moving on Lincoln from Nottingham. Lee deliberately arranged for this to be proclaimed at the fair, where it was guaranteed to have maximum impact.

And so it did, but not in the way that the Archbishop had evidently intended. Next day, 200 or 300 men, mostly recruited from Masham, Kirkby Malzeard and Nidderdale, advanced on the great Cistercian Abbey of Jervaulx, which had stood beside the River Ure, towards the eastern end of Wensleydale, since 1156, after its monks had spent eleven fruitless years further up the dale, near Askrigg, where the weather was more bitter, the soil relatively poor, and crops had failed with discouraging regularity. This was a house with very considerable landholdings, on which it had introduced intensive sheep farming to that part of Yorkshire,[5] wealthy enough to escape the first of Cromwell's inroads into English monasticism, unlike nearby Coverham Abbey, a much smaller Premonstratensian foundation, which had just been suppressed.[6]

The Abbot of Jervaulx, Adam Sedbar, subsequently insisted that the horde which descended on his church did so with two ends in mind: one was to commandeer the abbey's horses; the other to make him take the oath. His first response was to run for it on to Witton Fell, accompanied by his father and a young boy; and there he remained for the next four days, only going home each night, when the rebels had dispersed, in order to obtain

---

5 Jervaulx was also responsible for the beginnings of cheese-making in Wensleydale, from the milk of its ewes.

6 Coverham was close to the birthplace of Miles Coverdale who, the year before, had produced the first complete Bible in English, which he dedicated to Henry VIII.

some food. Presently, they came back and threatened to burn down Jervaulx if Sedbar did not surrender himself, which caused his community to send him a message begging him to return. When he did, he was severely knocked about, though it could have been a lot worse, for there were cries of 'Down with the traitor ... Whoreson traitor, where hast thou been? ... Get a block to strike off his head upon ...' The oath was forced upon him and then he was carried off, obliged to ride a horse bareback to Richmond and beyond, to Oxenfield beside the River Tees, just over the border in Durham, where a muster had been summoned by Robert Bowes, who was emerging as a leader of the dissidents in this part of the North.

It was a little later, at another muster in Barnard Castle, that an eyewitness gave an account of the Abbot's behaviour that was at variance with Sedbar's own. According to this source, 'there was an abbot, a tall lusty man ... which said that I hearsay the king doth cry thirteen pence a day and I trust we shall have as many men for eight pence a day; and, as he troweth, it was the abbot of Jervaulx, and his chaplain had a bow and sheaf of arrows'. If that was true, then Sedbar was in a much less supine mood than he admitted, confident enough of the popularity of this burgeoning cause to believe that it could attract manpower at almost half the rate of pay offered to the royal soldiery.

While they were waiting for Sedbar to come down off Witton Fell, the commons went over to Coverham, restored its little abbey and reinstated its canons who, lately dejected and confused, were so buoyed up by this turn of events that they sang a celebratory mattins, normally the dawn office in the monastic horarium, in the middle of that night.

Other activities during those four days were the burning of beacons at night and the imposition of oaths during the day; and by the end of this interlude not only the whole of Wensleydale was roused, from its junction with Garsdale in the west to its terminus at Bedale, thirty miles to the east, but also Coverdale, Nidderdale, Colsterdale and Ripon itself. And nothing much, so far, had been done to try to put down the rising. By 12 October Henry Clifford had heard from Christopher Aske of the doings in the East Riding and he had been told by his son-in-law Lord Henry Scrope that the beacons had been fired in Wensleydale, where his home was at Bolton Castle, and that the insurgents were coming to take him there. Yet all Clifford did at this stage was to despatch his son Lord Clifford to join George Talbot's forces in Nottingham, and to tell Sir Christopher Metcalfe, at Nappa Hall in Wensleydale, to alert other local gentry to the trouble that might come their way. Lord Scrope, who didn't need this advice, promptly fled from Bolton Castle to Skipton, by a circuitous route through Westmorland, leaving his wife Katherine, Clifford's eldest daughter – he called her his bedfellow in a letter to her father – and their infant son to face the music alone. She herself waited for the rebels to appear, having hidden the child, together with his nurse, in a poor man's house.

Someone else also decided that it might not be a good idea to stay put any longer, and he was Edward Lee, Archbishop of York. Lee was the grandson of a lord mayor of London, was distinguished by having studied at both Oxford and Cambridge, and had served Henry in a number of foreign embassies while he was ascending the hierarchy of the Church. His inclinations were conservative and he is thought to have had a hand in the composition of Henry's book attacking Martin Luther, as is John Longland, Bishop of Lincoln, but Luther thought it was all Lee's work. In the 1520s he had had a long-running theological dispute with Erasmus, who became so irritated by Lee's attitude to him that he dismissed the Englishman as a pushy young man (he was then in his late thirties, in fact) who simply wanted to be famous. By 1531, when he was Chancellor of Salisbury, just before his elevation to York, he was in a delegation sent to Rome to lobby Clement VII about Henry's divorce, but he somehow managed to square this with his otherwise traditional beliefs. He was highly critical of the abrogation of holy days and he particularly resented the new calendar of permitted festivals being regulated by the vagaries of the Westminster law terms. But he preached against papal supremacy in York Minster in 1535 and had the timing of services in the city's parish churches altered in order to ensure a bigger congregation in the Minster, which included the mayor and the city's aldermen.

In some senses Lee was growing into a very middling Anglican prelate, in spite of his dislike of Cranmer's influence. He wrote to Cromwell, with whom he was generally on good terms, in the autumn of 1535, complaining about the new radical preachers who were beginning to stride the land, and followed this up six months later with an assurance that nobody would be allowed to preach 'novelties' in his archdiocese unless they had the King's express permission. Some of these men, he added, 'say they have licence of my lord of Canterbury: but I trust they have no such, and if they have, none shall be obeyed here, but only the King's and yours'.

Lee was not only antagonistic to the men of reform who uttered extreme views; he wanted none of the opposite variety, either, and pointed out that he himself had lately stopped a friar from preaching in defence of Purgatory. Henry, however, had begun to wonder whether Lee really was reliable by the summer of 1535, to the extent that the odious commissioner Richard Layton was sent to find out his views on the royal supremacy. He evidently passed that test but soon afterwards found himself under a slightly smaller cloud, when he approached Cromwell on behalf of Hexham Priory, which was within his archdiocese. He asked that it should be spared suppression, on the grounds that 'wise men that know the Borders think that the lands thereof, although they were ten times as much, cannot counter-vail the damage that is like to ensue if it be suppressed ... and men fear if the monastery go down, that in process all shall be waste in the land'. The Prior of Hexham himself went to London to plead his cause with Cromwell. It was while he was on his way home that Lee received him on his barge in the River Ouse and urged him to accept the decision that had been made. They were together there when the confrontation in Hexham took place.

After Lee was enthroned as Archbishop in 1531, following the removal of his predecessor Cardinal Wolsey, his principal domi-cile became Cawood Castle, on the south bank of the Ouse, not far from where the Wharfe pours into that river, midway between York and Aughton. Cawood had been associated with the second-highest-ranking priest in the Church for nearly 600 years and, although by the sixteenth century there was a certain amount of crenellation, it was essentially a two-storey palace built of brick, with forty rooms and various ancillary buildings, includ-ing a brewhouse. There were also extensive gardens and a seven-acre orchard. All this had become run down by the time the disgraced Wolsey was deposed from the archdiocese and Lee was loud in his complaints to Cromwell about the expense this was going to involve him in, not to mention the fact that he had found there no horse or even provisions awaiting him. In fact, he had inherited a position which rapidly made him the wealthiest man in Yorkshire, after the King and the Earl of Northumberland, a small part of his income coming from the tolls on the ferry crossing the river at this point; he would also be the last Archbishop of York to mint his own coins.

But life had suddenly become more difficult than ever. He had got himself into a dispute with the citizens of Beverley, whose lord of the manor he was. This was to do with the procedure for electing the town's governors, known as the Twelve Men, who traditionally served for one year only, elected from one St Mark's Day in April to the next. The stumbling block was that old Sir Ralph Ellerker, having served his time, was determined to stay on for another twelve months and, being an important figure locally, received the support of the other governors. Lee had therefore put up twenty-four of his own nominees, to share their civic responsibilities and powers (and outvote them in the town's council), and one thing had led to another, including violence by Ellerker's supporters. The upshot was that Lee had complained to Cromwell, who had summoned a group of townsfolk to appear before Star Chamber, the court which sat in the Palace of Westminster under the direct jurisdiction of the King and his councillors, to deal with perjury, riots and serious misdemeanours which might be considered somewhat less than criminal. The court had found in Lee's favour, Ellerker was forbidden to take any further part in elections and was fined 500 marks, the townsmen having to part with twice as much.

This dispute still had some way to go by 10 October when that shadowy character William Breyar – 'the pretended King's servant' – turned up at Cawood to announce that people were coming from Beverley to kill the Archbishop. And Lee had already been alarmed by news of a rising in Malton, which had resulted in two of his officials being taken by the insurgents. No sooner had Breyar delivered his warning, been given a horse and twenty shillings to take a message to the King, than yet more information came in, this time that the Marshland commons were on their way to press the Archbishop into service as their captain. If he had entertained any doubts about the peril which might face him before, Edward Lee had none whatsoever now. He must leave Cawood forthwith, before either the men of Beverley or those from Marshland arrived. His initial reflex was probably to think of the King's castle at Scarborough as a bolthole, but that would involve a hazardous journey through an area that was now inflamed and becoming daily more belligerent. He would, therefore, make off in the opposite direction, to one of the monarch's other great fortifications at Pontefract.

THE REBEL ARMIES

Pontefract (or Pomfret) Castle had stood on a rocky knoll a little to the south of the River Aire since the end of the eleventh century, having been granted to the de Lacy family, together with wider estates, by William the Conqueror. Apart from the de Lacys, it was held by a number of figures over the next three centuries, including John of Gaunt, until it fell to the Crown in 1399. A year later, King Richard II died in captivity there, having been overthrown in a power struggle with his cousin Bolingbroke, who thereupon became Henry IV. Pontefract had always been a place of imprisonment and execution for the high-born, and Shakespeare would one day pronounce upon it resoundingly: 'O Pomfret, Pomfret! O thou bloody prison, Fatal and ominous to noble peers!' It was a massive fortification, with a keep and nine other towers around the walls of its inner bailey, all built of huge limestone blocks with an infilling of rubble and mortar; the stone had probably come from local quarries, the distinctively pink-tinged mortar had certainly come from local sand. The lofty keep was quite different from the other constructions, which were rectangular, but its own several linked towers all had curved walls, a novelty introduced to England by returning Crusaders, who had been impressed by the military effectiveness of this design in France and the Middle Fast. The castle had a number of subsidiary buildings, such as a magazine, a treasury, a kitchen, a brewhouse and a bakery; and stables which could accommodate almost 700 horses without too much difficulty, maybe as many as 1000 at a pinch. It had a couple of wells from which good water could be drawn and twelve deep garderobe shafts for the disposal of sewage. There was a garden inside the walls, and a bowling green situated between that and the bailey. It was, in every way, a dominant and self-contained presence in this part of the West Riding, and it was well recognised that whoever wished to be confident of his authority throughout northern England needed to secure Pontefract first.

Henry VIII, however, had neglected it. Not only had he never visited it, but he was so apparently uninterested in its function or its condition that its masonry had been allowed to decay. It was still a great bastion but it would need overhauling before long if it was to retain its reputation as a fortress that no one could breach. In the absence of kings, its custodians were a series of trusted noblemen and, by 1536, its commander was Thomas Lord Darcy, whose family seat was a few miles away at Templehirst, on the north bank of the Aire, just to the south of Selby. Darcy was, in fact, supervisor of all the royal castles in Yorkshire and had a long record of service to the Crown, stretching back to before Henry's accession. As a young man he had been indentured to Henry's father and he had often campaigned with or for his new sovereign, though he tends to be remembered best for the military fiasco that took place in 1511.

Henry had been requested by his father-in-law, Ferdinand of Aragon, to supply 1500 English archers – unequalled for accuracy with their extremely long-range bows – in a North African campaign against the Moors and Darcy had asked to lead this expeditionary force. What happened next is not very clear. Either Ferdinand made a truce with the Moors and told the English they were no longer required, or he used this as a pretext to get rid of Darcy's force, who had got seriously drunk and run riot one day, doing much damage to Spanish property in the process. In any event, the English sailed for home a fortnight after arriving with not much of a reputation left and nothing at all of booty, at great expense to Darcy and his friend Sir Robert Constable, who had to share the cost of victualling and paying the men out of their own pockets.

Darcy was not a tremendously wealthy man, though he was a powerful figure in his part of the world: his landed income of £333 was only a quarter of Henry Clifford's and not even as much as a large monastery like Jervaulx collected in rents. He remained steadfast in his devotion to the King, however, long enough to draw up the indictment of Thomas Wolsey, but shortly afterwards the relationship cooled over the matter of the King's divorce. Darcy had gone along with the idea to the extent of being a signatory to the great petition submitted to Clement VII, but his deep religious convictions soon began to trouble him and he asserted his belief that the future of the marriage with Catherine was a spiritual and not a temporal matter. He was a naturally outspoken man with a great sense of honour and on this occasion it resulted in his being told that he would not be needed again that Parliament. Much worse, the King forbade him to leave London for another five years, which was perhaps the worst thing he could have done, for it gave Darcy a long time to brood on injustice and to resent his enforced absence from home.

According to Eustace Chapuys — and we must treat his evidence cautiously — Darcy supped in London one evening in the summer of 1534 with Sir Robert Constable and Lord Hussey. As a result of whatever conversation then took place, Darcy got in touch with Chapuys and asked him to sound out the Emperor about a possible invasion of England, landing troops at the mouth of the Thames so that Henry's devoutly Catholic daughter Mary, who was confined in Greenwich, could be whisked away to the Continent, presumably as a focal point of English discontent. Darcy is supposed to have given Chapuys a token of his esteem during this transaction, an enamelled gold pansy, the emblem of the old Yorkist nobility, which had survived the Wars of the Roses, to which Darcy belonged. This rings true, because Darcy certainly had a taste for badges and symbols. As far back as 1496 he had been charged at the quarter sessions for having distributed something called the Buck's Head among his people (kings, on the whole, disliking their subjects wearing any insignia but their own) and in the Spanish campaign, such as it was, Darcy's archers were equipped to go into battle wearing a device called 'The Five Wounds of Christ'.

He was now sixty-nine years old, suffering from a rupture he had incurred in one of Henry's French adventures and from a chronic bowel disorder, which may be why his humour has been described as grim. He had four sons by his first marriage to one of the Tempests of Ribblesdale but after her death he had remarried the widow of Ralph, Lord Neville, which meant that he had united with one of the traditionally most influential families in the North, whose head (another Ralph and grandson of the aforementioned) was the fourth Earl of Westmorland in 1536. Whichever way you looked at Thomas Darcy – Old Tom, as he was known to his familiars – he was a northcountryman through and through.

And he had been somewhat restored in the royal favour after being permitted to go back to where he belonged. Not only did Henry allow him to retain his official positions, but they had been in correspondence about the signs of dissent that were beginning to gain strength up there. It was Darcy who, on 6 October, told the King about the seditious talk in Dent, Sedbergh and upper Wensleydale, about the 500 men who had been sworn in with 'oaths to suffer no spoils nor suppressions of abbeys, parish churches or their jewels &c, and to pay no more money'. Two days later Darcy and his family moved to Pontefract from Templehirst. Mindful of his responsibilities as a commander, and with a soldier's nose for advancing danger, he then informed Henry that there was 'not one gun in Pontefract Castle ready to shoot. There is no powder, arrows and bows are few and bad, money and gunners none, the well, the bridge, houses of office etc for defence much out of frame.' The garrison numbered about 260 men.

This was the situation when the Archbishop of York arrived from Cawood and besought Darcy to give him refuge there, together with the thirty people in his retinue. Nor was Lee the only person who felt threatened enough to look to Pontefract for sanctuary. The Archdeacon of York, Thomas Magnus, had already beaten him to it and so had eight knights, among them Darcy's sons Sir Arthur and Sir George, and his friend Sir Robert Constable, together with one of the Neville family. A number of gentry – according to one account, maybe as many as 140 – were also soon sheltering within the castle walls and there they waited, while the gathering storm steadily rolled towards them from many directions.

In the next ten days, seven more rebellious hosts would be formed, to add to the one already assembled under William Stapleton's captaincy, and they were organised in virtually every part of the North. The most important of them was the contingent led by Robert Aske himself. As we know, he had assumed the leadership of Marshland and Howdenshire in his proclamation of 11 October, the day Edward Lee abandoned Cawood in favour of Pontefract. This was substantially a rising of the commons with a leavening of gentlemen – a pattern that was to be repeated everywhere – but an attempt was made early on to involve the nobility as well. The disgraced Lord Dacre was approached in his Yorkshire residence of Hinderskelfe, near Malton and close to the boundary between the North and East Ridings.[1] The inducement offered him was that the rebels would support him in any claim he might make for compensation from the Crown connected with the losses he had sustained after his trial three years earlier. But Dacre would not be drawn and, perhaps deciding it would be better to take himself out of harm's way, left the North Riding soon afterwards for his other home at Naworth Castle in Cumberland. Lord Darcy became another target, but when some insurgents turned up on his doorstep at Templehirst it was to find that he had already left for Pontefract. The biggest fish they were hoping to land was the sixth Earl of Northumberland who, although he was a feeble and deranged man, still in his thirties but with not much longer to live, was still the most potent symbol of power in the North-east. Doubtless because Aske had once worked for Henry Percy, he himself led the party which rode to Wressle Castle, between Aughton and Howden, and shouted encouragement outside its gates. 'Thousands for a Percy' was the cry, but this was another barren exercise because Northumberland, too, was not at home.

Aske's entire following therefore made shift with its existing resources, though it managed to acquire a number of other gentlemen and a priest, Thomas Maunsell, Vicar of Brayton, near Selby, who was pressed into attending the Skipwith Moor muster after being required to swear the oath whether he liked it or not. And, in the manner of William Morland in Lincolnshire, he was soon a willing member of Aske's small army, scurrying

1 Thirty-five years later this became a Howard property, after the Duke of Norfolk's son married a Dacre. At the end of the seventeenth century, when there was a disastrous fire, it was rebuilt as today's Castle Howard, to designs by Vanbrugh and Hawksmoor.

here and there, in his case as a recruiting officer. After discussing tactics and policy on Skipwith Moor, Aske's column set off for Market Weighton, marching behind the cross of Howden Minster and a vanguard of priests. The intention was to agree upon a joint strategy with William Stapleton and his men, and when the two old friends met the next day they formed a joint council of four gentlemen from each host. According to Guy Kyme, who was there, it was at this meeting that Aske 'bade God be with them, saying "they were pilgrims and had a pilgrimage gate to go"'. This was the first time Robert Aske expressed the sentiment that presently took more memorable shape as the Pilgrimage of Grace.

Second only in importance to Aske's own host was the one that arose in Richmondshire under the leadership of Robert Bowes. The first intimation that trouble was brewing over there came with the occupation of Jervaulx Abbey, another memorable event of that 11 October; and, at that stage, almost no one but commons were involved, though it was a minor gentleman from Bedale way, Leonard Burgh, who administered the oath to Adam Sedbar when the Abbot finally came down from Witton Fell. Shortly afterwards, however, these commons imposed the oath on Lord Latimer of Snape, also at that end of Wensleydale, and on Sir Christopher Danby of Masham, some distance downstream of Jervaulx on the banks of the Ure. Like many men in their position, having been pressed into allegiance, they very quickly assumed the habit of command. Another group of gentry quickly became involved in a rising in Richmond itself two days after Jervaulx was occupied and, as an early priority, restored the Premonstratensian monastery of Easby, which stood beside the Swale just outside the town and had been suppressed at the same time as Coverham. The two separate groups decided to amalgamate as soon as they became aware of each other's existence and proceeded to recruit more gentlemen to their cause, an exercise which was so successful that, only four days after the affair at Jervaulx began, 10,000 rebels mustered in Richmond, representing all sections of society apart from the nobility.

It was at this meeting that Robert Bowes was elected leader of them all. He came from a family who had done well for themselves by marrying into the Balliols in the fourteenth century, which produced substantial estates around Barnard Castle, though Robert himself lived at South Cowton, some miles beyond Richmond, his wife being one of the Metcalfes of Nappa. He was another lawyer and had been a Justice of the Peace, when such figures were not nearly as common as they became later in the sixteenth century. He had also had some military experience, when doing his stint of service on the Borders. Before long, he would have a host so large that it made sense to divide it into two, with one army made up of the Richmondshire rebels, the other consisting of men from Durham and Cleveland. It was they who provided one of the most potent symbols of the entire rebellion, the gorgeous white and crimson velvet banner of St Cuthbert, with the saint's cross embroidered in gold and silk in the middle, which was kept in Durham Cathedral and brought out only on high feast days and in time of war; by 1536, it had several times been flourished against the Scots and always on the winning side.

Aske's attempt to enlist Henry Percy had failed, but his brothers Sir Thomas and Sir Ingram proved to be more amenable. There were complex reasons for this, involving family animosities and the troubled relationship that the Percies had long had with the Crown. Over many generations and with the accumulation of much wealth, they had built up a position of virtually unassailable strength in the North-east, based on the possession of several tremendous castles, great powers of patronage, and vast landholdings throughout the North and even in distant places like Sussex, Kent and the south-west of England. Their power was such that, quite simply, they posed a potential threat to the stability of the Crown. Kings could not do without them, because they were a form of reliable insurance against incursions by the Scots, but the same monarchs were also well aware that the power of the Percies might one day be turned against the throne.

The Tudors were especially conscious of this danger and Henry VIII was determined to limit it drastically; if possible, to eliminate it altogether. Henry Percy had played into his hands. He was a malleable unfortunate who had long suffered from a form of ague and who had always been subjected to bullying, first by his father, then by Wolsey, now by Cromwell and the King. His wife had left him in despair, possibly because, on top of everything else, there were no children. He was also deeply in debt and this was partly the reason why he came to an extraordinary arrangement with the Crown whereby, in exchange for a pension and other assistance that he had been receiving for some years, he made the King his sole heir and legatee in 1536.

Something else that weighed with him was the animus that had always existed between him and his brother Sir Thomas, who in the circumstances might have expected to inherit the Percy estates when Henry died, as the second of the three brothers. No one knows what first caused the rupture between them, but it had long since passed the point at which it might have been healed. Sir Thomas was as unlike Henry as it was possible for brothers to be. He was a swaggering buccaneer of a man, popular, decisive, straight and very strong, where Henry was devious and miserably weak. He was much like their domineering father, the fifth Earl – sharing, among other things, a taste for flamboyant dress – who in his time had been known as Henry the Magnificent. And Sir Thomas had ample reason, in 1536, to be an embittered man.

In the events that followed, the youngest brother Ingram played little part, remaining at Alnwick Castle to swear the gentry of Northumberland in fidelity to the cause and not once to take up arms himself. But Thomas was different from him, too. He was staying with their mother at the manor of Seamer, near Scarborough, when news of risings in Yorkshire came to him, and his first instinct was to make for Prudhoe Castle on the Tyne, where his wife and children awaited him. As he left, disguised as a servant, he was accosted by two men who failed to recognise him and told him that if they hadn't found Thomas Percy within the next few hours they were going to burn the Seamer house down. So he returned to the manor where, that afternoon, a large number of commons came for him and swore him in. Next day he and sixteen of his men were at an assembly on a hillside to the south of Seamer, where several thousand had gathered; and, although we do not know this for certain, it was probably here that Thomas Percy was made captain of a new host, whose first act was to attack and despoil property belonging to the Cholmley family, as a punishment for its refusal to join in the rising, although Percy would later claim that he had tried to

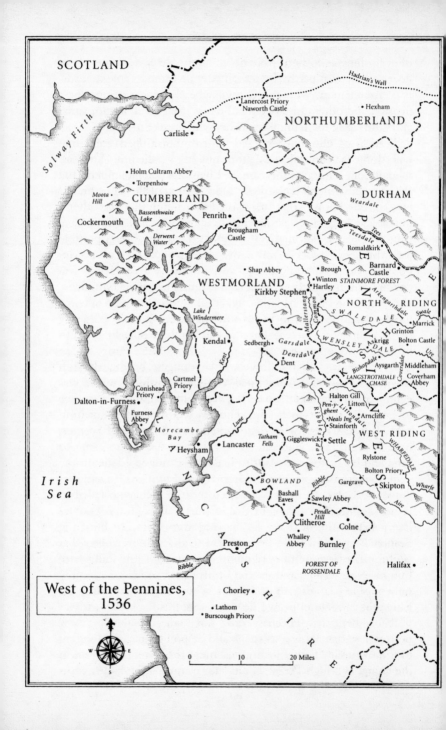

West of the Pennines, 1536

SCOTLAND

Solway Firth

Hadrian's Wall

• Lanercost Priory
• Naworth Castle   • Hexham

Carlisle •   NORTHUMBERLAND

Eden

• Holm Cultram Abbey   DURHAM
  • Torpenhow   *Weardale*
Moota
Hill   CUMBERLAND   Penrith •   *Tees*
         Bassenthwaite   *Teesdale*
         Lake   Romaldkirk •
Cockermouth •   Barnard
         Derwent   Brougham   • Brough   Castle
         Water   Castle   *STAINMORE FOREST*
                                        • Winton   P
                    • Shap Abbey   Hartley •   E
                                    Kirkby Stephen   N   NORTH RIDING
         WESTMORLAND   N *Arkengarthdale*
                                                   Swale •
                  Lake   S *SWALEDALE*   • Marrick
                  Windermere   *WENSLEY*   Grinton •
                                             DALE N Bolton Castle •
                   Kendal •   Sedbergh • *Garsdale* Askrigg   I
                            Dentdale   Aysgarth • *Coverdale* Middleham •
                            Dent •   *BISHOPSDALE*   Coverham
                                          LANGSTROTHDALE *Ure*   Abbey
         Conishead   *CHASE*
         Priory • Cartmel   Halton Gill •
Dalton-in-Furness • Priory •   *Pen-y-* Litton •
       Furness   *ghent* • Arncliffe WEST RIDING
       Abbey   • Neals Ing
              Morecambe   Stainforth •   *WHARFEDALE*
              Bay   *Tatham* Giggleswick • Settle
             ⚓ Heysham • Lancaster *Fells*   Rylstone •
                                                          Bolton Priory • Skipton •
Irish   *BOWLAND*   Gargrave •   *Wharfe*
Sea   Sawley Abbey •   *Aire*
                              Bashall
                              Eaves • *Pendle*
                                       Hill
                              Clitheroe • Colne •
                  Preston •   Whalley   Burnley •
                  Ribble   Abbey •   Halifax •
                                        FOREST OF
                              Chorley • *ROSSENDALE*
                              • Lathom
                              • Burscough Priory

0   10   20 Miles

stop this happening. But before long he would be riding towards Pontefract at the head of 5000 men.

On the day that he was sworn another host was taking shape over in Westmorland. Twenty-four hours earlier, at the parish church in Kirkby Stephen – a town which owed its name to the dedication of the church – the Sunday worshippers had done what John Hallam did at Watton: object to their priest's failure to announce a feast, in this case, St Luke's Day, which fell on the following Wednesday, the 18th. Once again, a cleric was pressed into submission, the church bell was rung and, on the Monday, a muster took place on Sandford Moor, some distance away to the west of Brough and evidently chosen because it was the usual place of assembly when the locals were summoned for border duty by the Lord Warden of the West March.

Once more, we have to approach what is said to have happened cautiously, because the only eyewitness account of these proceedings was given by Robert Thompson, the Vicar of Brough, when he was in deep trouble and trying to disengage himself from suspicion of having been involved himself. He failed to mention what had probably roused the Westmorlanders even more than the affront to their religious instincts, which was a letter that had almost certainly arrived first in Brough from the Richmondshire rebels, whence it had circulated throughout the district, urging all who heard its contents to join forces without further delay. The Westmorlanders, moreover, were instructed to send four gentlemen to Richmondshire and told that if they failed to respond to the letter, they would be regarded as 'enemies to the Christian faith and the Commonwealth'. And respond they did, except in the matter of the emissaries. The oath was sworn on Sandford Moor and four men were chosen as captains of the new host, though very quickly the command was in the hands of only two of them. One was Robert Pulleyn of Ormside, between Brough and Appleby, who was not much more substantial than a commoner; the other was Nicholas Musgrave, a yeoman from Kirkby Stephen.

The immediate concern was to enlist more gentlemen, their principal target being Sir Thomas Wharton, the Earl of Northumberland's principal officer in these parts. His home was just south of Kirkby Stephen, but when they reached Wharton

Hall its owner was missing, so the insurgents spent the night on his premises, had second thoughts about burning it down and seized his son instead. The next morning, St Luke's Day, there was a great gathering in Kirkby Stephen before men set off in various directions to dragoon more people of Wharton's calibre. Arriving at Lammerside Hall, the family seat of the influential Warcops, they drew another blank, the house being populated only by servants. With Robert Pulleyn in command here, these were told that if Wharton and Warcop didn't show up soon they would live to regret it. Pulleyn and his men then made themselves at home, and used Lammerside as a base from which search parties were despatched to root out commoners who had failed to respond to the muster call and to confiscate their goods. Next day the host marched towards Penrith along the River Eden, Musgrave leading a party down the west bank, Pulleyn in charge of the rebels advancing opposite them. When they reached Penrith, just across Westmorland's boundary with Cumberland, it was to find that the town had already risen under four captains of its own. The rebels never did manage to get their hands on Wharton and had to make do with pressing his eldest son to take the oath instead. Sir Thomas simply vanished and did not surface again until he turned up at Skipton Castle in January.

Though this was not the original formation, the four captains were all commoners, this rising being singular in its lack of gentlemen leaders. One was Gilbert Whelpdale, a prosperous man for one who was not rated among the gentry, and brother-in-law to Robert Thompson, whom he appointed as a chaplain to the host. Two more were the yeomen John Beck and Thomas Burbeck; and the fourth was a man named Robert Mownsey, of whom we know nothing apart from the fact that he acted under the alias of Charity and that he had quickly replaced Anthony Hutton, gentleman, because the commons wanted none of that rank in the leadership. The other three had likewise adopted similar pseudonyms: Beck was Faith, Burbeck was Pity and Whelpdale rejoiced in the title of Captain Poverty, a suggestive name that was by then widely recognised throughout the North, to which we shall return shortly. When these four captains attended any kind of gathering, they were not only preceded by a crossbearer, but also boasted a crier, who was there to make announcements. And each one had his own chaplain. Apart from Vicar Thompson's attachment to Whelpdale, there was the Rector of Caldbeck and sometime Chancellor to the Bishop of Carlisle, Barnard Townley, the Vicar of Edenhall, Christopher Blenkow, and the Vicar of Castle Sowerby, Christopher Slee. With the exception of Thompson, who seems to have been willing enough, none of them appears to have been enthusiastic about his role, which each had accepted after being told that he would be executed by the commons if he failed to come up to scratch.

But the religious element was important to these Cumbrians. They had a special ceremony known as the captains' mass, which was first celebrated in Penrith church with Robert Thompson officiating, leading the four captains in a procession with their swords drawn, before embarking upon the service, which was notable for his recitation of the Ten Commandments and his accompanying observation that 'the breaking of all these was the cause of all that great trouble'. In this way, in a series of musters spread widely across Cumberland from Penrith itself to Moota Hill far away to the north-west, the captains made themselves and their cause known all over their recruiting ground. And gradually the rising gained strength there, and was joined by a number of the gentry, most notably by Cuthbert Hutton of Greystoke, who had been the Sheriff of Cumberland until a few months earlier. Another important catch was John Legh of Isel, a cousin of the notorious commissioner Dr Legh, a former Constable of Carlisle Castle and a Member of Parliament for Cumberland. So was Barnard Townley, though his participation was doubtless encouraged by a threat of execution if he failed to join the host. The Dacres, however, proved just as elusive here as they had been when Robert Aske tried to involve one of them in the East Riding revolt. Gradually, too, the Cumbrians began to focus their attention on Carlisle, both because it commanded the borderlands – where trouble from the Scots was always likely to emerge – and because its royal garrison was perfectly placed for the repulse and punishment of local insurgents.

Immediately to the south of the Pulleyn–Musgrave host's stamping ground was the barony of Kendal, the Lancashire hundred of Lonsdale and a large slice of the West Riding which fell within the wapentake of Ewcross. The whole area therefore stretched south from Kendal, included all the land around Morecambe Bay east of the River Duddon and down to the mouth of the Lune, and everything west of the Ribble between Sedbergh and the Tatham Fells. Apart from some low land immediately beside the Bay, it was entirely hill country, which also took in the length of Windermere and the town of Dent. Dent was the focal point of discontent in this part of the North, where the first rumblings of thunder had been heard even before Lincolnshire arose and a couple of weeks before Robert Aske's East Riding rebellion began. Right at the start of October, local gentry were being approached to take the oath and it was a minor gentleman, John Atkinson, whom the commons of Dent elected as their chief captain early on, though he is thought to have come from either Sedbergh or Austwick; and he may have been related to the Towneleys of Burnley, a family of purely local significance at this time, whose great days as patrons of the arts were yet to come and who would supply a Catholic martyr in a much later rebellion.[2]

Atkinson's first recruitments were within the extensive parish of Sedbergh, which incorporated the winding miles of both Dentdale and Garsdale, but within a few days the Dent men were casting their net more widely. Kendal was raised because it was promised a hostile visit by 10,000 men if the citizens didn't sign on and, though their first inclination was to resist, they eventually chose from among themselves 500 to parley with the Dent host at Endmoor to the south of their town. There they capitulated and pressure was now brought to bear upon the local gentry, who were ordered to attend a meeting in Kendal on 24 October. The rebels were especially interested in enlisting Sir James Layburn of Cunswick, the principal figure in the area, but he never showed up; whereupon the Dent men went to his home and, even though an attempt was made to buy them off, did such damage there that, within forty-eight hours, Layburn and other gentlemen rode into Kendal and were sworn. He was in the party under Atkinson's command which then advanced upon Lancaster, which submitted at once, its townsfolk obediently swearing the

2 Colonel Francis Towneley was executed in 1746, in the aftermath of the Jacobite rebellion.

oath en masse; with the exception of the mayor, who fled south to take refuge with the Earl of Derby. Given that the town was dominated by a royal castle overlooking the wharves and quays of the Lune – Leland in 1539 thought it 'strongly built on a hill and kept in good repair' – this was a strangely easy acquisition, which the garrison seem to have made no attempt at all to obstruct.

The hundred of Lonsdale, too, was effectively under Atkinson's control, his host having mopped up recruits everywhere on their progress from Kendal. Their presence in the vicinity secured the immediate future of two religious houses in this area, which had recently been suppressed, their fates sealed by Drs Legh and Layton, who had worked over the Furness region with their usual thoroughness. Both were Augustinian priories: Conishead, which stood above the shoreline where the River Leven pours into Morecambe Bay, and Cartmel, perched on higher ground some distance across the Leven estuary. The only certainty is that, within a month or so of their occupants being ejected – seven canons at Conishead, with a wretched history of incontinence, and another ten at Cartmel, who had led something closer to an approximately blameless life (though one of the canons, according to Layton and Legh, had fathered five children) – they were back in their houses and functioning as before. But these foundations had less lurid claims to fame than their sexual activity. Cartmel possessed a fragment of what was said to be the True Cross, and the men of both houses were charged with arranging guides for people who needed to cross the treacherous quicksands of the Bay, where lives could easily be lost when the tides turned with exceptional speed in relatively shallow waters.

Fifteen days earlier another house had been restored, the Cistercian abbey of Sawley, which stood on the banks of the Ribble, in the lee of Pendle Hill's long whaleback, a mile or two above Clitheroe. The circumstances of its suppression were unusual, to say the least, because with an income of at least £467 from its substantial holdings in Ribblesdale and the Forest of Bowland, it was well outside the limit defining which houses should go forthwith and which would be allowed to linger for a little while longer. But the King had done a secret deal on New Year's Day with Lord Darcy's youngest son Sir Arthur whereby, in exchange for an estate in Northamptonshire which passed to the Crown, Darcy was granted the monastery, its goods, its estates and its advowsons (its right to present suitable persons to benefices, which was also worth much money). In other words, a procedure which should not have taken place before the agents of the Crown had finished the statutory processes of suppression occurred without them playing any significant part in the handover of Sawley to secular hands, other than actually evicting Abbot Bolton (who was awarded a pension of £20) and twenty-one other monks, three of whom decided to transfer themselves to distant Furness Abbey, the rest continuing their lives much closer to home with their Cistercian brethren at Whalley. The evictions had taken place in May and they appear to have been the smouldering tinder which finally ignited on 12 October, when some very angry men from Percy Fee in Craven appeared, to reinstate the monks and forty monastic servants who had also been dismissed. The monks later told Robert Aske that they had been 'by the good and loving commons of the country there assigned, admitted and entered into their house by virtue of the said commons'.

For several more days it was commoners alone who began to organise themselves into a force which, it was said, in seventy-two hours grew from 300 to 3000 men, belonging to upper Ribblesdale, Langstrothdale and Littondale. Its first muster was held at Neals Ing on the bleak hillside above Stainforth in Ribblesdale, beside the track which ran past the leonine shape of Pen-y-ghent, to Halton Gill in Littondale. For once, no bells had heralded this rising, perhaps because the fells were so steep and so tightly packed hereabouts that the sound of bell-ringing would not have carried very far. Instead, attendance was assured by notices tacked to all the church doors in the district, including one at Giggleswick, which announced that the muster on Neals Ing would take place the following day. But once again, after the oath-taking, the next stage was to enlist the gentry. High on the commons' list was the steward of Percy Fee, Sir Stephen Hamerton, who was taken from his Ribblesdale home at Wigglesworth, sworn to the cause and made the host's captain at once; 300 armed men had arrived on his doorstep, led by Richard Fawcett of Litton and John Jacks of Cray, both of them more well-to-do than many commoners.

Next day an even bigger armed gang, led by John Catterall, who was lord of the manor of Rathmell, Anthony Talbot of West Halton, who was another gentleman, and Richard Hamerton, who was Sir Stephen Hamerton's brother, descended on the deputy steward of the Blackburnshire hundred, Nicholas Tempest. He lived at Bashall in Bowland and he tried to duck the invitation until his visitors threatened to execute his son. Three hours later he was their man. He was, in any case, sympathetic to their action at Sawley, for when the monks returned to their abbey they found awaiting them an ox, a sheep and some geese, which Tempest had given. But he, too, could be rough when something stood in his way. He was given the job of raising the large parish of Whalley, while Hamerton led the recruiting expedition to Burnley and Colne. The monks of Whalley were reluctant to admit the rebels, but when Tempest turned up with 400 men and threatened to set the place on fire, they were led out by Abbot Paslew and promptly took the oath.

Eventually, there must have been at least 40,000 men under arms and hostile to the government across the North of England; maybe as many as 50,000. Overwhelmingly, they were commoners, who eventually managed to attract to their cause, by one means and another, six members of the nobility, twenty knights and thirty-five lesser gentlemen (though a more recent assessment has suggested there were 300 nobles and gentlemen). It is nearly impossible to be exact in any of the other relevant figures, because the head-counting of the individual hosts would have been an imprecise business, almost certainly given to a degree of exaggeration. Such realistic estimates as can be made, therefore, depend wholly upon the muster rolls, which the government itself required periodically from each administrative district in the kingdom. They listed every male between the ages of sixteen and sixty who was liable to be summoned to the defence of the realm, and they indicated each man's ability to provide arms, according to his income; there were ten separate grades to keep a tally of this, the most exalted consisting of men who could supply no fewer than sixteen horses, eighty suits of light armour, forty pikes and thirty longbows, another example of Tudor administration at its most admirably efficient.

The general musters were summoned by the lord-lieutenant

of each county, or his deputy, at least every three years, much more frequently in time of trouble, and they generally lasted two or three days, which allowed time for the tally to be brought up to date, for manoeuvres to be held, for any shortages or defects to be exposed and for matters to be put right before the recruits were sent home. A typical muster of the 1530s, supervised on Middleham Moor by Lord Scrope and two justices of the peace, indicated that at that time the parish of Askrigg could supply seventy-nine men, Bainbridge 188, Leyburn thirty-four and Aysgarth twenty-six and that the numbers for Wensleydale as a whole amounted to 'Archers horsed and harnessed 455, billmen 326, archers without horse and harness 286, billmen 377, spearmen 7. In all 1451.'

The London musters were, as might be expected, much more of an occasion than anything arranged in the provinces and, instead of a lord-lieutenant being responsible for the troops turning out, the Lord Mayor and aldermen fulfilled this duty. And very lavish affairs they usually were, often graced by the King himself as an interested spectator. At one muster, which Henry attended, the accoutrements of the participants were all white, including white caps with feathers. 'These were all commanded to be in white hose and cleanly shod. When it was known that the King himself would see the muster it was a joyful sight to every Englishman to see how gladly every man prepared himself.' The principal event began before six o'clock on a May morning, with everyone mustered in order of battle in the fields between Whitechapel and Mile End. 'About 8 a.m. they marched forward, the first "battle" led by 13 pieces of light ordnance on carts with powder and stone, followed by drums and fifers, and after them the standard of the city arms. Then came Mr Sadler, alderman, captain of the guns, well horsed and in coat of black velvet, followed by the guns, five in a rank, five feet apart, and every man's shoulder even with his fellows "which guns shot all together in divers places terribly, and especially before the King".' After the gunners came the archers, the pikemen, the billmen – and the surgeons, whose white coats were decorated with green bands. This considerable force entered Aldgate before nine and marched through the city to Westminster, 'where the King and all the nobility stood and beheld the muster, before whom the great guns and hand-guns of every "battle" shot very terribly'. Then it was through the Great Sanctuary at Westminster, round St James's Park into St James's Field, to Holborn, Cheapside and Leadenhall, 'and so severed about 3 p.m. To see the numbers of lords, ladies and gentlewomen at the windows, and how the streets were crowded, men would have thought that they that mustered had rather been strangers than citizens.'

The weakness in correlating the figures on the muster rolls with the strength of the Pilgrim hosts in 1536 is obvious, though by the time this rebellion reached its peak, there could have been relatively few commons in the North who had not become involved. On the basis of the muster rolls at this time, therefore, it is possible to estimate that Yorkshire alone raised 33,000 men, Cumberland over 7000 more; but this takes no account of the men under arms in either Westmorland or in the parts of Lancashire that were implicated in the rebellion, none of their records having survived to our own times. On the available assessments we can even extend the picture a little and it is a very patchy one. Yorkshire could supply 10,000 horsemen, Cumberland 2300 and, in the case of the Yorkshiremen, the North Riding was far better off for cavalry than the East or West Ridings. As far as individual protection was concerned, most of the horsemen were fully harnessed, but the foot soldiers were often without any armour at all. In Cumberland almost three-quarters of the fighting men were harnessed, which was a reflection of their periodic front-line deployment in conflict with the Scots, but even in Richmondshire well over half the available forces had some pieces of equipment – a helmet, a jacket designed to resist arrows, something to protect their arms and suchlike – that would minimise the degree of serious injury.

As for weapons, the gentry came off best, as might be expected, being armed with spears, short lances and poleaxes as well as the bow and the bill, which was carried by horsemen and footmen alike. Very few commons at the rebellion's lowest and most hard-pressed level possessed swords or anything else that was more sophisticated than a bill, a weapon for slashing and thrusting, with its antecedents in agriculture. They had not a single arquebus, that new-fangled firearm with a long barrel, which could only be obtained by importing them from abroad. Among all the rebels, it seems to be the case that only six of them could even have been the owners of pistols.[3] And it was not only in the matter of arms that the rebels were self-supporting: what they required for food and other necessities during the revolt often came from funds provided by the local communities as a result of voluntary taxation.

These people may have been united in their revolt, but they were by no means as one in the grievances that had roused them though, in some degree or other, what was seen as an attack on religion in some shape or form occurred everywhere. But secular issues which greatly agitated one part of the North might be a secondary cause for complaint, or even absent altogether in another area; and when people eventually gave reasons why they had rebelled it was sometimes found that men in the same host could have different emphases even when they were agreed upon the main matter of their discontent.

Taxation, for example, did not seem to be a primary concern in that part of the East Riding which centred on Beverley, where the government's intervention in what was regarded locally as the town's internal affairs was deeply resented and where there was much anger about the changing composition of the King's Council, in which men of lowly birth were taking the place of those with noble blood, who had previously enjoyed exclusive membership; and part of John Hallam's particular grudge against Robert Holgate was that the Prior of Watton was Cromwell's placeman. In Robert Aske's own territory immediately next to the Beverley hinterland the same complaint about the Council existed, but the prospect of new taxes was also a high priority, as were the other depredations of the Crown, both in a spiritual sense and as an act of licensed plundering. The lawyer in Aske was much concerned with the way Parliament had been repeatedly manoeuvred into making legislation that would be convenient to Henry but not necessarily to anyone else, and he had engaged the interest of the men he led in this topic, too. Both there and around Beverley the rebels had clearly taken their cue from Lincolnshire, in making not only a religious protest but

3 The figures have been extracted from Appendix I in Michael Bush's definitive study of the Pilgrim hosts.

with almost identical secular concerns, including a belief in a hierarchy of social orders; which is why, on both sides of the Humber, the commons who had either started their revolts or been very ready to be stirred up were anxious to have gentlemen (or, even better, noblemen) as their leaders.

Something akin to the very localised Beverley complaint about government intervention cropped up among the men of Richmondshire, who objected to Cromwell's meddling in the legal process which had followed a recent murder just south of Barnard Castle. Its corollary was their demand that all people living north of the Trent who became involved in serious legal proceedings short of treason should henceforth be subpoenaed to appear before the authorities in York and not in faraway Westminster; and it is possible to see the guiding hand of Robert Bowes, another lawyer, in that. Taxation also exercised these people, especially those who lived in Wensleydale, whose inhab-itants, together with those of Swaledale, were particularly hostile to the imposition of gressums – money paid to landlords on taking up a tenancy – whereas in neighbouring Nidderdale they simply wanted a revision of the amount paid. There was, too, the issue of whether tithes should be paid in cash or in kind, and the tenant right provision which obliged men to defend the border without pay and which, again, the commons of Swaledale and Wensleydale were more concerned about than others who rose with them. The Percy host shared many of these complaints, but singled out the Statute of Uses, with its drastic effect on the tra-ditional rules of inheritance, for attack. Further south, in Halifax and the other woollen manufacturing towns of the West Riding, there was huge resentment of government attempts to eradicate the local habit of 'flocking', which was the adulteration of loosely woven cloth by the introduction of small clippings and other fibres. Many signed up with the Pilgrimage for that reason alone.

Notably lacking in its catalogue of woes was any great evidence of agrarian concerns in the North-east, which figured hugely in all the resentment that had been building up in the higher North-west. In Westmorland they were moved to action by very little else of secular significance, but in this matter their complaints were many and various. They were hostile to the enclosures of land and other processes which restricted the grazing of animals belonging to the commons, and the Clifford family were a particular object of their anger, both because they enclosed and because they had raised gressums, which encouraged lesser landlords to follow suit. The exaction of tithes was also an issue here, but there was a curious absence of complaint about the government's fiscal policies.

In Cumberland, on the other hand, discontent had been concentrated on the issue of tenant right and it is easy to see why, when Cumbrians were pressed into military service against the Scots more frequently than anybody else except Northumbrians. They also protested against the habit of tithe-farmers – leaseholders who paid a fixed rent to a patron, in this case the Church, in return for extracting what profit they could make out of the revenue from tenants – from requiring payment in kind, which in some mysterious way helped to push the price of foodstuffs up for those who were on the receiving end of the demand. Below these two counties, in the territory raised by the rebel leader John Atkinson, the tenant right was another principal grievance, though in the Blackburnshire hundred they were more worked up against improving landlords; and taxation, too, was a vexed question hereabouts. As for the insurgents of Percy Fee, who became the host led by Hamerton and Tempest, they were as one with Robert Aske's own people in their detestation of the way traditional society was being dismantled, and especially of the way that people of inferior breeding had wormed their way into the confidence of the King. But, above all things, the suppression of Sawley Abbey had weighed most heavily here. Not only its actual closure, but the fact that it had passed into the hands of an outsider, as Sir Arthur Darcy was perceived, who clearly had seen it as nothing more important than part of a commercial transaction with the King.

The many repercussions of Henry's breach with the papacy, his attack on the Roman Church's traditions, its wealth, its liturgies and beliefs, its monastic and other social structures, was the one thing common to all the uprisings. Almost all the hosts were indignant at the suppression of the monasteries and, to the men of Richmondshire, as with the rebels in Percy Fee, this appeared to be the reason that weighed above all others. Around Beverley they were sorely put out when they heard that the Lincolnshire folk hadn't bothered to restore any of their suppressed houses, for in Beverley one of the most important aims of the revolt was to 'put religious persons in their houses again'. Only the people of West Cumberland, who were led by Gilbert Whelpdale and the other three captains, and those of Westmorland, under Pulleyn and Musgrave, did not even take the suppressions into account: the main thrust of their religious complaints was to do with more general changes in Church life that had been imposed upon them, including the reduction in holy days, and the severance of ties with the Vatican.

The issue of holy days cropped up almost everywhere, but was noticeably missing in Robert Aske's area, where the principal vexation was the prospect of the parish churches suffering as the lesser monasteries had. Interestingly, though, the people of Howdenshire and Marshland were made angry by the suppressions not on religious grounds, but because they were a manifestation of government greed. As for the rejection of the papacy, people in Richmondshire, like those in Westmorland, singled out 'the alteration of the power of the Bishop of Rome' as a matter of great concern. And, as with certain secular dissatisfactions, different emphases in the same community could be detected in the religious bitterness. Thomas Percy's people were as apprehensive as anyone at the rumoured prospect of increased taxation that would be levied in matters spiritual as well as temporal; but whereas this man was anxious about an impost on christenings and ploughs, that one was dismayed by the prospect of the government collecting a revenue from the sacraments and from bread. Such anxieties were scarcely surprising when it was said that the tax on every baptism would be 6s 8d, with the same levy on each plough. These were huge sums for a peasant to find.

One other thing pulled this great variety of dissidence together and that was the phenomenon of Captain Poverty. Its origins have been seen in the long allegorical poem *Piers Plowman*, which the Shropshire cleric William Langland had composed in the fourteenth century, whose theme was the familiar one of a quest for the meaning of life on earth, and how this was related to the life hereafter. In a modern translation it begins, 'One summer season, when the sun was warm, I rigged myself out in shaggy woollen clothes, as if I were a shepherd; and...I set out to roam far and wide through the world, hoping to hear of marvels.' Piers dreams of Reason preaching to the whole realm and rousing all the people to confess their sins, and eventually his progress becomes a pilgrimage to the castle of Truth. Whether or not this was actually in the mind of Yorkshiremen in 1536, there is a certain resemblance between Piers's dream and a stirring up of the people into a crusade, though the object of the sixteenth-century reality was not to discern the truth about anything, but to obtain redress from the government of King Henry VIII.

Captain Poverty first appeared at the massive Richmond assembly of 15 October, which elected Robert Bowes as the leader of the Richmondshire host. A document emerged from this event, signed by the pseudonymous Captain, which called for oath-taking as a prelude to action and listed a number of grievances, including a restoration of smaller monasteries (such as the locals had already achieved in the previous week at Coverham and Easby) and an end to the imposition of gressums; it made it plain that Captain Poverty's concerns included both religious issues and matters affecting the commonwealth. This word, which was to be much bandied about during the next few months, carried slightly different meanings, depending on who was using it and where. It could mean the wealth of the commons or the wealth of the whole country as distinct from that of the King; it included such things as church treasures, which were seen as possessions of each local community whose inhabitants, after all, had raised the money to pay for them. What the word commonwealth never meant was a condition of holding all things in common.

Directly or by way of imitations, Captain Poverty's letter was responsible for raising all but two of the eight rebellious hosts that were mobilised that month. From the North Riding, copies were despatched in a number of directions, to Northumberland and Durham, into part of the West Riding, to Cumberland and to Westmorland. It never went to the East Riding or to the adjacent Marshland area of the West Riding, because there they were marching to the instructions which had been composed in Lincolnshire and brought over the Humber by Guy Kyme and his associates, not that there was any fundamental difference between the two calls to arms. As for the North Riding version, Sir Ingram Percy received his document at Alnwick Castle, summoned the local gentry and made them all listen to the contents. Another copy, as we have already seen, went through the Pennine pass at Stainmore from Richmond to Brough, whose vicar, Robert Thompson, may well have been the first recipient. Soon, he was known as Captain Poverty's chaplain, and Gilbert Whelpdale's choice of *nom de guerre*, together with those of the other three captains in Penrith, was clearly influenced by the incitement to rebellion which had come out of Richmondshire.

Before long, other versions of the original letter were being concocted and spread further abroad. John Atkinson is thought to have been responsible for one issuing from Dentdale and the Vicar of Clapham, Christopher Howden, for another that began to circulate round Lonsdale. And all these compositions came under the imprimatur of Captain Poverty, or variants of that name. North Lancashire was summoned to arms by Master Poverty, Kendal by the Captain of Poverty, and other versions of the pseudonym that cropped up elsewhere were Lord Poverty and Brother Poverty. And, just as there was some small variety in the identities, so, too, were there slight differences in the complaints that were mentioned and in the wording of the oaths. A whole range of local issues were dealt with in this way, demanding among other things the abolition of sergeant corn and noutgeld, a switch from compulsory to voluntary tithes, the conversion of gressums to fixed sums if the complete abolition could not be achieved.[4] The defence of the Borders, however, was a very common theme. And though the wording of the oaths, too, might not always be absolutely identical, it is thought that the version circulating in Cumberland and Westmorland, 'to be true to God, to the faith of the Church, to the King and to the commonwealth of this realm' was fairly typical.

Two other things were composed at this time, and both were the work of religious. As in Lincolnshire, so in the North, there were examples during the rebellion of clerics taking up arms, sometimes under duress, sometimes not. But mostly the parish priests and the religious preferred a background role of incitement

4 Sergeant corn was a payment in oats to feed a sheriff's horses; noutgeld was a cash payment to the Crown imposed upon freeholders.

or simply one of providing sustenance of one sort and another. One such cleric was a Dominican friar from York, Dr John Pickering, who had made his base in Bridlington. There he wrote a song, based on certain seditious ditties supplied by John Hallam, and this circulated so widely that the Prior of Bridlington subsequently told how many copies were 'spread abroad as well about Bridlington as also about Pomfret and the same was also almost on everyman's mouth thereabouts'. The song urged that there was no animus towards the King, but for Thomas Cromwell there was a vicious hostility, which likened him to 'the cruel Haman' and his cronies to 'those southern Turks perverting our laws and spoiling Christ's Church'.[5] The underlying sentiment was expressed in a couplet which suggested that

> If this Haman was hanged, then dare I will say
> This realm then redresed full soon should be.

The other composition was almost certainly by a Cistercian monk of Sawley Abbey and achieved even wider popularity. It ran to sixteen verses, beginning with

> Christ crucified!
> For thy wounds wide,
> Us commons guide!
> Which pilgrims be,
> Through God's grace,
> For to purchase
> Old wealth and peace
> Of the spirituality.

It went on to complain of being 'robbed, spoiled and shorn, from cattle and corn ... that grace is gone and all goodness', and claimed that the commons had no alternative but 'to mell, to make redress'. It asked God to 'send them good speed, with health, wealth and

---

5 Haman was an Old Testament figure who planned to kill all Jews for an injury done to him by one Mordecai. He was outwitted by Mordecai's cousin Esther and finished up on the gallows himself, but remained an object of hatred throughout Israel.

speed' and to give them 'joy endless, when they be dead'. It ended resoundingly with the hope

> And that Aske may,
> Without delay,
> Here make a stay
> And well to end!

Although the Sawley Ballad has survived in its entirety, we do not, alas, have any idea what the tune was that went with it. But it, too, played a significant part in the events of 1536–7. The rebels had a cause, they were becoming very well organised under an inspiring leadership. Now they had a marching song as well and very soon its words were on thousands of lips as the hosts began to advance across the North of England, to do battle with whatever lay in their path.

VII

VICTORIES AND SURRENDERS

By the time the original Captain Poverty letter was written, the first real action in the East Riding had already occurred. At their meeting on Weighton Hill on Friday the 13th, Robert Aske and William Stapleton had decided on a two-pronged attack. Aske's host would advance forthwith upon York, while Stapleton and his men would make for Hull and effect its submission to the rebel cause. The towns so dominated that part of the North that it was vital to the ultimate success of the rebellion that they should not be allowed to stand in its way.

Hull was by far the younger of the two, having no history to speak of before Edward I acquired the small settlement there in 1293. Thereafter, it had increased in prosperity, though its population had remained remarkably static since the end of the fourteenth century, when it was recorded as about 3000 souls. It was a town with little industry and therefore only a small handful of craft guilds, and its wealth was based almost wholly upon its flourishing trade as a seaport. Vessels plied between Hull and Iceland, the Baltic, Hamburg, Portugal and Gascony, and there was also a brisk commerce with other ports along the English east coast. As we have already noted, it had nature to thank for its substance more than anything, in attaching it to the river system that had denied Beverley any comparable prosperity by the sixteenth century. Among other things, this meant that the profitable export of lead, mined in the Pennines of Yorkshire and Derbyshire, was largely in the hands of Hull. Beverley, indeed, had more than one reason to be jealous, and there had been a dispute between the two towns, because merchandise from the first had long been faced with tolls imposed by the second before it was allowed to pass down the Humber and so on to markets, at home and abroad, that were supplied by shipping. Things had become so one-sided that a number of the old Beverley mercantile families – the Alcocks, the Holmeses, the Hadelsays and the Bromptons – accepting the reality of their situation, had at one time or another moved their businesses to take advantage of the profit that could be made in the upstart port. As good an indication as anything of Hull's substance was the fact that its Holy Trinity Church, though still technically no more than a chapel of ease dependent on Beverley, was larger than any other parish church in the whole country.

York's importance was otherwise. Its history reverberated more than that of anywhere else in the kingdom, with the possible exception of London. It had been the Roman fortress of Eboracum, headquarters of the crack Ninth Legion until this was replaced in 122 by the Sixth, and it was where Constantine the Great had been proclaimed Emperor in 306. Its Minster had been founded on Roman remains by King Edwin, after his baptism by Paulinus, Bishop of York, in 627. In the eighth century, under the influence of the scholar Alcuin, it became a place of learning so renowned that people spoke of it as *Altera Roma*, the other Rome. Since that same time its archbishop had been the senior prelate in the Northern Province of the Church, and for 300 years there was a struggle between York and Canterbury for ecclesiastical superiority over all England, until Pope Innocent VI decided in the latter's favour in the middle of the fourteenth century. Not that this did much to diminish the opulence of everything connected with the Minster. Its chief residentiary priest in 1536, Dean Higden, was invariably 'attended to the church on the Christmas Day by 50 gentlemen before him in tawny coats garded with black velvet and 30 yeomen behind him in like coats garded with taffeta'.

The city's religious occasions were never less than memorable. Its cycle of Mystery Plays, which had been performed by the local guilds on the Feast of Corpus Christi for almost 200 years, were famous throughout the land and that same day included a procession through the streets, whose householders hung out 'coverings of beds of the best that they can get and strew before their doors rushes and other such flowers ... for the honour of God and worship of this city'. But York also had a secular importance because the Crown delegated to it a number of functions that were normally the responsibility of Westminster alone; and, with the North of England so distant from the nation's capital in perception, perhaps, even more than in travelling time and in miles, this was a case of convenience rather than generosity. As a result, for eight of the northern counties, York was where the most pressing matters of government and justice were handled by bodies like the King's Council in the Northern Parts, though this had gradually become less effective than was at first intended, partly because of what was perceived as the monarch's indifference to the region; and, certainly, no Tudor king had been seen in the North since Henry VII ventured there in 1487, the second year of his reign.

York's prosperity had always been closely connected with the Ouse, a very considerable waterway at that point, which not only gave it a valuable outlet to the sea, but also allowed goods to be shipped, through connections with other rivers, to and from Boroughbridge, Ripon, Northallerton, Knaresborough, Middleham and even as far as Halifax, which was on the farther edge of the Pennines and had a great reputation for the manufacture of woollen broadcloth. But the prosperity had failed in the 1530s, owing to a decline in the textile industry and a faltering foreign trade. There were a number of reasons for this. One was a dislocation of the cloth trade which England enjoyed with the Netherlands and Spain, as a result of the hostilities that broke out between Henry and the Emperor in 1528–9 and the subsequent cold war. Another was the high-handed attitude of the north German merchants who were banded together in the Hanseatic League and had become powerful enough to dictate the terms of trade across the North Sea and into the Baltic. A third was Thomas Cromwell's commercial policies, which were more and more increasing London's seaborne trade at the expense of its several English rivals.

Then there was the cold fact that Hull, in times of anxiety as well as contentment, was somewhat better placed than it was for the import and export of goods. York, therefore, had seen much better times than it was going through in 1536. It was still, however, the sixth largest city outside the capital, the second in eminence, with a population of about 8000, and in some ways it continued to thrive. It contained no fewer than forty parish churches whereas Exeter, with about the same number of inhabitants, had only half as many. It was home to three Benedictine communities, a Gilbertine priory and four friaries; and many other Yorkshire religious houses owned property in the city. Drs Layton and Legh, of course, had visited York in January and produced their customary withering report. There was friction in the air that summer, when a riot occurred 'at the acting of a religious interlude of St Thomas the Apostle…owing to the seditious conduct of certain papists who took a part in preparing for the said interlude'. And in September there had been a quarrel in the Merchants' Hall, involving one of the aldermen, who was accused of being 'false both to God and to the King'.

In these circumstances, then, Robert Aske set off for York, William Stapleton in the opposite direction. As Stapleton and his host were marching down to Hull from Market Weighton, a number of the gentry were riding hard to get there ahead of them, because the town was regarded as loyal to the Crown and would put them, they thought, beyond the reach of rebel pressure to join the revolt. These fugitives included old Sir Ralph Ellerker and two members of the powerful East Riding clan of Constables, Sir John of Burton Constable and his cousin Sir William of Great Hatfield, a younger brother of the Sir Robert Constable of Flamborough and of Holme-upon-Spalding Moor, to the east of Aughton, who was now safe inside Pontefract Castle. As things turned out, their hopes were not quite as well founded as they had supposed, though it was true that, the day before, messengers from Hull had gone to Beverley to explain why the citizens could not join in the rising; at that stage, in fact, most of them were probably not sure which way to turn. But the arrival of Sir Ralph and Sir John, in particular, certainly seemed to stiffen the idea of resistance.

When Stapleton sought an interview with the town's chief dignitaries he was at first rebuffed, but was later invited to meet the mayor, aldermen and the fugitive gentlemen in Holy Trinity Church. And there he was told that 'they would keep their town as the King's town' but that, if anyone wanted to leave and join the rebels, 'they should have liberty, but neither horse, harness, meat nor money'. Sir John Constable, in fact, swore that he would die rather than join the rebellion, but old Sir Ralph Ellerker was in a more difficult position because, as he had just learned, his sons, young Sir Ralph and Thomas, had been pressed into service on the other side and could be used as hostages if things turned nasty. So he temporised by offering to take the articles of rebellion to the King if Stapleton so wished, as long as he didn't have to be sworn. The offer was not accepted.

By this time the countryside around Hull was raised and the town was isolated in its defiance. With Holderness (the fenland between the town and the coast) also up in arms, Hull was beleaguered on three sides, only Humberside being empty of its adversaries. Richard Cromwell, awaiting further instructions in Lincoln, wrote to his uncle about the defences of Hull which, he reckoned, was now under threat from about 6000 insurgents, and short of 'vital gun powder and other such necessities as they need to defend themself'. As a result of this call for assistance, Charles Brandon was ordered to despatch some guns and ammunition from the Midlands and, though these at once came lumbering north, when they eventually reached Hull it was too late and everything fell into rebel hands.

For the commons were in no mood for a prolonged stand-off outside the town walls. Tension had built up between themselves and their gentlemen – it was never far away at any time, among any of the hosts, during the next few months – whose caution at all times seemed to them to be deeply suspicious, possibly a preliminary to betrayal. For a fortnight they even refused to allow William Stapleton, whom they held in higher regard than most, and his nephew Brian to dash home to Wighill to collect harness which, astonishingly, they had neglected to bring with them. At the same time, when an irritated Stapleton said he'd be glad to be shot of all this responsibility, a great shout went up that they would have no other captain but him and that whoever spoke against him would be struck down. But what the commons wanted above all was instant action: fireboats to be floated down the Humber, or even a barrel of flaming pitch, which might set shipping ablaze in the docks at Hull, or some other such drastic remedy to stalemate. The men of Beverley were in a particularly truculent mood, for they had some old economic scores to settle with Hull. They were doubtless made anxious as well by the news that the Lincolnshire rising had failed. But for once, intelligence about what was going on over there was not brought to them by Guy Kyme. He and a companion had left for home on the evening tide, a few hours after they had been with Aske and Stapleton, talking tactics on Weighton Hill. The two Lincolnshire men would never see Yorkshire again.

The siege, in fact, lasted no more than five days and the town surrendered on 19 October. The balance swung in favour of the rebels because Hull started to run out of provisions and because there was a genuine fear that the place might be burned down. Another important factor was that Sir Ralph Ellerker decided to negotiate and there is some reason to suppose that he had received a persuasive message from Sir Thomas Percy, who had now joined the rebellion himself. With Ellerker in conciliatory mood, the pressure on Sir John Constable to yield increased, to the point at which he agreed to join in the talks. The meeting took place in the Charterhouse outside the walls and, after further consultation between Ellerker, Constable and the civic leaders, two aldermen marched out and offered to give in, provided no one was forced to take the rebel oath. The terms were accepted but, by mutual agreement, the gates of Hull were not opened until the following morning, to forestall the possibility of looting during the hours of darkness.

There was good enough reason for this fear. While awaiting the surrender, Stapleton had set up his headquarters in the mayor's own house at Sculcoates, just outside the walls. There, his men took what they wanted of fodder for their horses. They seized, too, a crane, a peacock and some swine, together with a number of wethers which were being driven into the hungry town, and seventy-five oxen belonging to Archbishop Lee's brother, who also lived thereabouts. But Stapleton, honourable man that he was, made sure that everything was returned in due course and also set a trap for two rebels he suspected of theft. Caught in the act, they were allowed to think that they would be put to death for their crime and a friar was even sent to confess them before they were taken to Humberside, where a concourse of people had gathered to watch what happened next. Which was a good ducking for the major culprit, with a rope round his middle and an oar shoving his head under again every time he surfaced, and a reprieve for his mate. But both were banished from the host and told not to come near it again. There would be no more looting under Stapleton's command.

Hull was secured, old Sir Ralph was told to guard well the Hunsley beacon, Sir John Constable was left to take care of the town for the time being, while his cousin Sir William joined the host, which now set off to rendezvous with Robert Aske and his men. Aske, in fact, had enjoyed an even easier conquest than his friend. When the two parted at Weighton Hill, he and his host proceeded along the old Roman road that connected Lincoln and York, but they took a couple of days to reach the city, which may be thought very slow progress, when the distance was less than twenty miles. One reason for this is that Aske was probably hoping for reinforcements from Stapleton, after Hull was taken, whenever that might be; another is that he was certainly recruiting along the way; and it is possible that he took the opportunity to visit a couple of suppressed religious houses, the Augustinian priory of Warter and the Benedictine convent of Nunburnholme, at the same time. He would also be anxious about the reception that awaited him, for he was not yet aware that the commons in the adjacent wapentake of the Ainsty, which was normally obliged to send troops to defend the city, had already joined in the rebellion and had, indeed, restored the suppressed Augustinian house at Healaugh. Prudently, therefore, he sent a couple of reconnaissance parties ahead of the main host to secure the hump-backed bridges over the Derwent at Kexby and Sutton, the first directly in his path, the second just a mile or two downstream, so that loyalist forces would not be able to destroy them and impede his advance. The river was not very wide that far up from its junction with the Ouse, but it was certainly too deep to be fordable and, after heavy rain, its current could be dangerous. That October was a very wet month.

After Aske and his army had crossed the Derwent and were nearing the city without incident, he simply wrote to the mayor, requesting that they should be allowed to pass through York; and he attached to his letter the Lincolnshire articles, which had been a sort of steering orders for the men of Howdenshire and Marshland so far, together with a copy of the oath sworn in Beverley. If this was a kind of softening-up tactic it worked on a dignitary who was fearful of attack by the Richmondshire rebels and the notoriously rough crowd from Beverley, as well as by Aske's army, which by now consisted of between 4000 and 5000 men. Mayor William Harrington had already made sure that the King's treasury was safely out of reach, having despatched it, a couple of days earlier, down to the royal castle of Tickhill on the other side of Doncaster. With it he sent a desperate plea for the monarch's help, which went unanswered. And now, without consulting any of the city fathers, he agreed to let the rebels into York, provided no injury was done to any citizen and all victuals were paid for at the going rate of tuppence a meal. Aske agreed to these terms and, to show that he could be relied upon, instructed his footmen – by far the larger part of his host – to stay outside the walls when they reached them on 16 October. These rebels waited there, each company of them gathered around its own cross, which had been brought from its local parish church.

The surrender having then been formally offered and taken, Aske himself and his chief gentlemen went straight away, at five o'clock in the evening, through the narrow, winding streets to the Minster. There, the chief captain was met at the great west door by the Archbishop's treasurer and the two men shook hands, before a procession of all the Minster's clergy, and its choir, led Aske up the nave towards the altar – between the soaring pillars and walls from which gargoyles looked down, beneath the embossed vaulting dimly visible in the twilight high above the floor, past the elaborate tombs of archbishops long since dead, past the great grey lancet windows which were known as the Five Sisters, through the stone screen of the pulpitum with its statuettes of fifteen English kings, from William the Conqueror to Henry VI, finally to stand before the emerald, ruby, gold and sapphire panes of the great east window, which had taken three years to glaze, as huge as a tennis court. Up there, at the high altar, where the candle flames swayed and the incense drifted upwards in delicate wraiths, and the priests and acolytes circulated in their appointed tasks, was held a celebratory mass, with a bell to announce the consecration of the Host. It must have felt, to Robert Aske, as if he were part of something quite close to a coronation that Monday evening in York.

Afterwards he spent the night in the house of Sir George Lawson, one of the city's aldermen, and stayed there for two days while he awaited news from Stapleton in Hull. It was during this interlude that he composed the oath which was put before all the gentry in his army on Tuesday morning and quickly despatched for similar swearings throughout the North, turning up in Swaledale and Wensleydale within twenty-four hours. The travelling versions were, of course, copies of the original and therefore there were small but essentially insignificant differences in the wording of each. Aske called this 'The Oath of the Honourable Men' and it was to be sworn on the Bible, as follows:

> Ye shall not enter into this our Pilgrimage of Grace for the Commonwealth, but only for the love that ye do bear unto Almighty God, his faith, and to Holy Church militant and the maintenance thereof, to the preservation of the King's person and his issue, to the purifying of the nobility, and to expulse all villein blood and evil councillors against the commonwealth from his Grace and his Privy Council of the same. And ye shall not enter into our said Pilgrimage for no particular profit to your self, nor to do any displeasure to any private person, but by counsel of the commonwealth, nor slay nor murder for no envy, but in your hearts put away all fear and dread, and take afore you the Cross of Christ, and in your hearts His faith, the Restitution of the Church, the suppression of these Heretics and their opinions, by all the holy contents of this book.

The rebels had a cause which they believed to be just, they had the fervour to carry it through regardless of any obstacles, and now they had its principles expressed in the noblest of terms. Aske had already, at the weekend, composed a proclamation which was addressed to the 'Lords, knights, masters, kinsmen and friends' of York and which enlarged on the principal sentiments in the Oath.

For as much that such simple and evil disposed persons, being of the King's Council, hath not only insensed his Grace with many and sundry new inventions, which be contrary to the faith of God and honour to the King's majesty and the commonwealth of this realm, and thereby intendeth to destroy the church of England and the ministers of the same, ye do know as well as we: but also the said Council hath spoiled and robbed, and further intending utterly to spoil and rob the whole body of this realm…Wherefore, for a conclusion, if ye will not come on with us for reformation of the premises, we certify you by this our writing that we will fight and die against both you and all those that shall be about towards to stop us in the said Pilgrimage; and God shall be judge which shall have his grace and mercy therein; and then you shall be judged hereafter to be shedders of Christian blood, and destroyers of your equal Christians.

Again, as in his very first proclamation, made on the eve of St Wilfrid's Day, he ratified his position as 'chief captain'; only this time he was claiming leadership of 'the conventual assembly on pilgrimage for the same, baronage and commonalty of the same'. Consciously or not, he was acknowledging his wider responsibility for everyone who marched to the beat of his drum, for everything that happened to them all from now on. His primacy, in fact, had already survived its one and only challenge when two gentlemen of his inner circle, Thomas Metham and Thomas Saltmarsh, both of whom had been with him since the outset of the rebellion in Howdenshire but who seem to have been relegated somewhat in the pecking order of minor captains since, expressed what sounds much like a grudge. They, 'disdaining that he should be above them', declared their opposition to the strategy that he proposed to pursue after York. But pursued it was. Robert Aske was not just a physically robust man.

Determined to show that his leadership would be honourable, he issued an order forbidding damage to property, before he left York. He also declared his interest in the religious houses by having a notice tacked to the Minster door, announcing his sympathy for monastic restorations. At the same time he sent word to a number of wealthy foundations that this Pilgrimage would need funding if it were to succeed, and doubtless the various abbots and priors regarded his plea as an oblique demand for protection money. Soon, York would be teeming with Pilgrims, as more and more rebels arrived from all parts of the North-east, among them Sir Thomas Percy, astride a bay gelding and gorgeously dressed with feathers decorating his harness, and a retinue wearing the black and white Percy livery with the silver crescent across the chest. Percy's host was led reluctantly in procession by the Benedictine Abbot of St Mary's, carrying his most treasured cross; and, though he was subsequently allowed to go, his cross stayed with the Pilgrimage. Young Sir Ralph Ellerker turned up, too, and spent some time with Aske in Sir George Lawson's house.

Meanwhile, only a few locals refused to accept the Pilgrimage, or fled at the rumour of its coming; among them the sometime clerk to Drs Layton and Legh, together with Henry Percy's doctor and the priest of St Mary's, Castlegate, who had been presented to the living by the Earl earlier that year and was therefore much in his debt. They, and others like them, were given twenty-four hours to get out of town with whatever they wished to take with them, before any other of their goods were seized. Only occasionally thereafter did anything but harmony reign among the inhabitants and insurgents alike. Once, there was a small commotion when certain Pilgrim gentlemen discovered Thomas Cromwell's coat of arms decorating the front door of the man who had welcomed Aske into the Minster; whereupon the treasurer not only removed the offending tablet but invited the various captains to sup at his house as long as they were in York. He also contributed, handsomely it was said, to the rebel funds.

Aske's disputed strategy was to make for Pontefract now that York was taken. But first he sent the priest Thomas Maunsell ahead in order to find out what he could about the castle's defences and, in his alternative role as recruiting sergeant, to raise up the country round Pontefract and Wakefield. After pausing overnight at Ferrybridge, Maunsell went on to Pontefract and ordered its mayor to muster the commons there, before proceeding to Wakefield and doing the same thing. He then rode enthusiastically to Doncaster where, before he actually reached it, half a dozen aldermen came out to meet him and escort him to the mayor and other senior citizens. So keen was everyone, from His Worship downwards, to be sworn, that Maunsell was able to report to Aske: 'Never sheep ran faster in a morning out of their fold than they did to receive the said oath.'

This was not the only intelligence that came the chief captain's way. Lord Darcy's steward, Thomas Strangways, also came to him in York, having been sent there by his master in order to obtain some clear idea of the grievances that lay behind this revolt. Strangways, in making this request, gave Aske to understand that a head captain might be found 'if the articles pleased his mind'. He was naming no names, but the hint was obviously that Darcy would offer himself to the cause if he was satisfied about certain things. It was during this discussion that one of Aske's minor captains, Thomas Rudston, burst out with the accusation that he thought Strangways was nothing less than a spy; and he might well have added who wanted a head captain anyway, when they already had one who seemed competent enough. Aske heeded this to the extent that he insisted on Strangways leaving York before the next morning's musters took place, so that he would be in no position to assess the strength of the forces likely to march on Pontefract, but he made sure that Strangways was given what he said he wanted before he turned his horse for home. So he left with a copy of the oath and the Yorkshire articles, which complained about taxations, asked that the Statute of Uses should be repealed, and warned the King that people like Cromwell and Sir Richard Riche were up to no good. It was also stated that 'By the suppression of so many poor houses the service of God is not well performed and the poor are unrelieved… There are bishops of the King's late promotion who have subverted the faith of Christ, viz. the bishops of Canterbury, Rochester, Worcester, Salisbury, St David's and Dublin. We think that the beginning of all this trouble was the bishop of Lincoln.' There was not one word of criticism directed at the King himself – except, of course, by implication – though the leading Pilgrims never wavered in their belief that Henry was personally innocent of all the troubles which beset them. The exchange between Darcy's steward and the rebel commander was probably not one way. It is likely that Strangways, deliberately or accidentally (we do not know which), gave Aske much useful information about the state of things at the castle. At any rate, when the chief captain set off for Darcy's stronghold, it was with an impression that certain people serving there might well be sympathetic to the cause.

Darcy's position was a difficult one, made worse because he was being pulled in several directions at once. He was above all things a man of honour and he was in a position of royal trust – including membership of the King's Council in the North – which he, of all people, would be extremely reluctant to betray. But by now he must have been feeling let down by his sovereign. On 10 October he had received instructions from the Sheriff of Yorkshire, Sir Brian Hastings, to send troops to York in anticipation of the rebels' arrival, 'to overawe their faction in the city', but replied that he was awaiting the King's pleasure, as indeed he was. He had received a communication from the Earl of Shrewsbury, written on the day that Aske and Stapleton were discussing strategy on Weighton Hill, telling him that the business in Lincolnshire was over and that if there was any more of this nonsense – from Yorkshire, for example – somebody was going to have a fight on his hands. This was conveyed by Sir Arthur Darcy, who was acting as messenger between Pontefract and Nottingham, and who was advised by Shrewsbury to 'Go bid your father stay his country, or I will turn my back upon yonder traitors and my face upon them'. Lord Darcy was also at this time receiving reports from Lancashire and from Wakefield, to say that not only was there great discontent in those areas, but that weapons were being sent to them from York; indeed, it was said that no one was quite sure whether the Earl of Derby himself, over in Lancashire, was for or against the rebels. But from the King, all Darcy had received in response to telling Henry the poor state of Pontefract's defences, and asking for supplies and funds to improve matters, was a tetchy letter marvelling that an end had not yet been put to unlawful assemblies in Yorkshire and suggesting that if Darcy was too feeble to do anything about this himself, then he'd better hand things over to his son Arthur. It said nothing at all about Pontefract's requirements.

A number of reasons can be cited for Darcy's failure to respond to Hastings's urgency and his appearing increasingly indecisive as time went on. In the first place, every day made it less likely that any force he might have been able to raise could have got through to York without being intercepted and very seriously damaged, when this rebellion was clearly no longer a localised matter: Hastings himself reckoned that by that week no fewer than 40,000 men were up in arms. Darcy's instinct was to pacify the rebels, not to do battle with them – emulating Shrewsbury's policy, perhaps, in dealing with Lincolnshire – and he evidently hoped that after York they would march straight towards London (as some of them, indeed, wanted to) instead of heading in his direction. News had reached him, too, that the rebels had threatened to destroy the property of any gentlemen who took up arms against them and Darcy had many such potential victims with him at Pontefract. Then there was the matter of his deep religious convictions, which had already been sorely tried by Henry's freebooting ways with the Church, not to mention his insistence on banishing Catherine of Aragon. After Thomas Strangways arrived from York with the grievances of the Pilgrims in black and white, Lord Darcy could have been in no doubt that he shared many of their convictions. It is very likely, by then, that he wasn't at all sure whose side he was on. But he made one more attempt to obtain assistance from the King, getting Sir Arthur Darcy out just before the newly risen commons of Pontefract sealed off the castle from the outside world. The message he sent with his youngest son laid out the position in the starkest possible terms. It told Henry that 'we in the castle must in a few days either yield or lose our lives', that there was 'no likelihood of vanquishing the commons with any power here'.

Robert Aske had obviously decided that he was in no danger of blundering into a trap when he and Thomas Maunsell went ahead of the army to see Darcy in Pontefract. He was canny enough, however, to make sure that Darcy's eldest son, Sir George, was sent out to wait in the custody of the rebels while Aske was in the father's hands. On Thursday the 19th, the day Hull was surrendering to William Stapleton, the rebel leader rode up the approach to the castle gatehouse, from whose adjacent battlements, it may be imagined, several score of soldiery looked down at the one-eyed figure coming towards them out of the throng of local insurgents. The gates were opened, he and Maunsell entered and were conducted to where Darcy, the Archbishop of York, Sir Robert Constable and the other notables, about fifty people in all, awaited them. And, far from being at all daunted by the probably hostile power that was latent in such an assembly, Aske at once took the initiative, telling them roundly the business that had brought him there and where it placed them, whether they liked it or not. He indicted the nobility above all for their failure to warn the King of what had been done in his name. The lords spiritual (that is, the bishops) had not told His Highness how best to end the current heresies swiftly and how to silence the preachers of them. The lords temporal had failed to inform the King how the North Country was being bled by one imposition after another, all Thomas Cromwell's policies, to the extent that northcountrymen would soon have to make terms with the Scots, having no resources left to fight wars with, unless something drastic was done to remedy matters.

Having delivered what was essentially a blistering attack on those present, Aske coolly demanded that they join the Pilgrimage forthwith and surrender Pontefract. Archbishop Lee, subsequently describing the occasion, added 'that if we refused, he had ways to constrain us, and we should find them people without mercy'. Darcy asked the Archbishop to reply on behalf of all of them, but Edward Lee was not the man to expose himself to danger, or even to the risk of rebuke, if he could avoid it, so he declined the invitation. Darcy therefore told Aske that he neither could nor would deliver the castle to the King's enemies, but that he was ready to discuss all the grievances with his friends and let Aske know in due course what he thought should be done about them. When Lee did at last find his voice, it was to suggest that he himself might act as a strictly neutral intermediary, provided, of course, that he was given a safe conduct in his dealings with the insurgents.

Aske not only turned down the offer, but added a few more crisp comments about the dereliction of bishops in the recent past. There was some more parleying between the two sides and then Aske presented his ultimatum. They could have time to consider their position, but this truce would end at eight o'clock the following morning; after that, unless they had received a satisfactory answer, the Pilgrims would attack.

Darcy's predicament was threefold. His garrison had shrunk to much less than half its original size, partly because some of the gentry had left to protect their property, though there must have been other defections, too. Those who were left had only enough provisions to feed themselves for eight or ten days at the most and were now forced to watch food which would normally have been delivered to the castle being consumed by the rebels outside its walls. And, although Shrewsbury had hinted that he might be moving north from Nottingham soon, there was still no sign of his coming. So Aske was offered £20 for the rebel funds, not a small sum, if he would extend the deadline, but the chief captain of the Pilgrims was adamant. Darcy had much less than twenty-four hours in which to make up his mind.

If he had entertained the faint hope that either the King or Shrewsbury would come to his assistance in time, he must very soon have concluded that this was an expectation already doomed. A final council of war was held by Darcy and those closest to him, after which, according to Edward Lee, 'considering the danger of resistance, they determined with sorrow to yield, and repented that they ever came there, where they had expected to be as safe as if they were in London'. At 8 a.m. on Friday morning, therefore, Aske was informed that Pontefract Castle was his. All its occupants, from nobility to esquire, were presented with the Pilgrims' oath and, without exception, they swore themselves to it. Not only that: neither Darcy nor anyone else with him was prepared to accept the leadership, though Aske made it clear that he was perfectly willing to relinquish it to one of the nobility. But after dithering for so long, Darcy now became totally committed to his new allegiance, one of his first acts being to send the oath into Lancashire for further dissemination there. He also went rummaging in the storerooms of the castle when he remembered that somewhere or other he still had a set of badges that he had used on his ill-fated expedition against the Moors.

Badges and banners were an important element in denoting allegiance to one's sovereign, one's lord, one's faith, in the sixteenth century. Royal banners had been introduced to England by Edward III and the Tudors were especially fond of them, while the Crusaders had always gone about their business with a cross displayed prominently on their standards, their dress and their shields. Quite apart from coats of arms, each noble family had its own insignia, like the crescent of the Percies, the white lion of the Howards, the scallop shells of the Dacres, the cock of the Lumleys.

But no symbol was more potent or more evocative than the religious insignia of the Five Wounds of Christ, which depicted a bleeding heart (sometimes a Host) above a chalice, both being surrounded at the corners of the illustration by the pierced hands and feet. This derived from a cult that had developed across Europe over 200 years or so, which was attached to a legend that Pope Gregory the Great, in the sixth century, had seen a vision at the church of Santa Croce in Rome, in which Christ was displaying his injuries. Indulgences were granted to people who prayed before an icon there which portrayed the stages of the Passion, and the theme of the Five Wounds was reproduced everywhere when printing arrived, to enhance the rituals of Holy Week, to be venerated in the privacy of the home; and it was woven into or painted upon the various emblems of loyalty and devotion. The men of Lincolnshire had just finished creating their own elaborate version of it, to replace the Dymmoke banner, when their rising collapsed. 'The Five Wounds were to show the people they fought in Christ's cause; the chalice and the Host were in remembrance that chalices, crosses and church jewels should be taken away [i.e. hidden]; the plough was to encourage the husbandmen; the horn, according to the Horncastle men, was in token of Horncastle, but others regarded it as a symbol of the tax on horned cattle.'

Another version of the design was on banners which came down to Pontefract from the North-east – together with St Cuthbert's banner – later that week; while the form that Robert Aske preferred, which was soon adopted as the chief insignia of the Pilgrimage, simply carried the wounded hands and feet, the heart and the chalice, below the letters IHS (a transliterated abbreviation of the Greek word for Jesus). Darcy's own badges were also on these lines and, having found them, he distributed them among the Pilgrims, giving one of them in particular to

Aske. Then he set about organising the area surrounding Pontefract into a force capable of withstanding an attack by Shrewsbury or anyone else on the government side. This was, to say the least, a remarkable turnabout.

The first loyalist presence in the vicinity, in fact, was the arrival next day of Lancaster Herald from Nottingham, bearing a document in the King's name. He was but one of several office holders who were originally not much more than the announcers of the next bout in jousting tournaments. Since the fourteenth century, however, they had all been given titles which indicated the areas in which they normally arranged royal progresses and delivered royal proclamations. They were respectively known as Chester, Lancaster, Windsor, Richmond, York and Somerset Herald and they worked under the immediate supervision of three other functionaries – Garter King-of-Arms, whose principal job was attending to all matters pertaining to the Order of the Garter, Norroy King-of-Arms, who kept an eye on royal affairs north of the Trent, and Clarencieux King-of-Arms, who discharged the same office south of that river. Lancaster Herald at this time, appointed only in May that year, was one Thomas Miller, who has been described as 'a man of parts and conduct, as became the honourable bearer of messages from the King'. He fell in with a number of rebels marching towards Pontefract and they appear to have treated him with courtesy, while he explained to them that half the stories they had heard about new taxations and so forth were nonsense. He proposed to read his proclamation at the market cross, but before he got there he was told that the chief captain wished to see him in the castle. He was led up the causeway to the gates, then through successive inner entrances, at each of which stood men in harness who looked, according to Miller afterwards, very cruel.

He was conducted into the great hall of the castle, where he was about to start reading his script, when he was told to wait until Robert Aske was ready for him. After a few moments he was taken into another room, and there 'Aske, the Captain, sits in state, with the Archbishop of York and Lord Darcy standing each side of him' with other gentlemen gathered around. It was customary, when receiving a message from the King, for the recipient to kneel and kiss the seal on the document but Aske did no such thing, according to Miller. Instead, there he was, 'keeping his port and countenance as though he had been a great prince with great rigour and like a tyrant'. Edward Lee was later to report that Lancaster Herald, not Aske, was the one who made the gesture of submission: 'The poor man fell down upon his knees for fear and said he was but a messanger.' House-trained to observe the social niceties of the realm, Miller made to announce his tidings to the Archbishop or to Lord Darcy, whichever indicated his willingness to listen; but to his consternation they both told him to give it to the mere gentleman sitting between them. Who, 'with an inestimable proud countenance, stretched himself and took a hearing of my tale', held out his hand for the document and 'read it openly, without reverence to any person'. Having done so, Aske told Miller that in no circumstances could he read his message publicly; at which Lancaster Herald fell on his knees and begged to be allowed to discharge his responsibility as he had been ordered to.

But there was nothing doing, for a very good reason. The announcement was simply to the effect that the Lincolnshire rising was over. It wasn't even a demand that the Yorkshire rebels should give reasons for their own insubordination. Aske would have been stupid to spread this intelligence among his people, because of the effect it might well have had on their morale; and it is possible he took the view that the total lack of Henry's interest in the feelings of his subjects would simply inflame the Pilgrims the more, to the point where Lancaster Herald's life might be in jeopardy. Robert Aske seems to have been hoping to carry through this Pilgrimage without any more blood being shed than that which had already been spilled in Lincolnshire.

Aske promised Miller safe conduct both now and in any future meetings they might have, so long as he always wore the King's livery. He gave him a message for Shrewsbury and any other of the nobility he might have dealings with, to the effect that they really ought to be on this side of the fence, because it was partly for their benefit that Aske was on this Pilgrimage. He then told Darcy to give the man two crowns, and he himself took Miller by the arm and led him outside to where both of them could be seen by the crowds beneath the castle walls. Aske shouted down to them that no one must touch Miller, on pain of death. And when Miller discovered that someone had taken his horse, Aske ordered its return at once or, again, be in peril of their lives. Aske's final order of this episode was to tell off a company of horsemen to escort Miller safely out of town and to set him on his way. Then, for the time being, the two men parted company. Lancaster Herald headed back to Nottingham, and Aske went inside to discuss strategy with Darcy and his other new brothers in arms. One of the options they began to consider was a march down to London, to persuade Henry that their cause was just.

The Pilgrims had now enjoyed five days of unqualified success, between 16 and 20 October, when York, Hull and Pontefract Castle had been taken in turn, and when Lord Thomas Darcy and a number of other distinguished personages had been persuaded to join the Pilgrimage. Darcy was easily the biggest fish the rebels had landed, but not far behind in importance was his old friend Sir Robert Constable, who had shared the costs of the Spanish fiasco with him a quarter of a century earlier.

Constable had fought many times for his sovereign, most notably as a very young man, when he was knighted on the field of battle at Blackheath in 1497, after routing an army of 10,000 who had risen up against new taxations and marched to the very outskirts of London. He had also distinguished himself at Flodden Field, when he fought alongside other Constables against the Scots. He had a reputation for wildness in his youth when, among other things, he abducted a girl who was a ward in chancery and tried to force marriage with one of his retainers on to her. Most people agreed that he was a man with a very short fuse and a disposition to violence. Even Darcy was wary of him, to the extent that when his daughter married Constable's son and heir, Darcy made sure that the dowry was paid without delay. Constable was forever feuding with people, with the Ellerker family highest on the list of his antipathies, his sworn enemy above all others being young Sir Ralph Ellerker. Now, at the age of sixty-three, his temper not improved by perpetual gout, he had turned against the King. As in Darcy's case, he had been reluctant to switch sides, but he, too, had some reason to resent his treatment by the government. He had succeeded his friend as steward of the royal castle at Sheriff Hutton, in the North Riding between Malton and York, which carried many emoluments with it, but this had been removed from his jurisdiction a few years earlier and given to one of Henry Clifford's men. Worse, his stewardship of Holderness was taken away from him in 1532 and transferred to, of all people, young Ellerker. On top of all this were the facts that he loathed Cromwell and all he stood for, and that he was as deeply committed to the old religion as Thomas Darcy himself was.

In switching sides Constable, like Darcy, was putting himself under the command of a man half his age, from somewhere beneath him in the social scale and with no military experience whatsoever, whereas these two old sweats had spent long years of their lives fighting at home and abroad. What was just as remarkable was the fact that Constable and Robert Aske had been acquainted for a number of years and had no great reason to like each other: Aske had represented Henry Percy and too many other people in their various litigations with Sir Robert Constable for that to have happened. But at Pontefract the two men quickly settled whatever differences existed between them; they even shared the immediate task of drilling the companies of rebels who were beginning to arrive at the castle in droves, to find themselves rapidly being put through their paces on St Thomas's Hill, just outside the town. From now on, Aske and Constable were to work very closely together.

VIII

TO MARCH ON LONDON

By this time another siege was under way, but it was meeting much more resistance than the Pilgrims had encountered in Hull or York or Pontefract. It is not absolutely clear why thousands of rebels decided to attack Skipton Castle without, apparently, consulting Robert Aske. 'In one sense, it derived from the rebels' policy of seeking to bind the magnates to the cause and of punishing the ones who refused to comply.' On these grounds Henry Clifford, first Earl of Cumberland, was an obvious target, one way or the other. He was also, as we have seen, an unpopular landlord, which doubtless weighed with many as well, especially the ones who had long been involved in tenant disputes with him around Ripon and in Craven. Lord Scrope, of Bolton Castle in Wensleydale, was another potential acquisition or victim, though by now, and probably still unbeknown to the rebels, he had fled to Skipton. Most of the hosts obeyed Aske's instruction to head straight for Pontefract as soon as they could, but a large number of the men originally commanded by Robert Bowes did not. His army, it will be remembered, became so large as to be unwieldy, so it was divided into two, one half of it consisting of men from Cleveland and Durham, to which Bowes was still attached, the other of the Richmondshire insurgents under a separate command.

It was the Richmondshire men who now detached themselves from the combined hosts and marched on Skipton while the others followed instructions and made their way down to where Aske awaited them. Or maybe they were told by Bowes to go to Skipton because they, more than anyone else under his leadership, knew the lie of the land thereabouts, but the most likely explanation seems to be that there was pressure on the leadership from the commons, who doubtless wanted to settle some old scores: these were a particularly belligerent company, after all, who had threatened to sack Jervaulx Abbey at the beginning of that week and to blazes with Mother Church.

Jointly commanding the Richmondshire Pilgrims were three knights who had all either submitted to the rebels without demur or been pressed into service with them: Sir Christopher Danby of Thorpe Perrow and lord of Masham, Sir William Mallory of Studley near Ripon, and Sir Ralph Bulmer of Marrick in Swaledale, with a medley of gentlemen serving as minor captains, one of them Bowes's younger brother Richard. These now led their army from Richmond into Wensleydale, where they ascertained that Scrope was no longer at home in Bolton Castle. From there they marched up Bishopdale – or perhaps, but less likely, up the adjacent Coverdale – and down the length of upper Wharfedale until they came to the market town at the head of Airedale, where the barren and dramatically sweeping fells of the high Pennines gave way to the pale limestone crags of much lower hills that were flanked by many trees. Henry Clifford, a few days before they arrived, was setting out on his much delayed expedition to the troubled country round Hexham, but he had not gone far before he was informed that an army of rebels was coming his way, whereupon he turned his horse round and went back home to prepare its defence.

Skipton Castle was not nearly as dominant as Pontefract, either in its position or in its building. Instead of rearing above the town on a ridge of high ground, it simply stood halfway down a gentle slope, with the end of a wide street, where the sheep and other markets were held, running right up to its front door; though there was a steep drop on the far side of the castle, where the Eller Beck flowed past its walls. Nor was it in other ways nearly as commanding as Pontefract, where crenellated walls and towers stretched high into the sky. The round towers flanking Skipton's entrance were comparatively squat, the gatehouse scarcely less so, made to seem higher than it really was because the Clifford motto, Desormais (Henceforth), was conspicuously fretworked in stone and freestanding above the arch. There had been a fortification here since soon after the Conquest, built as a bastion against marauding Scots – which is why the most difficult approach, above the beck, was on the north side. The Cliffords had held it since 1310, when Edward II appointed Robert Clifford as the first lord of Skipton and Guardian of Craven. It was he who had begun extending the fortifications before he was killed at Bannockburn, just four years after coming into his new estate, but other Cliffords had carried on with this work, so that, by 1536, it was a very considerable obstruction in the path of any enemy wishing to get past. Curtain walls connected its four major defence-works, but there was little open space between one building and the next, and there was no keep – and this is why, as much as anything else, Skipton Castle looked more like a rather large and well-fortified manor house than something impregnably built for the conduct of war. This appearance, however, was deceptive, as the Richmondshire rebels quickly found out.

The full attack was preceded by a visit from a company of the Percy Fee rebels led by their own lately pressed commander, Sir Stephen Hamerton. The two men who had sworn him in, Jacks and Fawcett, sent him and a deputation of eight others to bring Henry Clifford in. When asked why they had risen against the King, they replied that it was because they were afraid of being ill-used by the commons of Bishopdale and Wensleydale. Clifford offered to see them right if they suffered in any way but made it perfectly clear that he had no intention of joining the rebellion. 'I defy you, and do your worst,' he told them, 'for I will not meddle with you.' A few hours later the men of Richmondshire arrived.

By the time the host reached Skipton a number of the gentry sheltering there had left Clifford in the lurch, probably intending to save their property after hearing of the way the rebels dealt with such as them. He had no more than about eighty people at his disposal for the castle's defence and one of these was Christopher Aske. As we already know, Aske and his elder brother John had set out for Skipton by separate routes, on becoming alarmed by rebel activities in the East Riding. John, in fact, seems never to have reached Skipton. He travelled by way of Cawood, arriving just after Archbishop Lee had fled to Pontefract, and was caught there by some of Edward Lee's tenants, but managed to escape from them across the River Ouse, probably returning to Aughton, certainly taking no further part in these events for several months.

Christopher, however, was much more Henry Clifford's man than his senior. He was held in high regard by the Earl, whose receiver he was, and lived at some ease in Skipton, which had become much more his home than the manor at Aughton by now. His room in the castle was full of books – of genealogy, of Scripture, and treatises on hunting, which was a particular interest of his, for which he kept falcons and a beagle named Oliver. He also had a large Mappa Mundi made of cloth, which depicted Jerusalem at the centre of the world, the topography festooned with illustrations of bizarre and mythical creatures culled from the bestiaries, like the Sciapod (which moved at remarkable speed in spite of having only one foot with ten toes), the Manticora (part-man, part-lion, part-scorpion) and the Phrygian Bonnocon (which discharged its fiery dung over three acres when chased and was generally pictured with a very smug expression on its countenance). Aske now set about organising the defence of the castle, collecting forty young men from the town to add to Clifford's resident staff.

After two or three days of stand-off outside its walls, the rebels concluded that they would make no headway without cannon, which they lacked. They therefore decided to take hostages in order to make Henry Clifford yield. Three of the Clifford women, and the small son of one of them, were staying a few miles away at Bolton Priory, an Augustinian house on the banks of the River Wharfe, and the besiegers threatened to use them as human shields in the next day's assault. Christopher Aske, however, assisted by the Vicar of Skipton, a groom and a boy, managed to get the women out of the priory before the insurgents arrived, led them over Skipton Moor into the town, spirited them through the host while it was off its guard and into the castle without the rebels realising that they had been outwitted for once. Aske then wrote to his brother Robert, reproachfully, telling him that Clifford would never give up and that if the castle were taken, not only the Earl but his womenfolk as well would probably be killed. To which Robert replied in due course that he himself would not march on the castle but that the Earl's enemies certainly would if he didn't yield. This was the first sign of hostility between the Aske brothers and it would end in tragedy. The siege of Skipton Castle, though, did not. After ten days all told, and after receiving a summons from Robert Aske to proceed south as soon as possible, the men of Richmondshire realised that its capture had become a forlorn hope and gave vent to their frustration by taking Clifford's cattle, pillaging his deer park and demolishing his houses at Barden and Carleton, 'which were so strong as to take three days in breaking'. They also, at last, managed to persuade Lord Scrope, one of those who had sought the safety of the castle but then decided to make a run for it, to change sides.

Skipton was not the only impediment in these early days of the Pilgrimage north of the Humber. When the rising began, a number of gentlemen had fled to Scarborough rather than Pontefract, having good reason to believe that they would be just as secure beside the North Sea as alongside the River Aire. Scarborough had been a Roman signal station and some of the Roman walls had been incorporated into the twelfth-century castle, which was even more spectacular than the other royal fortress down in the West Riding. For its Norman keep and surrounding battlements rose high above the town and its harbour, poised on a clifftop more than 300 feet above the sea, the only viable approach to it being along a narrow neck of land connecting it to the community over which it stood guard. If Pontefract was virtually impregnable, Scarborough was most certainly that against any enemy who was not well equipped with artillery. The Pilgrims had not yet acquired any ordnance by 13 October, when a particularly prominent group of gentry took refuge inside walls that were eleven feet thick and a group of rebels from the Percy host clamoured for an assault. In fact, nothing serious was attempted for another month, though the castle was blockaded to ensure that nobody who mattered was able to escape. Quite apart from the matter of its intimidating fortifications, Scarborough was probably not thought to be a high priority for the Pilgrimage at that stage, as it was not an obstruction on the way to anywhere else.

The same assessment may have been made in the case of Newcastle, some seventy miles further up the coast. Known as Pons Aelius when the Romans built a fort there beside the Tyne, it was soon linked to Carlisle, on the other side of northern England, by a road running below Hadrian's Wall. Its majestic castle was new in the twelfth century, its great keep crowning all else as a bastion which Henry II had erected against invading Scots, marauding bandits from the unruly Tynedale and Redesdale parts of Northumberland, and powerfully ambitious noblemen, of whom the Percies were only the most prominent. The city's prosperity as a port and as an outlet for the region's coal, which had been mined since the thirteenth century, had been well worth guarding by successive monarchs; so that, by 1536, Newcastle had a very long tradition of allegiance to the Crown. And it did not disappoint Henry VIII now, in spite of Durham county having risen in arms, making common cause with rebels who quickly secured the fortresses at Barnard Castle, Brancepeth and Durham city, and despoiled the palace of Cuthbert Tunstall, Bishop of Durham, a moderate man who had nevertheless incurred the displeasure of the insurgents by sub-scribing, with the Archbishop of York, to the Ten Articles. At their coming he fled to the safety of Norham Castle, overlooking the Scottish Border on the River Tweed, which had been a stronghold of the prince-bishops of Durham since the twelfth century. Brancepeth was an especially valuable acquisition to the rebels, because it was the ancestral home of the Nevilles, the earls of Westmorland, whose current head of the family, Ralph the fourth Earl, had taken the oath under pressure from a large rebel presence and promptly deputed his thirteen-year-old son to take his place with the host on its further progress south; to carry with him, moreover, the precious St Cuthbert's banner. Another important figure in the region was Lord Lumley, whose home was some miles north of Durham city and who also joined the Pilgrimage under duress.

Through all these rebel triumphs Newcastle remained loyal, though at one point this could not have been taken for granted. The mayor, Richard Braudling, and the corporation were stead-fast for the King from the beginning of the Pilgrimage of Grace, but they represented a relatively small and moneyed section of the community, which had long been at odds with the artisan class. Sir Thomas Hilton, Sheriff of Durham and one of the most influential men in the region, sent a couple of servants into the city from his home at Hilton Castle to test the temperature there, and they reported that the commons of Newcastle would almost certainly make no attempt to oppose the Pilgrims, if such came their way. But the city fathers made sure that there were enough provisions to withstand a siege and also acquired some guns, which they mounted on the walls, this causing some of the townsfolk to threaten that 'they might lay the guns where they would but they would turn them when the commons came whither they would'.

Mayor Braudling, however, was an astute fellow, and he seems to have pacified potential rebels by making small conciliatory gestures. A local man had been forced to recant certain heretical opinions – which included his belief that priests should be allowed to marry if they wished – before Cuthbert Tunstall, Bishop of Durham, as far back as 1531. Braudling now meted out punishment for this offence though, as there is no record of what this was, we may assume that it was not unduly harsh. The mayor also allowed a couple of mendicants, who had been banished to Scotland for their opposition to the King's divorce, to come back to Newcastle and take up residence quietly at the city's Greyfriars again. Such small gestures evidently worked, because Tyneside remained so faithful to the Crown that Charles Brandon, Duke of Suffolk, would eventually commend it for its loyalty, with a special mention for its mayor. And its walls never were besieged, for reasons we can only guess at. Certainly Sir Ingram Percy, though willing to canvass support for the Pilgrimage from his own fastness at Alnwick some thirty miles to the north, never once looked as if he were going to do more than that.

Another prominent figure, on the other side of the country, was beginning to take an active part in these events, however. Edward Stanley, third Earl of Derby, was something of an enigma, not least because his family had always been notoriously slow to declare their position on anything until they were very sure that they would not suffer as a result, holding it as a great principle in life never to join a cause for its own sake. They had originally been small landowners on the Cheshire–Staffordshire border but had risen to prominence following a fourteenth-century marriage into the Lathoms of Lancashire, who owned vast estates in that county. By the time Thomas, Lord Stanley, headed the family a hundred years later, they were important enough in north-west England for monarchs to beware of them whenever some contentious matter of state arose.

This happened most memorably in the struggle between Richard III and Henry Tudor, which was resolved at Bosworth Field in 1485. Richard had been counting on Stanley's support, but he and his troops stood aside from the battle until it was perfectly clear that Henry was winning: it is not at all clear that Stanley took any relevant part in the battle at all, though he was certainly at Henry's side when Richard was killed and may, indeed, have been the one who actually placed the crown on Tudor's head. As a result of this masterstroke, Stanley was ennobled with the earldom of Derby by the new King Henry VII and acquired yet more estates, most notably from the Pilkington family of South Lancashire, who had unfortunately backed the wrong side. With homes at Lathom House and at Knowsley, both in the flat hinterland of Liverpool, he had become easily the most powerful landowner in the region. In spite of this, family debts to the Crown amounted to over £3000 at the first Earl's death. By the time Edward Stanley inherited the title as a boy of eleven these had been reduced by no more than a half.

Now, at the age of twenty-six, he, too, was being asked to make up his mind which side he would take in a potentially catastrophic dispute. His reputation by this time was as a vacillating young man who was not very good at maintaining law and order in those parts of the realm for which he was held responsible by the Crown. In 1535 there had been riots involving the retainers of many leading Lancashire families which, it was thought in Westminster, Stanley should have been clever enough to have forestalled. The year before that, many Lancashire clergy had refused to pay the clerical subsidy; while up in the north of the county there was a great deal of agitation against the policies enacted against the Church, where people were taking their cue from the Cistercians of Furness Abbey. There was even a question mark against Edward Stanley's own religious allegiance. His family had always been devoutly Catholic and one of his relatives, indeed, was a priest who was certainly trying to secure the Earl's commitment to the Pilgrimage, though Robert Aske might not have welcomed this recruit, whom he regarded as a 'false, flattering boy'.

Cromwell himself was suspicious enough to ensure that he heard all the menial gossip of the household at Lathom and was informed that almost all Stanley's servants were scathing in their opinion of Henry's vicar-general. But instead of vindictively moving against Stanley, he persuaded the King to give the Earl of Derby full powers of royal authority throughout Lancashire, Cheshire and North Wales, as well as in those parts of Staffordshire which were not already answerable to the Earl of Shrewsbury. Cromwell by now knew his man very well indeed. Stanley's response was one of immense, almost childlike, pride in being the first member of his family ever to attain such an exalted position. As Cromwell had intended, this new and glittering responsibility made up Stanley's mind for him. He was definitely the King's liegeman from now on.

On 10 October Henry had instructed him to prepare for a joint advance into Lincolnshire with George Talbot's forces. Nine days later this plan was abandoned because the Lincolnshire rising had collapsed without armed intervention. The King, meanwhile, had heard of the goings-on at Sawley Abbey, lately restored by the rebels of Percy Fee, and he was probably also appraised of the inflammatory Sawley Ballad, which was being taken up as a marching song throughout the Pilgrimage. In any event, he sent Edward Stanley a stern injunction to raise troops in Lancashire, with the following furious conclusion: 'Having since heard of an insurrection attempted about the abbey of Salley [sic] in Lancashire, where the abbot and monks have been restored by the traitors, we now desire you immediately to repress it, to apprehend the captains and either have them immediately executed as traitors or sent up to us ... You are to take the said abbot and monks forth with violence, and have them hanged without delay in their monk's apparel ...' But it was raining hard in Lancashire, as it was everywhere else that month, so Stanley put off his move, excusing himself to Henry on the grounds that 'the ways and passages to Whalley and Salley be very cumbrous, strait, full of mire impediments by waters and otherwise'. He then received another despatch from his king, demanding action at once: 'If on your coming to Sauley [sic] you find the abbot and monks or canons restored again, of which they must have been authors or abettors, you shall at once cause the abbot and certain of the chief monks to be hanged on long pieces of timber, or otherwise, out of the steeple, and the rest to be executed in such places as you think fit ... You must have special regard to the apprehension of all such captains and let none escape.'

The bad weather notwithstanding, Stanley was not completely inactive between the receipt of these two orders. He set about complying with the very first instruction he had received and presently had raised 7000 men, with which he occupied Preston. This was a force big enough to intimidate the whole of Lancashire and goes a long way to explaining why it was that the rebellion never took hold there south of Lonsdale – which included an immense area lying inland of Morecambe Bay, and reached down to a line between Cockerham and Bowland – and the Blackburnshire hundred, whose southern limit was the head of Rossendale. Had enough of the gentry below those boundaries been so enthusiastic for the Pilgrimage as to challenge Stanley's authority, then Lancashire might have been as strong for the rebellion as Yorkshire; but such men never came forward, so a generally impoverished and cowed region remained dormant.

Much of it was land which the Stanleys had taken from the Pilkingtons as a reward for making the right choice at Bosworth Field and had totally dominated ever since. Once in control of things there, Edward Stanley found that a number of fugitives sought his protection. One of these was the Prior of Cartmel, Richard Preston, who had deserted his brethren after they were restored to their house because, according to him, they had pressed him into going back there unwillingly. Another religious who fled to Lathom House, which he reached by sailing down the coast and then cutting inland, probably by way of the Ribble or the Mersey estuaries, was the Abbot of Furness, Roger Pyle, who sounds as if he might have been hedging his bets in the great tradition of the Stanleys themselves. For before he left his abbey, he advised his monks to 'stick together and ... do their best that they can do to the commons', while he would do the best he could with the King. A charitable interpretation of this is that he abandoned them because, in all conscience, he felt unable to take the rebel oath himself, even if they were willing to do so, as they were. But, writing from Lathom, he then told them 'to be of good cheer, for he had taken such a way that he was sure enough both from the king and also from the commons'.

The collective loss of nerve by a gentry who failed to raise South Lancashire was just as well for Stanley because, even as things stood, he soon found himself facing two separate rebel hosts, each of about 3000 men. One consisted of insurgents from Percy Fee, who had been mustered thrice after their initial gathering at Neals Ing: twice at Monubent, between Sawley and Sir Stephen Hamerton's home at Wigglesworth, and once on Clitheroe Moor, where everyone between the ages of sixteen and sixty was bidden to turn up properly armed by nine o'clock sharp. The intention of these rebels was not only to defend Sawley against anything that Stanley might do there, but to prevent him from making any move to assist Henry Clifford in Skipton. Hearing that Stanley was at last about to leave Preston for Whalley Abbey, from whence he would strike at Sawley, the Percy Fee host at once made for some high ground overlooking the Sawley monastery, between the Ribble and the Swanside Beck, and there awaited the Earl's arrival. They would thus be at some advantage if an engagement took place, but it never did materialise.

For Stanley was deflected by the news coming from further north, where John Atkinson's host had taken Kendal and were marching on Lancaster, whose mayor, as we already know, was another of those who sought Stanley's protection. The usual threatening noises made by the commons when they weren't getting their own way were then transmitted to Preston by Atkinson's men, to the effect that they would burn down the mayor's house and smash all his possessions if he did not return. Stanley's response was that the mayor would be staying where he was, that the host had better clear off out of Lancaster, in which case he 'would be a means to the King's Highness to extend his pity and mercy to them'. To which Atkinson replied that he had a list of the mayor's friends, whose lives would be a surety against that functionary's return; and he supplied their names, to demonstrate that this was no idle boast. He added that they 'had a pilgrimage to do for the commonwealth', which they would accomplish or 'die in that quarrel'.

But for once, threats did not produce the intended result, because Edward Stanley was no longer the vacillating young man whom Robert Aske and many others had lately scorned. He sent word back to Atkinson that if he could demonstrate that a dozen of his principal rebels were prepared to fight the matter out here and now, Stanley would oblige them, 'promising to fight on Bentham Moor, which was the place where they were accustomed to muster and within their own strength', where the Earl 'would meet them on a day to be agreed upon, and determine the quarrel by battle'. So the commons' bluff was called, Atkinson declining the invitation on the grounds that they would not fight Stanley and his men unless 'he interrupted them of their Pilgrimage' or tried to join up with other forces of the Crown.

Having in this way disposed of one potential adversary, Stanley had very good reason to continue his unfinished business at Sawley, taking on the Percy Fee host with much more confidence. But again he was dissuaded, this time by a royal messenger's arrival in Preston, with news from George Talbot of an important turn of events in South Yorkshire. After he had consulted his leading aides, Stanley disbanded his army (they were an immediate burden on his purse, after all, and Henry was slow to meet debts for which he was ultimately responsible) and returned to Lathom House, to await whatever happened next. The men of Percy Fee received a similar message from Robert Aske, instructing them to hold their fire; which explains why they made no attempt to harry the dispersing royalists.

The strategy that Robert Aske and Lord Darcy discussed after Thomas Miller was sent on his way from Pontefract on Saturday, 21 October was for a general advance of the rebel hosts down to London. These were now arriving at the new headquarters of the Pilgrimage one after the other. Aske's own host from Marshland and Howdenshire were already in, having followed not far behind their captain and William Maunsell on the Thursday night. First after them came Thomas Percy and his cohorts – some 5000 men – from the North-east on Saturday, bringing with them some welcome funds which had been donated by the Augustinians of Kirkham, Newburgh, Guisborough and Bridlington, the Cistercians of Byland and Rievaulx, the Benedictines of Whitby, the Gilbertines of Malton and the Carthusians of Mount Grace. The Abbot of Rievaulx and the Prior of Guisborough, indeed, had offered to accompany Percy and his men to Pontefract but were told that they would not be needed on this expedition.

Next morning, William Stapleton and his Beverley host arrived from Hull, with Sir Ralph Ellerker riding beside the captain at the head of between 2000 and 3000 troops. Only a couple of hours behind them came Robert Bowes's force from Durham and Cleveland, together with such men of Richmondshire as were not delayed at Skipton. This army was variously estimated at anything from 4000 to 10,000 men and it, too, brought welcome sustenance in the form of three recruits from the nobility: the Lords Latimer, Lumley and the adolescent Neville. By that Sunday night there were still some conspicuous absentees from the ingathering at Pontefract: about 15,000 rebels directed by John Atkinson, by Pulleyn and Musgrave and by the four captains in different places north-west of the Pennines; some 6000 men of Percy Fee, otherwise engaged at Sawley; and perhaps twice that number of the Richmondshire host, who were trying to extract Henry Clifford from his fastness in Skipton.

It is not at all certain that Robert Aske was aware of all these forces at that time, nor they of him, but despatches were sent to those which were recognised by the high command and to other parts of the North so that everyone should be in no doubt where the rebellion now stood; and a copy of the oath accompanied each message, just in case there were any more people to be sworn. But even without its full complement of manpower, when the number of recent South Yorkshire insurgents was also taken into account, the Pilgrimage of Grace could muster between 28,000 and 30,000 rebels in Pontefract as the last full week of October began. What's more, they began to blend with every appearance of harmony, apart from some of the commons who became disgruntled when they learned of Robert Aske's strict attitude to any form of looting. Even people whose relationship in quieter times had been poisonous – as Constable's and Ellerker's had – either kept at a safe distance from each other or decided to forget their animosities, for the time being at least.

The victualling of such large numbers was but one of several things that Aske and Darcy had to settle now, but their principal concern was for a plan of campaign and an order of battle. The first major objective was Doncaster but a message which came from Talbot's camp – from a spy whose identity neither Darcy nor Aske ever disclosed – gave them pause to think. It was to the effect that Talbot and his troops had advanced as far as the very edge of Nottinghamshire, to a position near Scrooby, twelve miles south of the old town on the banks of the River Don. It added the ominous warning: 'Son Thomas, this night the Earl of Shrewsbury intendeth to take you sleeper' – and it is recorded that Darcy handed the letter to Aske with a sigh of resignation when he read that. There was, therefore, good reason to take precautionary steps first of all, in case Talbot made a night march to Pontefract in order to capture, or kill, Lord Darcy. It was decided that a host of rebels should march forthwith to the village of Wentbridge, in a gentle and wooded river valley four miles on the way to Doncaster, in order to block any such incursion from the south. The companies commanded by Robert Bowes were asked to undertake this assignment, but Bowes protested that his men were worn out after a long forced march from Durham and needed some rest before they did anything else; so Stapleton's host, together with Thomas Percy's men, became the temporary vanguard of the Pilgrim army and set off for Wentbridge on Sunday evening, for a night which passed peacefully, with Talbot and his army nowhere in sight.

The following day the rest of the available Pilgrims joined them there and the order of battle which Aske and Darcy had already planned for the campaign as a whole was adopted. The vanguard was to consist of Robert Bowes and his troops, plus Sir Thomas Percy and his men. There were two reasons for this choice. Between them they mustered the most experienced soldiery that the Pilgrim command had at its disposal just then, men who had been long mettled by fighting border skirmishes against the Scots. There was also an inestimable advantage to be gained from the fact that such an array meant the Pilgrim army, in its advance south towards the capital, would be led by quite an impressive clutch of the English nobility: Lord Latimer and Lord Lumley, together with the next Earl of Northumberland (Percy) and the next Earl of Westmorland (young Neville, even if he was scarcely more than juvenile). This, together with a full panoply of banners – St Cuthbert's, the Five Wounds and all the heraldic display that each noble family could provide – at the head of maybe 30,000 troops was bound to create a mighty impression on any adversary who stood in the way. And on the rest of England, as soon as the word got around.

The other dispositions were quickly settled. The middle-ward was to consist of Aske and his men, plus Stapleton and his host. The rearguard would presently be formed by the Richmondshire men still in Skipton, who had been told to break off the siege and come down to Pontefract without delay; and, if they could detach themselves from their business with Edward Stanley, the contingent from Percy Fee were probably going to join them as back-up troops. For the moment, Lord Darcy remained in Pontefract with his servants, because his age and his health no longer fitted him for the role of warrior. So did the Archbishop, who would have been no use at all on a battlefield.

Meanwhile, the commanders in the field adopted a rolling movement, which bore all the marks of long military experience – that is, it was almost certainly a tactic devised by Darcy and Constable. The vanguard was to move to an advanced position before the middle-ward vacated the ground already held and followed up, the rearguard being expected to do likewise in its turn; and in this way the Pilgrimage would steadily make its way in carefully planned stages down the country until it reached the capital, not only with its own reinforcements from the North at its back, but also with new recruits who would doubtless be picked up on the way as the strength and power of the rebellion became manifest to everybody when the Pilgrims passed by. The first phase of this strategy was completed by Wednesday night, 25 October, when Aske's host and Stapleton's were deployed around the village of Hampole, well on the other side of Wentbridge, where there was a priory of Cistercian nuns. The vanguard, meanwhile, had taken up a position further on, at

Pickburn, from which it was perfectly placed to enter Doncaster, now almost within sight.

But Thomas Miller, Lancaster Herald, had turned up again with a message from the joint commanders of the royal forces that caused the Pilgrims to delay their next move.

IX

A BATTLE WAITING TO BE WON

The government by now had no doubt about the magnitude of the problem facing it. The Sheriff of Yorkshire, Sir Brian Hastings, had shrewdly and accurately reckoned rebel numbers within the past week, and there were other sources which only confirmed his estimates, including Lord Darcy before he capitulated to Aske. A final assessment, when royal forces were on the threshold of Doncaster, the rebels not far away on the other side of the Don, was made by Lawrence Cook, Prior of the Carmelites in the town, who was ordered to cross the river on a scouting mission for the Earl of Shrewsbury's troops, and in the course of it even spoke with Robert Aske.[1] Quite apart from the fact that the rebels were evidently moving towards confrontation in much greater numbers than anticipated, the fall of Pontefract and the treacherous conversion of Darcy and Sir Robert Constable in particular, not to mention the increasing recruitment of other notables to this Pilgrimage of Grace, must have been a tremendous blow to Henry's self-confidence, enduringly buoyant though that invariably was. What had happened in Lincolnshire, it was becoming more obvious by the day, was almost trifling in comparison with this tremendous upheaval across the North, and the most immediately pertinent question was this: would a strategy of threats which had worked down there now produce the same result again and, if it was in doubt,

1 Cook's mission was of doubtful benefit, however. Privately, he sympathised with the Pilgrims and probably gave as much useful information to them as whatever he passed on to the royal commanders.

what was the alternative? A military solution would be admirable, provided the King could be sure that most of the blood would be shed in the rebel cause. But as he received reports about the deployment and low morale of his own armies, he could scarcely have been confident of that, in the immediate future at least.

For his soldiers were in some disarray, scattered across the Midlands of England, with the exception of Edward Stanley's force, which was itself isolated up in North Lancashire, not nearly within swift striking distance of Pontefract or anywhere else the main body of Pilgrims might be. In fact, there never had been a cohesive and well-organised military response to any threat facing the Crown, whether from the Scots or anyone else, and the fundamental reason for this is that there was no such thing as a standing army in Tudor England, only a requirement, codified in the Statute of Winchester since 1285, that every man had to keep some sort of harness at home, against such time as he might be called up to serve the Crown. All the sovereign had at his immediate disposal were his Yeomen of the Guard, who numbered anything up to 600 men, a handful of gentlemen in his household, and the garrisons at Berwick, Calais and in Ireland. If he required more troops to serve his purposes, for other royal garrison duties, or when hostilities seemed imminent, these were raised piecemeal by individual noblemen and gentry, from commons who were under a well-defined obligation to their masters. A list drawn up early in October 'of persons who are to supply men against the northern rebels' included landowners from seven southern English counties and a number of religious superiors from the same parts, whose liabilities were anything from 400 to a dozen men: Sir Giles Capel was down for fifty of his Essex tenants, the Abbot of Westminster for 100 of his.

Such was the backbone of the county militias, which would always be raised at royal command by the lords-lieutenant of England and whose numbers were regularly checked on the muster rolls. From their ranks came the northern soldiers who fought against the Scots at Flodden Field, while their counterparts in southern England would have been expected to stand to in the same way if there was ever any possibility of invasion from the Continent. It was an untidy system, with glaring weaknesses which were soon exposed in 1536, but it was necessary in order to avoid the huge cost of maintaining a permanent military machine capable of instant action under a unified command, which could respond to any eventuality.[2]

The difficulties had been apparent from the start of the rebellion in Lincolnshire. Thomas Howard, having received the call from Henry to bestir himself again, at once set about raising troops in his East Anglian dukedom, estimating that he could muster 2500 men but that this would take a few days. He reported that he had five pieces of cannon and twenty other brass firearms, but that he was sorely in need of gunners as well as equipment for his archers, and asked the King to send him some at once: 'two or three carts of bows and arrows are requisite'. A week later he was more specifically pleading for 'at least 400 bows and 500 sheaves of arrows. This were better than gold or silver for, for money, I cannot get bows nor arrows.' He might have added that there was a shortage of good horses for reconnaissance work, where it was essential to have animals that could move long distances across the countryside at speed, rather than creatures more suitable for the briefer lumbering business of the charge. His second plea for weapons was made after he had received orders to meet the King at Windsor, only to be told before he was halfway there that he should go to Ampthill instead, together with his troops.

The trouble with that was that Howard's soldiers, most of whom were on foot, could not move as fast as he could on horseback, but at least they were heading in the right direction, by way of Cambridge and Huntingdon, when Henry decided that he was not going to take personal command of his army at Ampthill after all and countermanded the order. Howard therefore met his sovereign at Windsor as originally planned while his by now understandably confused troops were awaiting fresh instructions, still somewhere in the fenlands. The day after meeting Henry – which was the day York surrendered to Robert Aske, who knew exactly what he was doing – Howard

---

2 The system was slightly different when overseas expeditions were mounted, foreign mercenaries generally being recruited to augment whatever army left these shores. Only a limited number of English troops could be ferried across the Channel because of transport difficulties.

was at last sent off to Ampthill with authority to raise 5000 men there as a preliminary to meeting the new danger in Yorkshire. His original forces, which Howard had left under the command of his son Henry, Earl of Surrey, reached Cambridge, where a despatch arrived from Cromwell with orders to stay their advance until further notice. So bewildered by this was the young Earl, who did not dare inform the soldiery in case they demobilised themselves on the spot, that he wrote to his father in desperation, asking what he ought to do next.

He wasn't the only commander whose troops had come to a standstill, not knowing what was expected of them. Charles Brandon, Duke of Suffolk, was probably the sole one of them whose instructions were clear-cut. He and his men were to stay in Lincolnshire and keep watch there lest rebellion should break out again, with the local spirit revived at the news that they were no longer alone in their readiness to take up arms against the throne. Nobody else could have been as confident of what they should be doing. Not the Marquis of Exeter, the dashing young Henry Courtenay, who was at Ampthill awaiting the arrival of 1000 men marching up from Gloucestershire to add to the 2000 he had already mustered in Bedfordshire. Not George Talbot, Earl of Shrewsbury, who was still up in Nottinghamshire, whose most recent instruction from the King had given him and Howard the joint command of all the royal armies, and who was wondering whether to get on up to Yorkshire at once or whether to await the laggardly Howard, the better to face what was beginning to sound like a formidable foe. And certainly Howard himself must have been thoroughly muddled by now, with so many orders countermanded and with no definite plan of campaign in sight. He was on edge, too, because he had come to realise that Henry didn't quite trust him completely. And, although he had offered 'gladly' to serve under Charles Brandon in his pleasure at being recalled from semi-retirement, at being felt wanted again, it rankled with him that resources he might reasonably have expected to come his way, as Henry's most experienced man of war, had been diverted to Brandon instead. The lack of bows and arrows was only part of it; there were 600 of cavalry as well and he was being instructed to send Brandon his ordnance on top of that. The final indignity came when

Courtenay was told to disband his 2000 troops at Ampthill and then, with these men well on their way home, ill-tempered at having wasted much time attending musters, another order came to say that on no account should they be dismissed. Howard, it was made clear, was expected to pick up the pieces.

He was perfectly correct in his belief that Henry was not quite sure where his sympathies lay, but the King, in fact, still admired him as 'the chief and best captain' in the land. Henry's summaries of all the principal figures who stood by him in 1536, which he subsequently committed to paper, make instructive reading. Brandon, who was in his fifties, was 'a good man and captain, sickly and half lame'. Edward Stanley was 'the greatest of power and land, young and a child in wisdom, and half a fool'. Henry Clifford was 'a man of 50 years, of good power, without discretion or conduct'. Top marks were awarded, in fact, to Courtenay: '36, lusty and strong of power, specially beloved, diseased often with the gout and next unto the Crown of any man within England'.[3] Whatever his other failings, Henry could be a penetrating judge of men, though Courtenay was to disappoint him greatly later on.

The King was, however, magnificently indifferent to the conditions under which the common soldiery obeyed his commands. An uncontrolled and unequalled spendthrift himself, he cared little for the pockets of his underlings. His father had paid the royal armies eightpence a day but Henry had reduced this to sixpence, which was tuppence less than the Pilgrims were given out of their own infinitely slimmer treasury; and, though he was begged by Howard and others to restore the old eightpence, Henry wouldn't hear of it.[4] It was not as though this was pocket money, or cash men could take home to their families: they were expected to pay for their own food when campaigning, which soaked up an increasingly high proportion of their wages. The cavalry also had to fodder their horses out of it, which made life for them all but impossible without a private income. Even the

3 The Earl of Shrewsbury does not appear in this assessment because he had died just before it was made, in 1538.
4 Parity was restored at some stage, however, though whether this was a grudging concession by Henry, or something arranged independently by a more sympathetic (and realistic) Cromwell, we do not know.

settled rate was not always paid on time, because the King was invariably slow to respond when commanders asked for the necessary funds. At one stage he was actually implored to lend his generals £1000 apiece, which they would pay back at the end of the campaign, so that they could get on with his bidding. At another, Howard was told £2000 had been sent his way, but when the money turned up it amounted to no more that £1200. He therefore had to spend £1500 of his own money in order to prevent something close to mutiny among his troops and Courtenay's. The balance owing him was promised within ten more days, to which Howard replied that 'neither I nor my lord Marquis will be able to keep our companies so long without money'.

A minor captain in the royal service, Richard Cotton, who brought up 200 horsemen to serve under Howard, wrote a letter to Cromwell that made perfectly clear the difficulties under which he and others like him were expected to lead their men into battle. He pointed out that some of his cavalry had been obliged to ride bareback because they had no saddles, so he had provided these out of his own purse, and other gear for the horses. He then added, 'Great murmur and grudging there was among your lordship's company because they thought the wages of eightpence by the day was too little to fund them and their horses ... either they shall mar their horses for lack of meat or else make such shifts for money that shall not stand well with your lordship's honour.' The government's resources were so stretched, in fact, that, when the truth of his situation finally dawned on him, Henry ordered Cromwell that, if need be, he should melt down and convert into coinage some of the precious royal plate.

There were other things that could have done little for the spirit of the royal armies. Due to the dreadful weather across the whole of England, roads everywhere were so muddy that twenty miles a day was as much as anyone could be expected to advance. And when they eventually closed in on Yorkshire, they discovered that most of the available fuel and food for man and beast had already been sold to the rebels, so that the day was not far off when they would need to disperse and make what shift each individual could for himself. It was scarcely surprising that for

Howard and his colleagues, an increasingly major problem was how they could continue to motivate their men enough to stand up in battle against an enemy who was fired up with zeal and bravado, taken care of by its commanders, well-led and well-disciplined by men with a clear vision of their objective and how they were going to attain it. In these circumstances, then, the royal armies made their haphazard way up England towards the moment of confrontation, which was clearly not going to be a repetition of the Lincolnshire triumph.

On 17 October, as Robert Aske was composing his Oath of the Honourable Men in York, Howard and Courtenay were in Ampthill, though their armies were at Cambridge and Buckingham respectively, with the contingent coming up from Gloucestershire no closer than Stony Stratford. Meanwhile George Talbot, who had shifted from Nottingham to Newark, was receiving instructions from Henry to advance into Yorkshire and 'to give them the stroke', but by then Talbot had discovered that the people of Doncaster were now committed to the rebel cause and he was also made aware of how many rebels were, in fact, facing him. He therefore paused at Southwell until Howard and Courtenay had caught up with him, then changed his mind and continued his march north so that he was no nearer than Scrooby the day Pontefract Castle fell. The next day, Saturday the 21st, he received further instructions from the King, ordering him to safeguard the bridges over the Trent at Nottingham and Newark. This was Howard's idea, part of a new strategy, a 'politic device', in which he urged that instead of seeking engagement with the rebels, it might be better to parley with them, in order to buy time and, with luck, to create division among the Pilgrims. The Trent, moreover, would be a far better defensive line if it came to needing one than the much smaller River Don; and there was always the possibility that the rebels could be held at bay there until winter set in, which might well have a discouraging effect and would certainly make campaigning even more difficult than it already was in this atrocious autumn.

This was not the first time Howard had suggested to the King that a cautious approach might be prudent; much earlier in the month, when policy was still being worked out against the rebels in Lincolnshire, he had advised that 'I think it unwise to be too hasty in giving them battle'. But Talbot now decided to press on, probably reckoning that Howard himself could handle the new Nottinghamshire assignment – provided he ever got there. By 23 October, when Sir Thomas Percy and Robert Bowes had led their Pilgrims south as far as Hampole, with Aske and Stapleton having taken the middle-ward behind them to Wentbridge, Talbot had advanced from Scrooby to the outskirts of Doncaster, while Howard had only just reached Newark and Courtenay was still making his way up from Bedfordshire. Realising that his strategy of making the Trent the royal defensive line had now become redundant, because Talbot had gone on ahead towards whatever awaited him at the Don, Howard spurred his horse northwards for what was becoming an urgent need for consultation between the joint commanders. But by the time he caught up with Talbot, his army was no further along the road than Tuxford, which was some twenty-five miles away.

Courtenay by then had managed to get as far as Nottingham. With Charles Brandon still in Lincoln, this meant that what might conceivably be the eve of a big battle would have to be fought with the King's men widely dispersed in relatively small companies of troops. Talbot had the biggest force, of about 6000 men, Brandon had 4000 or so, Howard was leading 3000 soldiers, Courtenay no more than 2000; and there was no way – there couldn't be any way for some days to come – in which they might be united in a coherent whole. They were sitting ducks for a determined enemy which, if it were led skilfully enough, would be able to pick them off one by one. Unless time was bought, and quickly, the situation was quite likely to become a royal shambles.

Howard, an essentially devious man, was the best possible person to handle a situation like this on his sovereign's behalf. At Newark he had composed a letter which was to be taken to the Pilgrim leadership, suggesting that there should be a meeting in Doncaster between them and Howard, in order to avoid an 'effusion of blood'. If the rebels would send 'four of the discreetest men of the north parts' Howard would despatch to the Pilgrims four of his own people as sureties while the talks went on, in which the insurgents were invited to air their grievances;

but he alone, it was made clear, would parley with the nominated captains. Apart from Lord Darcy's enquiry before he surrendered Pontefract Castle, this was the first time anyone speaking in the name of the King had shown any inclination to ask the Pilgrims the reasons for their taking up arms against the Crown. It was the message that Lancaster Herald brought to the Pilgrims from George Talbot on Tuesday, when they had advanced as far as Barnsdale, between Hampole and Wentbridge, and it could be construed as marking a significant shift in government policy towards the rebellion, for it hinted that Henry might be prepared to listen to his subjects at last instead of peremptorily putting them down. Robert Aske happened to be with the vanguard when Thomas Miller arrived, having detached himself temporarily from his own host – he was doubtless checking that all was going according to plan at the front line – and he immediately consulted Bowes, Percy and the other leaders of the van about the offer from Howard. Then, after deputing two gentlemen to take care of Miller and ensure his safety, Aske galloped back to Pontefract to see what Thomas Darcy thought. He also wanted him to join the rest of the Pilgrims on the way to Doncaster because the commons, ever suspicious of their social superiors who, they believed, could never be trusted not to betray them and their cause, were beginning to grumble at Darcy's absence in the security of Pontefract.

The likelihood is that Aske's colleagues at Barnsdale were in favour of rejecting Howard's proposal and fighting things out, whereas their chief captain, an essentially moderate man, wished to explore every avenue that might possibly result in a peaceful solution to their argument with the government. And, although we have no record of the consultation at Pontefract, it seems probable that Darcy advised a compromise between these conflicting views. At any rate, Thomas Miller was sent back to the King's commanders with the message that, though Howard's terms were not acceptable as formulated, the Pilgrims were willing to hold discussions 'betwixt the hosts, and there to declare their grievances and petition'. In other words, they wanted the talks to take place wherever the royal army was, rather than specifically at Doncaster. This was a counter-offer in which the wily Duke immediately sensed danger and it was the phrase 'betwixt the hosts' that alerted him, because the last thing he wanted was the rebels getting sight of his own comparatively slender resources, whereupon the essential weakness of the Crown's military position would be abundantly clear to his enemy. It would amount to an invitation to a battle that he would be unlikely to win. Something that happened next morning would only have confirmed his anxiety.

With the Pilgrim vanguard then encamped at Hampole, a royal scouting part of thirty horsemen or so appeared from somewhere across the Don, obviously bent on making a reconnaissance from beyond the range of longbows. They were allowed to get on with this uninterrupted until they came across a couple of rebel stragglers, seized them and began to ride away with two very useful captives. At this, a much larger body of Pilgrim cavalry leapt into the saddle and gave pursuit, so hotly that the King's men released their prisoners in order to escape more effectively. But they were chased until they had crossed the only bridge into Doncaster, when their pursuers paused to take stock from the higher ground of Scawsby Hill on the north side of the Don. From there the Pilgrims overlooked the town, where the Romans had created their fortress settlement of Danum in order to protect the river crossing and to safeguard an important line of communication from the south. Their legions habitually paused there, on their way to garrison duties at Eboracum or somewhere along Hadrian's Wall; and the Conqueror's army had passed that way during William's great northern campaign of 1068–9. To the rebel skirmishers that Wednesday morning, however, it seemed to be unprotected; indeed, to be well within their grasp if they made a sudden and unexpected attack; and many of them made it plain that they thought this was what they should do, with their enemy so conspicuously in retreat. But Robert Bowes, who was with them and who feared that, if they attempted an attack with their limited numbers they might thereby be riding into a trap, managed to stay their impetuous desire to come to grips with the King's men at last.

His initial overture rebuffed, Howard now resorted to the fall-back tactic that he had already thought out and conveyed to George Talbot, to be adopted in the event of the first ruse failing. Thomas Miller was sent to the rebels yet again, this time with an ultimatum to the effect that unless they withdrew and went on their ways peacefully, they could assume that they would have a battle on their hands. If they did as they were told, on the other hand, the royal commanders would press their suit upon the King, but if they did not disperse, 'then do your worst to us for so we will do to you'. This was the most tremendous bluff, just as Howard's entire strategy was based on a profound dishonesty. For he had written to the King before launching his first initiative, so that Henry should be in no doubt where Howard actually stood if he received independent news of the Duke treating at all leniently with the rebels: 'Sir, most humbly I beseech you to take in good part whatsoever promise I shall make unto the rebels (if such I shall by the advice of others make) for surely I shall observe no part thereof...' This was the communication of a man who was not only willing to double-cross his adversaries, but also prepared to shift all possible blame on to other shoulders if things did not go as planned. It was essentially the word of a calculating timeserver who, in the same document, assured the King that his one wish was 'to serve you mine only master and sovereign', that he 'shall rather be torn in a million of pieces than to show one point of cowardice or untruth to your majesty'.

The immediate effect of the ultimatum was that the senior Pilgrims conferred at Hampole Priory, which offered shelter from the downpouring rain that incessantly soaked man and beast, and everything else in the open air. All the commanders were present and so was the Archbishop of York, who had come down from Pontefract with Darcy, though probably not from choice. But both Darcy and Aske still hoped to engage him in the cause, to provide it with some spiritual substance and leadership. Darcy had asked Lee about the possibility of the Pilgrim manifestos being printed on the press at York if it was still available, the better to spread their intentions as widely as possible; but the Archbishop had pooh-poohed the idea. Aske had particularly pressed him to contribute a spiritual element to a revised set of articles, but Lee had ducked out of that one as well. He had no intention of incriminating himself by doing anything so committed, though the Pilgrims retained a touching belief in his good faith towards them, when he had done nothing at all beyond trying to keep himself out of harm's way.

But at least, at Hampole, he sided with Aske, with Darcy and with Sir Robert Constable in their agreement to pursue negotiation for the time being, rather than violence. What they were after, still, was not a humiliation of their sovereign, certainly not the national bloodbath which might well ensue if it was seen that a royal army could be defeated by common Englishmen, thus offering encouragement to all dissidents in the country at large. What they wanted was simply the removal of Cromwell and others like him who had, the Pilgrims devoutly believed, usurped positions which should never have been theirs and in doing so had poisoned the King's mind on a whole range of matters, which had resulted in this Pilgrimage of Grace. There were others with a different outlook on things as they stood, especially the belligerent fellows who led the van, and Robert Bowes represented their views fluently.

Although Thomas Miller was obviously not party to this conference, certain assurances he gave after delivering the message from his master must have been taken into account. He led the commanders to believe that if only they accepted Howard's offer, Cromwell would be deposed and the King would grant 'all other their demands'; and, one day, Miller would pay dearly for this gratuitous piece of advice. Darcy may have produced the clinching argument with a military assessment of the situation they were in. Though it was true that many things were on their side, including almost certainly superior numbers, better morale and greater motivation, it was also true that the men of Richmondshire who were the designated rearguard of the Pilgrim host had not yet obeyed the order to drop what they were doing in Skipton and get down to Pontefract: the rebel army, in short, was lacking about a third of its potential manpower. Darcy further suggested that the onset of winter meant that it would be more sensible to have a 'garrison war' in the next few months rather than any other sort. Why, it was even possible that by temporising they would be buying time for the possibility of assistance coming from the Pope and other sources overseas. Henry VIII, formerly Defender of the Faith, certainly wouldn't be able to obtain reinforcements that way any more.

Not for the first time, a willingness to be calmly reasonable prevailed over the impulse for instant action; and perhaps one look at the weather outside the priory windows was enough to dissuade any waverers from a determination to start fighting at all costs and without further delay. In spite of the fact that it might be interpreted as a climb-down, and therefore a sign of weakness, it was proposed that Howard's first offer should be accepted, with nothing in their reply to be said about the possibility of battle, and the four discreet men were chosen to represent the Pilgrims at the meeting with the Duke. They were to be Robert Bowes, young Sir Ralph Ellerker, Sir Thomas Hilton, who had been press-ganged by the rebels up in Durham, and Robert Chaloner of Wakefield, another of the gentry who had made the apparently effortless transition from fear of to wholehearted support for the Pilgrims. Having been one of those who fled to the sanctuary of Pontefract when it was still held by Darcy in the King's name, on its surrender he quickly became one of the inner circle around Aske, which planned all strategy from then on. These four, then, were readied to go forth to a meeting with Howard, Lancaster Herald being sent on ahead to inform the Duke of what was afoot and to set in motion the arrangement for the exchange of the royal hostages, who were to be in the custody of the Archbishop at Hampole while the truce talks were going on.

The meeting took place on Friday the 27th, the day after Howard had reached Doncaster himself, having ridden through much of the night from Newark. He was not, in fact, alone in receiving the four Pilgrims in Lawrence Cook's priory. With him were George Talbot, together with the Earls of Rutland and Huntingdon, and these heard Robert Bowes enunciate five requests to the King; oddly enough, they weren't written down until Howard asked for this to be done, after Bowes had first spoken from memory. The Pilgrims begged that the faith should be truly maintained. Likewise, they asked for the ancient liberties of the Church to be kept safe. They wanted unpopular statutes repealed, so that the law would stand again as it was when Henry came to the throne. They wanted the 'villein blood' to be expelled from government and noble blood restored to the King's Council. Finally, and adamantly, they wanted Cromwell, Richard Riche and the heretic bishops banished and punished as subverters of God's and the commonwealth's laws. In all essentials, therefore, these were the articles that had motivated the Pilgrims from the outset. The delegates added that if Henry would but grant these requests, they besought his pardon and would gladly return to their homes peacefully.

Later that day there was a second meeting, the reason for which is indistinct, though it went some way to satisfying the rebel demand for discussions 'betwixt the hosts', for it took place in sight of both armies on Doncaster bridge and more people were involved – about thirty on each side – than had been present at the first encounter. Leading the Pilgrim delegation, in addition to the original four negotiators, were the Lords Darcy, Latimer and Lumley, together with Sir Robert Constable and Sir John Bulmer, member of a prominent North Riding family, who had once served under Howard in Ireland and had been pressed into the Pilgrimage by the rebels coming down from Durham and Cleveland on their way to a muster at Northallerton.

Although the absence of Robert Aske from either of these truce talks seems on the face of it to be unaccountable, given his position as captain in chief, it is consistent with the policy adopted by the rebels from the start: to secure the allegiance of as many nobles and knights as they could and to parade them as prominently as possible in order to impress upon the King (and everyone else who was not a committed Pilgrim) the fact that this was not simply a rising of the commons and a sprinkling of gentry, but something that was socially much more impressive than that. In its way, it was a statement of a deeply held belief in a society of orders. Aske's absence may also, of course, have been a desire – subconscious or otherwise – on the part of Aske himself to deflect attention from his own person; to take cover, in case things went amiss, as much as possible behind the more substantial figures of the nobility and others scarcely less exalted.[5]

The talks may have been a genuine attempt by both sides – for vastly different reasons – to reach a peaceful solution to their confrontation, but a great deal of sabre rattling went on in the background of these comings and goings of Thomas Miller, the various delegations, the persons of high consequence. There

5 It has recently been suggested that the chief captain was deliberately sidelined by colleagues whose problem was 'what to do with Aske'. This, too, can be no more than speculation.

were other skirmishes besides the one that had finished with the royal scouts being chased back into Doncaster, and though they never amounted to anything that might precipitate a major battle, being more in the nature of military irritants, they did result in the killing of an unfortunate Pilgrim belonging to the Bowes host: he was speared from behind by one of his own comrades, who mistook the black cross of St Cuthbert on the man's jacket for the similar red cross of St George worn by the royal soldiery – and this resulted in the order that such badges should be discarded, that instead every Pilgrim should wear, back and front, either the badge of the Five Wounds or the one with IHS blazoned upon it. Apart from such minor engagements, there was a calculated display of its power by the rebel army on the Thursday morning when, at first light, the entire force of some 30,000 men was deployed at Scawsby Leys, where everyone in Doncaster would have a good view of them, including a contingent of royal soldiery amounting to no more than one-fifth of the rebel strength. They repeated this belligerent display the next day and there they stayed until after the delegations had come back to them. No one called up to the royal service could have been anything but extremely apprehensive at the sight.

Company after company was drawn up in battle order, their captains riding up and down their ranks, encouraging, correcting, maintaining a strict discipline among their men. Priests moved among them, too, exhorting them to have no fear of dying in defence of the faith. Each man wore his Pilgrim badge proudly and all of them were further sustained by the great crimson and silver banner of St Cuthbert which, together with that of the Five Wounds, billowed and rippled in the most prominent position of all, at the head of this dauntingly impressive array of troops. The crescent of the Percies was also to be seen, as well as the insigniae of the other nobility. And it may well be that this enormous combination of hosts sang the Sawley Ballad from time to time, with a choral lustiness that could never have been heard before, for it would have been an excellent way of stirring their own blood and making the enemy even more nervous than he was already at the sight of this intimidating presence.

Many of the rebels, certainly, still wanted to engage with their royal adversary and some doubtless felt that a golden opportunity had been lost when they were restrained from pursuing the royal scouts right into the town, which they might easily have over-come with a lightning raid. For the moment, there was no question of attempting that. The royal artillery had now arrived and the only bridge into Doncaster, part of the old Roman road from Lincoln to York, lay under the muzzles of a hundred pieces of ordnance, commanded by a gentleman of the Privy Chamber, Peter Mewtas. If conditions had remained as they were on the day of the pursuit it would have been possible to ford the river, which was normally only a couple of feet deep, to work round behind the guns and turn them to the rebels' own advantage. Torrential overnight rain had ruled out that tactic, the waters having risen so much that the Don was quite impassable. As Howard himself reported to the King, seeing Providence itself working on their behalf: 'God of his infinite goodness sent, that night, such a Rain that it was not possible without swimming to pass the water.'

We do not know exactly what went on at Doncaster bridge, though whatever it was, it went on long enough for the commons on the north bank to have their everlasting suspicions of a treacherous upper class raised again. They might have been even more cynical had they been aware of an exchange that took place between Lord Darcy and the Earl of Shrewsbury. There was by now – and there was ample reason for it – some antipathy between the two men, so that when Darcy told Talbot to 'Hold up thy long claw and promise me that I shall have the king's favour and shall be indifferently heard, and I will come [in] to Doncaster to you', the Earl's dismissive reply was, 'Then ye shall not come in.' But it was true that Darcy had aligned himself with the rebel party that preferred a peaceful solution if one could be found, as did everyone among the Pilgrim leaders except those in the vanguard, and there could have been very few commoners in any of the hosts who did not want to go on to London now that their blood was up; not now that many of them had seen for themselves how very much stronger they were – guns or no guns – than the undernourished army that was supposed to stand in their way.

There were hawks and doves on both sides, in fact, and while

Talbot certainly fell into the first category among the royal commanders, there is reason to suspect that Howard did not nearly share his views. His religious sympathies, insofar as he had any, lay with the rebels and he hated Cromwell as much as any of them; only expediency, perhaps, had held him thus far to his sovereign's side. What is also certain is that he was profoundly relieved at the prospect of avoiding battle for, the next day, he wrote to the King that 'The pestilence is in our army. We want victuals and money. The country is theirs. They have made it desolate. These considerations (as that we cannot force them to a battle but when and where pleaseth them) have made us condescend to a treaty with them...' The meaning of 'condescend' in the sixteenth century did not necessarily carry the patronising overtones of our own day, but it now sounds a perverse usage, given the reality of the Duke's circumstances that weekend. And though it is very likely that Howard, on the bridge, made an effort to undermine the pledges that had so far held commons, gentry and nobility together in the Pilgrimage, it is also possible that he made various concessions, though whether from goodwill or his habitual cunning is more difficult to estimate.

The rebel delegation seem to have come away from the meeting with the impression that a number of desirable things were now on the cards: a special sitting of Parliament to consider their grievances, an offer that the Crown would listen attentively – and would be open to persuasion – to complaints about certain statutes and a general pardon for everyone who had risen against the government, including the insurgents in Lincolnshire. They may have been sworn to secrecy on these points, in order to protect Howard's position at court in the immediate future, until their suit was laid before the King; and if this is so, it certainly betrays a degree of trusting *naïveté* on the part of supposedly sophisticated men. But the Duke of Norfolk was better than most at the tortuous art of dissembling.

The openly agreed outcome of the two parleys was that Howard and the Earl of Shrewsbury's son, Francis, Lord Talbot, should go south without delay, accompanied by Robert Bowes and Sir Ralph Ellerker representing the Pilgrims, to present the petition and further arguments to the King himself. They would then return with the royal response to their overtures.

Meanwhile, there would be a truce, in which both armies would disperse over the next couple of days to await further events when the King's pleasure was known. This was certainly a blow to the Pilgrim vanguard, who by now had become so confident of victory that they scoffed at the prospect of doing battle against opponents led by old men. 'They wished the King had sent some younger lords against them than my lord of Norfolk and my lord of Shrewsbury.' It is probable that they only consented to the truce and the approach to Henry because some sort of internal deal had been negotiated by the rebel leadership whereby, in exchange for their restraint over a limited period, they were rewarded by having two of their own captains, Bowes and Ellerker, represent the entire Pilgrimage in London, where their most adamant concerns would not be misrepresented or allowed to go by default. But there were others who also needed pacifying, which is why Darcy and Aske rode straight back to Pontefract on Friday evening, the moment the bridge talks were over and agreement had been reached by the principals.

For the men of Richmondshire had finally come down from Skipton and, deprived of their quarry there, were more than ready for a fight at Doncaster. Next morning they were told about the truce and ordered to make their way home, being no longer required as the rearguard. And while the commanders who, by now, were Lord Scrope and Sir Christopher Danby, could appreciate the reason behind this sudden about-turn, the ordinary dalesmen of their host most certainly could not. They were well aware, no doubt, that if they had been where they were supposed to be when the peace talks were going on, the outcome might have been otherwise; for they were of the same background, with the same cast of mind, as those of the vanguard commanded by Robert Bowes and had they been united they might have created an irresistible pressure on the Pilgrim leadership for war without further delay. With this frustration added to their failure to bring down Henry Clifford and to all their other grievances, they were very angry indeed at the order to disperse. Sir Robert Constable was later to speak of 'the fury of the commons' and Lord Darcy of 'wild people' from the dales. It was with difficulty, and after much argument, that Aske, Darcy and the others persuaded these commons to be on their way. But, that

Saturday, all the hosts eventually began the return journey north and east, just as the royal soldiers simultaneously dribbled away to the south. William Stapleton told his men to remain well-behaved as they made their way back to Beverley, after he had parted company with them at Tadcaster. Then he went home to Wighill, where he resumed the life of a country gentleman, with its seasonal pastimes of shooting birds and hunting the fox.

Up to a point, everything now depended upon the probity of Thomas Howard and no one had ever been sure of that. As he and young Talbot and the two Pilgrims rode out of Doncaster that Saturday, the only certain thing about him was that he was very far from elated at the way things had turned out. He was, in fact, almost dropping with exhaustion, having covered much more ground even than Robert Aske in the previous week, and he twice the rebel leader's age. It showed in a letter he wrote to Henry from Tuxford at five o'clock on Sunday morning. He pointed out that he had arrived the night before 'as weary a man as can be' and since then had been allowed only three hours' sleep, what with being woken twice to receive messages from the King and from Charles Brandon. In being forced to treat with the rebels 'my heart is near broken. And notwithstanding that in every man's mouth it is said in our army that I never served his Grace so well as now as in dissolving the army of the enemy without loss of ours, yet fearing how his Majesty shall take the despatching of our band, I am the most unquiet man of mind living. All others here are joyful and I only sorrowful.' He explained the circumstances which had caused the truce rather than bloodshed.

Foul weather and no housing for horse nor man, at the most not for the third part of the army and no wood to make fires withal, hunger both for men and horses of such sort that of truth I think never English saw the like. Pestilence in the town...on Friday night the mayor's wife and two of his daughters and one servant died in one house, how many others in the town I know not, but of soldiers nine, and if there were left in the town or within five miles one load of hay or one load of oats, peas or beans, all the purveyors say untruly.

There was then an admission that all was not well with the commitment of his common troops. 'Though never prince had a company of more valiant noblemen and gentlemen, yet right few of the soldiers but that thought and think their quarrels to be good and godly ...' As he must have known by then, or at least suspected, a large proportion of the royal army sympathised with the rebels. Had there been a Pilgrim victory at Doncaster, they would have gone over to the other side in droves. Was the Duke obliquely trying to tell Henry something that he didn't have the courage to say outright?

It was a typical Howard response to a difficult situation: self-regarding, self-justifying, expecting sympathy, obsequious, just a little enigmatic. It even included a damning flick at someone he didn't like and knew would be a particular object of Henry's vindictive wrath. 'Fie, fie upon the Lord Darcy,' he wrote, 'the most arrant traitor that ever was living, and yet both his sons true knights.' This was misleading or ill-informed in its assessment of loyalties within the Darcy family; for although Lord Darcy's youngest son, Sir Arthur, had not only done business with his King, but remained true to him throughout the rebellion, the eldest boy, Sir George, took the Pilgrim oath at the same time as his father and stayed firm in his commitment to the insurgent cause until the issues at stake were no longer as clear as they had been then. Nevertheless, the royal commander at this time gave the impression of a man who had struggled bravely with an intractable problem, which had brought him close to the end of his tether. But that would have been deceptive. Thomas Howard, third Duke of Norfolk, still had plenty of energy left, and zeal, as everyone would see for themselves in the next few months.

BACK FROM THE BRINK

Though the Pilgrim hosts dutifully – and, in most cases, reluctantly – went their ways home, their commanders made sure that
they could be mobilised again, at very short notice if necessary.
In response to Robert Aske's message that they should break off
their engagement with the Earl of Derby, the men of Craven
certainly 'kept every man his own house ready to be and come
together at an hour's notice'; and it is likely that the same state of
readiness was maintained elsewhere, given the disposition of the
overwhelming majority to go to war anyway, regardless of the
arrangements made at Doncaster. A further precaution was taken
to ensure a swift response throughout the North, should a
changing situation warrant it. That last weekend of October
Robert Aske ordered that beacons should be set up within sig-
nalling distance of each other 'in divers places, to give warning to
rise again, if need be' and he also instructed the men of the East
Riding to keep a perpetual night watch from their church
towers, lest the royal forces in Lincolnshire tried to mount a surprise attack across the Humber. This was a prudent move
because Charles Brandon, with 4000 troops still at his disposal in
spite of the truce, was busily despatching many of them from his
base in Lincoln to garrison Grimsby, Barton-on-Humber and
other towns along the Humber and the Trent. News could
scarcely have failed to reach the Pilgrims' chief captain that
Barton, in particular, was being reinforced and that efforts were
quite openly being made to accumulate as many boats as possible
on the south bank of the river.

A substantial number of insurgents, of course, had played no part whatsoever in the occupation of Pontefract and the advance on Doncaster. Apart from those in the North-west who were fully occupied with the potential threat to Sawley, the host of Cumberland were similarly engaged in the developing situation outside Carlisle, which in many respects resembled the sideshow of the Richmondshire rebels at Skipton. It is possible, however, that a number of the Westmorlanders took part in besieging Henry Clifford's home, too, in which case they would almost certainly have then marched south to Pontefract with their comrades in arms from Richmondshire. We cannot be sure of this, because no record of their presence in either Skipton or Pontefract exists, though two things are highly suggestive. One is Lord Darcy's estimate that when the rearguard eventually caught up with the main Pilgrimage it numbered 20,000 men and it is known that Skipton was initially besieged by no more than 10,000 rebels. The addition of 8000 from Westmorland at some later stage is perfectly plausible because Clifford was regarded with as much hostility there as anywhere else, as an absentee landlord whose impositions of one kind or another had become unbearable. The other reason for assuming that Westmorlanders had marched south in some numbers is that one of their two captains, Robert Pulleyn, was certainly in Pontefract either when or immediately after the truce was announced, because he met Aske there on Saturday the 28th and presented him with a document which assured the leader of absolute support in his region; and it is highly improbable that Pulleyn would alone have made a journey that any messenger could have undertaken, much more likely that he had brought an armed contingent with him.

A further assumption about the Westmorland host seems possible if these two premises are accepted. It is that the army commanded by Pulleyn and Nicholas Musgrave had deliberately been divided, in much the same way that the men of Richmondshire and those from Durham and Cleveland had been reorganised before them, in order to spread their effectiveness. If this was indeed the case, Pulleyn had doubtless headed south with part of the host and, as Skipton lay directly on their route to Pontefract, had dallied with the Richmondshire men there before Aske's orders were finally obeyed. Musgrave, meanwhile, had taken the other half of their army in the opposite direction. One of the things we do know is that Clifford's nineteen-year-old son Lord Henry, who had taken refuge in Carlisle Castle after being deflected from his intended destination in Berwick by rebel troop movements, informed his father and through him the King on the last day of October that the town was threatened by a mixture of Westmorlanders and Cumbrians.

The Cumbrians had the more obvious reason for concern about Carlisle and a lot of it was to do with their constant awareness that they were exposed, as no one else but Northumbrians were, to the possibility of engagement with the Scots, either to repel an invasion from north of the border, or to do the King's bidding and themselves move aggressively against an old enemy. One of the things that Anthony Hutton did, before he was replaced as a captain by the commoner Robert Mownsey four days after the initial rising in Penrith, was to compose a proclamation setting out the intention of the Cumbrians. It was clearly influenced by the Captain Poverty letter which had reached the area from Richmondshire – though it said nothing about suppressed monasteries, or even of oath-taking – but it made a particular point of urging Cumbrians to be ready for action 'when the thieves or Scots would invade us'; the thieves being the dangerous reivers whose only motivation was the acquisition of plunder throughout the Debatable Lands flanking the border on both its sides. Cumbrian bitterness towards Henry Clifford included the fact that he did not, in their view, properly discharge his duties as Earl of Cumberland for their protection against such marauders, seated as he was too far away in Yorkshire and generally much too absorbed in his family feud with the Dacres to be bothered. Carlisle, therefore, was the very logical focal point of these various discontents and anxieties, for it was an absolute necessity as a protective shield against all the alarming possibilities that might beset the region.

Its strategic importance against the Picts had been well recognised by the Emperor Hadrian when he ordered the building of the Roman Wall from one side of the country to the other in AD 122, but for more than thirty years before he proposed to make it the Wall's major garrison close to the western terminus, Luguvalium had been a civil settlement, a market place which thrived on the rich agricultural land of the Eden valley, and on the lead and silver mined in the North Pennine hills overlooking it. For decades the town was actually held by the Scots until William Rufus recaptured it in 1092 and built its first castle of stone to supersede a fortification made of wood and to ensure that such an indignity would not easily befall Carlisle again. Besieged unsuccessfully by Robert Bruce in 1315, Carlisle Castle had been well taken care of by successive monarchs as one of the most important outposts in the defence of the realm, and only in Henry VIII's time had it fallen into serious neglect, because he thought he had better things to do with his funds. It was, nevertheless, still a commanding presence on a mound overseeing the town walls, its Norman keep brooding squatly above its own battlements. Like other fortresses belonging to the kings of England, it had a long history of use for imprisonment, and for well over 200 years its inmates had tried to lighten their captivity by chiselling graffiti on its dungeon walls, which were by now notable for 'dragons and mermaids, coats of arms, the Crucifixion and the Virgin, Justice and the Wheel of Fortune, and stags and the fox preaching to the geese'.

There were a number of other inducements to taking Carlisle apart from the acquisition of its castle, including its associations with the Clifford family and the fact that its capture by the rebels would send a powerful signal to all those in the region who were yet unsworn. It was also vital that the royal garrison should either be nullified or, better still, converted to the cause. But its pre-eminence as a defence in troubled times was always reason number one.

This, then, was the object of a council of war held by the Cumbrians the day after the Doncaster truce was agreed, of which they were then ignorant, on top of Moota Hill, a rocky knoll 750 feet above the nearby sea level a little to the north-west of Bassenthwaite, the northernmost expanse of water in the Lake counties. Because of its altitude and because it stood well clear of the much greater Cumbrian mountains, Moota was perfectly situated for a sweeping view of the Solway Firth and the Eden estuary, of Carlisle itself, and of all the territory adjacent to them. And there a number of the most influential gentry in the region assembled, including John Legh and Sir John Lamplugh, formerly lieutenant in the Honour of Cockermouth. Also present were the four commoner captains of Penrith and Thomas Carter, the Cistercian Abbot of Holm Cultram, which was the richest religious house in Cumberland and consequently a notable prize for which the houses of Clifford and Dacre had long contended. He was, in fact, sworn to the cause that day on Moota Hill, but there is good reason to believe that he had attached himself to it at least several days earlier, though the evidence for this partly comes from a rival of his in the monastery and therefore could be tainted. It does seem very probable, however, that, even though he carefully absented himself from the occasion, Carter had ordered his brethren and their monastic tenants to attend one of the Cumbrian musters held in the very early stages of the local rebellion, on the day that the four chaplains of Poverty were being appointed by the newly elected captains in Penrith.

Though he appears to have been chiefly motivated by a fear for the future of his abbey if the Pilgrimage of Grace failed, another consideration might have been the opposition of Henry Clifford to his election as abbot a couple of months earlier. There was further religious support for the rebellion from the Augustinian house in Carlisle, whose former prior, Christopher Slee, now Vicar of Castle Sowerby, was one of the four chaplains to the local rebel leaders. Carlisle's adherence to the traditional Church was symbolised by its possession of St Thomas Becket's sword, its most venerated relic, and by the inclusion of the Pope's name in the daily prayers of the canons, a habit which they continued, astonishingly without detection, not only throughout the rebellion but until Henry had suppressed the priory and promoted the premises into a cathedral in 1541.

The Cumbrian leaders had received a setback to their plans the day before when, at a muster on Sandale Moor, they had been told by a delegation from the town that the citizens of Carlisle would not swear the oath, even though they were sympathetic to the Pilgrimage. The decision was therefore taken to force them and the garrison into submission by blockading Carlisle and starving it of victuals. A commission of four was chosen to ride there and inform the mayor and senior citizens that this was going to happen unless they took the oath, and the point about a defence against the Scots and the reivers was also emphatically to be made. The men selected for this task with a fine sense of balance were two gentlemen, Richard Blenkow and Thomas Dalston, the first a client of the Cliffords, the second in a similar relationship with the Dacres; and two priests, one of whom was Thomas Carter, the other Barnard Townley, the Rector of Caldbeck and one of the four chaplains. They were to enlist the support of someone already in Carlisle, Sir John Lowther, deputy sheriff of Westmorland, where he had already been sworn under pressure from Nicholas Musgrave's men, though he had hitherto always been a Clifford stalwart.

But the nominated four refused this commission because they were afraid of being thrown into the castle dungeons, which caused so much anger among the commons that the familiar threats of execution were soon disturbing the air. A difficult situation was only ended when the official crier of the four captains, Thomas Berwick, loudly ordered a fresh muster after the weekend in the Broadfield, just outside Carlisle on the road from Penrith, a place where military assemblies had always taken place. The muster duly went ahead, attended by 15,000 men, on Monday the 30th, and it was then that those present were informed that a truce had been called in Doncaster, which they refused to believe, rejecting it as 'but craft and falsehood' designed to throw them into disarray.

The following Thursday the rebels mustered again in the same place and, once more, a quartet of representatives chosen by the four captains, which included only Townley of the original nominations, jibbed at the dubious honour that had befallen them. So two canons of Carlisle, the recently sworn Richard Huttwyth and William Florens, were enlisted instead and returned with a couple of leading citizens, bearing the official proclamation of the truce and the assurance that it was indeed a reality. This was still not enough for a large proportion of the commons, who made it plain that their patience was rapidly running out. At this point an unprecedented collusion between the house of Clifford and that of Dacre played a crucial role in what happened next.

Henry Clifford's heir, the young Lord Clifford who had lodged himself secretly in Carlisle Castle the best part of a week earlier, had not revealed his presence until the penultimate day of

October, when he came out of hiding to announce that he would act as his father's deputy; and this had produced a response from Lord Dacre, who had been securely sitting at home in Naworth Castle, just below the Roman Wall near Lanercost Priory, ever since the earliest days of the Pilgrimage, in spite of all the efforts made by the rebels to extract him, either by threats or by persuasion. Dacre now announced that he would join Clifford in the defence of Carlisle, provided the Cliffords would come to his assistance if Naworth was attacked – though within a few more days his promise could be seen as a hollow one, for he suddenly left Naworth for his Yorkshire seat at Hinderscelfe, where things appeared to have simmered down, certainly compared with the doings in Cumberland. His departure resulted – and this possibly had some bearing on his decision to get out while the going was good, as he had done from Yorkshire some weeks earlier – in his tenants forthwith declaring themselves for the Pilgrimage. The family, however, was not entirely indifferent to its Cumbrian responsibilities. Lord William's uncle, Sir Christopher Dacre of Gilsland, a committed royalist but more highly regarded than most of the King's adherents in the area, came to see the rebels on the Broadfield under safe conduct and persuaded them not only to end their blockade of Carlisle, but to disperse for the time being. In return, he assured them the gates of the town would remain open and that the garrison soldiers would not take action against them.

This was to be only a temporary lull and, though the rebels accepted a truce for the moment, all the old discontents quickly surfaced again and a number of Cumbrians, on their way home to other parts of the county, decided to take out their frustration on someone else. He was Peter Middleton of Castlerigg, a rack-renting landlord with an unpleasant history of tenant evictions ever since his acquisition of estates in the district five years earlier. His manor house was situated on Lord's Island, just off the thickly wooded eastern shore of Derwentwater, and some rebels made for it straight from Carlisle. Middleton subsequently said that 'most of the tenants and inhabitants dwelling on this manor' attacked him but that he and some friends managed 'to keep and defend' the house, thus implying that the impetus for this action came from very local dissidents. It seems rather more likely that he was blockaded in the lake from stepping ashore for provisions or any other reason than that his home was actually in danger of being destroyed. It would be menacing enough, however, to know and to be able to see that a large number of hostile men were permanently waiting only a few hundred yards away for you to make a false move. Whatever actually happened on or about Lord's Island in the autumn of 1536, it continued for almost four months: the besieged Middleton was not to enjoy a respite until the Duke of Norfolk and his troops arrived in Cumberland in the middle of February, to settle the royal account with the rebels up there.

But it was now the first week of November and Robert Aske was bound to a schedule that had kept him permanently on the move since the declaration of the original truce. The day that happened he rode from Doncaster to Pontefract, to tell the Pilgrim rearguard to go home. Within thirty-six hours, by Sunday, 29 October, he was in York, issuing instructions about the keeping of the truce, making sure that everything was otherwise as he had left it there. Next morning he rode to Wressle Castle to try to solve the continuing problem posed by the Earl of Northumberland's steadfast refusal to have anything to do with either the Pilgrimage or his two brothers. Henry Percy was in his now customary invalid condition and had suffered a further tribulation when some of the commons from nearby Snaith intercepted two chests full of clothes which were coming to him from London. He warmed to Aske when the chief captain prevented the commons from destroying these goods – though, apart from a gown and a doublet of crimson satin, they seem not to have been very valuable – had a careful inventory of them made and arranged for the chests to be returned. Percy was so impressed by this decency that he presented the chests and their contents to his benefactor. But on the larger matters he still refused to budge. So Aske went back to York to talk to Sir Thomas Percy, stayed that night with him and continued discussions next day. While they were dining at St Mary's Abbey, William Stapleton arrived in York, on his way to Wressle to pay his respects to Henry Percy, whose attorney he was, supervisor of transactions in the Earl's Yorkshire lands. Aske and Thomas Percy themselves repaired to Wressle the following morning, and Aske then tried once more to persuade Henry to make Thomas lieutenant of one of the Marches in his stead, nominating the youngest brother, Ingram, to the other one at the same time. When Stapleton arrived, it was to find the Earl 'weeping, ever wishing himself out of the world' and quite clearly in no state to make a decision on anything important.

On the first day of November, after staying overnight at Wressle, Aske made one more attempt to win Percy over and was at last successful in obtaining some sort of agreement that he would do nothing to injure the Pilgrimage, while remaining a dutiful liegeman of the King, but all efforts to effect a reconciliation with the brothers were adamantly rejected. It is perhaps as clear an indication of his mental instability as anything he did in this twilight of his life that Percy consented to move out of Wressle and leave it in Aske's hands. Before November was halfway through he had, in fact, formally and legally made over the castle to Aske for as long as the captain needed it; and thus it became a convenient base for the subsequent direction of the Pilgrimage. The King never forgave Percy for that and it may be only because the Earl was obviously dying by inches that he escaped a charge of treason.

By then, Aske had made other excursions. He rode up to Watton to settle the affairs of its priory, which had been made almost destitute by John Hallam's old enemy Robert Holgate, who had decamped in search of protection by his master, Cromwell, taking all the money he could get hold of and leaving behind 'three or four score brethren and sisters of the same house without forty shillings to succour them'. Aske did what he could for their survival and suggested that they would do well to elect the sub-prior as Holgate's successor.

Next day found him in Hull, which he placed under the authority of Sir Robert Constable, the two together taking steps to prepare its walls for serious defence and to instal a garrison of 200 men. They also secured as many boats as possible, just as Charles Brandon's people were doing on the other side of the Humber, where it was thought that the Pilgrims might be preparing seriously to break the truce. In fact, the collection of boats was all of a piece with Aske's instruction to keep a precautionary watch from the church towers along the river, lest the King's forces should suddenly come at them from the southern shore or from somewhere out at sea. And, surprisingly perhaps, Constable's deference to Aske seems to have been genuine, in spite of their working together as equals on this occasion and the very real difference in their social standing, where Constable, the soldierly knight, clearly outranked a lawyer without any property to speak of, whose eyesight was seriously defective.

A small instance of Constable's regard for the younger man occurred during this period. On Sunday 5 November, Aske probably left Hull to return to Wressle, because next day Charles Brandon sent to the mayor of the town for the surrender of four Lincolnshire men, two of whom had been among the first messengers from south of the Humber to Beverley at the beginning of October. They had been put into the prison at Hull because they were suspected of betraying a man named Woodmancy, a Yorkshire messenger to Lincolnshire who had been taken by Brandon and now stood in danger of his life. Constable, however, informed Brandon that the four held in Hull would not be released unless there was a specific order to that effect from the absent chief captain.

By this time Thomas Howard, young Talbot, Bowes and Ellerker were at court after a journey from the North made slower than usual because the elderly Duke was so weary that he could by now manage no more than thirty miles a day on horseback. While they were on the way, the Bishop of Worcester, Hugh Latimer, one of the prelates most vilified by the Pilgrims, preached a Sunday sermon in which he described the rebels as agents of the devil. They were men who decorated themselves with 'the Cross and Wounds before and behind' so that they might deceive 'the poor ignorant people, and bring them to fight against both the King, the Church and the Commonwealth'. His text was St Paul's injunction to 'Put on the whole armour of God' and this he urged his congregation to do in order to repulse Satan, whose work was being done for him by those masquerading as the King's loyal subjects, but who were no such thing.

Less controlled stuff would be heard from Henry himself by the time Howard and his companions reached Windsor, where they arrived at ten in the morning on Tuesday the 2nd. Howard had written ahead to the King, to enquire whether he should bring the two Pilgrim delegates into the royal presence straight away, or whether he should lodge them in London until he and young Talbot had had a chance to report to their sovereign in private. The reply was that all should proceed without delay, though Howard was granted an audience alone before the others joined him in the presence of the King after dinner that night. The moment he set eyes on Bowes and Ellerker, the monarch flew into one of his famous tempers, which continued for some time until Howard and other royal counsellors managed to calm him down. It is possible that they succeeded in this only because Henry still did not realise the seriousness of his predicament and believed that after getting explosive anger out of his system he could resume the role of cool and lofty monarch whose birthright was always to have the upper hand, enabling him to dispense justice, generosity or punishment as and where it pleased him without regard for anyone else's claims. Had he been aware how very insecure his throne really was that night in Windsor, he might seriously have considered making some concessions to the Pilgrims. But he assumed that his position was as strong as it ever had been when, in fact, he stood on ground that had been drastically undermined and might easily be swept away in the next flood.

As it was, Henry composed a very long letter to the Pilgrims, which displayed amazement, deeply injured innocence, self-justification, vanity, reproachfulness, truculence and contempt before a final spasm of anger against 'your shameful insurrection and unnatural rebellion' and a pompous gesture of regal paternity. He began by treating the rebel articles as something scarcely worth noticing because 'the terms be so general, that hard they be to be answered'. He marvelled 'not a little that ignorant people will go about or take upon them to instruct us (which something have been noted learned) what the right Faith should be' and he dismissed the entreaty to maintain the liberties of the Church on the grounds that 'this is so general a proposition that without distinctions no man can answer it neither by God's laws nor the laws of the realm'. He reminded them that, far from being high-handed in his attitude to the Church 'whereof we be the Supreme Head here in Earth, we have not done so much prejudice as many of our predecessors have done upon much less

grounds'. As for the matter of the religious houses and their suppression, 'I cannot but reckon a great unkindness and unnaturalness, in that ye had liever a churl or two should enjoy those
profits of their monasteries, in supportation of vicious and abominable life, than I your prince for supportation of my extreme
charges, done for your defence.'

He claimed, moreover, that 'there were never in any of our
predecessors' days so many wholesome, commodious and beneficial acts made for the common wealth' and asked 'what King
hath given you more general or freer pardons? What King hath
been loather to punish his subjects, or showed more mercy
among them?' He pointed out that, far from the nobility having
once enjoyed exclusive access to the monarch, at the start of his
reign he had inherited a Privy Council which included only two
genuine noblemen, the Duke of Norfolk's father and the present
Earl of Shrewsbury, its other members being 'but scant well born
gentlemen; and yet of no great lands till they were promoted
by us and so made knights and lords; the rest were lawyers
and priests, save two bishops, which were Canterbury and
Winchester'. He repudiated any suggestion that Cromwell and
others were 'subverters both of God's law and the laws of this
realm; we do take and repute them as just and true executors
both of God's laws and ours as far as their commissions under us
do extend'. He dismissed the North of England and its ignorance
in these matters, saying that the Pilgrim slander against his counsellors and bishops was untrue 'because it proceedeth from the
place which is both so far distant from where they inhabit, and
also from those people which have never heard them preach nor
yet knoweth any part of their conversation'.

The ending of Henry's anathema should be heard in full. It was
particularly addressed to 'ye our subjects of Yorkshire' whose
rebellion, he declared, professing amazement at the very idea, he
could not believe to have been declared out of malice or rancour,
'but rather by a lightness given in a manner by a naughty nature to
a commonalty and a wondrous sudden surreption of gentlemen'.
He then concluded:

> We must needs have executed another manner of punishment
> than (ye humbly knowledging your fault and submitting

yourselves to our mercy) we intend to do. And to the intent that ye shall know that our princely heart rather embraceth (of his own disposition) pity and compassion of his offending subjects than will to be revenged of their naughty deeds; we are contented, if we may see and perceive in you all a sorrowfulness for your offences and will henceforth to do no more so, nor to believe so lewd and naughty tales or reports of your most kind and loving prince and his Council, to grant unto you all our letters patent of pardon for this rebellion; so that ye will deliver unto us ten such of the ringleaders and provokers of you in this rebellion, as we shall assign to you and appoint. Now note the benignity of your prince. Now note how easily ye may have pardon, both gentlemen and other if ye list. Now note how effusion of blood may be eschewed. Now note, what this little while of your rebellion hath hindered yourselves and country. Now learn by a little lack to eschew a worse. Now learn, by this small warning, to keep you true men. Thus I, as your head, pray for you my members, that God may light you with his Grace to knowledge and declare yourselves our true subjects henceforth, and to give more credence to these our benign persuasions than to the perverse instigations of maliciously disposed persons.

This could be regarded as a declaration of war on the rebels, even though it did not speak bluntly of revenge, as Henry had when responding to the rising in Lincolnshire; nor did he now demand as many rebels for punishment as he had on the earlier occasion. But in its failure to concede a single point, its haughty insistence on Henry's own excellence, its dismissal of Pilgrim claims as being without foundation, it offered nothing at all that the Pilgrim leadership could pass on to the belligerent commons with a recommendation that these terms met at least some of their grievances and should therefore be accepted, if only as a possible starting point for further dialogue with their king. And although Howard certainly, other members of the Council probably, would have been dismayed by the tone of the document, recognising that it was unlikely to pacify a North of England that was only with difficulty being restrained from further action, they were unwilling to say so to Henry in his present mood, lest his smouldering rage should be turned upon them: when he lashed out, as they well knew, it was often indiscriminately.

So the letter, composed immediately after the delegation had apprised him of the rebel position, was handed over to Bowes and Ellerker, and other letters were written, thanking all those gentry who had remained loyal to their sovereign. Inducements were to be offered to those who had rebelled, as an incentive to changing their allegiance: they were to understand that they would be rewarded with property seized from those who remained obdurate. All these tidings were to be taken north by heralds, whose further assignment was to make public the King's reply everywhere, and to report on their return the way Yorkshiremen and others had responded to it.

Bowes and Ellerker set off home from Windsor on Sunday the 5th. They were only a morning's ride along the road when some of Cromwell's men caught up with them with orders that the two Pilgrims must be allowed to go no further, and so they were escorted back to the royal headquarters, though they were allowed to send servants on to Yorkshire, to convey news of how events in the South were shaping up. For Henry had suddenly had second thoughts, as a result of a communication that had meanwhile reached him from the North, which has not, unfortunately, survived. It may have told the King that Robert Aske had started stirring up trouble in the far North-west – where the stand-off outside Carlisle was still unresolved at the time of writing – in which case it was a piece of misinformation or something more malicious: Aske had indeed sent a message to the leaders of the Pilgrimage in Lancashire, Cumberland and Westmorland, but it was simply to inform them of the doings in Doncaster and the validity of the truce. Whatever the contents of the disturbing message from the North may have been, they were enough to make Henry consult his Council again and, as a result, he decided it was necessary to buy some time. If Bowes and Ellerker could be delayed long enough, provided the northern rebels did not become more hostile than ever by assuming that their safe conducts had been violated, it might be time well spent in allowing tensions to ease up there, time in which enough of the insurgents might begin to question a number of things about this Pilgrimage of Grace and the way it had been led. Henry therefore retrieved from the two emissaries his reply to the Pilgrims and bided his time, a decision which smelled strongly of Thomas Howard's advice. But the letter that made Henry change his plans may have signified the moment when it first began to dawn on him that he was in very great trouble.

The truce, in fact, was not being strictly observed by either side, though not all reports of this were accurate. Charles Brandon was certainly moving his men around Lincolnshire, and the defences of Nottingham and Newark were being repaired. Both the royalists and the rebels were making their dispositions along the Humber, as we have seen, and reports began to come in of other Pilgrim activity. One of them reckoned that a man named Leonard Beckwith had been roughed up so badly that his mother had taken to her bed in a state of shock. Beckwith was the Yorkshire receiver of the Court of Augmentations and, as such, had an official role in the disposal of monastic property. The story was that he had accumulated in his home at South Cave, not far from Hull, valuables confiscated from two religious houses and that these had been plundered by a gang of sixty insurgents, possibly the same ones who stole Henry Percy's clothes. And it was perfectly true; but it had happened some time before the truce was declared. Three days after the truce, Sir Marmaduke Constable of Everingham, a cousin of Sir Robert, fled to the sanctuary of Lincolnshire when a number of commons turned up and threatened to spoil his house if he would not take the oath. Aske had written to him, too, offering him the protection of Wressle Castle, but Constable evidently decided that Charles Brandon was a safer bet.

There was also substance in a report that a muster had taken place at Furness Abbey at the very start of November, with the blatant encouragement of the monks, apart from their recently departed superior – and Furness could muster 850 armed men, many with horses, if need be, from their tenants. But that remote cul-de-sac on the west coast was no more likely to be abreast of developments further south than were the commons then still threatening Carlisle. It was said that there was a great deal of coming and going by the northern gentry in general and so there was: there was much to discuss about events so far and many contingency plans to be made just in case they became necessary.

Apart from such infractions, real or supposed, there was a widespread state of alertness on either side of the dividing line. Aske was not the only one to tell his people to remain prepared for action again at short notice. The Earls of Derby and Shrewsbury maintained themselves and their retainers in similar states of readiness. George Talbot had also been told by the King to keep a particularly sharp eye on the bridges at Derby and Burton-on-Trent.

Meanwhile, the rebel leaders took the opportunity in this lull to replenish their treasury. Sir Robert Constable paid most of the money needed to garrison Hull out of his own pocket, but he seized some more from the local collector of customs and acquired the rest as a loan from one of the gentry. But some parishes had levies imposed upon them, in order to maintain Pontefract Castle in a full state of alert. The suppressed priory at Marton, a mixed house of Augustinian canons and nuns north of York, had already been stripped of the lead from its roof by the King's men: this was now looted by the neighbouring commons and sold for £9 13s 4d, which was forthwith put into the Pilgrim exchequer. Aske used his new-found amity with Henry Percy to obtain permission from the Earl to raise money from the sale of some plate which was kept at Watton Priory, whose acting superior, James Lawrence, Prior of Ellerton, had been pressed upon the Watton religious by John Hallam to replace Robert Holgate. After some hesitation, and some heavy hints from Aske that this would be but a small return for all the efforts he had been making on their behalf over the past few weeks, Lawrence delivered the plate to the rebel leader in person. Other monasteries more willingly gave what they could to the Pilgrimage.

Robert Aske's next move was to call for a general council of Pilgrim captains, together with representatives of both commons and gentry, which was to meet at York in the third week of November; this would give ample time for a proper consideration beforehand of the King's response to their overtures, whenever that might be made available to them. But by now Aske was a marked man, above all others, and the King was seriously thinking of ways to be rid of him. Although the names of the ten exceptions to Henry's pardon were still unknown outside court, Aske's was at the head of the list, which also included that of

Thomas Maunsell, the priest who had accompanied Aske to Pontefract, Thomas Hutton, who had led one of the earliest risings, round Snaith, Roger Kitchen, one of the ringleaders in Beverley, William Ombler, one of the three captains in Holderness, Henry Coke, a Durham shoemaker who was implicated in the rebellion up there, and four others whose names were not specified.

The King was also by now determined to make an example of Sir Robert Constable, as well as Aske, though Charles Brandon doubted whether this could be done because those two, with Darcy, 'have most credit among the rebels'. But the threat of assassination certainly hung in the air. Two of the Lincolnshire men held by Constable in Hull had managed to escape across the Humber and were then conveyed to Lincoln, where they were accused by Brandon of being 'principal beginners of this rebellion in this shire'. At this, one of the two, Anthony Curtis, a lawyer who was reported by Brandon to be 'a kinsman of Aske's', evidently tried to save his life with a dramatic undertaking – 'and for malice that Aske has accused him, offers to go and kill Aske'. Brandon declined to accept, being deeply suspicious of the man's integrity and sensing that this might be a ruse by Curtis in order to escape from his startlingly new captivity.

The King, meanwhile, was making calculations of his own. Lord John Hussey had been sent down to him after putting himself at the mercy of George Talbot in Nottingham, and one of his servants, Percival Cresswell, was now summoned by the Duke of Norfolk to write under dictation a letter purporting to come from Hussey, which Hussey was then obliged to sign, to give it authenticity. Cresswell was instructed to take this, under the seal of the Privy Council, to Lord Darcy in Yorkshire. He was to catch up with the servants of Bowes and Ellerker, and ride with them the rest of the way in order to reach Pontefract without molestation from the commons, and if he didn't manage to overtake them and reached Yorkshire alone, then he must certainly obtain a safe conduct before proceeding any further. What must on no account be allowed to happen was anyone but Darcy finding out what was in the letter.

In fact, Cresswell made such good progress that he got to Doncaster on Friday the 10th, before the servants, made contact with Darcy and from him received an assurance that he would be brought on to Templehirst without any interference. The two met in the garden there and, because others were present, Cresswell dutifully passed the forged letter, and another in the hand of Thomas Howard, to Darcy when no one else was looking. Darcy went inside to read them alone, leaving Cresswell on the lawn with a number of commoners, who made it plain that they regarded him with something more than disdain. They interrogated him about the dispositions at court, being especially scathing about Cromwell, and when Cresswell informed them that the Lord Privy Seal had not been seen at Windsor for several days, but that a number of the nobility were certainly in attendance on their sovereign, the Yorkshiremen shouted 'God save the King and them all! For as long as such noblemen of the true noble blood may reign and rule about the King, all shall be well.' They assured Cresswell that the 'thing that moves us to this [action] is the faith we bear unto God, to the King's person, and all his true noble blood and the commonwealth'.

Darcy's immediate instinct, on reading the letters, was to send someone to fetch Robert Aske, who happened to be only a couple of miles away in Selby. For the communication from Howard had complained about rebel breaches of the truce, had said that the King's replies were by now composed and answered the situation perfectly, and that some nasty things were being said down south about Darcy's loyalty, though Howard always told such malicious gossips that Darcy had acted as he did under duress. He then dropped his bombshell. The best way for Darcy to refute these unworthy suggestions would be to secure Aske and despatch him to Windsor 'dead or alive, but alive if possible, which will extinct the ill bruit and raise you in the favour of his Highness'. Howard, moreover, assured Darcy that he would stand by him, whatever the consequences, if he did this. The letter which was supposed to have come from Hussey was not as long-winded as the other one but it conveyed the same message. The unhappy Lord said that he had been landed in such great trouble because he was thought to be an associate of Darcy's and that he would take it kindly if Darcy would deliver Aske 'quick or dead'.

Having digested all this, Darcy returned to Cresswell, who added his own three ha'p'orth by telling Darcy that it would be prudent to do as he was asked. To which Darcy replied: 'I cannot do it in no wise, for I have made a promise to the contrary, and my coat was never hitherto stained with any such blot. And my lord's Grace your master knoweth well enough what a nobleman's promise is, and therefore I think that this thing cometh not of his Grace's device, nor of none other nobleman, and if I might have two dukedoms for my labour I would not consent to have such a spot on my coat.' It doubtless occurred to him that he himself was probably another target for assassination.

Robert Aske duly arrived from Selby and after dinner all the Pilgrim leaders who were available at Templehirst sat down in council. Next day, Cresswell set off on his return journey south with letters for Howard from both Darcy and Aske. That from the chief captain explained the supposed rebel breaches of the truce, saying that letters he had written were no more than restraints on the commons in different areas, or offers of protection to individuals like Sir Marmaduke Constable and Sir Thomas Wharton, who had received threats from the insurgents in Cumberland. Any goods or money that had been taken in this period with or without his knowledge would be restored as far as possible. Darcy wrote to Bowes and Ellerker, making the point that their continued detention was itself a gross violation of the truce, that their return with their own news from the King would do much more good than any correspondence from other hands. His letter to Howard began by refuting the charges that had been made against him and reminding the Duke that repeated requests to the King for help in fortifying Pontefract against the approaching rebels had been ignored. He then produced his most considered response to Howard's invitation. He was, he said, perfectly ready to serve his King in the lowliest position imaginable without recompense, but 'alas my good lord that ever ye being a man of so much honour and great experience should advise or choose me a man to be of any such sort or fashion to betray or disserve any living man, Frenchman, Scot, yea, or Turk; of my faith, to get and win me and mine heirs four of the best duke's lands in France, or to be king there, I would not do it to no living person'.

Four centuries later, we may well think that no words more truly noble have ever been uttered by an Englishman. For even as he penned them, Old Tom Darcy must have known that they would be read by his King as an insult so insufferable that he could expect no mercy whatsoever if Henry retained his grip on the throne.

THE KING'S GREAT BLUFF

November was a month in which the weather improved, in which foreign intervention in the affairs of England became a distinct possibility and in which Henry was made to realise that he was very close to utter humiliation. It was a nervous time for both sides, full of uncertainties, in circumstances that promised a desperate outcome for either if things went the wrong way for them. The rebel leadership was for the most part anxious to maintain the truce, in spite of hostility from the majority of the commons, because it believed that negotiation with the Crown was the best way of achieving the aims of the Pilgrimage, and in negotiation also lay the greatest hope of ultimate safety for themselves. At this tense time, it would not be a coincidence that Robert Aske, normally impervious to fatigue and strain, was flattened by colic in the days after the York conference. As for Henry, he wriggled and squirmed and looked to every device that might preserve his honour; which, in his terms, was something different from the code that regulated Thomas Darcy's life. It simply meant not having to climb down before his subjects, and the infliction of punishment on those he held responsible for the present indignity. As the days passed, anxiety became the norm, for the monarch and his opponents alike. But at least, by the middle of the month, the torrential rain, which had kept the land and everything struggling across it sodden for several weeks, had eased off – though this proved to be no more than a brief interlude before the onset of an exceptionally bitter winter.

The King's proclamation that, provided the Pilgrims submitted unconditionally, all but ten rebels would be pardoned, was made public on 11 November, more than a week after it was composed. It was announced in every town in Yorkshire and, in Skipton market place, 'after three long *Oyez*', the man who carried out this task at the Earl of Cumberland's behest with armed men by his side was Christopher Aske, who was immediately faced with an angry crowd of more than 3000 people, who had come in from the surrounding countryside for the annual Skipton Fair – even Aske later admitted that his announcement was 'much to the commons' indignation'. Lancaster Herald was supposed to go north on the same errand, with further instructions to convey the monarch's paternal disappointment at the behaviour of his northern subjects and his great forbearance in not ordering 50,000 men into battle, when the royal army was all ready and waiting to attack the rebels mercilessly at one word from the King. This was taking bluff to ridiculous heights, as would have been transparently obvious to everyone in the North, the rebel hosts having by now dispersed to their own homes, where they were informing all the neighbourhood how things had really been at Doncaster. The truth was that Henry had certainly been trying to raise a force capable of serious engagement with the rebels, which, for the second time in this conflict, he proposed to lead himself; but after the Ampthill fiasco this was an optimistic hope, which was effectively getting nowhere by the last week in October, and the plan had been cancelled immediately he heard that the Pilgrims were homeward bound after the truce. Thomas Miller, however, did not embark on another northern excursion, because Henry countermanded the order that would have despatched him, in the same cautionary mood that caused him to delay the return of Bowes and Ellerker. Instead of proclamation by Lancaster Herald, therefore, the job was entrusted to Henry Clifford and to the rest of the loyal nobility in the North.

Meanwhile, George Talbot, Earl of Shrewsbury, was faltering. His health was poor, he had lost his appetite for warfare and he said as much to Cromwell after receiving the instruction to prepare the defences at Derby and Burton-on-Trent. He produced a number of reasons why this was asking too much, tactically because there were too many fords and bridges across the

The parish church of St James, Louth, whose Perpendicular spire is admired as one of the most elegant in England. From its pulpit on 1 October 1536, its Vicar, Thomas Kendall, preached the sermon that initiated the Lincolnshire Rising, which was the preliminary to the Pilgrimage of Grace.

Anticlockwise from the top: **Henry VIII** in a portrait (after Holbein) which was painted in the year of the great rebellion against his throne. Once, he had been admired as the most handsome monarch in Christendom: later, his features would coarsen even more; **Thomas Cromwell**, Henry's Lord Privy Seal and the greatest power behind the throne. He became the most detested man in the kingdom for his supervision of Henry's policies, especially for the Dissolution of the Monasteries (portrait after Holbein); **Thomas Howard**, Third Duke of Norfolk, who was Henry VIII's principal commander in 1536–7. He originated the cunning plan that persuaded the rebels to accept a truce at Doncaster, instead of fighting a battle they would almost certainly have won and which might well have led to Henry's downfall (painting by Holbein); **Charles Brandon**, Duke of Suffolk, childhood friend of the King and subsequently husband of Henry's younger sister Mary. He was in charge of operations against the Lincolnshire rebels, and of the executions following the failure of the rising there (artist unknown).

Jervaulx Abbey, Wensleydale, which was seized by the Crown in 1537 after it had become implicated in the rebellion. It was the monks of this and other Cistercian monasteries who introduced commercial sheep-farming to England.

The Badge of the Five Wounds of Christ was the most potent symbol of the Pilgrimage of Grace. It was embroidered on a banner (above) which was carried at the head of the rebel hosts as they prepared to do battle at Doncaster.

Adam Sedbar was the sixteenth Abbot of Jervaulx and had been installed three years before the Pilgrimage of Grace began. For his part in the revolt, he was sent to the Tower of London – where his name and title were carved on the wall of his cell (above) – before he was executed at Tyburn.

Top: Pontefract Castle c. 1625–30, which Lord Darcy surrendered to Robert Aske before he himself joined the Pilgrimage. It was regarded as a key to political and military supremacy in the North of England (painting attributed to Alexander Keirinx, 1600–52). *Bottom:* Lancaster Castle, which surrendered to the rebels and was subsequently one of the places where some of them were executed. It has remained a prison to this day.

Left: The ruins of the Cistercian Sawley Abbey, which stood beside the River Ribble on the border of Lancashire and Yorkshire. Its monks were responsible for much of the incitement to rebellion in 1536–7. From the ridge behind, rebel forces prepared to attack the Earl of Derby and his troops. *Right:* Skipton Castle, Airedale, home of Henry Clifford, First Earl of Cumberland and loyal servant of the Crown. Pilgrims besieged it without success, one of those organising its defence being Robert Aske's brother Christopher, who held an appointment in Clifford's household.

Bolton Castle, Wensleydale, home of Lord Scrope, who fled at the approach of the Pilgrims, was later persuaded to join them, but became stoutly royalist again after the Doncaster truce. Many years later, Mary Queen of Scots was imprisoned here.

Top: Scythe blades mounted in the South aisle of St Mary's parish church, Horncastle. They were almost certainly carried as weapons during the Lincolnshire Rising. *Bottom:* Christopher Aske caused this carving to be worked into the rebuilding of the church tower at Aughton sometime after his brother was executed for leading the Pilgrimage of Grace. It refers to the events of 1536 so ambivalently that no one is quite sure what it means.

THIS... ETH THOMAS LORDE DACY OF THE NORTHE AND SVMTYME OF THE ORDER OF THE
GARTER SIR NICHOLAS CARREW KNIGHT SVMTYME OF THE GARTER AND LADY ELIZABETH CARREW
DAVGHTER TO SIR THOMAS BRIAN KNIGHT AND SIR ARTHVR DARCY KNIGHT YONGER SONNE TO
THE ABOVE NAMED LORDE DARCY AND LADY MARY DARCY HIS DERE... THE DAVGHTER TO SIR
NICHOLAS CARREW ... WHO HAD TENNE SONNES AND FIVE DAVGHTERS HERE LIETH
CHARLES WILLM AND PHILLIP ...MARY AND VRSVLY SONNES AND DAVGHTERS TO THE
SAIDE SIR ARTHVR AND MARY HIS WIF WHOSE SOWLES GOD TAKE TO HIS INFINIT MERCY AMEN

Alabaster monument to the executed Lord Darcy in the porch of St Botolph-
Without-Aldgate, in the City of London. It is almost the only memorial to
anyone who took part in the Pilgrimage of Grace.

Top: John Paslew, Cistercian Abbot of Whalley, going to his execution in 1537. The background is his abbey, but he was more probably put to death in Lancaster (etching by Charles Cattermole dated 1886). *Bottom:* The hamlet of Hanging Lund in Mallerstang, south of Kirkby Stephen. Along this valley, ten men were selected for execution after the failed attempt to capture Carlisle. A total of 76 rebels from Cumberland and Westmorland were put to death without trial in reprisal for this action.

Trent to make it defendable except by at least 10,000 men, which he knew he could never raise himself and which the King was unlikely to provide. He also asked the Lord Privy Seal to appoint someone else as joint commander of the royal forces with Thomas Howard, and he cited his age and his ill health in support of this plea; but he was turned down. The only concession made to him was that Thomas Manners, Earl of Rutland, was given the job of defending Nottingham, which he soon decided was as near impossible as anything Talbot was being asked to do. Manners, too, pointed out the difficulties on the ground and also pleaded military inexperience – which was true enough, his acquaintance with the martial arts being limited to his part in the short French expedition of 1513, which produced victory at the Battle of the Spurs – and begged that someone more qualified should be sent to advise him. Advice presently came in the shape of the local gentry, who sat down with him once a week to discuss tactics for the Nottingham garrison, which consisted of 400 men or so, who were gradually becoming more and more disgruntled as Rutland's money began to run out.

Thomas Darcy now decided to let bygones be bygones as far as possible between himself and the Earl of Shrewsbury, and it is very probable that George Talbot was in much the same frame of mind, given the withdrawal symptoms he was experiencing that week. Darcy wrote, as one old friend to another in spite of their recent differences, to make plain the overall situation as he saw it. He pointed out that the royal forces, just as much as the rebels, were failing to observe a strict interpretation of the truce and he enumerated the offences one by one, including Sir Brian Hastings's efforts to prise a number of gentlemen away from their allegiance to the Pilgrimage, and most certainly not forgetting the King's failure to release Bowes and Ellerker which, he said, constituted the biggest single impediment to a settlement of the conflict. He asked Talbot to use his good offices to speed their journey home, so that the Pilgrim leadership could hear at first hand, unfiltered through messengers, what the situation was at court, and how Henry's temper and intentions seemed to them. Their detention was only increasing the strain on the northern leaders, especially those in Cumberland and the North Riding, who were having the greatest difficulty in holding the commons there back. In the far North-west the situation was especially tense, because the Cumbrians had never been party to the Doncaster appointment and therefore saw little justification for observing a truce arranged by others without their consent. After making these points, Darcy asked his old comrade to tell him candidly what he needed to know about the government's intentions. Would Charles Brandon remain in Lincolnshire or not? Was there likely to be a sudden strike by agents of the Crown, a surprise attack, or an attempt on the life of men singled out for eradication? These were the matters that, unrealistically perhaps, he hoped to be told.

Talbot's reply was largely a defence of the violations of the truce by loyalists and an insistence that the royal troops were observing it to the letter. He promised that Bowes and Ellerker would shortly be back in the North, and he softened enough to thank Darcy for what he had done to hold the more aggressive commons in check. Next morning, Talbot sent his account of this correspondence to the King, together with a despatch from Hastings, which had just come in. He added, as a footnote to Darcy's request to know what the royalists proposed in the immediate future, a very delicately worded expression of distaste for the very idea of the truce being broken by anything as dishonourable as an attack without warning, on either the Pilgrim dispositions or any individual. He had not, he said, hitherto 'been accustomed to make answer to any such causes' as Darcy had raised.

That same day, Bowes and Ellerker were given leave to return home. They reached Templehirst in the evening of Friday the 17th, a day short of three weeks since they had set off for the South. Aske was at Wressle when they arrived, but rumour had already reached him that the two envoys had returned with instructions to take him prisoner. This was false, as Darcy told him in response to Aske's cautious enquiry, adding that the chief captain was badly needed at Templehirst in order to discuss what to do next. So Aske rode over, accompanied by William Babthorpe, one of the East Riding gentry who had fled to Pontefract, had been converted to the Pilgrimage there and had since become a member of the inner council. Next morning

Aske, Babthorpe, Darcy, Constable and a small handful of other captains gathered to hear the latest news. Which was that Bowes and Ellerker had not brought anything in writing from the King, but a verbal message to the effect that Henry would send Thomas Howard to Doncaster, where the Duke would deliver the sovereign's considered response. The Pilgrims were to send 300 representatives to Doncaster to hear him and they would be given safe conduct if they wished. Beyond that, the envoys could only add that they were convinced the King was acting in good faith, that he would be merciful, and that it was safe for the rebel hosts to forget about more strife and put their weapons away for good. Darcy was prepared to believe them and suggested that they write at once to Henry, accepting his terms. But the others were more sceptical, in spite of the assurances Bowes and Ellerker had given, and it was decided that nothing should be done until after the general council at York, which would be given all the information available before making up its collective mind what the future should be.

It is perhaps as good an indication as any, of the uncertainties that now beset the rebellion, that Darcy's mood had swung from belligerence to reconciliation within the space of a few days. He had generally, as we know, been among the strongest advocates of peace, so long as it was a decent peace and not an abject surrender of principles; there had never been any doubt that the old warrior would fight to the death if he deemed it necessary. The previous Saturday a report had come to him that royal troops had been spotted assembling in some woodland near Snaith, where Darcy had another home. This was accompanied by a warning that Sir Brian Hastings and Sir William Fitzwilliam, the King's Lord Admiral and one of the royal generals who had lately been with Charles Brandon in Lincoln, were on their way to take Darcy, with 5000 men at their command.[1] This was plausible and Darcy reacted characteristically. He sent a counter-threat to Hastings to the effect that if the Sheriff of Yorkshire so much as put a spark to tinder at Snaith, Old Tom would 'light him with a candle to all the houses he had'. He sent off simultaneous messages to warn Pontefract of impending trouble and ordered that

1 The Lord Admiral merely supervised Henry's navy; it was not a seagoing appointment.

beacons should be lit. Darcy then summoned his servant William Talbot to bring him harness and sword, swearing that the King of Heaven meant much more to him than twenty sovereigns on earth. He was so exuberant at the prospect of imminent battle, increasingly infirm though he was, that he grabbed Talbot in horseplay and began to wrestle him around the room. But now he was looking for peace again, because what he wanted to believe of his king seemed to be on offer at last. And Hastings had replied that the reported troop movements were in reality a gathering of his neighbours to help him protect his cattle, some of which had recently been lost to local rustlers, who were said to be coming back for more.

But there had been further violations of the truce elsewhere, with the promise of yet more to come. In Beverley some hot-heads had been trying to stir up another rising, and in both Cumberland and Westmorland anger was beginning to mount out of control. Down in Lancashire, a couple of men wearing harness went round Chorley with blackened faces one night, swearing people to the Pilgrimage. Some of the King's deer had been taken in the East Riding and around Goole, possibly by the same cattle thieves who had made inroads into Hastings's herd. Darcy's steward in Wakefield, Thomas Grice, who had led the uprising there after his master changed sides, was now reported to be harassing the tenants of Sir Henry Saville, who was a deeply committed royalist in the district. The demonstration by the commons of Skipton against the announcement made by Christopher Aske had involved between 3000 and 4000 people, and for a while looked as if it might develop into a second attempt to take the castle; as it was, it at least constituted the same sort of threat to Henry Clifford that Peter Middleton was facing up in Derwentwater.

Something more serious actually was happening in Scarborough. The keeper of the royal castle there was Sir Ralph Evers the younger, scion of a family almost as influential along the east coast as the Constables, who would one day be described by a Scottish general as 'a fell cruel man and over cruel'. He certainly seems to have been an overweening man who, it was said, had stripped lead from the roof of some of the castle towers, which he then exchanged for French wines. Otherwise, he took great care to maintain the castle as best he could for his sovereign, and repulsed all attempts to take the fortification in the middle of October in spite of the hardship of having 'no sustenance but bread and water for the space of twenty days'.

It was in an attempt to remedy this enforced fasting that, after the truce, he wrote to Charles Brandon asking for urgently needed supplies. In mid-November, therefore, a man named Edward Waters embarked at Grimsby in a crayer, a small vessel built for the coastal trade, with victuals, some ordnance and £100, together with a letter of encouragement from Cromwell, which was to play an important part in deciding Pilgrim attitudes at the York conference. For it was seized, together with the boat and its other contents, before the crayer had even docked in Scarborough, by John Hallam, who had with him some of the Beverley men and others who came from the Wolds. Hallam, aggressive as ever, threatened to decapitate Waters if he didn't talk, which extracted the confession that Cromwell was behind this mission to Yorkshire. Hallam's men kept the supplies and the guns for their own immediate use, and resumed the siege of Scarborough Castle. The money found on board they sent to Robert Aske, together with Waters and Cromwell's letter; apart from some loose change which, when divided among themselves, amounted to three shillings apiece for their trouble.

A number of the Pilgrim delegates had already reached York, having started to arrive the day Waters was boarding his ship in Grimsby, which was almost a week before the conference was due to begin. Eventually 800 men assembled in the city, and they included nearly all the rebel leaders with the exception of Darcy, who had been given permission to stay home because he was not well enough to travel even the relatively short distance from Templehirst. It was otherwise a representative gathering, with someone there to advance the views of every wapentake and hundred across the affected parts of the North. The Abbot of Sawley's chaplain, Richard Estgate, also attended so as to be sure that his community's interests were not ignored. Straight away, a rather cumbersome committee of 200 was selected to lead the discussions and this, too, was chosen on a regional basis, with, for example, William Stapleton and eleven others nominated to speak for one district of the East Riding. Robert Bowes told the assembly what had gone on at court while he and Ellerker were there, what had passed between them and the King, and their conviction, already expressed to the leadership at Templehirst, that Henry was genuinely sympathetic to the rebel demands and that 'the goodness of my Lord Privy Seal to the commons promised by his word' could be trusted as well.

The two envoys were immediately asked to leave the room by Sir Robert Constable, who then produced the letter from Cromwell which had been seized by John Hallam in Scarborough. It had been composed on 10 November and at its heart was the assurance – intended only for the eyes of Sir Ralph Evers – that if the northern rebellion continued it would be crushed so completely that 'their example shall be fearful to all subjects whiles the world doth endure'. In the crescendo of indignation which followed this disclosure, Constable added his own angry response that the fight must continue before there could be any more parleying with the King at Doncaster: 'as he had broken one point in the tables with the King he would break another, and have no meeting, but have all the country made sure from Trent northwards, and then had no doubt all Lancashire, Cheshire, Derbyshire and the parts thereabout would join them. Then, he said, he would condescend to a meeting.' Aske, Babthorpe and others still spoke in favour of a continued peace, and they were able to advance Darcy's proxy vote as well. They argued that nothing would be lost by talking to the Duke of Norfolk again and that he was an honourable man, as Thomas Cromwell most certainly was not. But they hoped that the balance of power at court was shifting in favour of Howard, which meant that the King would soon receive better advice with the removal of the upstart's pernicious influence.

There were other matters to discuss, the first of which was the King's dismissal of the Pilgrim case on the grounds that its details were vague and obscure. To obviate this complaint, it was decided that every district in the North should send someone to another conference, this time at Pontefract, a couple of days before the second rendezvous at Doncaster, each bringing with him a list of detailed grievances, which could then be assembled into a coherent whole and offered to Howard as a supplementary statement to the original rebel articles. The Archbishop of York, who was still lurking apprehensively in the background of the Pilgrimage, was to be asked to fortify this new statement with theological arguments in support of the religious complaints. There and then, a letter was composed, suggesting arrangements for Doncaster to Howard. The Pilgrims wanted the meeting on neutral ground, on the Eve of St Nicholas, which was 5 December, and they asked that there should be a truce for two weeks after that date. There should be safe conducts for all the Pilgrims taking part, but to ensure Robert Aske's own protection, he being the rebel whose life seemed to be most at risk, hostages should be exchanged. Beyond this, the document made a special point of complaining about the truce being breached by the escapade involving Edward Waters. Other details to do with Doncaster, and the preliminary meeting in Pontefract, were reviewed, including the method by which the 300 Pilgrim representatives at the new appointment with Thomas Howard should be chosen.

Any other business conducted by the delegates across the four full days in York included discussions about other infractions and they resulted in another letter being written, this one to the Earl of Cumberland, asking him to yield Skipton Castle. News had come in that the Earl of Derby had been ordered to melt down the bells and the lead of the suppressed Burscough Priory, an Augustinian house on the coastal plain of Lancashire, by the end of the month, but that he was reluctant to do so in case it caused new trouble in the area. To this Sir Robert Constable, now in full sabre-rattling mood, urged support for anyone in those parts who was inclined to defend the canons and their property. The outcome of the debate was Darcy being charged with communicating the feelings of the conference to George Talbot, with a request that the Earl of Shrewsbury should restrain Edward Stanley; Darcy had already been asked to speak to his old colleague about all the breaches of the truce. The petitions of other religious were heard, including one from Sawley, asking for guidance in their troubles – they were told to make their case a week hence in Pontefract.

The delegates then moved on to two matters which had from the start of the uprising been among their deepest concerns. One was the revised Act of Succession, the legislation which had first been drafted to enable any child issuing from Henry and Anne Boleyn to become sovereign, but which now empowered Henry to nominate whomsoever he chose to succeed him. Insurgent England naturally saw this as a device by Cromwell to secure the succession for himself, and there was even a story going the rounds that he was planning to marry the Princess Mary, though this had subsequently been modified to a rumour that he had his eye on the King's niece, Lady Margaret Douglas, instead. The conference now wanted this act repealed forthwith, with a firm undertaking that Mary would one day be queen.

The other matter exercising the Pilgrims gathered in November was to do with pardon. They insisted that their pardon must come by Act of Parliament, which would give it the full force of English law, and not be left at the whim of the King. What's more, there must be a Parliament legislating for the North and situated somewhere more accessible than Westminster to all northcountrymen; in other words, in York. So much did this matter to them that a voice from the conference floor, addressed to Robert Aske on this particular point, shouted, 'Look you well upon this matter, for it is your charge, for if you do not you shall repent it.' John Hallam, who did not attend the conference, being otherwise engaged in Scarborough, but who made his views known in a letter to the delegates, put it another way. The commons wanted a general pardon by Act of Parliament, 'or else we are fully determined to spend our lives and goods in battle, as knoweth our God and St George'.

Those four days had their moments of rational discussion but, such were the conflicting emotions assembled there, tempers sometimes ran high and hard words were exchanged. In the end, the peace party prevailed once again, in spite of Sir Robert Constable's relentless opposition to accepting any terms that Henry might offer. Many imponderables were still hanging in the air, though, and one of the greatest concerns Christopher Aske.

He had visited his brother at Wressle a few days before the conference began, ostensibly to make a complaint on behalf of Henry Clifford about the behaviour of the Richmondshire rebels at Skipton Castle. It was an argumentative meeting and it is difficult to believe that it did not involve a certain amount of acrimony about the different loyalties of the two Askes, though they are only recorded as having exchanged words about the castle and whether it could or could not have been taken if the Pilgrims had been commanded by Robert himself, backed up with a battery of guns and enough ammunition to conduct a proper siege. Christopher then told his brother that he would do well to seek the best terms he could extract from Henry, otherwise he was likely to finish up, as a number of rebel leaders had done before him, being killed or handed over to the authorities by their own followers; who, in this case, were at that moment cantankerously objecting to having their dinner interrupted by the arrival of the message from Darcy, summoning Robert to the preliminary meeting at Templehirst. Christopher was left behind at Wressle after Robert and his bodyguard of sixty bellyaching commons had ridden off, and took the opportunity to go through Robert's papers which, among other things, contained a number of contingency plans that had been drawn up against the possibility of war. The elder Aske had come to Wressle under safe conduct and for some reason this appears to have been extended. At any rate, he was allowed to be in York during the conference as, effectively, a royal spy; a decision which is quite unfathomable. Did the Pilgrim leaders think that he might be won over to their cause after reconsidering his position, as many a hostile gentleman had been before him? Did they optimistically believe that a report of their deliberations might in some way influence the King in their favour? Or was this simply a matter of honour again, carried to a degree which is quite unimaginable in our own day, an acceptance of the fact that a safe conduct was what it purported to be and which, whether or not it was abused by the recipient, must certainly not be violated in any way by those who had given their word for it? Whatever the reason was, it resulted in Christopher Aske returning to Skipton with an exact and detailed account of where the Pilgrimage now stood.

The contingency plans, which were revised and refined at Templehirst, fell into two parts. The first of these considered arrangements that should be made at home, including instructions for the full garrisoning of Hull, Pontefract and elsewhere, together with their victualling and arming adequately enough to withstand full-scale hostilities. The entire Pilgrim strength would be divided into three armies and these would advance across the Trent at three different places, to rendezvous somewhere deeper inside Nottinghamshire yet to be decided.

The second part of the planning was much more ambitious and even more dangerous to Henry. The rebels decided that they would send an envoy to the Netherlands to see Mary of Hungary, who was the Emperor's Regent there, and ask her to provide them with money, 200 arquebuses and 2000 of cavalry. He was also to seek her intercession on their behalf with the Pope himself. The emissary was to be Dr Marmaduke Waldby, Vicar of Kirk Deighton, near Wetherby, and Prebendary of Carlisle, who was selected because he had become acquainted with certain members of the Dutch nobility during overtures made to the Emperor in 1534, after Lord Darcy's clandestine meeting with Sir Robert Constable and Lord Hussey in London. Thus, for the second time in two years, there was a very real possibility that England might be invaded in a combined operation between imperial troops and English dissidents, which the King would have been most unlikely to survive. The threat from the Continent had always been there, of course, as had an English invasion across the Channel; these were among the recognised facts of medieval European life. But the threat had become more acute ever since Henry's quarrel with the papacy began nearly a decade earlier and the King had been made well aware of it through the behaviour of Reginald Pole.

Pole had Tudor blood in him on his mother's side and he had been greatly helped as a young man by Henry, who paid for his education in England, presented him with a number of lucrative benefices and subsidised his further studies in Italy where Pole, a bookish and diffident layman at this stage of his life, made many lasting friendships, including that of the nobleman who subsequently became Pope Paul III. After five years on the Continent, Pole returned to England just as the question of Henry's divorce from Catherine of Aragon was first being raised and, not wishing to become in any way involved in it, after a short stay in the Charterhouse at Sheen, in Surrey, he moved to Paris, again with the King's assistance. Henry's quid pro quo for this bounty was to require Pole to canvass the unversity there for authoritatively favourable opinions that would help him to obtain his divorce from the Vatican; and when Pole tried to dodge this obligation, the King sent one of his courtiers to Paris to help him change his mind, which Pole eventually did. Back in the royal favour, he could have become Archbishop of York after Wolsey's fall if he had wished, because Henry offered it to him. Alternatively, if he preferred it, he could have the see of Winchester; but Pole declined both and stayed in France. By now, he had become one of those with a deep dislike of Thomas Cromwell and, simultaneously, his attitude to the divorce had hardened.

He spent two years writing a book, *Pro Unitatis Ecclesiasticae Defensione* (*In Defence of the One Universal Church*), which was based upon his unshakeable belief that the leadership of Europe resided in the Pope and the Emperor, to whom all things spiritual and temporal must be referred. The King had actually commissioned it, this somehow leading Pole to believe that above all things he wanted honesty. That is what Henry got, such honesty that it is hard to know whether one should stand in awe of immense courage or be dumbfounded by the simple-minded *naïveté* of the author. For Pole not only insulted his sovereign by comparing him with a dirty barrel, but openly advocated foreign intervention in the affairs of his own native land and claimed that Englishmen would be totally justified in taking up arms against their king. Henry, understandably enraged, did what he could to entice Pole back to England, where he would undoubtedly have been charged with treason, but Pole was at least worldly enough to realise the gravity of his situation and stayed put. And now, just as the English Pilgrims were drawing up their contingency plans in Yorkshire, his old friend Paul III sent for him, lodged him with great honour in the Vatican, priested him and announced that Reginald Pole would be made a cardinal after the feast of St Thomas, just a few days before Christmas. Within six months, Henry would be offering 100,000 pieces of gold to anyone who would bring him home, dead or alive. Preferably, he was to be seized, 'trussed up and conveyed to Calais', and then sent across the water for trial.

Pole had obviously become a very dangerous man to the throne, someone who could act as a powerful intermediary between the English Pilgrims and both the Emperor and the Pope. But there were other factors in foreign relations which the King must take into account as well. One of these was the possibility of a marriage between the Princess Mary and the Duke of Angoulême, which had been considered by both the French and English kings for some time, with Francis more openly pleased with the idea than Henry, who was playing hard to get. While negotiations between the two courts were still in their opening stages, the Emperor let it be known that he wanted to see a match between Mary and Don Luis of Portugal, which she herself was said to prefer.

The third strand, in a tangle of matrimonial propositions, was the prospect of Scotland's James V marrying the French King's daughter Madeleine de Valois. This was a distinctly threatening union from Henry's point of view because, although James was his nephew, relations between them were at best strained and might become very much worse than that: there was too much bad blood in the historical relationship of the Scots and the English for it to be otherwise. It took little imagination for Henry to see in such an alliance the makings of a crisis in which he could easily be attacked on two flanks by extremely determined foes. Moreover, he had good reason to be alarmed, for the papal nuncio at the French court was doing all he could to encourage the match, and the senior French prelate, Cardinal Jean du Bellay, was dropping heavy hints that, as James's father-in-law, Francis might well be induced to move against the apostate English King. Early in November the Pope had expressed his pleasure at the impending marriage, and his hope that neither Francis nor James would help Henry to put down his rebellious subjects; to which the young Scottish King replied that he would always, if possible, be at the service of the Pope.

It was in these circumstances, therefore, that Henry did what European monarchs were always doing with their sons and, especially, their daughters. He simply used Mary as an instrument of policy that might be crucial to the future of his throne. He let it be known that she was on the market with his blessing and, through long weeks of ambassadorial contact and bland assurances of goodwill on all sides, he kept both the Emperor and Francis waiting for his decision. The two were always on the verge of open enmity and, as long as they could both be kept guessing, it was less probable that either would become hostile to him than if he offended one of them.

Had he been wise enough, he would have realised that he was less likely to be left to the mercy of James, with a divided kingdom, than exposed to danger from any other foreign adversary. For there is nothing more touching in the Pilgrimage of Grace than the repeated insistence of the rebels, even when they were pressing their case upon the King most vehemently, that if he ever needed them to fight the Scots, they would be there for him alongside everybody else. In the event, the marriage between James and Madeleine went ahead, while Mary disappointed both her suitors by, eventually, marrying Philip of Spain. This did not completely reduce the threat of continental help for the English rebels. The Pilgrims believed that the Emperor favoured their cause and the Pope was certainly on their side, never delivering as much as he might have done, but taking a number of practical steps to encourage them. He subsequently claimed to have sent some money to the rebels through intermediaries, though there is no record that it ever arrived. What certainly happened is that the new Cardinal Pole was told to establish a base in Flanders, where he would be better placed to influence events in England than if he remained in Rome, and from where he might, when the moment seemed propitious to him, actually lead an army across the Channel. And in congratulating Francis on his daughter's forthcoming marriage, the Pope had urged him to join other monarchs in a crusade against Henry.

Meanwhile, Cromwell was alive to the notion of arms being smuggled to the North from the Low Countries and asked his agent in Brussels to investigate, but the man reported that if this were indeed happening it could not be on a very large scale, because English customs officials inspected all vessels coming from Europe too thoroughly. Cromwell may well have been alerted to the possibility by information received (from Christopher Aske, or from some other royal spy in York?) about the intention of Dr Waldby's projected journey to the Netherlands. But Waldby only got as far as Hull before a message from Darcy told him to delay his departure until further notice. The mission may have been cancelled because news had come in that the Regent had indicated her willingness to assist Henry and not the Pilgrimage.

One other consideration affected Henry's judgement at this

time: the uncertain temper of his subjects outside the North of England and Lincolnshire. Both he and Cromwell were wary enough of discontent spreading to the south and the west of the country for a number of arrests to be made on suspicion of provoking trouble, including that of Sir Robert Constable's son and the lad's schoolmaster, who happened to be in Buckinghamshire at the wrong time. Anyone with Lincolnshire connections was automatically seized, wherever in the country they might turn up, usually after they were reported by someone to the authorities for uttering seditious talk. A number of parish priests who still held to the old ways found themselves in trouble for various infringements in Hampshire, in Hertfordshire and on the Isle of Wight, and one of them, the Vicar of Wickham, fled after he, too, was accused of sedition. In Bath and in Worcester, men were imprisoned for having spoken out against Cromwell in public. Many copies of the Pilgrim oath, articles and other pronouncements had been made by now, and these were circulating far beyond the northern heartland. One turned up in Bromsgrove, another surfaced in King's Lynn, where it was declaimed at the Bell before an audience of attentive customers. It was then copied and these versions went from place to place elsewhere in Norfolk, as well as to a group of Cornishmen who were on a pilgrimage to Walsingham.

Inevitably, the message was also getting through to London and not just to the common citizens of the capital. Sir John Clarke sent a copy to his friend Sir George Throgmorton, after the pair had supped at the Horse Head in Cheapside, where they had discussed the rebellion, and Sir George duly passed it on to Sir William Essex, whose servant subsequently made another copy for himself, which he lent to an innkeeper in Reading and, before long, several rebel documents were circulating in the Berkshire town. No doubt all the insurgent papers which made their way south started similar chain reactions of their own. So alive was the government to the possibility of the rebellion spreading to the South, that the collection of the subsidy was suspended in order to pacify all those in danger of being infected by events in the North. That created its own problems, however, by resulting in such a shortage of income that the perpetual problem of paying the royal armies became more acute than ever. As if all this weren't enough for the authorities to worry about, there was the matter of undoubted sympathy for the Pilgrimage among men who were expected to serve the King as soldiers, which usually became evident in unguarded talk at musters, as Thomas Howard had discovered when he reported that he did not feel he could trust the troops under his command.

For a little while longer Henry kept up his bluff. The Pilgrim resolutions at York had been sent to the Duke of Norfolk and Howard had passed them on to the King, who chose to reply, on 27 November, not to the rebel leadership but to Bowes and Ellerker. He upbraided them in his first sentence, for 'the great slackness of you twain that were messengers from the whole company of that assembly to us, especially that you have not made us a full answer to your instructions'. In short, the two envoys, after being carefully coached for the part during their extended stay at court, had not produced the effect on the Pilgrims that Henry had intended. In a relatively short document, he still managed to deploy his customary rhetorical devices to indicate his all but divine status, his displeasure and his astonishment – 'we are much surprised...contrary to God's commandment...what madness...ashamed to call yourselves humble subjects'. He told them plainly that 'the commons be now down, and perhaps not so ready to rise again as some pretend'. What had been happening was not the behaviour of dutiful subjects 'but like war between princes' and if they carried on like this they 'will destroy themselves and utterly devast those parts which they inhabit'. He, Henry, would be sorry to repress them by force 'but if they persevere, will take measures to cut them off as corrupt members'. He then went for the principal object of his wrath and the man he saw as the chief cause of his by now deeply injured self-esteem: 'We think it no little shame to all you that have been accounted noble to suffer such a villain as Aske...who was never esteemed in any of our courts but as a common pedlar in the law.' Their honour was besmirched by this misplaced loyalty, and 'It is only his filed tongue and false surmises that have brought him this unfitting estimation among you'. Henry was, he declared, still inclined to be merciful, but if they wanted mercy they had better start working for it. There must be no repetition of the doings in Scarborough and no interception of government letters; the ship that had been seized must be returned to Sir Ralph Evers and they must 'withdraw their men from our towns and castles, which they now keep contrary to the duties of good subjects ...' Unless they demonstrated their submission to the King by their deeds 'we do not intend my lord of Norfolk to common any further with them ...'

It was another desperate attempt to drive in a wedge that would split the insurrection; in this case, between those noblemen and gentry who constituted the bulk of the Pilgrim leadership and those few, above all Robert Aske, who had, in Henry's view, been stirring up trouble among the common people from the start. The King was also making the ultimate threat, in almost the same language as Cromwell had used in the letter seized in Scarborough, which had been written seventeen days before Henry put his own pen to paper. Hand over the people he really wanted to make an example of or else, was the message. Not for the first time, Henry had quite miscalculated the depth of real loyalty that by now existed in the Pilgrimage of Grace, that was not to be intimidated, or bought, or weakened by making men feel guilty about their chosen allegiance, with spurious talk of honour. Beyond that, this was perhaps the first time it occurred to Aske and the other leaders of the peace party in the Pilgrimage that maybe their sovereign prince was not as trustworthy as they had always believed, as they had fervently wanted him to be. Surely, he had a mind of his own, even though it had been skilfully manipulated by the Lord Privy Seal? But, now, the two seemed to be speaking with exactly the same voice. Robert Constable and others like him had, of course, reached this conclusion a little earlier. Except Robert Bowes, who had been one of the most aggressive captains before and at Doncaster, but who now seemed to have entered a no man's land which he shared only with young Sir Ralph Ellerker, who had also changed his allegiance more than once.

XII

TO DONCASTER BRIDGE ...

So eager were the Pilgrim delegates to move their business forward that once again they began to turn up several days before they needed to, this time for the weekend meeting that was to draw up their agenda for Doncaster. When the leaders arrived in Pontefract on Saturday, 2 December, they found the district representatives awaiting them and some of these made a bonny show: York had sent its sheriff and six burgesses, together with their servants, and each was clad in a new coat for the occasion, all displaying the city's livery. Others came in harness, as a reminder that the outcome of the approaching parley with the government might go either way, and a novelty of military engineering was also to be seen: a bridge, designed by 'one Diamond of Wakefield, a poor man', which would 'shoot over any arm of the sea in this realm'.[1] Robert Aske's colic had been relieved by a few days of 'using himself tenderly', as he had hoped when he called off a meeting with Darcy after York because he 'would rather die than be sick at Pomfret'. Apart from Aske, the inner council on this occasion consisted of Darcy and five other lords, Sir Robert Constable and twenty-two other knights, Robert Bowes and twenty-five other gentlemen, plus sixteen men to represent the commons, led by Robert Pulleyn and Nicholas Musgrave from Westmorland. The only two big names missing were those of Sir Thomas Percy, who was busy with affairs in Northumberland,

---

1 This can be seen as an ancestor of the prefabricated Bailey bridge, which served the British Army well in World War Two. It was obviously made in order to cross unfordable rivers.

and Sir Thomas Tempest, who was a cousin of Robert Bowes and was still suffering the effects of a chill he had caught on his way home to Durham from York. As a demonstration of his goodwill, however, Tempest had set down in writing his opinions on the matters to be discussed – which was a risky thing to do in the uncertain circumstances of that month – and Bowes conveyed these to Pontefract.

The principal matter for discussion being an amplification of the original articles, which the King had rejected as too vague to discuss, they made a start by collecting the numerous submissions that each delegation had brought from its home territory. Above all other topics was the religious issue, so central to the ethos of the rebellion that Aske had made a special point of canvassing the northern clergy for their views, in order that these should be heard in Pontefract.

Archbishop Lee, as usual, tried to find a way out of any commitment that could be held against him by anyone: his subsequent explanation to Cromwell was that he had only gone to Pontefract so as to act as a deterrent to the hotheads in the rebellion. As it was, he and his colleagues managed to dodge a question that had been put to all the clerics by Aske, which was to do with the vastly important matter of oaths. What was the spiritual position of someone who took an oath which contradicted an earlier oath, though it was worded in such a way as to evade the charge of repudiation? The rebels were scrupulously thinking in terms of their Pilgrim oath, taken after swearing allegiance to the King. The priesthood avoided answering because it would have reflected uncomfortably on the similar state they themselves had reached when they solemnly acknowledged Henry as Supreme Head of the English Church, after plighting their troth to the Pope as leader of the Universal Church. A number of these leading clergy had been invited to come to Pontefract with their opinions, supplemented by those they had brought from the junior priesthood. Their collective answer seemed to be that no one was quite sure where they stood with the Holy Ghost on this matter.

Many submissions had been made to the conference on the subject of the Supremacy and some of them came in Latin. There were a number of different opinions on this matter and a majority on the council wanted the Act to be repealed in its entirety. But Aske, thoughtfully cautious as always, advised that it was important to make a reservation in order to take into account two forms of ecclesiastical authority that just might be acceptable to Henry. He proposed a compromise which would acknowledge the King's temporal supremacy over the Church in England, while making it clear that the *cura animarum* (the care of souls) belonged in a different sphere. This was the Pope's responsibility to the Universal Church, but it could perhaps be delegated by the pontiff to the two English primates in this case, 'so that the said Bishop of Rome have no further meddling'. Aske was, in short, proposing the kind of solution that would become almost a caste mark of Anglicanism down the ages, even when this way of circumventing problems left it open to ridicule by more inflexible critics.

There was then the problem of the suppressed monasteries, in which Aske took the lead eloquently. He requested that they be restored, with full possession of their lands and goods, in a document whose length indicates how much the subject mattered to him personally. The suppression was resented by everyone, he claimed, 'because the abbeys in the north parts gave great alms to poor men and laudably served God; in which parts of late days they had but small comfort by ghostly teaching. And by occasion of the said suppression the divine service of almighty God is much minished, great numbers of masses unsaid, and the blessed consecration of the sacrament now not used and showed in those places, to the distress of the faith and spiritual comfort to man's soul ...' The North of England, he argued, was something of a special case, because 'divers and many of the said abbeys were in the mountains and desert places, where the people be rude of conditions and not well taught the law of God, and when the said abbeys stood, the said people not only had worldly refreshing in their bodies but also spiritual refuge both by ghostly living of them and also by spiritual information, and preaching; and many their tenants were their fee'd servants to them, and servingmen, well succoured by abbeys ...'

He went on to enumerate a number of other deprivations that had resulted from the suppression: 'of meat, cloth and wages ... neither carriage of corn and merchandise ... neither horsemeat nor mansmeat ...' He concluded by mentioning some factors that might easily be overlooked by many.

> Also the abbeys were one of the beauties of this realm to all men and strangers passing through the same; also all gentlemen [were] much succoured in their needs with money, their young men there succoured, and in nunneries their daughters brought up in virtue; and also their evidences and money left to the uses of infants in abbeys' hands, always sure there; and such abbeys as were near the danger of sea banks [were] great maintainers of sea walls and dykes, maintainers and builders of bridges and highways [and] such other things for the commonwealth.

It is scarcely surprising that the King thought the man capable of such advocacy was possessed of 'a filed tongue'.

Other voices said much the same things briefly and with less passion. The monks, it was claimed, were good landlords who never enclosed land and who, in hard times, would frequently undercut the current market price of corn so as to give everybody but the big landowners a hand; and these matters appeared to weigh with the Pilgrims much more heavily than occasional sexual transgressions by individual religious or the even rarer instances of lawlessness by some who were supposed to know a lot better. John Hexham, the Benedictine Abbot of Whitby, for example, was said to be a man of some personal substance because he was notoriously in league with a couple of French pirates who regularly worked the east coast of England, and he seems generally to have been a thoroughgoing scoundrel who had entered the wrong profession.

Having reviewed the monasteries, the delegates then took issue with the King over the Act of Annates whose introduction, in Henry's opinion, meant that he was merely a more appropriate recipient of ecclesiastical first-fruits than the Pope, who had previously been enriched by them. The trouble was, as far as the Pilgrims were concerned, not so much the diversion of funds from the Vatican to the Tudor Treasury, but that the Pope had collected first-fruits at infrequent intervals, whereas the King exacted them much more often, sometimes several times a year if a benefice changed hands more than once for one reason or another. This could easily occur when patronage was sometimes traded like any other commodity, which is what had happened in the transaction of Sawley Abbey between Henry and Sir Arthur Darcy. A house of religious could be crippled in this way when, with each new appointment of a superior or change of ownership, it saw one year's income vanish at a stroke, leaving many mouths still to feed and other responsibilities to discharge. The clergy wanted the best possible deal for themselves, which would have been an abolition of all such imposts; but the Pilgrims would have been well content if the system had been changed to one in which the Church paid a fixed annual charge, instead of one that was not only variable, but sometimes liable to occur every few months. Among other advantages, it was thought that this would reduce the amount of money regularly drained out of the North, where it was felt that there was a damaging shortage of currency already.

Other religious grievances were addressed. The conference eventually petitioned 'to have the heretics, bishops and temporal, and their sect, to have condign punishment by fire or such other, or else to try the quarrel with us and our partakers in battle'. The yardstick of heresy was to be the Ten Articles promulgated earlier in the year, which the Pilgrims (and even Reginald Pole) were prepared to accept as a proper summary of the faith, their only caveat being that the articles implicitly ratified Henry's Supremacy. The caveat was, of course, crucial, and it was acceptance of the Supremacy that made Cranmer, several other bishops, Cromwell and the rest of the new establishment heretics in the eyes of the rebels.

'Condign punishment' was also to be inflicted on the infamous commissioners Legh and Layton 'for their extortions from religious houses and other abominable acts'. At the time of Pontefract the delegates were seething at some recent news that these two had used vestments from suppressed religious houses as saddle cloths, which may seem a paltry reason for sending men to the stake, but there was by then an enormous accumulation of fury against these particular agents of Cromwell who, as the delegates well knew, or would one day find out if they didn't know already, were perfectly capable of stripping the precious metals from a much venerated shrine and throwing away the bones of the incumbent saint.

Two other matters concerning the Church demonstrated the anxiety of the Pilgrims that the will of the nation's chosen representatives, not the whim of their king, should be the governing factor in all ecclesiastical legislation. They asked for the restoration of the Church's old liberties – that is, its jurisdiction over various lands and properties – and for its privileges and rights, such as sanctuary and the inviolable nature of the priesthood, to revert to the custom that had always been recognised before Henry ascended the throne. And they wanted the authorisation of both these matters to be sealed by Acts of Parliament.

Parliament also figured in many of the other conclusions the delegates reached after completing their review of religious grievances. It was invoked to ensure that the Princess Mary was legitimised as heir to the Crown, both because her demotion had been achieved by illegal means and because 'the said Lady Mary is marvellously beloved for her virtue in the hearts of the people'. But Parliament itself was the subject of a contention made by the Pilgrims that it was seriously in need of reform, so that it would be much less a tool of the sovereign and more of an assembly which genuinely represented the people and had an independent mind of its own. The procedures for election to the assembly should be revised, so that every burgess sent to Westminster should actually live in the borough he represented, that a seat should be declared void if its member died during a Parliament, and not simply be filled by a nominee of the Crown, that none of the King's servants should be allowed to sit in the House of Commons.

The Pilgrims also wanted more representation of the North in Parliament, where it had fallen off in Yorkshire alone from fifteen men representing boroughs, plus those for the shire and the city of York, which was the tally in Edward III's time, to no more than two in the present Parliament. This was not Henry's fault, as we have already noted, but the result of indifference by earlier generations of Yorkshiremen and the subsequent inability of many places to pay their way adequately. It is, however, significant that the Pilgrims wanted the situation rectified in the light of their new enthusiasm for the institution itself, as an instrument of the people at large. They repeated, of course, their insistence on a Parliament situated in York, 'and that shortly', but they were now prepared to accept Nottingham as a possible alternative.

They wanted no more interference by the King in elections and complete freedom of speech in both Houses, so that there would be no repetition of anything like Darcy's banishment in 1534 after he had taken Catherine's side in a debate on the divorce proceedings. They wanted spiritual matters to be handled by Convocation and not by Parliament, and they desired a couple of adjustments to procedures affecting the House of Lords: all bills put before the Commons should automatically be sent on to the Lords, they said, and the old custom of Magna Carta's first chapter being read to the peers following the mass that was always said before every session should be restored after an absence of some six or seven years. Finally, in this bundle of constitutional issues, they wanted reform of the legislation governing the laws of inheritance, an old sore for the upper classes in particular, and also of the statute which at present made it possible for the King to nominate his successor, instead of the throne passing by right to his natural heir. And if the hazard that everyone had in mind was not Thomas Cromwell, it was the possibility that the English throne might one day be occupied by James V of Scotland, or someone else whose principal allegiance belonged north of the Border. One of the potential candidates in this case was whomsoever James's half-sister, Lady Margaret Douglas, might marry, which was a well-grounded instinct as it turned out. For in 1544 she became the Countess of Lennox and therefore part of the Stuart dynasty.[2]

There was a great swathe of grievances about various other laws of the land and many of these, in the final drafting of fresh articles, clearly bore the imprint of Robert Aske's professional skills. At one end of the scale was a demand that the statute affecting ownership of handguns and crossbows should be repealed, except in the King's parks or forests, at the other a wish that 'the common laws may have place as was used in the beginning of the reign, and that no injunctions be granted unless the matter has been determined in Chancery'. On weapons, the law

---

2 Her son, Lord Darnley, would be the disastrous husband of Mary Queen of Scots and murderer of her confidant David Riccio. He was himself disposed of in mysterious circumstances after he and Mary had become estranged.

forbade the use of handguns and crossbows to anyone whose income was less than £100 a year, excepting people in certain towns and fortresses, and those living within seven miles of the coast or the Scottish Borders – there was total exemption, in fact, for everyone in Northumberland, Durham, Westmorland and Cumberland precisely because of the Scottish threat. This statute was designed to maintain proficiency with the longbow, which was still regarded as the most devastating weapon available to foot soldiers, but archers needed constant practice if their arrows were to be shot with maximum effect. One reason for wanting a change, especially in Yorkshire, was a smouldering resentment that the northernmost counties were treated differently from everybody else; more powerfully, there was a growing feeling everywhere that modern weapons which effectively were only available to the King's soldiers, put everyone else at a potentially alarming disadvantage.

The question of the Common Law was raised in order to curb the powers of Henry's Lord Chancellor, Sir Thomas Audley, in granting injunctions which secured an advantage for one or other party in a lawsuit and which were entirely a privilege of the rich. Inevitably, Audley was suspected of partiality in making these awards, which is why the Pilgrims wanted his role limited to interventions in cases which had already been heard before the Chancellor's own court, and not in any disputatious matter that might be raised before other judiciaries: before the court of Common Pleas, for example, or the County Courts of the provinces.

In between the concerns about weapons and the state of the Common Law came a legal matter that was related both to the limiting of the Chancellor's powers and to the Pilgrim feeling about the remoteness of the North from London and all its works. It was to the effect that anyone living north of the Trent who was subpoenaed to appear in any case that didn't directly affect the King should be able to obtain a hearing in York, or at least be represented in the capital by a lawyer and not have to trail down to London in person. Then there was the role of the King's escheators, the royal officers who administered forfeited goods and lands, and who stood accused of rapacity when dealing with people in the provinces. The Pilgrims wanted 'a remedy against escheators for finding false offices and extorting fees'. The memorandum that Sir Thomas Tempest submitted, because he was unable to get to Pontefract, laid the blame squarely on Cromwell's men, whose arrogance was such that they thought 'to have the law in every place here ordered at their commandment, and will take upon them to command sheriff, justices of peace, *coram* and of session in their master's name at their pleasure ...'[3]

Tempest remembered times past when contemplating taxation in general, which was among a number of economic considerations that were debated in Pontefract. In particular, he wistfully recalled the ways in which Henry's father had augmented his treasury, by encouraging foreign trade, by selling pardons and by deft transactions when an episcopal see became vacant: 'When a bishopric fell he would promote his chaplain, and thereby by such exchange he would have the profit of the temporalities of all the sees of the realm and content all his prelates by the same, for he amended all their lineage thereby, and hurt none, and yet increased his own riches marvellously.' His contribution on this point was taken into account before the Pilgrims drew up their considered opinion that 'the quinzine and taxes now granted by Act of Parliament' should be abrogated, and this included the subsidy which had, in fact, just been suspended in southern England on the grounds of political expediency, as well as the assessment which took a fifteenth part of the value of a man's possessions.

Two other matters were more a concern of the commons than of the gentlemen, though they were aired in the name of the whole Pilgrimage. One was a desire that 'the lands in Westmorland, Cumberland, Kendal, Dent, Sedbergh, Furness, and the abbey lands of Mashamshire, Kirkbyshire, Netherdale, may be by tenant right, and the lord to have, at every change, two years' rent for gressum, according to the grant now made by the lords to the commons there. This to be done by Act of Parliament.' The other was a demand for a drastic revision of the law regarding the enclosure of the land, which was not directed against the King so much as the monied class, who, whenever

3 *Coram judice* was a hearing before a judge.

possible, converted the fields tilled by their tenants into far more profitable pasture for sheep farming.

When Monday morning came and the conference broke up, the Pilgrimage had rearranged its collective thoughts into Twenty-Four Articles, which not even Henry could have dismissed as vague, but which crisply made point after point in a long catalogue of dissatisfactions. They were notable, moreover, for the frequency with which the Pilgrims were open to compromise – a Parliament in Nottingham if not in York, the King's acquisition of first-fruits acceptable within certain limits, his Supremacy over the Church in England endorsed provided it was recognised as only a temporal power, the Ten Articles of Religion approved so long as the Supremacy claim was clarified, the King's own private lands to be exempted from a revision of the laws regulating the possession of weapons. Compromise had also been reached in attending to the particular interests of the commons and their social superiors, when these did not obviously coincide. There may have been a certain amount of horse-trading in Pontefract, which resulted, for example, in the inclusion of the articles affecting the laws on gressums, enclosure and other matters of concern only to the non-landowning class, this perhaps being absorbed by the gentry in exchange for a general acceptance of a revised law of inheritance, which did not have much bearing on the life of the commons.

Other matters that were considered by the inner council, to do with arrangements for the forthcoming parley with the Duke of Norfolk and the strategy to be pursued thenceforth, did not admit any form of appeasement, however. One of them was an unqualified insistence that 'Richard Cromwell nor none of his kind nor sort be at our meeting at Doncaster' and there were a number of grounds for this, including the likelihood that if the commons at large heard of anyone connected with the Lord Privy Seal being present at the second truce talks, they would almost certainly attack the government delegation and destroy any possibility of a lasting peace. Another, the most important by far in the entire catalogue of new submissions, required 'Pardon by Act of Parliament for all recognisances, statutes and penalties new forfeited during the time of this commotion'. They were telling Henry what he could do with his ten exceptions to the amnesty.

Pontefract was notable for one other thing, apart from the Twenty-Four Articles. It was during the conference that the Archbishop of York was at last flushed out of his non-committal hiding place, where he had carefully sheltered ever since taking flight from Cawood three weeks earlier, even though he had returned to the archiepiscopal palace as soon as the truce began. Not only that, but he now placed himself in a position where he could no longer try to extract incriminating evidence from the Pilgrim leadership while refusing to reveal his own position on any of the issues involved. He was obviously the first priest Aske had turned to before the conference began, in canvassing the northern clergy for their opinions on various matters affecting the Church, and Lee had very craftily required the captain to set down in writing what topics he wanted the Archbishop's views on, including the important subject of dual oaths, which clearly troubled a number of the more tender Pilgrim consciences. The unsuspecting Aske complied with the request, which enabled Lee to convince Cromwell later that this was the warning signal that caused him to go to Pontefract, to do what he could for the King's cause. He would, even so, have much preferred to stay at home, but Sir Robert Constable, ever more worldly than Robert Aske, made it plain that he could only do that if he put down his own views on paper. So Lee went to the conference, though he rejected the hospitality offered him at the castle and stayed at the Cluniac Priory instead. He was still as non-committal as ever, but eager to acquire any more evidence he could that would help his own position if the Pilgrimage failed. He sent his principal chaplain, John Brandsby, to see Lord Darcy and ask him if he, too, would give Lee a written opinion on the matters pending. But Old Tom, like Constable, could smell bad fish when it was placed in front of him and gave his answer by word of mouth – robustly, no doubt.

Edward Lee's self-exposure occurred on the second day of the conference, after he had been invited to preach at the principal Sunday service in the church of All Saints, at the bottom of the hill on which the castle was built. It was a very early mass that day, because the conference was due to reassemble at nine o'clock and the rebels wanted to take their spiritual nourishment first. All Saints was packed when the service began, the body of the church full of gentry and priests, such commons as could be accommodated being lodged in something described as a gallery, which was maybe the clerestory, 'up a height in the church'. Almost as soon as Lee arrived in Pontefract, Lord Latimer had asked him to give his congregation some guidance on the subject that probably exercised the more sensitive Pilgrims more than anything, that was at the heart of their scruples about oaths: was it, or was it not, lawful for them to wage war on their king? It was an indication of how closely he had so far kept his opinions to himself that the question even needed to be put to him at this stage of proceedings and it is a matter of some astonishment that Lee had managed to keep so many intelligent men in the dark so long. But they seem to have been quite unprepared for what was about to happen after the Archbishop had mounted the pulpit and begun to speak. Robert Aske said later that he would never have allowed Lee to preach if he had known what was coming. The Archbishop's chaplains must have had some idea of what was in his mind, however, because they appear to have tried to dissuade him from preaching at all. And it may be that he intended to mouth some neutral platitudes, yet again evading the question of where he himself stood in this rebellion, if something had not caused him to be candid for the first time.

His text has not survived, but Robert Aske's eyewitness account suggests that he began his sermon by talking about the sacraments, about the Creeds, about the Ten Articles of Religion, none of which was going to stir anybody's blood. He then spoke of the Church's liberties and declared that they must under no circumstances be used for any purposes contrary to the teachings of the Church; and this was a conclusion with which everyone present would certainly concur. He went on to condemn priests who took up arms, which may have caused a small ripple of unease in a congregation that included a number of clerics deeply committed to the cause, not all of whom were reluctant to march with a bill over their shoulder alongside everybody else. He began to say something about pilgrimage … then stopped, visibly startled, because the church door had been flung open and Lancaster Herald walked in.[4] The Herald had, in fact, simply arrived with

4 According to Aske, some people in the congregation thought the Archbishop had fainted.

the safe conducts for Doncaster, but he dutifully sat down to share the mass with everybody else. It has been conjectured that Thomas Miller's arrival, certain evidence that the King's men were comfortingly close at hand, gave the Archbishop the courage to state his position in front of these people, as he had not done before, and this may be so. Alternatively, it has been suggested, his courage may have failed him at the moment when he was about to tell the rebels what they had from the start wanted to hear from his own lips. At any rate, he continued his unfinished sentence ... to the effect that no man might take up arms except by his sovereign's leave. Bedlam broke out at once and, had the commons been situated nearer to the prelate than they were, things might have gone very ill indeed for him. As it was, amidst angry shouts denouncing him as a vile cheat and worse, Lee was hustled out of the pulpit by Robert Aske and other gentlemen, to the relative safety of the Priory, whence he later returned to Cawood.

Their intervention was, in a sense, unfortunate. They may have saved Edward Lee from being lynched, or at least from being severely manhandled, but in doing so after such a sermon they placed themselves in an invidious position. For their protection of the Archbishop reawakened the perpetual suspicion of the commons about the integrity of the gentry, an instinct that perhaps they had been playing a double game all along. From where the commons were standing, ostentatiously separated from these conceivably duplicitous people in the body of the church, it was easy to conclude that those they had been glad to accept, and had often enough dragooned into service as helpmates, were about to do a deal with the Crown in order to save their own skins at the expense of their lowlier comrades, in much the same way that the Lincolnshire gentlemen had independently sued for terms with Charles Brandon when it became clear that the rising there was on its last legs. Not knowing at that moment the purpose of Lancaster Herald's latest mission, many may have read something ominous into his sudden arrival: they would have been aware, after all (Aske and Darcy certainly were), that ten ships loaded with ordnance had left the Tower of London during the last week of November and it required little imagination to guess where they were bound for and to what end.

These suspicions of the commons could only have been fuelled by an incident that occurred after Lee had been escorted from the building, while the uproar continued inside. For one of the burgesses in the colourful representation from York, a man named Richard Bowyer, was not wearing the city's livery, as he had been when he and his colleagues arrived in Pontefract, but a coat bearing the royal insignia of red crosses, which he had doubtless retained from his official position in charge of the fortification at York's Bootham Bar, before the city was handed over to the rebels. Robert Aske's servants could now clearly be seen cutting the St George's crosses from Bowyer's coat, and what could that be but a desire to conceal a careless mistake and an extremely incriminating piece of evidence? We may well wonder why the commons did not then take action more drastic than continuing to bellow with outrage, but something – perhaps an unwillingness to face a potentially grave situation for which at that moment they were not properly prepared – for the time being stayed their hand.

The main business of Pontefract may have been concluded, but Aske was still anxious to have the opinions of the clergy he had canvassed and these clerics gathered in the Priory church on Monday, to begin a debate which went on until the following day. Even without the Archbishop, they were an impressive assortment of divines, including his chancellor, his vicar-general, his principal chaplain, the Chancellor of Beverley Minster, the Abbot of Kirkstall, the Archdeacons of Cleveland and Nottingham, the Prior of Pontefract and others, among whom were the rebel song-writer Dr John Pickering and Dr Marmaduke Waldby, who still had not gone on his errand to the Emperor's Regent in the Netherlands. They were not of one mind on any of the topics raised, and their response to the question of the Supremacy and the nature of Henry's role in the Church was typical. Only the Chancellor of Beverley appeared to be much at ease with the King's self-promotion. While some were totally inclined towards the primacy of the Pope, others wanted the pontiff's authority limited and three men thought the entire matter should be referred to a General Council of the Church; which in effect meant that they looked to someone other than themselves to shoulder the responsibility for offending the English Crown.

Another question that was handled with extreme caution concerned the King's divorce, to which their united response began 'we be not sufficiently instructed in the facts...' They were outspoken enough on some other topics, though. On the subject of ecclesiastical taxes they thought that 'no temporal man hath authority by the laws of God to claim any such tenths or first fruits of any benefice or spiritual promotion'. They were at one with the conference delegates in their feelings about the Church's liberties – 'we think the lands given to God, the Church or religious men may not be taken away and put to profane uses...' And they were adamant that 'the examination and correction of deadly sin belongeth to the ministers of the Church by the laws of the same, which be consonant to God's laws'. But a final statement which included the resounding thought that it would be a good idea if the Church's laws were read in the universities, as in times past, finished with another careful disclaimer: 'And we said clergy say it for lack of time and instruction in these articles and want of books, we declare this our opinion for this time referring our determination in these premises to the next Convocation.'

That evening, these conclusions were taken to Cawood for the Archbishop's endorsement but he had retreated once more into his prevaricating mode and began to quibble over the article touching on the Supremacy most of all. Even though they might have taken encouragement from Lee's unexpected lead on the matter in church, the attendant divines never did give a straight answer to the question that troubled the Pilgrim leaders above all else, though Pickering and Waldby, at least, must have been quite clear where they stood by then on the validity of oaths.

By the time the clergy dispersed, the second appointment in Doncaster was only a matter of hours away. This was, in fact, then put back until the Wednesday, because the Duke of Norfolk had wanted the Earl of Shrewsbury to be at his side when he treated with the rebels, but Talbot was indisposed again and was unable to get over from his Derbyshire seat of Wingfield in time for Tuesday. Moreover, Howard was in the middle of an endless correspondence with the King, in which Henry's intentions became ever more devious with the arrival of each despatch from court, which was now at Richmond in Surrey. The Duke had come north once more with orders to secure the total submission of the rebels, in exchange for which he would affirm the pardon which was promised to all but the ten men reserved for punishment, and he would at last announce the names of the chosen ten, including that of Robert Aske. No hostages were to be exchanged for Aske's presence in Doncaster, nor was there to be a truce of fourteen days. The submission having been obtained, the Duke was to administer to all involved in the Pilgrimage the same oath that had been required of the Lincolnshire insurgents, one of total loyalty to the Crown in future. That was the position when he arrived at Hatfield, near Doncaster, on Sunday, while everyone in Pontefract was still recovering from the Archbishop of York's sermon.

But Howard had also been told what to do if the Pilgrims refused to take the oath on those terms. He was to play for more time and prepare to attack as soon as he judged conditions were such that a victory for the Crown's forces was assured. One way of buying a further breathing space, Henry suggested, was to tell the rebels that he, Howard, was not authorised to offer more than the limited pardon but that he would sympathetically put their case for a full pardon to the King, which should afford him at least a week's grace, given the time taken for messages to travel from one end of England to the other. As Henry craftily put it, Howard must ask for a delay that might plausibly seem to the rebels 'as though you should send hither unto us'.

By Saturday, 2 December, when Howard had reached Welbeck in Nottinghamshire on his way to Hatfield and Doncaster, Henry had received a letter from the Duke that was intended to remove any illusions the King might still have about the magnitude of the task facing him in the North, whether he hoped to pacify the rebels with cunning diplomacy or defeat them face to face in battle. If the second option were taken, then a great deal would depend upon the weather and the effect it might have on water levels along the Trent and other rivers that were strategically important. If the King was bent on diplomacy, he had better bear in mind that the leaders of the Pilgrimage were quite clearly not the sort of men who could be cheaply bought. The fact was that Howard had lost his taste for battle, especially hostilities which might cost him dear but allow the despised Cromwell to profit from his endeavours behind his back; but he also wanted his sovereign to understand the reality of his situation on purely pragmatic grounds. Sensing that Henry did not completely trust him, because of his enmity for the Lord Privy Seal and because of his own vulpine nature, Howard was anxious to place himself beyond suspicion of going soft on – or even becoming sympathetic to – the Pilgrimage. He didn't want to take the blame for something that might go catastrophically wrong because the King was unbending in his arrogance and immovable in his obstinacy. His letter, in fact, had largely the opposite effect from what he intended. Henry wrote back the day he received it, all but accusing the Duke of cowardice and asserting that his information about the rebels contradicted all the reports that were coming in from royal spies. This response was despatched with a covering note from the Privy Council (which, of course, included Cromwell) that was intended to soothe any hurt feelings Howard might have, but also repeated Henry's original order that if the rebels did not submit as demanded, they must be attacked at once.

A few days later, the Council sent another letter to Howard, dropping the hint that while the King wanted the matter settled once and for all on the battlefield, his closest advisers still believed that this could be avoided by skilful negotiation. If the Duke could bring this off, then he was to make a progress through Yorkshire with as impressive an entourage as possible, administering the oath to all local populations with due ceremony. This must not, of course, be too costly an exercise, because the King's expenses were already far too high and needed curtailing. With the letter the council sent a copy of the Ten Articles, for reference in the oath-taking, together with a document which Henry had circulated among the bishops in November. This required them to explain the Articles to their congregations from the pulpit, while at the same time urging obedience on their people. They were also to come down heavily on all unlicensed preachers and on all unauthorised rituals and other religious practices. The document was intended as a sop to those who deplored the religious legislation that had taken place in Henry's separation from Rome. The Privy Council's communication ended with the following advice: 'There remains one thing to be considered which the King has much to heart and we all no less desire – the preservation of his Grace's honour, which will be much touched if no man be reserved to punishment.' Sir Robert Constable was particularly mentioned for this treatment, his presumably being one of the four unspecified names that Henry had in mind when the limited pardon was drawn up.

The very same day that he sent his angry letter to Howard, Henry also wrote to George Talbot up at Wingfield, instructing him to start talking to Aske and Darcy about a possible switch in their loyalties. If they seemed at all interested he was to give them each a pardon, which had already been separately prepared and which were enclosed with Henry's despatch. Enclosed, but not signed or dated – Talbot was to fill in the blanks if and when the pardons were needed to gain advantage, 'but you must do so in such sort that there appear no diversity of hands'. In short, Henry wanted his old general to commit forgery on his behalf, so that either or both these documents could be repudiated if the King later deemed it expedient to do so. He was so intent on this deception remaining a secret between him and the Earl that not even the Privy Council, much less the Duke of Norfolk, were made aware of it. He was still hoping to smash the Pilgrimage of Grace by force or any other means that would serve his purpose, but on the evening of Sunday, 3 December, Henry was at last compelled to understand exactly how bad things now looked for him. Another letter arrived from Thomas Howard, stating even more emphatically the position as he saw it. More tellingly, a despatch came in from Charles Brandon, Henry's closest friend from boyhood and his brother-in-law, which also emphasised the seriousness of the position and asserted that unless a complete pardon was offered, together with a Parliament freed from the King's direct attention, the royal cause in the North was lost.

And, for once, Henry listened. He dictated fresh instructions, which included the ritual threats and reproaches, and a casual reminder of Howard's own duplicity: 'You said you would esteem no promise you should make to the rebels nor think your honour touched in the breach of it.' Henry then made it clear that negotiation could only take place if the numbers on both sides were equal – that is, the number of armed men waiting in the wings, while the talks went on. If the initial offer was turned down, then Howard, as already instructed, was to prevaricate under the pretence of seeking further instructions from the King, during a truce of no more than a week or so. But he must first obtain the assurances of the rebels that they would be content with an unqualified pardon and a Parliament, which would open on the last day of the following September at some place which Henry himself would nominate. They must not later ask for anything more than these two things from their king. If they were still not prepared to accept even this revised offer, the Duke was to extend the truce to twenty days and immediately inform His Majesty of what had happened, as well as Edward Stanley up in Lancashire and Charles Brandon down in Lincoln. The King, meanwhile, would issue three different safe conducts, for sixteen, twenty and forty days respectively, to take care of any eventuality. He would also compose the pardon of last resort and send that north without delay.

In fact, two versions of the same document were written down, one on 3 December, the other six days later, the first being sent direct to Brandon, who was to convey it to Henry Clifford in Skipton and to have it proclaimed in Yorkshire and all the other affected counties but Lancashire, though somehow or other it appears eventually to have surfaced there. Brandon did not, in fact, obey Henry's instructions immediately, evidently preferring to await the outcome of events in Doncaster before making a move; he may have been made cautious by his sovereign's obvious and extreme reluctance to climb down, which was clear in the King's observation that 'we thought the granting of such a pardon would only encourage others' to rise up against him elsewhere in his kingdom. Brandon was also preoccupied with planning Henry's alternative scenario, which in his case was an order to increase his military strength to 8000 men and, the moment he received Howard's signal, to take Hull after an assault from the other side of the Humber; presumably an amphibious attack, for which boats had been steadily accumulating along the Lincolnshire bank of the river for some time. After that, he was to march on York. But then, true to the pattern of contradictory instructions he had given his commanders from the earliest days of insurrection, Henry countermanded this order and told Brandon to do nothing until further notice.

After that first weekend in December there was a great deal of coming and going between Doncaster and Pontefract. The first people to cross the Don were Sir Thomas Hilton and nine others, who included Bowes, Ellerker, Babthorpe and Sir Robert Constable's brother, Sir William; these were sent on Monday to deliver the new Twenty-Four Articles to the Duke of Norfolk and to return with the safe conducts for the much larger body of Pilgrims who were to be present at the negotiations planned for the next day. They were also to pass on the message about Richard Cromwell being *persona non grata* and to ask for a general pardon. On receiving the ten emissaries, Howard went into his elaborate charade about needing to consult the King further, but he appears not to have revealed Henry's instruction that no special security should be offered Robert Aske. He may not then have known, but he certainly wouldn't have been surprised when he later learned, that while he was meeting Hilton and his companions, Charles Brandon was writing to the King asking him to supply guns, gunners and ammunition (including arrows for bowmen) and saying that he was awaiting the arrival of the two ships from London, part of the flotilla that had sailed from the Tower the week before.

The emissaries rode back to Pontefract with Howard's response and with an agreement that 300 Pilgrims should return the next day, from whom twenty gentlemen and twenty commons would be chosen to do the actual talking with the Duke and his own company. Tuesday's talks being cancelled, however, the Pilgrims didn't arrive in Doncaster until that evening and spent the night at the local Franciscan friary, which may have been chosen with a thought for their safety, because it was located on an island between the Don and the even smaller River Cheswold, and was therefore effectively surrounded by a natural moat. Leading the larger Pilgrim company were Aske, Lord Darcy, Lord Scrope and Lord Latimer, the three other lords in the Pilgrimage – Neville, Lumley and Conyers – staying in Pontefract to keep an eye on the best part of 3000 commons who were now assembled there, waiting to hear what their fate was likely to be.

Before they left the Franciscan house next morning the negotiating team decided that Aske should be their spokesman. Then the forty delegates crossed the moat into town and went to its other friary, belonging to the Carmelites, where the Duke and the other royal representatives awaited them. Howard had only just received the despatch from Henry empowering him to prolong the truce and, after a seemly interval, to offer the full pardon and a Parliament if he was incapable of getting a better deal for his king. Had the talks gone ahead as intended, twenty-four hours earlier, there is no telling how they would have proceeded, with Howard having only an approximate idea, much of which would have been based on guesswork, of what Henry was prepared to accept. As it was, he could parley with a certain vision of the boundaries within which he was permitted to speak for the Crown. Armed with this new confidence, he and his counsellors received their visitors. The forty delegates were led into the room by Aske, who described what happened next in the following terms: on behalf of them all he made there 'three low obeisances and then, kneeling on their knees, all did humbly require of the said lords to have the King's most merciful, liberal and free pardon, for any [of] their offences committed or down against his Highness or laws, with his Grace's high and benign favour to them to be showed ...'

The debate that followed was a detailed discussion of the Twenty-Four Articles, with Howard answering each clause point by point. He was able to cite Henry's circular to the bishops and, as he expected, it went some way towards mollifying the Pilgrim anxieties on the religious issues: Darcy subsequently told the Archbishop of York that in these answers 'all true Catholics may joy'. Matters not covered in the King's circular, it was agreed, could be settled by Act of Parliament – and Howard, disobeying instructions to play his last cards close to his chest for the moment, made it obvious that he was speaking of the free legislature for which the Pilgrims had campaigned. Only one religious matter stood between the two parties and general agreement: the suppression of the monasteries. The Pilgrims were adamant that the monasteries should remain untouched until the new Parliament had adjudicated upon their future; there was no moving them on that one, and so it was left on the table as a matter to be taken up again later, the two sides agreeing on an interim and face-saving compromise. Accordingly, religious superiors must submit to the royal commissioners, whereupon the King would graciously restore their monasteries for the time being.

Unresolved, too, were many other demands, covering everything from the constitutional reforms sought by the Pilgrims to their wide range of economic grievances. No serious discussion therefore took place in Doncaster about the Princess Mary's position, while impasse was reached on the date and location of the new Parliament, the Pilgrims being just as reluctant to wait another nine months before it was summoned as Henry was determined to dictate the terms of a deal he was being forced to concede. The matter of increased Parliamentary representation for Yorkshire was batted back and forth between the two delegations but it, too, was left hanging in the air. Howard also dangled the prospect of impeaching Cromwell, Audley and Riche as an appropriate form of punishment and there can be little doubt that he was perfectly genuine in wishing thus to dispose of his greatest enemy, though whether he believed it to be a realistic proposition is another matter. Certainly, he could be in no doubt at all that, whatever was negotiated, Henry was immovable in his insistence that the already suppressed monasteries and all that accrued from them were his to have and to hold in perpetuity; this was the minimum that his notion of honour – not to mention his appetite for wealth – demanded.

When Wednesday's deliberations came to an end, Aske and his companions returned to their Franciscan retreat, to report progress to the rest of the 300 stationed on the island. Being informed by the negotiators that they would thereby gain the free pardon, the assurance of a new Parliament and the holding operation on the monasteries, these agreed to the deal that had been struck with the Duke of Norfolk and his colleagues. That night, therefore, Aske rode back to Pontefract, to lay the terms before everybody waiting there. He spoke to the leaders first and then, on Thursday morning, he sent the bellman round the town to call all the commons together at the market cross to hear the news from Doncaster. So it was before a vast audience that the chief captain began to speak. According to his account later on, when he had finished, 'the said commons were very joyous thereof, and gave a great shout in receiving of the same'. The joy, however, certainly Aske's own interpretation of it, was a little premature. But with this supposed affirmation of the agreement ringing in his ears, he set off straight away back to

Doncaster to tell Howard the good news from his side of the argument.

He was beginning to inform the Duke of what had happened, when a note arrived from Lord Lumley to say that all had not gone quite as well as he might have supposed. For the moment Aske galloped out of sight from Pontefract market place, the commons there started asking some big questions about what had been put to them. The old suspicions, in other words, were bubbling to the surface again and the leading commons present, most notably John Hallam, who was supported by Robert Pulleyn from the gentry, were inciting them to light the beacons and get Yorkshire stirred up for another campaign unless they could see the pardon bearing the King's seal, have the promise of full protection of the monasteries down in black and white and be assured that the Parliament, *their* Parliament, would be held in York and nowhere else that the King might find more convenient. The atmosphere became so heated that Marmaduke Neville thought it quite possible he and the other gentlemen might have a fight on their hands. The Duke of Norfolk certainly believed that things had reached a stage at which the hostility of the commons flared up whenever they saw two gentlemen conversing in private.

Understandably, there was dismay in Doncaster when the report of this dissidence came in. But both sides at the Carmelite friary agreed that Aske must return without delay and use all his skill as an advocate to set the fears of the commons at rest. So off he went again, back the way he had come. We have, alas, only Aske's own explanation, written to satisfy the King's curiosity some weeks later, of how this hitch in proceedings was then overcome, and it is distinctly unenlightening, merely telling how, that same night, he 'so persuaded the said commons that they were all contented to abide the said order at Doncaster, favourable, without any denial'. Whatever it was he said, and whatever the degree of Hallam's and Pulleyn's acquiescence in the updated version of the deal, this time it held as far as the commons in general were concerned. Aske sent word to Howard that the pardon under the King's seal should be conveyed to Pontefract as soon as possible. His old friend Lancaster Herald had, in fact, just arrived with it, and brought it up from Doncaster that very same night. On Friday morning the Herald, Aske and the 300 representatives who had accompanied him to the talks, rode to the top of St Thomas's Hill, just outside the town, and there Thomas Miller read the pardon to the multitude assembled below them on its slopes. Again, the chronicle lacks a decent contemporary description of how those 3000 or more insurgents behaved when the precious document was recited from the hill; after all, it quite possibly meant the difference between life and death for at least ten of them, maybe even more. But, again, there is nothing but the blank and briefest information that the crowd 'received the King's most merciful pardon, and so departed to their houses and countries, and after, the said lords and knights, by the commandment of the said Aske, repaired again to Doncaster...'

Where a number of fine details, relatively small matters left over from Wednesday, were worked out after the Duke had produced a list of Henry's own questions and quibbles. Howard wanted to know how the King's rents were to be collected in Yorkshire and was told that they already awaited him. He wanted to know when the ship captured in Scarborough three weeks earlier, together with its artillery and other weapons, its crew, Edward Waters himself and the money taken at the seizure, were going to be returned to the Crown, and was told that everything was ready for delivery apart from the outstanding money, which had unfortunately been divided up and spent. Aske could have added that, since his capture, Waters had been comfortably accommodated in a proper room, furnished with a feather bed, and with a servant at his beck and call; that he had, in other words, been treated like a gentleman. Darcy might have said that he personally was reluctant to hand over anything taken at Scarborough unless he had an assurance that the Lincolnshire rebels would be included in the general pardon as well: he wrote to Charles Brandon a week later to say that, as far as he was concerned, there would be no ship unless this was done.

Some other trifling things were settled before the meeting came to an end dramatically. For, with all the loose ends tied up, Aske went on his knees and begged everyone present to understand that he wished to be relieved of the Pilgrim leadership and no longer wanted to be known as Captain. His companions assented to this –

again, we have no means of knowing with what degree of enthu-siasm – whereupon Aske tore from his tunic the badge of the Five Wounds, which he had worn ever since Darcy gave it to him after the surrender of Pontefract Castle. Everyone else wearing the badge did likewise, 'saying all these words – We will all wear no badge nor sign but the badge of our sovereign lord.' Howard immediately made out an authorisation for the King's farmers to enter the monastic lands, in accordance with the first part of the face-saving agreement on the suppressions.[5] Then the meeting broke up, the delegates from Pontefract dispersed and Robert Aske went home to his brother John's manor house in Aughton. The Pilgrimage of Grace, it seemed, was over. And, though the rebels could not yet be certain that everything they wanted would be delivered, they had been promised enough to cost the Crown a great deal in prestige and in the King's own self-esteem. As news of the settlement spread across England, every one of Henry's sub-jects would well understand how much he had been humiliated, by a handful of noblemen and gentry, and host upon host of quite ordinary people.

---

5 The King's farmer was a leaseholder who paid a fixed rent to the Crown, in exchange for permission to take all the revenues (which might be variable) that he could extract from a monastic or other property. His profit, therefore, to some extent depended on his powers of extortion.

A SMOULDERING FIRE

Henry was very angry at the latest turn of events. His first impulse on hearing the news from Doncaster was to compose a stinging letter to Sir William Fitzwilliam and to another of his commanders, Sir John Russell, both of whom had been in the Duke of Norfolk's negotiating team. It is significant of his suspicions about the Duke's enthusiasm for the job he had been given that the King wrote to them and not to him to demand a detailed account of what had happened at the talks: Thomas Cromwell was not alone in his appetite for potentially incriminating evidence, wherever it could be found. In writing to Fitzwilliam and Russell, Henry denounced the ambivalent arrangement that had been made in his name to safeguard the religious houses for the time being and declared that under no circumstances whatsoever would he relinquish his claim to the monasteries: 'In that point touching the abbeys, we shall never consent to their desires.' He was even more wrathful and astonished that the negotiators had not managed to preserve that part of his honour which mattered to him most of all, the part that required the punishment of those who had offended him. This letter, in fact, was never despatched from court, for reasons on which we can only speculate. It may well be that someone in the King's Council – perhaps Cromwell himself – had advised him that there were subtler ways of obtaining what he desired than blasting away at subordinates when things had not gone quite according to plan.

Within a few days a memorandum was circulating among those closest to the King, reviewing the situation they were now faced with and ways of resolving it to the entire satisfaction of His Majesty. It included an ominous passage to the effect that, though Henry would treat the northerners with goodness, clemency, wisdom and affability, 'his grace shall also by little and little find out the root of the matter'. And then the King could act accordingly, in whatever way he chose. People whose possessions had been taken from them by the rebels would provide one way of gratifying His Majesty, by suing the insurgents for the recovery of their goods, 'so that some of them shall yet come to punishment and the beginners of the rebellion do better appear'. The problem was to be resolved and the solution was to be achieved by stealth, not direct assault. At the same time, dispositions were made for rapid reaction this time, should further trouble break out. Most notably, Howard was to return to Yorkshire with 200 troops, Fitzwilliam was to occupy Pontefract Castle with fifty men, Sir Ralph Evers to have 100 at Scarborough, and young Sir Ralph Ellerker enough manpower to garrison Hull effectively. Charles Brandon was to return to his duties in Lincolnshire and the Earl of Shrewsbury to muster forces that could move at very short notice. The gentry of Lincolnshire and Cheshire were also to be readied for swift action if need be.

The royal proclamation was taken north for announcement in the traditional fashion. Lancaster Herald was sent to the North-east, Thomas Miller's commission being to read the document in all the principal communities, starting with York and finishing in Berwick-on-Tweed. Meanwhile, Clarencieux Herald, Thomas Hawley, was to begin his assignment in Wakefield and work his way up to Carlisle, then come down again to Lancaster. It was to be a laborious business for both of them, Hawley reaching the West Riding on 12 December and not completing his itinerary until the day after Christmas, which was when Miller, too, arrived at his own terminus. Charles Brandon's instinct in delaying his response to Henry's original instructions in proclaiming amnesty had been sound, for his original brief had been modified. His responsibility for disseminating the pardon was now limited to Hull, Beverley and the rest of the East Riding. Issued under the King's seal at Richmond on 9 December, in the twenty-eighth year of Henry's reign, the pardon was couched in familiar and florid terms. It berated all who had taken part in the insurrection, 'whereby was like to have ensued the utter ruin and destruction of those whole countries to the great comfort and advancement of your ancient enemies the Scots ... to the high displeasure of God, who straightly commandeth you to obey your sovereign lord and King in all things ...' It declared that His Highness 'is pleased that you and every of you [*sic*] from time to time shall and may have upon your suits to be made hereafter in the King's Chancery his said most gracious and free pardon' and the attachment of the King's seal to such precious documents would come free of charge. It required humble submissions to be made first to the Duke of Norfolk and other of the King's representatives before these gratuities would be made available, however. And it charged all who received the pardon never again to rise up against their sovereign but henceforth to conduct themselves as true and faithful subjects. The most important words of all were contained in an extremely long-winded sentence which came after the admonition about the Scottish threat, and which read as follows:

Nevertheless, the King's royal majesty, perceiving as well by the articles of your pretences sent to his highness, as also duly informed by credible reports that your said offences proceeded of ignorance and by occasion of sundry false tales never minded nor intended by his highness or any of his council but most craftily contrived and most spitefully set abroad amongst you by certain malicious and seditious persons: thereupon his highness, inclined to extend his most gracious pity and mercy towards you, having the chief charge of you under God both of your souls and bodies, and desiring rather the preservation of the same and your reconciliation by his merciful means than by the order and rigour of justice to punish you according to your demerits, of his inestimable goodness, benignity, mercy and pity, and at your most humble petitions and submissions made unto his highness, is contented to give and grant, and by this present proclamation doth give and grant, unto you all and to all and every your confederates where so ever they dwell, of what estate, degree or condition so ever you or they be, or by what name or names so ever they or

you be or may be called, his general and free pardon for all
manner treasons, rebellions, insurrections, misprisions of treasons, murders, robberies, felonies and all accessories of the
same and of every of them, unlawful assemblies, unlawful
conventicles, unlawful speaking of words, confederacies, con-
spiracies, riots, routs and all other trespasses, offences and contempts done and committed by you or any of you against the
King's majesty, his crown or dignity royal within and from
the time of the beginning of the said rebellion whensoever it
was until the present day of proclaiming of this proclamation,
and of all pains, judgements and executions of death and all
other penalties, fines and forfeitures of lands, tenements,
hereditaments, goods or chattels the King's said highness of his
special grace and mere motion by these presents giveth to such
as you as have or should have forfeited or lost the same by
occasion of the premisses [*sic*] or any of them.

On the face of things, there could scarcely have been a more
comprehensive wiping clean of the slate than this. It can be seen
as a massive climb-down from Henry's stance before the negotiations at Doncaster began, a total withdrawal from all the domineering positions he had previously and so publicly held.
Doubtless it was seen as such by a majority of Englishmen. And
yet, from where the rebels stood, there was a serious flaw in this
great act of clemency, in spite of the fact that they appeared to
have secured a considerable victory. For none of the terms
agreed upon with the Duke of Norfolk had been put in writing:
they had nothing tangible to show for their endeavours – no
promise of a Parliament, no deal about the monasteries, none of
the other matters which Howard had led them to believe would
be agreeably settled later on. They had only his word for it that
there would be a free Parliament which would presently adjudicate upon the most important things. Once again, the Pilgrims
had put themselves at the mercy of the Duke's integrity and of
their king's very distinctive notion of honour.

Indeed, the clemency was more an undertaking that a pardon
was available than it was itself a pardon which became fully valid
simply by being announced. For there was a condition attached to
it: namely, that each individual had to sue for his pardon in the

King's court after submitting to the Duke or any of Howard's representatives and pledging his unqualified loyalty to the Crown in future. Few commoners had the time or the substance (or, indeed, as often as not, the sophistication) to engage in such legal matters, which were settled in London. Only the upper classes were equipped to take advantage of the offer. This vital caveat in the King's proclamation could not, of course, have been foreseen by anyone and it would have come as news when it was publicly declared. But it is very hard to understand how the Pilgrim negotiators had allowed themselves to be outmanoeuvred in another important respect, by failing to get everything that mattered to them down in black and white. They were going to have to wait until the Duke of Norfolk returned to the North with the King's authorisation for the limited concessions he had made, for all the hints he had dropped, without first obtaining Henry's approval.

It has lately been suggested that the gentry of the North, imitating their counterparts in Lincolnshire, began to distance themselves from the commons in December and the New Year, having been far less concerned with securing the concessions the Pilgrimage had campaigned for than with clearing their own names in the eyes of the Crown; and this has a certain appeal in view of some subsequent events. For, when the Duke of Norfolk and his entourage headed south again after the talks were over, a number of gentlemen who had associated themselves with the revolt began to follow in his wake, as well as others who had managed to avoid its stain. Sir Ralph Ellerker was soon among those who went down to make their peace with the King or to improve their reputations for loyalty at court, as was Robert Bowes, Darcy's eldest son Sir George, the Earl of Westmorland, who had sworn the Pilgrim oath before sending his adolescent son to represent him at the taking of Pontefract, and Sir Oswald Wilstrop, who had forced an unwilling Abbot of St Mary's to lead the Pilgrims into the surrendered York behind his most expensive cross and who was subsequently a member of the rebel council that had done the planning for Doncaster. Another member of that council, Marmaduke Neville, a younger brother of Lord Latimer, went south at about the same time as the Duke, after having asked if he might do so and been told that no permission was required. This was not quite true, as Latimer subsequently discovered when he set out for London and was turned back at the King's express command.

The end of Neville's journey was to be much more wretched, however, for in his euphoria at the great crisis being over, he forgot the first rule of survival in Cromwell's time, which was to be very careful what you said in public. First in King's Lynn, later in Colchester, he spoke enthusiastically of what had been accomplished by the Pilgrimage, of how the monasteries had been saved and how a free Parliament would soon solve everything else. But his biggest mistake was to reply to a mild taunt about traitors with a pointed remark about heretics, in the hearing of some justices of the peace, who had him arrested and sent to the Tower, from which he never emerged.

More cautious men put out feelers towards their friends and acquaintances at court in letters rather than by riding south optimistically. Darcy wrote to Talbot, to Howard and to Fitzwilliam, and began the procedures with which to sue for his pardon, which was eventually issued on 18 January. Even Edward Lee, leaving nothing to chance in spite of a sermon which must have commended itself to the King, wrote directly to Cromwell the day Robert Aske and the others removed their badges in front of Howard and his friends. 'There is now some hope of quiet again,' the Archbishop said. 'Very sorry I am to see them so bent against you ... if I could have foreseen that such an office should have fallen on my head, I had rather been your priest than a Bishop ...' The office he referred to was the collection of the clerical tax known as the tenth which, he protested, 'the most part of the year occupieth me, when I should be occupied with better things'. He counselled Cromwell that the collection, which was due about Christmas, might be better postponed, lest it inflamed some still smouldering embers of the rebellion. Within the week, he was writing an ingratiating letter to Darcy, protesting at his sermon having been misrepresented by some. 'I trust you have a better opinion of me than to think that I would say anything in that place but what I know to be true ... When I came into the pulpit I came into it indifferent to live or die.'

As soon as Robert Aske finished his work at Doncaster, he helped to supervise the arrival of the King's farmers at the Augustinian priories of Haltemprice and North Ferriby. He thus kept his bargain with Howard over the monasteries, even though this was extremely unpopular with the commons, who believed that Leonard Beckwith had looted these East Riding houses the moment they were suppressed. Then something totally unexpected – indeed, highly improbable – happened to Aske. December was at its halfway stage when Henry sent Peter Mewtas, the man who had brought the guns up to Doncaster bridge when a pitched battle there was a likelihood, to Aughton with a message for the newly retired leader. It was to the effect that the King had 'conceived a great desire to speak with him and therefore commands him to come with diligence ... and trusts that Aske at his access will, by his plainness and frankness, deserve reward'. Aske was invited to court, then, but his visit was to be made in secrecy 'making no man privy thereunto'. Mewtas also handed him a safe conduct, which would protect him until Twelfth Night on 6 January. Having fallen into a sly man's trap before now, Aske was sufficiently cautious about Henry's intentions to seek Darcy's advice, while making it clear that he intended to go with proper precautions and begging his friend to make sure that nothing untoward happened in the North while he was away. It was subsequently alleged that Old Tom told him to take six servants with him, dropping one off in Lincoln, another in Huntingdon and a third in Ware, the idea being that these men would be in a position to relay a message at speed back to Templehirst, where some sort of response could be started if Henry were base enough to tear up the safe conduct, putting Aske at the mercy of the King's vindictive temperament.

There is probably a grain of truth in this story, which was put about by Darcy's steward, though it is as well to remember that its details are unconfirmed. It has been suggested that it may have originated in a Darcy jest, which was simply made as an encouragement, a reminder that while the younger man was at court he would not be forgotten at home. Nevertheless, when Aske rode off to London soon after Mewtas had delivered his message, he was accompanied by six of the Aughton retainers. He reached the capital just before Christmas, which Henry proposed to keep at Greenwich with his new, but as yet uncrowned, Queen Jane Seymour. They had been forced to travel downstream by land on 22 December, instead of by water as intended, because that bitter winter of 1536–7 was already so cold that the Thames's upper and middle reaches had frozen over. The royal couple made their progress, therefore, through streets that were richly decorated with textiles, between ranks of cheering citizens, and priests upholding crosses, and thurifers swinging censers, which sweetened the air with the fumes of incense. 'Such a sight,' it was recorded, 'has not been seen since the Emperor was here…It rejoiced every man wondrously.' The King had taken all possible precautions against his southern subjects knowing exactly what had been achieved by those in the North. He was determined to convey an impression of exuberant and unassailable sovereignty.

He even let it be known that he intended to make a much more impressive progress through the North in the New Year; nay, that his new queen Jane would be crowned in York Minster as a special mark of the sovereign's gracious forgiveness of recent errors in the region. Most of those who had been in error optimistically assumed that this was to be the moment when the King would also open the northern Parliament they longed for, though Henry very carefully avoided committing himself to any such thing. The progress and the northern coronation were, in fact, cancelled because of the queen's pregnancy; and thereafter both progress and coronation were overtaken by other events. But preparations had reached the stage where the city's corporation was making lists of all the spare beds and stabling that would be needed for the King's entourage and for the vast number of other visitors expected in York on this unique occasion. They would not be required until 1541, four years after Jane Seymour's death in childbirth, when the King went forth with 5000 horsemen, a thousand foot soldiers and much artillery in order to impress the natives; whose apologies for surrendering York to Robert Aske were offered to the King by nearly 200 principal citizens, abjectly, upon their knees. Archbishop Lee and his diocesan clergy had already made their own submissions to the monarch the day before in Pontefract, with a most welcome gift of £600 to the royal coffers.

Aske was received graciously at court in December 1536 and lodged there comfortably, according to Antonio Guaras. He was a Spaniard who dwelt in England when Edward VI was briefly on the throne and he then put together a chronicle of Henry's reign, obviously from information supplied to him by people who had lived through those years. He is therefore as useful a reporter as – and a little more unreliable than – the imperial ambassador Eugene Chapuys, who was at least in the country during these events; but his account of that Christmas encounter at Greenwich is the most comprehensive we have. Guaras says that as soon as Aske entered the room where the King awaited him, Henry stood up and threw his arms round the Yorkshireman and declared, 'Be ye welcome, my good Aske; it is my wish that here, before my Council, you ask what you desire and I will grant it.' To which Aske replied, 'Sir, your Majesty allows yourself to be governed by a tyrant named Cromwell. Everyone knows if it had not been for him the seven thousand poor priests I have in my company would not be ruined wanderers as they are now. They must have enough to live upon, for they have no handicraft.' Then the King 'with a smiling face' took a great gold chain that he wore and transferred it to Aske's neck, saying, 'I promise thee, thou art wiser than anyone thinks, and from this day forward I make thee one of my Council.' He told someone to make sure his guest was given £1000, a sum that would recur every year as long as he lived. Henry's final words were that Aske should return to the North, get his people to disperse and go home (they already had, of course), and then he should come back to court and join the King's Council. Meanwhile, the priests in the arch-diocese of York whom Aske had championed would be given an allowance of £10 a year to live on, and each parish would support two of them at the same time. 'When Aske saw the good tidings he had to take back he determined to return at once...' and so on. Henry also assured his guest that he intended to hold a Parliament in York and that he would have his new Queen crowned in the city.

A great deal of this, especially the dialogue, is obviously bunkum: it reads quite remarkably like the script in a modern pantomime. It is not credible that even a sturdy northern lawyer who had captained an armed rebellion resolutely would have summoned the courage to denounce Cromwell so crudely to his patron's face, although he might well be prepared to convey the essential message in some quieter way. It is most unlikely, too, that Henry could have convinced someone of Aske's intelligence that he was about to be incorporated into the higher reaches of the Crown's apparatus after what he had just done; very doubtful that the King would have made the attempt, even as an extravagant blandishment. But the Spaniard's chronicle should not be dismissed completely and may well have faithfully represented a contrived mood in the encounter between Henry and the biggest thorn in his flesh. The gift of money may have been somebody's fabrication, to make a good story even better, but there is some small corroborative evidence that Aske was at least given 'a jacket of crimson silk' by the King.

Henry's other requirement was that, while at Greenwich, Aske should compose for him a full narrative account of the Pilgrimage. This the visitor did, eventually producing a long memoir which must have taken two or three days to complete. It has been described as 'the first and best history of the Pilgrimage', and it is also an oddity in that it refers to its author throughout in the third person. Entitled *The manner of the taking of Robert Aske in Lincolnshire and the use of the same Robert unto his passage from York*, it begins, 'First, the same Robert Aske sayeth that he, being accompanied with his two brothers John and Christopher Aske, in the house of his brother-in-law William Ellerker in Yorkswold, had appointed to meet on hunting with Sir Ralph Ellerker, the younger, knight, at the fox.' Thereafter the writer's references are occasionally to 'Robert' or to 'Aske' but much more often than not to 'the said Aske'. It is as though the piece was being dictated to someone else, and two copies were indeed made of the original, which went to the King himself. The memoir records the events of October and November 1536 in enough detail for a reader to see what was happening to its author almost day by day, and who else was involved in his various encounters and communications, but it gives only the sketchiest idea of what Aske was thinking all that time.

Thus, at his first meeting with the Lincolnshire rebels, as a result of which he became captain of their Axholme company, he describes the appearance of the Caistor leader George Hudswell ('having a black coat and a grey beard') and recounts their exchange on the subject of oaths, but he is very blank about why he capitulated so quickly to their demands. Was it from fear, which would be perfectly understandable, or sympathy, or a sudden urge simply to find out what was going on that week in Lincolnshire? But he tells us only that Hudswell declared, '"Ye shall take this oath or else not pass undangered." And so the said Aske, as enforced, was contented to be sworn'; which can be read as both a defence and an incrimination at one and the same time. There are then several almost inconsequential sentences before he is back across the Humber where, 'having knowledge that he was taken in Lincolnshire and a leader there' the men of Howden received his instructions about the ringing of the bells. Scarcely ever does he plead extenuating circumstances for any of his unlawful acts; there is merely a hint of that when he says that, on first hearing of the Lincolnshire rising from the ferryman taking him across the Humber, 'the same Robert could not conveniently return, nor the tide of the water would not conveniently so serve him for that purpose'. And only once does he deny something that had or might have been attributed to him, when he was stuck on the wrong side of the flooding Trent for two days, 'and during that time, there was a letter forged in the name of the said Aske to the town of Beverley, which letter the said Aske utterly denieth to be his deed or consent'. Otherwise, he does not even make any attempt to minimise his actions or his statements in such serious circumstances as his capture of Pontefract Castle, and his subsequent condemnation of the nobility and their version of loyalty to the Crown. He is not boasting about his behaviour at such times, he is simply describing it.

There are things that we should like to know, quite apart from his state of mind, which are missing from the narrative: the reason why he was not in the Pilgrim delegation that first treated with the Duke of Norfolk in Doncaster, for example. But on the whole, Aske's memoir reads like the report of certain events, told emphatically from where he himself was standing in the middle of them, by an essentially truthful man whose greatest fault was perhaps his almost adolescent *naïveté*. It does not read, as has recently been suggested, like a form of self-promotion by someone anxious to curry favour with the King. For, in the semi-detached act of writing rather than speaking, Aske makes no bones at all about where the responsibility for the Pilgrimage lies: it is with 'the Lord Cromwell, being reputed the destroyer of the commonwealth ... and also ... certain bishops of the new learning, reputing themselves and their sect as heretics and the great causers of this late commotion; and also against the Lord Chancellor, for so general a granting of injunctions...' These were the King's own appointments and his Majesty was the begetter of the notorious sect. Aske could not have been more offensive without bluntly calling Henry himself a heretic too.

He ends with an attachment to the narrative, *A brief showing whereby his Grace may obtain the hearts of his subjects in the north parts, and that before the coming down of the Duke of Norfolk*. This advises the sovereign that there should be free elections of knights of the shire and burgesses, that the King should confirm his pardon and acknowledge the loyalty of his northern subjects, that when the Duke returned to the North he should declare where and when the new Parliament would sit, that a number of places which for a long time had not enjoyed parliamentary representation should have it restored. Is it conceivable (even if we accept what Antonio Guaras alleged in his Spanish Chronicle) that the author of this narrative was addressing the monarch as though he believed himself already to be a well-established member of the King's Council? Was Robert Aske really so inflated with hubris? Or was he, like Reginald Pole before him, innocently taking the King at his word when Henry asked for an honest account of things as he saw them? He may have been, probably was, highly flattered, but that is not the same thing as toadying.

While Aske was in London, the dark sounds of the commons going their own way could be heard rumbling ever louder in the North. Within days of the Doncaster agreement being brokered, it had become clear that, whatever the Pilgrim leadership made of the negotiated settlement, the rank and file of the rebellion were deeply dissatisfied with it. And even some of the men higher up the chain of command were prepared to defy the arrangement made over the monasteries. One such was Dr John Dakyn, rector of Kirkby Ravensworth in the North Riding, whose conversion to the rebellion is a paradigm of the experience that many men of his social standing went through in the back end of 1536. His first impulse on hearing that Aske was stirring trouble in the east of the county was to put himself out of harm's way, but he had been menaced and pressed into taking the oath by 500 rebels and thereafter became part of the insurgent hierarchy, first at Jervaulx

Abbey, where the Richmondshire men established a secretariat after Adam Sedbar joined the revolt, later as Richmond representative at the council in York; and he was one of the clerics who made their depositions at the conclave in Pontefract. In some ways he was ambivalent in his reaction to Henry's religious reforms but one thing he totally rejected was the suppression of the monasteries, as might be expected of someone who had once been a Benedictine monk, though his objection was partly based upon the loss to a local economy that the dispersal of a community could and usually did have.

Apart from his parochial office, Dakyn was also the Archdeacon of Richmond's vicar-general, and in this capacity he supervised one of the most extensive ecclesiastical districts in England, which stretched out of Yorkshire into both Lancashire and Cumberland. It was as vicar-general that he was informed of the situation at Cartmel and Conishead, whose monks had been restored by the commons, except for the Prior of Cartmel, who had declined the opportunity to go home. Only two days after the submission of Aske and his colleagues, Dakyn wrote to these communities, instructing them to stay where they were until the new Parliament reviewed their case; which was not quite what the Doncaster agreement had just sanctioned. His adjudication was also sought by the abbeys at Easby and Coverham, and there again he told the monks effectively to ignore the first part of the temporary provision for the religious houses.

Yet he did not defy the government on all matters concerning the Church. December also saw Dakyn admonishing the priest of Romaldkirk, in Teesdale, one of those northern clerics who had not shrunk from donning harness and marching like a soldier alongside his secular comrades in arms. This William Tristram was evidently still in so belligerent a mood after Doncaster that Dakyn not only told him that harness and bill did not go well with a clergyman's calling, but that he should stop trying 'to get the favour of the parishioners' by acting as though he were something other than a simple man of God. That the parishioners of Romaldkirk rather liked the idea of a soldier-priest saying their masses is clear from the fact that Dakyn thought it necessary to preach a sermon in the parish on New Year's Eve, in which he not only told them to calm down and be content, but to return various things that had been stolen from the Bishop of Durham when his palace was ransacked by rebels from the Palatinate during the early days of the Pilgrimage. He nearly provoked a riot.

For by then the commons everywhere were increasingly indignant at what had been agreed in their name. Attacks were being made on messengers travelling in the King's name. The first of these took place on the very day the pardon was announced, when Henry Alonby, bearing a communication from Henry Clifford's son in Carlisle to various of the local gentry, instructing them to be watchful for any more unrest, was seized by some of the commons and locked up in Cockermouth Castle. He appears to have been released unharmed in due course, but his captors escaped punishment only because there was so much tension in Cumberland that it was thought a counter-strike against them might provoke a fresh rising. Cumberland's response, a few weeks later, was to set about another messenger, Robert Wetley, who happened to be the detested Dr Legh's servant but who on this occasion was thought to be bringing letters of reassurance and gratitude from the Crown to the local gentry. He was seized by a mob of 500 men and taken to Egremont before being exposed to mockery and threats in Cockermouth market place, where a great pantomime of searching him for the correspondence was enacted, only to reveal that the letters were from his employer to various people and said nothing at all about the King or the commons. Nevertheless, there were calls for his execution on the spot and he was only spared that by the intervention of a gentleman who was still well thought of by the local commons, and who pro-posed that instead he should be tried publicly in the market place the following week. The trial did take place, but no more was heard of the hapless man after it, or of the verdict that was reached by twenty-four jurors.

Thomas Miller, Lancaster Herald himself, was roughed up while he was wending his way through north-eastern England, proclaiming the pardon at regular intervals. He had reached his final destination in Berwick so confident that his mission had been successful that he sent a breezy message back to London, informing his masters how the people up there were extremely sorry for what they had done and were 'right joyous' at the prospect of the Duke of Norfolk arriving later to 'do justice to the poor'. Miller spoke a little too soon, however. Unfortunately for him, it was necessary to return the way he had come and some of the commons were awaiting him when he got back to Durham. It seems that his proclamation there had differed somewhat from the version he announced in Newcastle – possibly an impromptu piece of editing by an over-zealous man, anxious to make the message more acceptable to a potentially hostile crowd – and this had been spotted when people from the neighbouring towns compared notes. On entering Durham a second time, therefore, Miller was 'ungodly handled and did not escape without danger', saving himself only by spurring his horse into a rapid getaway.

Trouble was brewing again down in Craven, where the Earl of Cumberland was informed that a fresh bill of incitement had been attached to the church door at Gargrave, which was followed by others at Rylstone, Lynton and Burnsall. Each one of them urged all parishioners in that part of the West Riding to assemble at Rylstone on 12 December for the purpose of killing all the deer in Skipton Forest, which belonged to Clifford. The instructions were very detailed: the local clergy, working with their parish constables, were to order every household to supply one able-bodied man, who was to muster at nine o'clock that Tuesday morning, which meant that a considerable force of the commons were being summoned to engage in a mass slaughter across an area which included not only the immediate hinterland of Skipton itself, but the westernmost parts of Nidderdale and the length of Langstrothdale to the north. This can be seen as no more than an indirect attack on the government and its reaction to the Pilgrimage, the immediate target of Craven anger being Clifford and his autocracy as a landowner: disputes about free-ranging deer, which destroyed everybody's crops if they got the chance, consumed good pasture and ring-barked the trees on common land, went back a long way in the area, and men had been held in Skipton Castle's dungeons before now for having even a tenuous connection with acts which were a cross between poaching and lawful self-protection.

On this occasion Clifford managed to have 200 of the commons dispersed at Rylstone by his retainers, who in his name promised various concessions, but a couple of the constables were seized in order to find out the names of those responsible for the bills, the mass of commons evidently doing nothing at all to assist these unfortunates, who remained in captivity until well into the New Year. And although this may be regarded as no more than an essentially local dispute, the fact is that Clifford's first reaction was to inform the King, who replied that the prisoners should be held until further notice, and that the Earl was 'to take all malefactors'. It is an indication of how much anger was still smouldering in Craven, in spite of the pacification, that Clifford's son, who had come down from Carlisle to spend Christmas at home, found himself fleeing from the commons when they objected to his presence at mass in Giggleswick.

The monks of Sawley were behind much of the bill-posting, though Clifford preferred to see in it the hand of 'certain gentlemen, some of them the King's servants', who had offended him in a number of land disputes. But his suspicions may well have extended to Nicholas Tempest, who was very close in his sympathy for Abbot Thomas Bolton and the other monks. They were in a high state of discontent in December, after being told by Aske to take their troubles to the preliminary meeting of Pilgrims in Pontefract. This seems to have provided them with little comfort, the agreement with Howard about the King's farmers even less, because they enquired after the conclusion at Doncaster what they should do until the York Parliament was summoned. Aske, replying to 'the special brethren in this our Pilgrimage of Grace for the commonwealth', told them that they must observe the provisions of the agreement and do nothing, 'behaving as religious persons should'.

About ten days later they heard of another communication, which this time Aske had sent just before leaving for London to Sir Stephen Hamerton, joint leader with Tempest of the Percy Fee rebels who had restored the monks at Sawley. It said that if and when the King's farmers arrived, the monks must leave their house in accordance with the Doncaster agreement. So unhappy were they with this further instruction that Abbot Bolton composed a letter to Sir Thomas Percy, who was both a Pilgrim captain and putative head of the family which had founded and endowed the monastery. This was taken to Prudhoe Castle, where Percy then was, by one of the abbey's servants, George

Shuttleworth, who was given ten shillings to cover his expenses on the way to Northumberland; and he spent some of it before he even left Sawley, at the inn just across the lane from the abbey gates, on refreshment to fortify himself for the long journey ahead. He also carried a token from the Abbot for Thomas Percy, a gold royal worth ten shillings, this particular coin being deliberately bent, which may have been meant to signify the abbey's plight, or monastic disillusionment with Robert Aske.

Percy was out hunting when Shuttleworth arrived four days later, so the messenger had to kick his heels until the next morning. The letter which he then handed to Sir Thomas was both a supplication and a prediction of more trouble unless something was done to help the Sawley community. It begged him 'to consider their present need' and told him that 'the whole country supports them in entering their house and is ready to extend the pilgrimage of Christ's Faith and the common wealth...' the commons being most willing 'to proceed in the said pilgrimage without any other delay or stay to be had or made to the contrary'. It referred to 'our most sinister back friend' Sir Arthur Darcy, who had acquired Sawley for gain from the Crown and would doubtless make his own deal with the King's farmers, for he 'yet intendeth to the uttermost of his power and diligence to put us to great inconvenience and destruction, if he may so obtain'. In short, it made it clear that the commons of Percy Fee were ready to rise again, implicitly at a word from the monks. The letter could be read as an incitement to further rebellion – and subsequently was, when the Duke of Norfolk returned to the North and, in her husband's absence, Lady Percy innocently handed it over with other papers. It helped to incriminate Percy who, in his reply to the Sawley messenger, had simply underlined Aske's instruction to the monks: that they should do nothing to resist the King's farmers when these came.

A curious encounter that took place before Shuttleworth left for Prudhoe adds to the suspicion that the letter was something more pointed than a general cry for help. For it was first taken to Sir Stephen Hamerton, who was hunting outside Settle, by Abbot Bolton's chaplain, Richard Estgate, one of only three monks who were privy to its contents, and he began to read it until he was curtly told that 'ye may do as ye list'. Before reading it, however,

Estgate offered Hamerton some woodland belonging to the abbey which Hamerton had tried to purchase a couple of years earlier; he offered it at no cost, as a goodwill gesture, in other words a bribe, which the knight carefully refused before telling the monk that he and his brethren must get on with things as they chose. The letter, and the events attending it, reinforce the belief that the Cistercians of Sawley certainly had much to do with the bills that were appearing on church doors at this time, even if they did not themselves compose the texts, though this cannot by any means be ruled out. Circumstantial evidence includes the fact that two of the churches involved, including Gargrave, were Sawley benefices, so that what happened in them would have been most unlikely without at least the abbey's tacit approval. The other church was at Tadcaster, outside York, where a bill similar to Gargrave's was tacked to the door just after George Shuttleworth had passed through the town on his way north. Was he conveying something else, as well as the letter for Thomas Percy?

The Sawley monks were, in fact, left in peace for a few more weeks, most probably because there was a very real threat not only that the men of Percy Fee would rush to their assistance again, but that the commons as far away as Kendal and Lonsdale, who had not been involved in the original rising to restore the monks, would also take up arms on their behalf; and, with only the troops under Charles Brandon's command still on active service, the government was not well placed to mount a counter-attack just yet. The Augustinians of Cartmel and Conishead priories, however, had the King's farmers to contend with some time before 19 December, when Clarencieux Herald arrived in the area with his royal proclamation and was asked to adjudicate in a dispute which had just broken out between the Cartmel monks and the leaseholders. The brethren had resisted the claimed entitlement of the farmers to both rents and corn, and the row had got to the stage where it could be said that there was 'like to have been murder between them about the same'. The man who offered that assessment was William Collins, wine merchant and bailiff of Kendal, who had been one of the leaders during the rising there. He had, in fact, been quietly inciting the monks to stand firm in their houses ever since Doncaster, telling them – as Dr Dakyn had already done – that this was in accordance with His Majesty's pleasure.

When Thomas Hawley turned up, two of the canons asked him to write an order which would authorise them to stay put until the Duke of Norfolk arrived some time in the New Year, when a conclusive adjudication would be made. They needed this authority in black and white, they said, so that they would have proof that they remained on the right side of the law. But the herald was in a hurry to get on with his King's commission, and simply gave a verbal opinion that the possession of lands and tithes should stay 'in like case as they were at the last meeting at Doncaster'. He then told Collins to write the order, in his capacity as bailiff of the Kendal barony, before continuing his journey to Carlisle. This Collins did, addressing the document to people in the neighbourhood as requested by the monks, who relied upon local goodwill to supply them with food and other necessities; such people obviously needed an assurance that they would not be breaking the law if they continued their donations. 'Neighbours of Cartmel,' wrote Collins, with all the weight that his office as bailiff could give him, 'so it is that the King's herald hath made proclamation here that every man, pain of high treason, should suffer everything, as farms, tithes and such other, to be in like stay and order concerning possessions as they were in time of the last meeting at Doncaster, except ye will of your charity help the brethren there somewhat towards their boards, till my lord of Norfolk come again and take further order therein.' In effect, this gave both the monks and the farmers a little of what they sought, by leaving the brethren in place and the farmers nominally in charge, with a heavy hint that the latter should take care of the community's needs for the time being.

There was also friction to the east, though this was a case of citizens in general refusing to pay the King's taxes, which were already in arrears because the rents due to the Crown at Michaelmas had not been collected, the Pilgrimage of Grace having got in the way. Because the Pilgrim leadership at Doncaster had, rashly perhaps, informed the Duke of Norfolk that the taxes were ready and waiting to be picked up, the great fiscal process was now launched throughout the North. In some places the tax collectors experienced no difficulty, Doncaster, Wakefield and Sheriff Hutton being among those that paid up promptly. But the officials drew a blank at Barnard Castle, where it was said that no one paid a penny of the money owed. The tenants instead asked that the process should be delayed for another twenty days, by which time January would be half gone, while those in the lordships of Richmond and Middleham, who also demurred, asked for almost another fortnight on top of that. And they were all granted the extensions, perhaps because the auditors, too, thought that this was a matter which could easily get out of hand if they pushed too hard, with little available to enforce their authority.

Edward Lee certainly thought along these lines, when the King ordered him to start collecting the clerical tenth at the end of the year, even though Lee had already warned Cromwell that this would be inadvisable. The Archbishop's distraught response to his sovereign's demand was to ask Lord Darcy for his opinion on what to do, and Darcy advised him to try the Earl of Shrewsbury instead, which the Primate did, Darcy meanwhile telling George Talbot that all sorts of trouble might break out north of Doncaster if the King insisted on the collection going ahead. Talbot forwarded both letters to court, with a covering note suggesting that the collection of the tenth should be delayed. At the same time he informed the Archbishop that he could not advise delay, but that he would get in touch the moment he heard that the King was prepared to wait. Which Henry was not in the least willing to do, though his brusque response was quickly overtaken by other events.

So, as 1536 began to turn the corner into another year, the tension in northern England was mounting again. Rumours were flying everywhere, including one that Robert Aske had been executed in London and, much less plausibly, that the Duke of Norfolk had been sent to the Tower for his failure at Doncaster, a story that was garnished with a further titbit: it was said that when the Duke's half-brother William was denied access to him, he was so angry and distraught that when 'he came along Chancery Lane he met with Richard Cromwell ... and took out his dagger and did stick him therewith, and turned him with his hand and so killed him' (on hearing this, crusty old Sir Robert Constable said it was a pity Howard hadn't killed young Cromwell's uncle instead). The rumours were not confined to the North, either: in London they were saying that the King was taxing baptisms, in Buckingham that the churches were to be demolished and all their valuables sold, while in Rochester people were being told that the Earl of Cumberland had turned against the King.

News had also started coming up to Yorkshire that sympathy for the Pilgrimage was growing in other parts of the country, that it had apparently been latent throughout the rebellion. Someone who arrived in the East Riding during Christmas week reported that people from Nottingham had told him that if the northerners had only pressed on south, they could have counted on them, too. The same messenger had needed his shoes repairing in London and the cobbler he went to near Smithfield had said, 'Because ye are a northern man ye shall pay but sixpence for your shoes, for ye have done very well there of late: and would to God ye had come to an end, for we were of the same mind that ye were.' Priests in Cambridgeshire, in Suffolk, at Windsor and at Stafford were all arrested in December for various offences, ranging from disseminating propaganda against Cromwell to denouncing the Ten Articles from the pulpit. More clergy repeated these and similar offences in the New Year, at Bristol and at Worcester, in Kent and in Oxfordshire, while in Oxford itself a scholar predicted that 'if the northern men should continue rebellious, his Grace would be in great danger of his life, or avoid his realm before the end of March'.

A little later in 1537 the Walsingham pilgrimage made by some Cornishmen at the end of October would at last have a political effect in the West Country. The seditious bill and the Pilgrimage's Five Articles which they picked up in Norfolk had been taken home, but their inflammatory sentiments had remained dormant until a couple of fishermen, mindful of the fact that the feast day of one of the great local patron saints had been proscribed under the new order, decided to make a stand against the abolition. They got someone to paint a banner for the parish of St Keverne, on which 'they would have first the picture of Christ with his wounds abroad and a banner in his hand, Our Lady on the one side holding her breast in her hand, St John à Baptist on the other side, the King's Grace and the Queen kneeling, and all the community kneeling, with scripture above their heads, making their petition to the picture of Christ that it would please the King's Grace that they might have their holidays'; that is, their holy days. In view of what by then was happening throughout northern England and also in London, this was an exceedingly brave as well as an exceptionally foolhardy act. No one could do that without incurring the worst sort of trouble and, while one of the men managed to evade arrest, the other was thrown into gaol; but he was never brought to trial, a court of Cornishmen subsequently declaring that they had no jurisdiction in cases of treason. Why the fisherman was not sent up to London for sentence and execution remains a mystery, but it may have been because solidarity was something more than a watchword in an extremity of the land which had always seen itself apart from the rest of England.

On New Year's Eve the tension finally exploded at Kendal parish church when Robert Applegarth, the curate there, refused a demand from his congregation that he should include in their prayers one for the Pope. Not only that, but they wanted the pontiff acknowledged as the head of the Universal Church. At the service were 300 people, including women as well as men, all clamouring for the priest's submission in the most violent way. William Collins, the Kendal bailiff, was also the object of their wrath, when he insisted on reading out the King's pardon in church. He was, in fact, in much greater danger than Applegarth, who was merely promised a ducking in the River Kent, which flowed past the building, unless he complied with these demands, whereas Collins was left in no doubt that he would be put to death unless the service was conducted in the old-fashioned way. And yet, as on so many other occasions in the previous three months, tremendous anger and vicious threats by the commons were suddenly pacified by soothing words from someone who wore even the most modest trappings of authority. On this occasion they appear to have been supplied by another clergyman, Nicholas Layburn, who had the additional status of brother to Sir James Layburn, acting steward of the barony. He suggested that the curate should carry on as he had been accustomed to for another month, leaving the matter to the Duke of Norfolk's adjudication when he came north. Remarkably, the congregation accepted this proposition and even allowed William Collins to get away, though he had to do so in such haste that he left the pardon behind.

Five days before this happened, on 26 December, a different sort of meeting had taken place that would lead to a new uprising and turmoil in the North which, this time, would bring great anguish with it as well. It involved the familiar figure of John Hallam, the principal firebrand in the East Riding, and William Nicholson, a small farmer from Holderness, who had been another of the petty captains in October and November. They met at Watton Priory, which Hallam by now regarded as his base for the planning of anything that would advance the rebel cause, and this he did with the full blessing of the resident Gilbertine community, who were as deeply hostile to the government as anyone in the religious life. The conversation between these two focused on the status of Hull and the potential threat it would represent if the government garrisoned it again. Having been in the hands of the Pilgrims since the third week in October, for most of that time under Sir Robert Constable's command, it had been relinquished into the hands of the mayor and town governors in the general dispersal that followed Doncaster. Neither Hallam nor Nicholson trusted the intentions of the civic leaders, and they agreed that 'Hull was false to the commons'. Among the rumours soon doing the rounds hereabouts was one that reckoned the Crown had already started to arm the port by bringing in ordnance from the sea, though the only shipping coming up the Humber at that stage was carrying the normal cargoes of trade. Nevertheless, the potential danger was manifest and the two conspirators decided that the only way to obviate it was by attacking Hull and taking control of it for a second time. Otherwise, not only would it be a government fortification that threatened a large area of Yorkshire and controlled all the traffic along its most important river, but a perfect refuge for gentry who wished to disentangle themselves from the commons once and for all – both Hallam and Nicholson were among those who now distrusted their erstwhile accomplices the most. They were also bent on revenge against those gentlemen who had never submitted to pressure from the commons in the autumn and who, they were determined, were not going to get away with non-cooperation a second time.

At Watton, they formulated only the notion of an aggressive move and considered how many men would be needed to achieve its aims. Nicholson said he could be sure of bringing between 200 and 300 commons from Holderness, and thought that if Hallam could produce another 100, that should be enough to pull the thing off. Four days later they met again in Beverley and enlarged upon this idea by deciding that they must also take Scarborough hostage and hold both towns until the Parliament sat in York and resolved all the rebel grievances. They were not interested at this stage in raising another huge army to do battle against the royal forces and then victoriously march down to London to confront the King; that was something that might have to be considered later on, but this was not the time. For the moment they only wanted the commons to take charge of two strategically important places and to hold these in pawn through a winter that was already so hard that a season of campaigning in the field was not to be thought of. And they were now clearer than they had been in Watton how this should be done. Rather than staging a full frontal attack on Hull which, like anywhere else of some size, had defensive walls that could only be breached at the cost of much blood, they would accomplish their objective by infiltration instead. A market day would be a perfect time for small groups of commons to mix unnoticed with the crowds that normally surged through the open gates of Hull to buy and sell things at that point in the week. No one would be aware of what was happening until it was too late to resist, until all the men mustered by Nicholson and Hallam were safely inside the walls. Then they would strike.

THE FATAL DIVISION

Robert Aske left London on 6 January, which was the day that his safe conduct from the King expired. By the 8th he was back in Aughton, where unwelcome news quickly followed him. It came in the form of a letter from Sir Marmaduke Constable, who belonged to the same East Riding clan as Sir Robert but had been one of the King's most devoted liegemen in the area, to the extent that he had fled to Lincolnshire to avoid submitting to the commons in the early days of the Pilgrimage in Yorkshire. Now he was back home at Everingham, near Market Weighton, anxiously watching the same commons stirring with anger again. He was doubtless feeling isolated, so many of the gentlemen who might have given him a sense of camaraderie, if not of security, having left the area in order to pay their respects at court, with others still setting off on the journey of humble submission.

On the other hand, Sir Thomas Percy, whose word carried more weight than anyone else's in the North-east, had retreated to his Northumbrian fastness and appeared to be wholly preoccupied with local affairs. In fact, he was busy dealing with the reivers of Tynedale and Redesdale, who had made everyone else's life a misery while Percy was otherwise engaged in the Pilgrimage; and to this end a muster of all Northumbrians was held at Morpeth on 17 January. But without the controlling leadership that Percy and the other absentees might have been able to exercise, as they had all the way to Doncaster, the commons were becoming answerable to no one but themselves, an extremely volatile and potentially dangerous mass who might easily wreck any chances of peacefully settling this dispute with the Crown. They were also becoming increasingly suspicious of the circumstances in which the Doncaster deal had been struck, as well as of the agreement's substance – or lack of it. The departure of so many leaders for the capital in the wake of what might turn out to be empty promises, led them to conclude that they were being left in the lurch, and even Aske himself was no longer exempt from this criticism. For every rumour that had him executed by a treacherous King, another reckoned that he was probably feathering his own nest at their expense. Why had he gone so secretly to see the King, telling no one but Lord Darcy that this was what he was about? Sir Marmaduke, however, reasoned that Aske was still the best hope of staying the commons from open rebellion again.

The letter that arrived at Aughton soon after Aske returned home explained what had happened locally while he was away, and it dwelt particularly on the danger that Sir Marmaduke foresaw in the activities of John Hallam. Constable did not know precisely what Hallam and Nicholson were up to, but he was aware that Beverley was becoming agitated at the rumour that the government was shipping guns up the Humber; which, in fact, it was not, the suspect vessel carrying nothing more hostile than a cargo of grain and wine. He doubted that he could prevent any fresh disturbance in the East Riding from bursting out into something much more aggressive and widespread, such as a march on Hull to seize the reported ordnance, probably led by the notoriously belligerent Hallam, and he besought Aske to use his much greater influence to pacify the hotheads.

The letter carried so much conviction that Aske promptly cancelled a planned visit to Templehirst next day, to tell Darcy of his experiences at court, and prepared to go to Beverley instead, sending a note to Hallam to meet him beforehand and alone. Aske clearly wanted to test the water before going in at the deep end in a town which, only three months earlier, he had roused to action and was now being asked to tranquillise. In fact, they did not meet until they got there independently, which meant that Aske did not quite know what to expect when he faced Hallam, the Twelve Men and a great number of other citizens. He did not know that, the day he got home, Hallam up at Watton was telling people that 'the gentlemen will deceive us, the commons, and the King's Grace intends to perform nothing of our desires and petitions, wherefore I think it best to take Hull and Scarborough ourselves betimes...'

Going into the meeting largely unprepared, therefore, Aske spoke words which might well be interpreted by his listeners as further proof that he had indeed been seduced by Henry's blandishments. 'The King's Highness,' he said, 'is good and gracious lord unto us, the commons all, and he hath granted us all our desires and petitions, and he will keep a Parliament shortly at York and there also, for the more favour and goodwill that he beareth to this country, he purposeth to have the Queen's Grace crowned.' After 'adding more good words on the King's behalf', he told his audience that the Duke of Norfolk would be arriving shortly 'and bring a better report unto them from the King's Grace under his Great Seal'. At this point he was interrupted by Hallam, who wanted to know 'How it happens, then, if this be true, that the tenths be gathered, for I hear say that my lord of York hath received a letter from the King's Grace for the gathering of the tenths or some other payment, whereas it was concluded at Doncaster that there should be no more payments gathered till the Parliament time'. Aske was genuinely unaware of Henry's instruction to the Archbishop and said so, adding that he imagined the King was only demanding money already collected and in Edward Lee's safekeeping.

Surprisingly, given the temper of the occasion, this explanation seems to have been accepted, Aske's powers of persuasion evidently being undiminished, whatever reservations some of the commons were beginning to have about him. The meeting apparently ended without acrimony and afterwards Aske, together with everyone else there, was invited to supper by the acting steward of Beverley, Robert Creke, and the Twelve Men. Before the meal started, Creke took the abrasive farmer aside and said to him, 'Mr Hallam, I pray you stay the country about you. Ye see how good and gracious the King's Highness is unto us and will be undoubtedly. There be certain lewd fellows abroad in the country that would stir the people to naughtiness again, as Nicholson of Holderness and the bailey of Snaith. I pray you stay them and be not counselled by them.' And Hallam said that he would not start any trouble. Nevertheless, he did nothing to retrieve the Friar of Knaresbrough, Robert Esch, who had been despatched a few days earlier in a repeat performance of his October role as roving propagandist for the commons.

Beverley might have been deftly held in check for the moment, but disturbance elsewhere that week was not so easily forestalled. Over in the North-west, trouble had been spreading throughout the region ever since Christmas and it was becoming rather more serious than the New Year's Eve commotion in Kendal parish church: barns had been broken into or fired and this was especially rife around Cockermouth, where locks were smashed so that people could enter the buildings and plunder the corn. Musters had been illegally held in some places, perhaps because another rumour said that the Earl of Derby was preparing to raise a punitive force, to parry any attempt to move on Lancaster again and to quell rebel activity that was reported from the adjacent coastal village of Heysham. Things had reached the stage at which the Duke of Norfolk sent word up from London that anyone suspected of creating these incidents should be arrested.

In accordance with these instructions, Henry Clifford's bastard son Thomas, deputy to his legitimate sibling Lord Clifford in charge of Carlisle, rode down to Kirkby Stephen to arrest Nicholas Musgrave, who had been joint captain of one of the Pilgrim hosts and was thought to be the cause of such trouble as was happening in Westmorland. Having been warned of his coming, the captain and another man, Thomas Tebay, took refuge on the tower of Kirkby Stephen church, where a number of Musgraves – an extensive Westmorland clan – were buried, including the man who was said to have killed the last wild boar in England on a nearby fell.[1] Not daring to violate the principle of sanctuary, Clifford backed off and went home, but his excursion led to a fresh outbreak of lawlessness, with enclosures demolished throughout the parish and along the length of Mallerstang, the deep valley which wound beneath the craggy heights of Wild Boar Fell to link Garsdale and Wensleydale with the Eden Valley and the way to Carlisle.

1 This was Sir Richard Musgrave, who died in 1464 and whose tomb, when it was opened for restoration in 1847, was found to contain not only Musgrave's remains but a boar's tusk.

No sooner had Robert Aske done what he could to stay Beverley than Sir Marmaduke sent him further unwelcome news, this time of a disturbance around Ripon and a muster that had been held on a hillside close to Fountains Abbey. Captains had been appointed, in case it became necessary to move quickly from a state of readiness similar to the one that had been maintained immediately after the original truce in Doncaster. It was a sign of the deep alienation hereabouts, from the upper classes as well as from the government, that the local Pilgrim leaders Lord Latimer and Sir Christopher Danby, who had both been in the thick of things since early October, now found it expedient to clear off so as to be out of harm's way. Having been pressed into service in the first place, they had no wish to undergo a similar but probably more unpleasant experience again, not with everything in the peace process so finely balanced that a false step by any gentleman might this time be fatal. So they set off on the by now well-trodden trail to London, Latimer by this time having been informed by Henry that he was at last required at court. No sooner were these two on the road south than their properties at Snape Castle and neighbouring Thorpe Perrow were invaded by the commons from Bedale and Masham, who made inventories of the contents and let it be known that they would not hesitate to wreck the premises as the whim took them; someone, in fact, swore that the commons 'were utterly bent to destroy their houses' if the two men did not return.

A variant on this form of intimidation was practised further north on Robert Bowes, whose cattle were driven off his property in his absence from South Cowton. In the West Riding, a lot of hot air was exhaled in talk of a conclusive march on London with an army of 40,000, which would settle Cromwell's hash once and for all. But Aske intervened again after Sir Marmaduke Constable informed him that the trouble there and in the North Riding was mostly caused by the rumour of Aske's execution, and that a personal appearance by him would instantly reduce the tension. So he went off to Ripon to prove that the reports of his death were greatly exaggerated, and to assure his old comrades there that the King really would abide by the terms of the pact that he and the Duke of Norfolk had made in Doncaster.

Another reason for the unrest in this part of Yorkshire had nothing to do with Aske's imagined plight or with suspicion of the gentry. Just after Christmas Adam Sedbar, back in his abbey beside the River Ure, had sent one of his servants, Simon Jackson, to Lincolnshire, to find out what was going on there, under the pretext of collecting rents which were due from properties that Jervaulx owned near Boston. Jackson returned on 6 January and reported that things were very bad over the water, the rebels there being treated cruelly by Charles Brandon's men in defiance of the Doncaster agreement, and that when the Duke of Norfolk came north again he would be bringing a huge army with him. The Lincolnshire insurgents were, in fact, being treated very cruelly indeed. Following the King's insistence that he wanted 100 victims to expiate the treason of the county, no fewer than 140 were held in Lincoln gaol by mid-November. Louth alone yielded fifteen of the local ringleaders, including Captain Cobbler and Thomas Kendall, the Vicar having vainly tried to obtain refuge in the Coventry Charterhouse, whose order was in enough trouble already without harbouring such a notorious rebel. Horncastle had surrendered its own quota, and the rest had been taken into custody more or less at the whim of Charles Brandon and his men.

As active as anyone in rounding up these victims was Sir Edward Dymmoke, who had recently been leading the Horncastle rebels and had done nothing to prevent the death of Dr Rayne. He was to do very well for himself when normality had been restored in England but another of the Lincolnshire gentry, Thomas Moigne, was one of thirty-four prisoners brought to trial early in March and he was executed in Lincoln the next day, together with the intermediary Guy Kyme and the Abbot of Cistercian Kirkstead, Richard Harrison. In all, forty-six Lincolnshire men were to die for their part in the rising, a figure that fell some distance short of Henry's target because Brandon feared that greater savagery would only encourage the county to rise again and make common cause with Yorkshire, which by then was everywhere up in arms and in a position of growing strength. A dozen of the men taken by Brandon were sent down to London, including Kendall who, in a sense, had started it all. Thirty-one of the executions took place at Louth and

THE PILGRIMAGE OF GRACE

Horncastle, whereas Kendall was to die at Tyburn, in spite of the fact that one of his choirmen (William Mann, bass) deposed that nothing would have happened at Louth 'had it not been bruited [rumoured] that the church jewels should be taken away'.

Some of the Jervaulx monks were so incensed and alarmed by Jackson's news that they urged the raising of the commons to fight off the Duke and his troops, 'to destroy the Duke of Norfolk, affirming that if he were destroyed, their abbey should stand as it did and so should Holy Church in such state as it was in Henry VII's days; and, if Norfolk came into the country and continued there, their abbey should be put down and they should go abegging'. With the collusion of William Thirsk, the former superior of Fountains, who had retired to Jervaulx after being deposed by a rival on dubious grounds, Sedbar therefore sent a message to Thomas Percy, asking him to bring down as many men from Northumberland as he could raise. But again, Percy declined to become involved. Nevertheless, the mood engendered by Jackson's news did much to provoke a fresh disturbance in Richmondshire towards the end of the month.

This was also exacerbated by the circulation of bills in the area, whose authors had more than one target in their sights. Cromwell was condemned as a heretic, as was everyone else who had caused the King to tamper with the old religion, but the greatest anger was directed against the local gentry and nobility in a flysheet which turned up at Richmond but was composed somewhere in Bilsdale, which cuts through the Cleveland Hills north of Rievaulx Abbey. The commons everywhere were incited by this to force such persons into more oath-taking and anyone who resisted was to be executed; one of the undertakings they were required to give was that they would no longer demand gressums, the fee which tenants paid on renting new land or when its ownership changed. Another bill was composed towards the end of the month by a couple of laymen from the Masham area and two of the more aggressive monks at Jervaulx, ordering a muster of every able-bodied man in the locality on Middleham Moor a couple of days later. This was not entirely a labour of love or even of anger, however, because the laymen made it clear at Jervaulx that they expected to be paid for their work in taking copies of the bill round Richmondshire. Adam

Sedbar refused point blank, but William Thirsk gave them two gold coins, one of which was said to be bent, with the promise of more if they could restore him to his position at Fountains.

Bills had been appearing in many other parts of Yorkshire by then. As in December, so again in January, a number of them are thought to have been composed at Sawley Abbey. One such, a lengthy paper which was probably written on 11 January, was nailed to church doors at Harewood and elsewhere, calling for a fresh uprising and implying that Robert Aske might not be the man to lead it this time, being one who 'was at London and had great rewards to betray the commons'. It linked him obliquely with a government plan to make Hull 'ready to receive ships by the sea to destroy all in north parts'. The bill repudiated the December agreement on the grounds that in reality there would be nothing in it for the commons, especially nothing which would solve the acute economic problems of ordinary people in the North, which followed from the wealth of the religious houses being removed to the South and from the abolition of traditionally reliable employers. It was also argued that Henry's supremacy over the Church would be undiminished by the agreement, and that the only hope of salvation for the monasteries was that they should be restored by the commons instead of being left at the mercy of the Crown. The document ended with a resounding call to action: 'Wherefore now is time to rise, or else never, and go proceed with our Pilgrimage of Grace or else we shall all be undone. Therefore, forward! Forward! Now forward on pain of death. Forward now or else never. And ye shall have captains just and true.'

Two days later another bill was nailed to a church door, this time at Arncliffe in Littondale, which stood at a bend on a tributary of the River Wharfe. The dale had always provided men willing to take up arms at a word of command, and on the north wall of St Oswald's nave was a great board which listed the local recruits who had fought at Flodden – the Knolles, the Atkinsons, the Franklins, the Tenants and the other families, together with a note of what each man had provided in the way of equipment ('a bowe, a bille, an able horse and harnish'd'). Another name on the list was that of a Richard Fawcett of Litton, and he may or may not have been the same Richard Fawcett of Litton who had helped to drum up the Percy Fee rebels for the defence of Sawley Abbey in October, twenty-three years after the great victory over the Scots. The Arncliffe bill was unlike others in the area in that it was directed specifically at the Vicar, Christopher Elyson, who was also the Dean of Craven. It read as follows:

> Master Dean: We recommend unto you, desiring you that ye bid beads and rehearse the points of cursing in your parish church as hath been accustomed aforetime after the true laws of God, as pray for the Pope of Rome, the head of our Holy Mother Church. And hath as hath been grant by holy Popes. And thus in the cause of Almighty God fail not to do, and we shall die and live with you as ye intend to have any duty of us, and if ye will not send us word to the contrary. By the whole assent of all the whole parishioners and tenants of my Lords of Northumberland.

In short, Vicar Elyson's parishioners wanted him to get back to the traditional form of service, which included anathematising the various offences which led to eternal damnation. Although there was no direct incitement to violence in this notice, the mood it expressed was clearly connected with the large-scale slaughter of deer which was at last taking place in nearby Langstrothdale Chase that very day, and which was probably inspired by the continuing detention of the two parish constables, who had been held in Skipton Castle since the abortive rally to kill Henry Clifford's deer a month earlier. As the slaughter began, Clifford was informing the King that 'throughout all these parts the people are so wild there is danger of further rebellion'.

The bills were not confined to the countryside. A number were circulating in the vicinity of Halifax and at Leeds many more began appearing on the same day that the Arncliffe bill was put up. This version reflected identical concerns to the one which appeared at Harewood and on other churches, and it seemed to have been composed in response to two particular rumours: one of these reckoned that the mayor of York had received the royal command to confiscate all weapons held by the commons of the city, while the other fed the increasing suspicion that the gentry who had led the Pilgrimage were now traitors to the cause. On both counts, therefore, the commons were now imperilled, their only remedy being to take up arms again. 'Commons keep well your harness,' it said. 'Trust you no gentlemen. Rise all at once.' If this was a less passionate exhortation than the one which had concluded the Harewood bill so emphatically, it nevertheless spoke with the same urgency. The ending of the Leeds bill struck another familiar chord with its assurance that 'God shall be your governor, and I shall be your captain'. It was as if something had lodged in the author's memory, a phrase, a nuance, whose pedigree went back to the Captain Poverty letters of October. Here again was the promise of leadership authorised by the will of God.

Aske was doing all he could to scotch the rumours that gave many of the bills their credence. Ripon was not the only place he travelled to after settling things down in Beverley. He galloped from one place to another across much of the West Riding after holding his postponed meeting with Darcy at Templehirst on 10 January. Sir Robert Constable was also there and the two were given a summary of Aske's dealings with Henry and were shown a copy of the Narrative he had written for the King. Darcy was particularly anxious to know what Henry had said about him and his activities, and Aske tried to reassure him that the sovereign regarded all of them in the same way, 'reckoning them offenders before the pardon and else little or nothing after'. Darcy's worry was what awaited him at court, for he had received the King's summons to go south just four days before this meeting, as had Constable, and he had been awaiting Aske's tidings before making any move. His young colleague counselled both that it was now much more important for the three of them to do what they could to keep the North calm until Norfolk arrived and the Parliament was set up, and said that he would write to the King and tell him as much. He suggested that Darcy, too, should write to Henry and make the same point, advice which Darcy only partially took. He did write to Henry, asking to be excused for the time being, but the reason he gave for his reticence was that his health was not up to a long journey in that fierce midwinter, except perhaps by sea. He therefore stayed and undertook to do what he could from his base near the boundary between the two Ridings, even if this was no more than despatching messengers with letters to Pontefract and other places. As the area of greatest disaffection seemed to be now clearly in the West Riding, Constable also threw his weight into the immediate task there, but sent letters of his own to Beverley, to Bridlington, to Howden, to Marshland and to other parts of the East Riding, including Hull, whose Pilgrim governor he had lately been.

They were not alone in these endeavours. Aske did as he had promised and wrote to the King, as a result of which Henry not only countermanded his orders to Darcy and Constable but despatched all the northern gentlemen home from his court, after meeting them in a special council on Wednesday, 14 January. They returned whence they had just come with his assurance – sworn by St George, whose red cross badge the sovereign now insisted that they must all wear, together with all their followers – that he had certainly pardoned everyone and had no intention of seizing arms and equipment or anything else. By that Sunday, virtually everyone who had been dribbling down to London in the previous three weeks was back in the North and helping to subdue the aggressive instincts that were now threatening them all.

Gentlemen who had never been anything but loyal to the throne, like Sir Ralph Evers, who had held Scarborough Castle for the Crown, worked alongside Pilgrim stalwarts like Sir Stephen Hamerton, who had never wavered in his commitment to the rebel cause and had been prepared to fight the Earl of Derby in Lancashire, and men like Lord Scrope, who had played both sides of the street in the months before Doncaster. Robert Bowes was again as indefatigable as Robert Aske, galloping tirelessly across the North Riding and the Palatinate of Durham, whose hosts he had taken down to Pontefract and Doncaster, where he had been readier than most to lead them into battle against the King. Most curiously, he found, as Aske had just done, that the very people who had spoken ill of him when he was away at court, had indeed stolen some of his property to demonstrate their anger at his most recent behaviour, were now quite willing to accept his word, coming from his own lips and not through any messenger, that things would be well if they were patient for just a little longer, and that their sovereign really did mean what he said. Nothing better illustrates the volatility, the sudden changes of mood, that possessed the mass of those who were not of such gentle birth.

Aske fully recognised, however, in his letter to Henry written on 12 January, how precariously things were balanced. He sent him comforting words about what had been accomplished in Beverley, but he said more plainly than Thomas Howard had ever done how seriously things were beginning to go awry again and spelled out the reasons for this, including the fact that the King had brought the northern gentry to heel and that they had meekly obeyed his call. He did not shrink from telling the sovereign that many of the northern commons were still inclined to doubt his word and would not be truly calmed unless Howard came soon with enough proof of goodwill to assuage their fears. His own particular fear he mentioned at the end of the letter. He had found, he said, 'that your Grace's subjects be wildly minded in their hearts towards commotions or assistance thereof', but begged to be excused for speaking so plainly, 'for I do utter in my poor heart to your Grace to the intent your Highness may perceive the danger that may ensue; for on my faith, I do greatly fear the end to be only by battle'. This was the clinching proposition that caused Henry not only to excuse Darcy and Constable from attendance at court for the time being, but to send the northern gentry home again.

There was one other factor, however, that influenced the King's decision. For the catastrophic figure of Sir Francis Bigod had just emerged from the wings and was now demanding to be noticed in the centre of the northern stage. Not yet thirty, Bigod came from a North Riding family with noble blood in its distant pedigree, which placed it only just below the peerage in the social scale. With seats at Mulgrave Castle, near Whitby, and Settrington, to the east of Malton, the Bigods were considerable landholders whose greatest assets were in the East Riding, though there were other properties in both the West and North Ridings, and in Lincolnshire as well. In spite of this, they had accumulated large debts by the time Francis came into his inheritance at the age of seven, both his father and his uncle having perished fighting the Scots. They may have had great estates in terms of acreage, but these produced little in the way of income, which had become quite insufficient to meet all the outgoings, including money periodically exacted by the Crown for the livery of the lands and other purposes.

As a juvenile, Bigod was placed in the care of Cardinal Wolsey, which meant that he was entering something between a training school for a life revolving round the court and an academy of instruction for a career in government. From there he was sent to Oxford, which was to shape his destiny to the end of his life. The university had lately received a transfusion from Cambridge of young men heavily influenced by Lutheranism and particularly by one of its principal exponents in England, the priest Thomas Gerrard, whose energies were spent on preaching the new gospel from the pulpit and distributing theological volumes wherever he could find a ready market for them. Bigod very soon became enamoured of a doctrine which asserted that any man might preach the word of God, that no temporal or spiritual law could stipulate anything that contradicted this. He emerged from Oxford not only with a much better education than the landed gentry of England normally acquired, but with a deep need to proselytise on behalf of the new religion.

Shortly after coming down, Bigod married into the nobility, his wife being the daughter of the first Lord Conyers, which meant that they were blood relatives only just distant enough to avoid their marriage being forbidden by the imperatives of the Church. He was now Sir Francis, but his economic circumstances were even more difficult than they had been when he inherited the Bigod acres and properties. In desperate need of cash he turned to the old money-lender Thomas Cromwell, with whom he had formed an attachment when both were in Wolsey's service. Bigod asked, in fact, for £1200 in exchange for a lordship worth £140 a year and a lump sum of £20 to Cromwell and his descendants for the next forty years. The Lord Privy Seal obliged, both then and on other occasions, for Bigod seemed incapable of running his estates as profitably as most Yorkshire landowners. He was obsessed with the obligation he felt to leave land to his two children and so was loath to sell any of it off; 'my heart doth even bleed in my belly to part with any of it for ever from my said children,' he told his benefactor. This was all very well, but at the same time he was running a substantial household, was constantly travelling expensively to London and back, and was supporting a number of Reforming clergy whom he appointed as his chaplains, one of them being Thomas Gerrard. He wrote a book at this time, *A Treatise concernyng Impropriations of Benefices*, which was an outright attack on monastic wealth, making the sharp point that if the religious were impoverished without the great income that came to them from impropriations, they would simply be fulfilling their monastic vows more adequately than at present.[2]

This was pleasing enough to the King and to his Lord Privy Seal, but it did nothing for Bigod's reputation in Yorkshire, where his neighbours increasingly saw him as a landowning failure, an incompetent manager of his estates who had been given more education than was good for him and had become a despised Protestant (though the word itself would not be attached to Englishmen for another twenty years, 'reformed' or 'evangelical' being the current usages for such people). Bigod was, in a peculiar sense, another form of upstart, just like Thomas Cromwell. He was also becoming obsessive to the point of eccentricity, once missing an appointment with Cromwell because he wanted to hear several sermons in London. On another occasion he wrote to his benefactor asking that, in spite of the fact that he was married with two children, he should be made a priest so that he could preach the new religion to the ignorant masses of the North.

Instead, in January 1535, Bigod became one of the Yorkshire commissioners whose task was to compile the *Valor Ecclesiasticus*, the great register of monastic wealth, which diminished his local standing even more. That same year he was instrumental in securing the arrest of a Cistercian monk, George Lazenby, who preached against the Royal Supremacy at Jervaulx Abbey when Bigod was in the congregation. Lazenby's indiscretion had evidently been fuelled by the Carthusians of Mount Grace, but it led him to martyrdom, whereas they in due course submitted meekly to the dissolution of their house. He was first held in

2 Impropriation meant the acquisition of a parish's wealth, most notably in its tithes, in exchange for appointing its incumbent and maintaining the fabric of the church.

Middleham Castle at Bigod's behest, then taken for trial to York, where he was executed in August. A more attractive side to Bigod's character emerged a few months later when he visited three men, two of them clerics, who had been imprisoned at York for treason. Convinced that they were repentant, Bigod interceded on their behalf with Cromwell and one of them certainly, the others possibly, survived an ordeal that cost most people their lives. He was not by any means a hard man; he was, in fact, a highly strung and somewhat unstable fellow who was given to unpredictable impulses, an erratic as well as an eccentric.

He was at home in Mulgrave when the Pilgrimage of Grace broke out in October. His immediate instinct, like that of almost all the gentry, was to get to a place of safety from God knows what might happen to him otherwise. He sailed from Whitby in a ship bound for the Thames, but the season of autumn gales was at its height and the vessel was blown northwards instead, so that Bigod was obliged to disembark at Hartlepool, from whence he made his way home. When the Cleveland host under Robert Bowes's command came down that way he was taken, to his great alarm, because his views as well as his activities as one of Cromwell's commissioners were well enough known by then. He was suspected, he later testified, 'because of my learning and much conversation with such a lewd one [sic] as they judged were enemies both to Christ's Church, the faith thereof and the commonwealth, by means whereof I was not only in great slander and obloquy, but also in great danger of my life...' Though he didn't realise it, at that stage of events he was, of course, much more valuable to the Pilgrims alive than dead and, after being sworn, he was, as usual, pressed into service as a company commander; and in this capacity he accompanied the host to York and then on to Pontefract.

He instantly underwent the familiar metamorphosis from adversary (or at least neutral) to zealot, though in his case the conversion was inevitably singular. He had become distanced from Cromwell by now because, while his own religious passion was growing, he was reaching the conclusion that the Lord Chancellor was a spiritually shallow man, whose deepest convictions were to do with politics and not with faith. And even while he was working for Cromwell, while he was writing his antimonastic tract, Bigod was never an enthusiast for the abolition of the religious life; he simply wanted it improved and cleansed of all stains. He told himself now that the Pilgrimage of Grace would be an excellent instrument to this end, a bulwark in defence of the monasteries, which would yet be free, emancipated and, in due course, Reformed. As an earnest of his new intent he quickly intervened in the affairs of the Augustinians at Guisborough, to the north-west of Whitby. Drs Legh and Layton had been there at the beginning of the year and had ejected the Prior, James Cockerell, in favour of their placeman Robert Silvester, on the grounds that he was, among other things, 'profitable'. Bigod decided that this manoeuvre must be reversed and he set about raising the commons locally to exert the same sort of pressure which had enlisted him into the rebellion. This plan, which was an obvious declaration of war on Cromwell's policies, backfired when the Pilgrim leadership intervened and directed the priory's steward, Sir John Bulmer, to sort things out at Guisborough, where the canons had divided into two factions; and, as a result of Bulmer's assessment, Silvester remained in place.

Bigod's *faux pas* there may have alerted Aske and others in the high command to one of the newcomer's most palpable weaknesses: his inclination to dash impetuously at a situation without first thinking of the consequences. At any rate, he never was incorporated into the Pilgrim hierarchy, did not even attend the great November council in York. Instead, he was sent to Scarborough to take part in the blockade of the castle held by Sir Ralph Evers, which he doubtless did with some relish, because there had been a feud for many years between the Bigods and the Everses, which had culminated earlier in 1536 in the murder of one of Sir Ralph's servants by Bigod's men, who then made for the sanctuary of Durham Cathedral. In spite of intercession by Bigod, they were retrieved on Cromwell's orders and put up for trial, though this had not yet taken place because the great rebellion had disrupted all normal procedures in the North. Evers, as we know, held the castle and the Pilgrims eventually withdrew, and Bigod next appears at the Pontefract gathering which thrashed out a programme before meeting the Duke of Norfolk in Doncaster.

He wrote a long and doubtless erudite opinion, which was circulated among all the delegates, though they appear not to have been much influenced by it, possibly being bored by exceedingly dense scholarship, or maybe because they had just heard something remarkably like Bigod's principal thesis in the compromise advanced by Robert Aske. Some of the commons even thought of him as a spy, so persistent was his reputation as another of Cromwell's creatures. His document has not survived but a number of eyewitness accounts have, and there is also another collection of writings that Bigod issued at this time which almost certainly reflect what he read out to his colleagues at Pontefract. They reveal a shift of position since the publication of his earlier book, to a stance which was not so very far from the one held by the unfortunate monk Lazenby. For Bigod now argued that the Royal Supremacy must be modified into a secular authority and that the Church in England should be spiritually governed by its own Reformed archbishops under the protection of the Crown. Henry, in other words, was to become an insular version of the Holy Roman Emperors.

At Scarborough, Bigod had the encounter that would eventually put an end to many lives. It was there that he first met John Hallam and they had become close in this working relationship, united in their grievance against the Pilgrim leadership for not giving them enough support to take the castle by storm. Bigod aired this resentment in a letter he subsequently wrote to Sir Oswald Wilstrop, in which he said, 'For my own part I have much to conjecture that you are not faithful to us, nor will not be, because I might well perceive, and so did all the soldiers at Scarborough, that you much more favoured Ralph Evers than ye did either us or yet our good cause.' By January, when that was written, he had also become extremely suspicious of the pardon and of the King's good faith, which isolated him even further from the majority of the Pilgrim gentlemen and drew him more into collaboration with the commons. He was actually going now in the opposite direction from the leadership. And his next known meeting with John Hallam was to be crucial.

Bigod had busied himself with the affairs of the Gilbertines of Watton just as much as he had with those of the Augustinians up at Guisborough. On 10 January, while Aske, Darcy and Sir

Robert Constable were conferring at Templehirst, Bigod and Hallam were putting their heads together at Watton Priory. In a sense it was a chance encounter, for Sir Francis had originally been on his way from Mulgrave to York, where he wanted to see the Archbishop's treasurer about the happenings at Guisborough. He first dropped by another Gilbertine community at Malton, in which he also took an interest, and discussed the pardon with its Prior, who told him of two prophecies he had heard. One said the King would flee England, the other that after suffering for three years, the Church would recover here. The Prior also passed on the rumour that Cromwell was hoping to marry Lady Margaret Douglas and become Henry's heir. He very probably added the wholly reliable information that Hallam had been dissuaded from action at Beverley the day before.

At any rate, something made Bigod decide to see Hallam at once and he went to the captain's house at nearby Cawkeld, which wasn't big enough to accommodate Bigod and his four servants for the night. They therefore walked over to Watton and supped together at the priory, at the same table as the canons. The talk during the meal was all to do with the pardon and whether or not it was genuine, but as soon as the food was finished Bigod took Hallam by the hand and led him over to a bay window, where they spoke alone for the next hour.

Bigod read what he had written about the Royal Supremacy, then suggested, according to Hallam, that 'he thought, as the most part of the country round about him did, it was best that Hull and Scarborough should be taken, for the country to resort to till the Parliament time...' Bigod even advanced the extraordinary idea that when the Duke of Norfolk came again he should be captured somewhere around Newburgh or Byland and sworn to the Pilgrim oath. Hallam said he doubted this would be possible, because too many people in the North regarded the Duke with favour and had done so ever since his brave exploits at Flodden Field. This was true, and it illustrates as much as anything the great fear northcountrymen had of the Scots, so that someone who brought them deliverance in 1513 was trusted even when he seemed to be working vigorously against their interests more than twenty years later. That was why so many in the Pilgrimage were prepared to believe almost anything that

Thomas Howard told them; that and the knowledge that he detested Thomas Cromwell as much as any of them.

But not Sir Francis Bigod, whose obsessions now included a fresh rising in which, he promised, there would be a leading role for John Hallam. Well, Hallam had already started plotting a move against Scarborough and Hull with William Nicholson, so that was an easy one to sell. He would later be assured by Bigod that something well beyond a holding operation against the two towns was possible, that a general rising was more than feasible because Swaledale, Wensleydale and other areas to the west and to the north were ready to move again, that Thomas Percy was coming down from Northumberland to take up a command. That night in Watton he simply contented himself with planting the idea in Hallam's head. Hallam was persuaded, particularly as, over the next couple of days, Bigod remained at the priory and drafted a legal document which would effectively close the door of Watton to the abhorred Robert Holgate for ever. Hallam had been looking for a new leader with fire in his belly, since Robert Aske's was now obviously quenched. In Sir Francis Bigod he thought he had found one.

On 14 January, a Sunday, Hallam made his way to Settrington at Bigod's request. Also there that day were the roving Friar of Knaresborough and a local yeoman, Ralph Fenton. Present, too, may have been George Lumley, who had been a captain in Sir Thomas Percy's company of troops, and whose father had been a leader of the Durham and Cleveland host, and was thereafter one of the Pilgrimage's inner circle. Or he may not have been incorporated into subsequent events until the day after, for the evidence is inconclusive and in some respects contradictory. However, at Settrington the outline of the plan which Bigod had sketched at Watton was developed into a full-blown strategy. Hallam was to lead his own men and William Nicholson's in the taking of Hull, but Scarborough belonged to Bigod, who had a score to settle with the keeper of its castle. After these objectives were secured – and Bigod appeared to think that this would be done in no time – the two companies would meet at Beverley and would then move on together to Pontefract and after that to Doncaster.

Hallam seems to have been worried by the sudden expansion

of his original ambition into a major campaign on the scale of the previous one: he was concerned lest the reinforcements Bigod promised from the Dales and elsewhere might not materialise, so the Friar was sent post-haste to check on the situation and next day reported that all was as Bigod had foretold. This was a gross exaggeration of the situation, whose reality was that there was much dissatisfaction with the pardon and the state of things generally, and a great deal of sword-rattling, but no organised move as yet under a credible leadership to create another military Pilgrimage all over again. Bigod, however, was now so fired up for action that he had become incapable of distinguishing things as they actually were from his own fantasy of what he would like them to be. He even composed a new oath to which his new army would be sworn and it was evidently influenced by the bill which had exhorted its readers to go 'Forward now or else never'. It was also tinctured with the old Piers Plowman mystique of a compelling quest for salvation, which in this case meant the capture of the Duke of Norfolk, a crusade to London and a triumphant confrontation with the King.

With the oath, Bigod composed several letters which were fired off in all directions to announce the plans and to rouse support. One went to Durham, another to Richmondshire, a third to Scarborough and a fourth to Percy by way of the dowager Countess of Northumberland, who lived outside Scarborough and who urged Sir Thomas to comply. She was doubtless influenced by Bigod's promise that he would see to it, if he came into his own, that everything Percy's brother the Earl had promised to the Crown at his death would now go to Sir Thomas instead. The only one of these missives to survive was sent by 'Francis Bigod, Knight, and John Hallam, Yeoman, in the name and by the commandment of all the commons…', though it curiously ended with the signature of Bigod alone. Was this a tacit admission that Hallam at least as much as Bigod was responsible for the grand plan, overtaken by a last burst of vanity because Bigod above all else saw much personal glory in what might be attained? Or was it simply a small oversight? One of Bigod's servants subsequently alleged that, far from his master having caused Hallam to break the promise he had lately made to Robert Aske and Robert Creke in Beverley, it was Hallam who, at Settrington, first floated the idea that they might aim for a full rerun of October 1536 instead of a limited tactical move on two towns. And certainly, if Bigod is to be believed, at Christmastide in Mulgrave – that is, before he met Hallam for the first time since the siege of Scarborough – 'there was no talk of further rebellions'. But it is as well to remember that all such statements about what happened during these months were made by men who were fighting for their lives before the King's interrogators and it would have been unnatural if the truth of things had not sometimes been distorted in order to place an individual in the best possible light. Bigod's letters, in any case, were written to little effect. No hosts arrived to reinforce the assaults on Scarborough and Hull, and Sir Thomas Percy decided it might be prudent not to follow his mother's advice. He was a much better judge of Sir Francis's character than she.

But on the basis of Bigod's fantasy and Robert Esch's exaggerations, a muster was held two days after the Settrington cabal, on Brough Hill, which overlooked the village. It was preceded by beacons at night as well as summonses by word of mouth and the result was an attendance of 300 or so, two-thirds of whom were either Bigod's tenants or in his service. Addressing them all, Sir Francis said that the gentry had deceived the commons, that Durham and Cleveland were already up, that the Duke of Norfolk was on his way with an army to seize Hull and Scarborough, 'which shall be our destruction unless we prevent him therein and take them before', and that they should all go with George Lumley to Scarborough 'to take the Castle and the town and keep the port and haven from any such as should come in there to be your destruction, as I have written a letter to the bailiffs of Scarborough that they should help thus to do with the aid of you the commons that I shall send unto them'.

Bigod was interrupted several times while he was speaking, but they were the shouts of men becoming excited by what he had just said, the interjections of people who agreed with his every word. He finished by pointing out: 'A Parliament is appointed as they say, but neither the place where nor the time when it should be kept is appointed. And also here is that the King should have cure both of your body and soul, which is plain false, for it is against the Gospel of Christ, and that will I justify even to my death. And therefore if ye will take my part in this and defend it, I will not fail you so long as I live to the utter-most of my power; and who will so do, assure me by your hands and hold them up.' At which a great roar went up and a unani-mous show of hands. It had been vintage rabble-rousing and it had done the trick. And, far from being prepared to share the spotlight with John Hallam, Bigod had presented himself as Messiah alone.

In the space of a few hours he had also changed his mind about leading the march on Scarborough and decided to go directly to Beverley instead. In his place he despatched Lumley to the seaside, armed with the letter to the bailiffs, which they received when Lumley arrived at the head of perhaps 140 men. Amazingly, the town capitulated without a shot being fired; and this was perhaps not so much because the sight of a few score men intimidated the civic leaders as because Bigod's letter promised the arrival of a much larger horde very soon, in which case things might become very dirty indeed. But Lumley refused to move on the castle, and this must have been in part because his family and the Everses had always been on good terms; he had, indeed, paused at the home of the elder Sir Ralph on the way to Scarborough and warned the old man that his son – still on his way back from seeing the King – ought not to go to Scarborough just yet or he might be roughly handled or even killed by men Lumley was not at all sure he could control.

He had been an inconspicuous and rather colourless young man before this, yet he was his father's son and he now acted as a commander by forbidding the commons to harm Evers's men in Scarborough, when the commons were eager to get their own back for the frustrations they had endured there in November. Instead, they were ordered simply to mount a guard which would stop anyone else from controlling the castle, and forbid-den to obtain food and drink in the town without paying the market price for it. Lumley then set about the matter of swearing the bailiffs to Bigod's new oath; after which he departed for his home at Thwing, to the south, some miles inland from Bridlington, where he proposed to raise more forces for the march towards London. Scarborough was left in the charge of a minor gentleman, John Wyvill, who had the yeoman Ralph

Fenton to back him up. It was now Wednesday, 17 January and the other conspicuous absentee, Sir Francis Bigod, had just made up his mind to go to Hull and provide extra stiffening, if it was needed, to John Hallam and his men. But even as Bigod was playing the great orator on Brough Hill, Hallam's company had already walked into a disaster.

Hallam had stayed the night at Settrington after the Sunday meeting there but went back to Watton the following morning, Bigod's parting instruction being that, the moment he gave the word, the two-pronged attack on the seaports should begin. In the meantime, Hallam held his own little council of war with a couple of men from Beverley, Roger Kitchen, a glover, and Richard Wilson, a draper, and it was agreed that when the moment came, Kitchen would hasten to Holderness to activate William Nicholson and his troops, while Wilson would get Beverley on the move; the three of them would then meet in Hull with whatever forces had been mustered. As Hallam and Nicholson had agreed, this combined company of new rebels would slip into Hull in small groups, and when all were inside the walls Hallam would shout 'Come hither to me all good commons!' and this would be the signal for the attack to begin. That night, Bigod's message came to confirm that everything was now poised for the campaign to go ahead, which meant that the combined operation would begin in the morning of 16 January. He also advised that he would be backing up Hallam instead of marching on Scarborough.

Before going to bed, Hallam sent Kitchen off to Holderness at once, and told everyone else that they must all rendezvous in Beverley at sunrise and then go on to Hull. They must not, however, wear full harness, otherwise they would be identified the moment they tried to enter the port and the plan to take it would come to nothing. Among those who would be setting out from the vicinity of Hallam's home were three men he already knew, with whom he had been drinking only the week before at the annual dragging of a plough from house to house, to raise money for the church. They were William Horsekey, Hugh Langdale and Philip Uty, and they were now given 3s 4d by the sub-Prior of Watton to tide them over the next couple of days.

And so, in the darkness before Tuesday's dawn, men began to

move off. As instructed, they all lacked body armour, though Hallam certainly wore the garments that went beneath full harness, which was a padded, resined linen jacket and some sort of skull cap on his head. He also carried a sword and a small shield, though how he expected to (and, in fact, did) pass himself off in Hull as an ordinary market day visitor when he was so conspicuously armed the sources fail to tell us. The rendezvous was made in Beverley on schedule and then, a few at a time, these commons rode on to the port, where they would reassemble at the house of man named William Hynde.

Somewhere ahead of Hallam were Horsekey, Langdale and Uty, by this time very uneasy about the whole enterprise. None of them trusted Bigod and they evidently had mixed feelings about Hallam now. The sub-Prior was later to testify that both Horsekey and Langdale had 'exhorted Hallam to live in quiet lest he should cast both himself and the country away', and the yeoman Horsekey claimed that he had only enlisted because Hallam had put him in fear of his life, a plea that was also entered by Langdale, who was a serving man at the priory. As they approached Hull they decided that they must do something to put themselves in the clear. They would go to some of their friends in the town and get these to tell the mayor what was about to happen, but under no circumstances must he learn the source of this intelligence. By eleven o'clock they were about this business, but when their friends went to the mayor they discovered that he was already aware of the plot. He had been told about it by one John Folbery, another of Hallam's acquaintances, who had been involved in the original Pilgrimage (had, indeed, been at the council in York) but, as a servant of Thomas Howard's son, the Earl of Surrey, had since decided that it was healthier to be a loyalist. He later excused his treachery on the grounds that, having accepted the King's pardon, he feared that if he offended again he would be 'torn with wild horses'.

When John Hallam turned up, therefore, he was already betrayed. Sword and buckler notwithstanding, he got through the Beverley gate of Hull undetected. Once safely inside, almost the first person he came across was William Nicholson, who seemed surprised to see him. Quickly the two went to Hynde's house, where Nicholson delivered the stunning news that he had only come into the town on some market day business. He had already left home, it seemed, before Kitchen arrived from Watton (the messenger had only travelled as far as Beverley the night before and didn't leave there for Holderness until six that morning). Nicholson was therefore unaware that the order had been given for the operation to proceed and, consequently, he had come to Hull alone; the promised 200 or 300 commons from Holderness were not with him. Hallam's strength, too, was much less than he had anticipated when the two of them had first spoken of this enterprise over Christmas: by his own reckoning no more than twenty people had arrived or were coming in from Beverley, though another estimate later on put the number at sixty. Whatever the true figure was, it was clearly inadequate to take a town whose citizens had gratefully accepted Henry's pardon and had no intention of getting into trouble once more. Since the Pilgrims had handed back the town to its own authorities, its vital seaborne trade had been restored to normality and no one was going to risk jeopardising that again; before long, it would be reported to Cromwell that 'Many men and children of the town wear red crosses'.

Quickly, the two men rethought their strategy and decided that they must postpone the action until the next day, by which time Nicholson would have gathered in his small army and Bigod would have arrived with back-up, together with the promised hosts from further afield. Hallam told his own people to disperse and be ready for the morrow. He himself slipped out of Hull through the Beverley gate that afternoon as casually as he had entered it a few hours earlier, in the company of two other men. Some distance down the road, beside a windmill, they paused to water their horses and, looking back, saw that the gates were being closed behind them. One of Hallam's companions was a canon of Watton named Thomas Marshall, who pointed out that their friends were still inside and urged Hallam to do something about it. 'Fie!' he said, 'will ye go your ways and leave your men behind you?' So Hallam wheeled his horse round and galloped back the way he had come. At the gate, he began speaking with the two officials in charge of it, telling them that he had friends still inside who needed to be on their way home, too. But John Folbery was there and identified him to the guards, who raised a general alarm and then made to seize the rebel leader.

For a few minutes there was a great hurly-burly at the gate, as other townsmen came to the assistance of the officials and one or two of Hallam's men rushed up to help their captain. He was attacked with daggers on both sides, but his resined jacket saved him from serious injury. One of the two who struck at him was unusually tenacious and slashed at the horse's bridle, which caused the animal to rear in alarm, to plunge into a ditch and to unseat its rider. Sword in hand and on foot now, Hallam still tried to fight off his attackers and wounded some, but they were too much for him and he was finally seized, together with two of his own men. As they were being led away William Nicholson attempted to stage a diversion, but he too was injured and taken. That night the two plotters were securely imprisoned in Hull, with a very bleak future ahead of them. And not a sign of help from the man who had promised so much and delivered so little.

XV

THE RETURN OF THE DUKE

We have no idea what Sir Francis Bigod did in the twenty-four hours after the fiasco at Hull. We don't even know whether he heard of it that same day or the day after, only that he wrote a letter asking for the release of Hallam, Nicholson and eight others – including Kitchen, who unwittingly walked into captivity there after his fruitless attempt to alert Nicholson – and that this reached Hull in the early afternoon of Thursday the 18th. He sent three men with his request, but only one of them returned with the reply that there was nothing doing and that Bigod's people should disperse immediately. It came on the authority of young Sir Ralph Ellerker, who had just arrived from London with his new commission from the King. To emphasise the point, the returned messenger's less fortunate companions were thrown into prison alongside the captive rebels.

This was not the only correspondence which Bigod was involved in that week. He also wrote to Sir Robert Constable with a copy of his new oath, explained what he was up to and asked for advice. The letter reached Constable when Robert Aske was with him at Holme and they both drafted replies which said more or less the same thing: that the King's pardon was genuine, that the plans for the York Parliament were being drawn up, that when Thomas Howard came north he would only have a private retinue. Constable's letter was specifically directed at Bigod and added that his new revolt violated the Doncaster agreement, that this was not a time of the year for fighting anyway. He said that he would have been willing to discuss matters but his gout prevented movement at the moment. Aske's reply was aimed at the commons, whom he called 'neighbours' and who were told that they had been foolish to listen to Bigod, whose actions might easily wreck everything that had been so carefully prepared for a peaceful settlement. He offered to come and tell them what the King had said to him, if they so wished.

It is possible that Bigod had spent Wednesday awaiting the arrival of the great force, which he imagined was coming down to help him from Durham and Cleveland. He had already arranged for a muster at Bainton, not far from Watton, and this went ahead as planned on Thursday morning, its purpose being a subsequent march in some direction to be determined by Bigod's latest whim. Scarborough? Hull? Beverley? All had been and still were possibilities, but Sir Francis kept changing his mind. It is conceivable – and his request for Constable's advice lends weight to this speculation – that it may have been dawning on an increasingly nervous Bigod that he just might have bitten off more than he could chew. However, there appears to have been a considerable gathering at Bainton, in view of what happened next and Bigod's claims about it. For a message came to him at the muster, to say that old Sir Ralph Ellerker had just gone to Beverley and was instructing the townspeople to resist any calls to rebel again. On hearing this, Bigod made for the town straight away and entered it at four o'clock that afternoon at the head, he reckoned, of 800 men. Shortly after arriving, he encountered Sir Thomas Percy's chaplain, who was the incumbent of nearby Leconfield, where the Percies had a castle. When the priest was asked how soon his master would be arriving with the expected reinforcements he replied, 'He will not rise for any man living and therefore it is but folly to send unto him for that cause.' In that one devastating sentence Bigod must have realised that all his high hopes of assistance from the Dales and elsewhere, all the information supplied by the Friar of Knaresborough, were quite false.

Predictably, he changed his mind yet again and decided now to take his company to Richmondshire, where they had always been ready for a fight and where he believed he would have no trouble raising a sufficient army to carry out a successful campaign. He and perhaps half his men stayed the night in Beverley (others who lived not far away probably went home to get some proper sleep), and it was there that disaster struck for the second time. Before dawn broke on Friday, old Ellerker suddenly attacked and routed 300 or 400 rebels, taking no fewer than sixty-two prisoners and some important papers that Bigod left behind at his lodging in his haste to get away. They included the tract which damned the Royal Supremacy and other views on matters to do with the Church. Even had he decided to make a proper fight of it, defeat would most likely still have been the result, for young Ellerker had promised to reach Beverley by noon, bringing with him reinforcements for his father from Hull and Holderness. When he arrived he seemed rather downcast at finding that no blood had actually been shed. If he had got there earlier, he assured the King, 'none of the prisoners taken at Beverley should have been taken alive by my will, to make others beware'.

Most of the defeated commons headed west out of town and then north to avoid running into Constable country, and thereafter they simply dispersed and were not heard of again. Bigod took off alone, apart from his posse of servants, and sent his horsekeeper, Harry Soulay, ahead to see how things were Settrington way. The fellow returned with the depressing news that Sir Francis stood accused of deserting his men and that the commons now regarded him as just another rotten gentleman who had betrayed them. This was alarming enough to make Bigod aim for Mulgrave instead and he rode all through Friday night to reach the sanctuary of his castle there. At this point the ominous figure of Gregory Conyers took a hand in his fate. He was a minor gentleman in the service of the dissolute and all but piratical Abbot of Whitby, and he had become Bigod's sworn enemy the year before after a dispute in which Bigod stood accused by the Abbot (to whom, almost inevitably, he was in debt) of fomenting a riot at the monastery. As a result, there had been a fight between Bigod and his men and some of the abbey's servants, including Conyers, who might well have been killed had not some other gentlemen intervened.

Ever since, Conyers had been looking for an opportunity to get even with Bigod and now that he had returned from paying his respects at court his chance had come. He not only spread the

word across a wide area inland of Whitby that Bigod had
betrayed everyone who trusted him, but he instructed all the
fishermen along that part of the coast to keep a sharp lookout,
lest this fugitive should try to escape by sea. After that he went to
Mulgrave, spoke offensively to Bigod's wife and walked off with
some of his possessions. He then discovered that Bigod was
hiding nearby, set off in pursuit with some others and surprised
the would-be rebel leader where he was resting before trying to
get home. Conyers actually laid hands on him, but Bigod slipped
out of his coat and raced into the cover of some woods, where
his pursuers lost track of him and had to be content with taking
his servants and his horse. Bigod then effectively disappeared and
was not heard of or seen again until he had been three weeks literally on the run, before turning up in Cumberland. His most
conspicuous achievement had been to provide the King with a
perfect excuse to repudiate all that had been offered by the Duke
of Norfolk at Doncaster.

The man who discovered the papers that Sir Francis left
behind in Beverley was Matthew Boynton, son-in-law of the Sir
John Bulmer who was steward of Guisborough Priory. Bulmer
had been pressed into the Pilgrimage under threat of having his
home burned down and played an unobtrusive role in the rebellion until he was included in the delegation which parleyed with
Norfolk at Doncaster bridge. He was in his late forties, the eldest
son of a Flodden hero, and he had married a daughter of Bigod's
grandfather, with whom he had six children, but subsequently
formed an attachment for another married woman, Margaret
Cheyney, who became his mistress. In due course, after both
Anne Bulmer and William Cheyney had died, Sir John and
Margaret, with whom he had a son, settled down together in
great happiness at Lastingham, north-west of Pickering and,
although they never married, he always thereafter referred to her
as his wife. His Peg was 'a very fair creature and a beautiful',
according to Henry's chronicler (and Windsor Herald) Charles
Wriothesley, and everyone acknowledged that this was a
genuine love match, as subsequent and tragic events clearly
proved.

After finding the papers, Boynton warned Bulmer that Bigod
was probably somewhere in his area and that whoever took him

would gain much favour in the eyes of the Crown. Bulmer was rather in need of some credit, in view of his Pilgrim past and the fact that he had sent his son and heir, Sir Ralph Bulmer, to London instead of going down to see the King himself. So he went scouting for Bigod and 'laid wait for him in Blackamore and Cleveland, but could not meet him'. He did, however, collect a number of bills that were both seditious and hostile to the gentry, which had been appearing in his territory; and these were later delivered to the Duke of Norfolk. One of the most violent was identical to the Bilsdale bill, which had turned up in Richmond earlier in the month. It was brought to Sir John by a man named Priestman, who asked him what he thought of it, to which Bulmer replied opaquely, 'Marry, very well, for when two dogs fight for a bone the third will take it up; for this will make the gentlemen and commons fall forth, and the King shall take up the matter.'

This was the wry jest of a rather worried man, who was anxious about his immediate future and not quite sure how to approach it. He was getting conflicting signals from his eldest son and from his youngest brother, Sir William Bulmer, who lived at Wilton Castle near the mouth of the Tees. Sir Ralph Bulmer had stayed down in London after making his obedience to the King, in order to keep his two elders abreast of the latest developments and news. A few days after Bigod fled from Beverley, one of Sir Ralph's servants arrived in Yorkshire to say that his master did not trust the King who, he thought, was not at all interested in peace but was determined to inflict punishment. Sir Ralph also said that thirty ships had just set sail for the North and that Norfolk was out to prove his loyalty to the Crown by complying with Henry's vicious instincts. He further warned his father that the Pilgrim leadership was in disarray and at each other's throats, with Robert Aske accusing colleagues of disloyalty and Sir Thomas Darcy's son, Sir George, now quite prepared to betray Old Tom and Sir Robert Constable. Unlike his brother Sir Arthur Darcy, who had obtained the lease of Sawley Abbey from the Crown and had always been a King's man, Sir George had been as committed to the rebellion as his father, but this appeared to count for nothing any more.

Sir William Bulmer had taken part in the Pilgrimage too and

was at the December council in Pontefract. But he had always been one of the doves there, had found no difficulty in taking the side of authority over the commons after Doncaster, and was one of those in charge of the forces that would have fallen upon Bigod had he not fled from Beverley. Not surprisingly, Bulmer was disposed to dismiss his nephew's intelligence, especially after an encounter he had in the last week of January. He had joined other gentlemen who supported the King in quietening a great muster of Clevelanders, about 1000 commons in all, that was held on Hambleton Hill on Thursday the 25th. Having done this, he went down to Richmondshire to confer with the old Pilgrim Lord Conyers at his home near Bedale but, at Northallerton on the way to Hornby Castle,[1] he ran into one of Cromwell's trusties, Sir Ralph Sadler, whose secret mission was to arrest Sir Thomas Percy and report to the Lord Privy Seal how things generally were in the North. Sadler told Bulmer that he was absolutely right to keep faith with the throne and to do all he could to prevent a fresh rebellion breaking out. On the strength of this Sir William dismissed Sir Ralph Bulmer's opinion when it came to his notice later that week and made plans to join the Duke of Norfolk's retinue, whose arrival was expected almost any day now.

Sir John Bulmer's problems were compounded by his knowing that letters had been sent to many of the Yorkshire gentry, including Matthew Boynton, inviting them to participate in Norfolk's progress round the North. Unfortunately, he had not received one; nor, for that matter, had his brother, though that didn't deter him from riding to Doncaster to meet the Duke. Doubtless confused and not sure which way to turn, Sir John then did something silly, given that he and his brother were evidently taking different paths, that there might even be a danger of their becoming as divided as the Darcys. He wrote to him, not only saying that he shared his son's scepticism about the King, but that Sir William should arrange coastal lookouts to give warning of the approaching thirty ships and to have beacons prepared for lighting the moment they showed up. 'I fear it is high time,' he wrote, meaning that it was imperative for such

1 Not to be confused with Hornby Castle in North Lancashire, home of the
  royalist Lord Monteagle, the Earl of Derby's cousin.

precautions to be taken. Sir William ignored this fraternal instruction and went on his way, while Sir John wrote to young Sir Ralph Evers, another who had lately returned from London, and sought his advice. He was told much the same as Sadler had told his brother, with the additionally heartening news that not only did the King wish him well, and craved his presence in Norfolk's retinue, but that Henry was actually writing him a letter of thanks for his 'diligent service'. Unfortunately, said Evers, he had departed from London in such a rush that he left this comforting document behind. This whole story was a lie. It assuaged Sir John Bulmer's immediate fears, however. But he had already given a hostage to fortune in the letter he wrote to his brother, which Sir William forgot to destroy.

And Sir John was not the only one to make such a fundamental mistake. A Nicholas Rudston of Hayton had been one of the Holderness captains in the Pilgrimage, but had rejected an attempt by Bigod to enlist him for further action, explaining that he was now the King's man. Like young Ellerker, who had been drifting further and further from the rebel leaders from the moment he was sent to court as a messenger with Robert Bowes, Rudston was keen to do anything that might enhance his reputation with Henry. Because he now obviously had some influence with the authorities, after inching his way towards them ever since Doncaster, Sir Robert Constable and Robert Aske had written to him after the calamity in Hull, to ask that the two Bigod messengers should be released because they were in no way implicated in Hallam's expedition, but had merely been on a harmless errand, as was recognised by Ellerker's return of their luckier comrade. Rudston at once passed the letter to Ellerker, who had a copy made and sent down to London; after which Rudston went to dine with Constable at Holme, with what purpose in mind is not at all clear, unless he coldly sought to incriminate Sir Robert even more. At Holme he showed Constable the letter and challenged him about its contents, at which the old soldier first tried to bluff his way out of a tricky situation, before confronting Rudston with 'And if so, what harm?'. To make matters worse, having realised the danger this now put him in, he tried to hide the letter in his clothing, which Rudston pretended not to notice. He was, after all, well aware that a copy had been made.

January was a waiting time in the North of England, with different expectations of what would happen when the Duke of Norfolk arrived. Because some people believed that he would come as a benefactor, while others thought that terrible things might befall them instead, it was also a time in which almost anything might occur virtually anywhere. The rumblings which had been heard ever since December had never died down: the agitation round Ripon, the disturbances in Craven, the bills circulating throughout the North, the various commotions on either side of the Pennines, had continued here and there with different degrees of intensity, in a number of shapes and forms, and what there had not been once was total peace and quiet. There had been that brief clap of thunder in the East Riding and along the east coast, but nothing to match it had followed anywhere, only a resumption of agitation in a minor key.

In Darlington there was a small to-do early one evening outside the inn where Sir Ralph Sadler was staying, when thirty or forty men assembled with clubs and wanted to know where things stood with the December agreement. Sadler suggested that they should be dispersed, but the innkeeper told him that would only make them angry instead of jumpy, that 1000 more would be on his doorstep within the hour. So Sadler told them that the Duke of Norfolk would be in Yorkshire by Candlemas, which commemorated the Purification of the Blessed Virgin Mary and fell on 2 February, and that he would be travelling with nothing more than his usual household staff. Whereupon, Sadler said, he 'heard no more of them'.

In Durham there was some trouble when the letter from Bigod arrived, urging people to fight the Duke of Norfolk and pressure the local gentry into taking a new oath. It was taken by the town's bailiff to the Earl of Westmorland's home at Brancepeth, where his wife the Countess was in charge during Neville's absence at court. Presumably with her consent, the bailiff composed a reply which rejected Bigod's demand and said they were all sworn to the King. This was given to one of Bigod's two messengers, to take back to his master, but the other man was held in custody at Brancepeth. As a result, a body of the local commons marched on the Westmorland home, made threatening noises and freed the prisoner. But before they could take any more action the news arrived of Bigod's great failure and their belligerence collapsed.

In Richmondshire there was a serious attempt to start another rising, following the agitation caused by the news from Lincolnshire which Simon Jackson of Jervaulx had brought back. This was exacerbated when the government tried to resume the collection of rents on 17 January, a move which affected Barnard Castle again, too, though not as ominously as it did the North Riding. The bills which were appearing everywhere added more fuel to an already combustible mixture, especially those which Sir Francis Bigod had originated before his flight to Cumberland. He may or may not have been behind one which promised that when Thomas Howard came, the brutality would be worse than in Lincolnshire, with people being hung, drawn and quartered for treason all the way from Doncaster to Berwick. It was in this atmosphere, towards the end of the month, that Jervaulx Abbey once more became a focal point of rebellious activity. The two laymen who had wanted payment for their bill-posting and had been given a bent coin by the ex-Abbot of Fountains, Ninian Staveley of Masham and Edward Middleton of Healey, had come up with their proposal that there should be a muster on Middleham Moor of all able-bodied men in the district.

The trouble with this was that the local commons, having to make decisions for themselves now instead of being firmly led by the gentry, simply could not agree on where they should assemble. Moreover, when a dozen men came knocking on his door, the Abbot of Jervaulx refused to let his monks attend the muster on the grounds that their vocation prohibited such behaviour. Adam Sedbar did, however, relent enough to give his visitors food and drink, and to authorise the abbey's servants and nearby tenants to join the assembly, which very nearly didn't happen because Staveley and Middleton were dismayed by all the discord. They were persuaded to go on when two of the Jervaulx Cistercians, Roger Hartlepool and John Stanton, turned up at Staveley's house in the middle of the night, clad not in their white habits but in harness and carrying battleaxes, and convinced him that it was absolutely necessary to start another rebellion. But no more than 100 people were eventually mustered on the moor and even they started arguing among themselves, before agreeing to try for a bigger turnout in Richmond the next day. The numbers there were not much greater, though they included people from a wider area, some coming from Kendal way and from Windermere. These decided that there should be a Pilgrim council in the town the following week, but that was to be a flop as well: 200 met, barely digested an agenda which emphasised the secular rather than the religious issues at stake, and evaporated the very same day without reaching any conclusions. By then, Adam Sedbar was safely under the protection of Lord Scrope in Bolton Castle, while Stanton and Hartlepool were on their way to seek refuge in Scotland.

People with strong opinions on how matters should proceed were unflaggingly busy in this period, attempting to push things in one direction or the other. Trying to maintain the peace in alliance with the King's men were former Pilgrims: noblemen like Lords Darcy and Scrope and Conyers, knights like Sir Robert Constable and Sir Oswald Wilstrop and Sir Richard Tempest, gentlemen like Robert Aske and Robert Bowes and Robert Pulleyn, clerics like Thomas Maunsell, the priest who had gone ahead with Aske to Pontefract (while the Archbishop of York, as ever, was trying to keep his head down and hoping that all this unpleasantness would soon go away). Counteracting the pacifiers were a number of commoners who moved menacingly from here to there, liable to pop up anywhere, inciting further rebellion, arranging assemblies, stirring up trouble as much as they could. John Hallam was obviously one of them and had been since the start of the Pilgrimage in Yorkshire. The thirty-four-year-old yeoman Ninian Staveley was another, having made his first appearance when terrifying Adam Sedbar into flight on to Witton Fell, after turning up at Jervaulx in October with other intimidating characters. He was notoriously as frightening as Hallam when in a temper and it is perhaps surprising that, in their January encounter, the Abbot found the courage to resist his demands, though by then he was probably so aware of some alarming writing on the wall by other hands that he closed his eyes and hoped for the best. Staveley had also been involved in damaging the properties of Sir Christopher Danby and Lord Latimer after hearing that they had gone to London, had written the letter that was sent from Jervaulx to Sir Thomas

Percy at Sedbar's request and had taken part in the abortive meeting at Richmond before moving over to Westmorland, where he was soon regarded as one of the local rebel leaders.

Also from the yeoman class was the Lincolnshire refugee William Leache, who had been in Louth when the people rose there, had started the rebellion in Horncastle, had forced Edward Dymmoke to take the oath or else face death and had been closely involved in the murder of the servant Wolsey, which followed the slaying of Dr Rayne. When Lincolnshire fell apart he evaded arrest, crossed the Humber and had never been far from trouble in the North of England, actual or potential, since. He was one of those who took part in the attack on Lancaster Herald up in Durham and he accompanied the Sawley servant George Shuttleworth on his errand to ask Sir Thomas Percy for help, having attached himself gratuitously to the messenger when Shuttleworth was having a drink before setting off. Later Leache, too, started operating in the North-west where, like Ninian Staveley, he soon made a reputation as one of the 'captains of Westmorland' with a price of £20 on his head, which was half as much as was being offered for the taking of Sir Francis Bigod.

Then there was Anthony Peacock, the bailiff of Arkengarthdale, who first got himself noticed by raising a contingent of men from his home patch to join the Richmondshire rising in October and took part in the restoration of Easby Abbey. Subsequently, he was involved in the refusal of people to pay the King's rents in the Barnard Castle district, both in December and in January, and almost any agitation there had Peacock close to its heart. He probably had something to do with the theft of Robert Bowes's cattle and other offences against property belonging to the acting-steward of the castle – in which capacity Bowes was responsible for the collection of the royal revenue – after the former Pilgrim leader had gone to London. And it may have been Bowes who, in his official role, was responsible for Peacock's arrest in February, after further disruptions near Barnard Castle. The bailiff was sent to York for trial, was condemned to death and was returned to Richmond, where he was to be executed. The night before this was due to happen a number of his friends were drinking at John o' Blade's alehouse in the Swaledale village of Grinton and one of them, Henry

Wycliffe, tried to organise a rescue party to get Peacock out of Richmond gaol. He upbraided his companions for their lethargy and said, 'Is your hearts done? Let me have 200 men and I shall give the Duke of Norfolk an onset, and I shall either save Peacock's life or have the Duke's chain...' But no 200 rescuers materialised, not one of the Grinton drinkers stirred and Anthony Peacock duly went to the gallows on Richmond Moor the following day. The commons of Richmondshire were no longer eager for anything but saving their own skins.

For, by then, the Duke of Norfolk was in command as the King's Lieutenant in the North. Since his exertions at the back end of 1536, Norfolk had been enjoying some well-earned leave on his estate at Kenninghall, knowing that he was not expected to be in Yorkshire again until the end of January. He needed to rest anyway, because he was not feeling very well. But he was summoned to Greenwich by Henry and there, on the 16th, he was given instructions for his next commission. They were issued, therefore, before word had reached London of Hallam's expedition to Hull, of Lumley's sally in Scarborough and of Bigod's abortive attempt to start a rising in Beverley. They were, in short, the King's response to a situation which had not changed in its essentials since Norfolk left the North in December and they should be read in that light. There had been distant rumblings in the meantime, but that first clap of thunder was only heard on the very day when Henry was meeting Norfolk in London, before it was audible down there. The Duke was charged with reaching Doncaster by Candlemas and there he would be met by the gentry who were most likely to serve his purposes. He would administer a new oath to them, the local commons would receive it next, and this swearing of obedience would be enacted wherever else in the North Thomas Howard went. From Doncaster he was to ride on to Pontefract, where more gentlemen would be waiting to join his progress, and after that he was to visit York, where 'he shall assemble the rest of the notable leaders and gentlemen of Yorkshire and the places adjoining, and give them the oath; and after that, command certain wapentakes every day to appear before him or his deputies and receive the oath; after that he shall pass through the countries that have rebelled, in such order as shall seem convenient'.

Before the oath was administered, people must confess and acknowledge 'their untrue demeanour towards their King, and submit themselves to his mercy'. They were to declare who the rebel leaders were, hand over all their arms, renounce all oaths they had made in the rebellion 'and swear to be true subjects and to maintain all Acts of Parliament made during the King's reign'. Because the oath was to be circulated by aides and henchmen of the Duke as well as by himself in person, a number of versions were eventually extant, though the thrust of them all was substantially the same. The original draft, with corrections and amendments made by other hands, insisted that 'First ye shall swear that ye be sorry ye have offended the King in this rebellion, and to repute vain all oaths made touching it ... to assist any commissioners for taking possession of any monasteries within the Act of Suppression, or for other purposes ... ye shall commit no treasons, murders, or felonies, but betray such to the King and in case any person move you to insurrection, or speak unfitting words of the King or his chief councillors, you shall apprehend them'. The palaver of oath-taking also included a homily which Norfolk and his assistants were to give everywhere, which 'shall enlarge upon the King's clemency and their offences'. The character of monks and other religious was to be vilified, for 'the Duke shall make a discourse to all men, and dilate how far they vary from good religious men – yea, from true subjects'. After settling the country, he was to 'restore the farmers to the houses already suppressed, endeavour to recover the goods of such houses, and aid any commissioners sent to dissolve others, causing all the religious persons of such houses to enter other houses of their religion, or to take capacities, or else punish them as vagabonds'. The arrears of rent everywhere were now to be collected.

That was the relatively lenient part of Norfolk's commission. But he and his council were also instructed that they shall 'everywhere search out the grounds of the insurrection, the setters forth, the devisers of articles put in at the last assembly at Doncaster and ... if any man refuse the oath, the Duke, if he thinks himself able, shall use him as the King's rebel'; that is, execute him. In the Lieutenant's progress through the North he and his aides were to 'inquire what persons have committed spoils, robberies, or other enormities since the King's pardon, and these he shall afterwards cause to be apprehended and executed, if it may be done without danger, especially if they have been ringleaders or captains. And if he may not do that without danger, he shall look through his fingers at their offences, and free them to continue till the King's Majesty's arrival in those parts, keeping watch that they escape not out of the country.' So, anyone who had offended since the pardon was granted was already a dead man, but these were not the only ones whom Henry had set his sights on. The whole commission reeks of a lurking desire for vengeance against those who had been active in the Pilgrimage from the start, even if they had not lifted a finger against the throne after Doncaster. It was also a licence for the unscrupulous to settle a few old scores by denunciation, whether or not their victims had held significant positions in the Pilgrimage. And not a word in it, from start to finish, about a new Parliament in York or anywhere else.

Just in case anything went amiss in a region which did not please him much even when it was tranquil and he was in good health, Norfolk made his will before leaving the South and lodged it with Cromwell who, though disliked by Howard, clearly had his uses for the Duke. The King's Lieutenant and his men were in Lincoln by the penultimate day of the month and reached Doncaster, as planned, on 1 February. Norfolk arrived without the army that so many had feared and half expected, travelling only with a body of servants who did not bear arms, in spite of the initial plan to provide him with 200 troops. Any other manpower he might need in the coming weeks would have to be raised on his behalf by the gentlemen who were now placing themselves at his disposal across the North.

Among those awaiting him at Doncaster were Sir Marmaduke Constable and Robert Aske's associate, the lawyer William Babthorpe, who had been nominated as one of the first captains of Howdenshire, had fled to the sanctuary of Pontefract and then became a member of the Pilgrimage's inner council after the castle was surrendered. Conspicuously missing was Aske himself, although he had written to enquire whether the Duke wanted him in the welcoming party: he was told, by Babthorpe, that York would be soon enough, that he must not be discouraged by this rebuff and that the reason for the delay would be revealed in due course. Another who was told (by Henry himself) to mark time until York was Sir Robert Constable, though Lord Darcy was encouraged to join the entourage at Pontefract, where he was installed again, in accordance with an earlier instruction from the King, to repair its defences and make sure it was properly provisioned. Dutifully, Darcy had done as he was told, and Pontefract was now well-stocked with food, including the beef from 'six stall-fed oxen at 20s ... muttons 6¼ at 2s 10d apiece ... 17 hens 4s 6d ... 17 partridges 2s 10d ... 131 eggs 13d ... 11 salt fish 9s 2d ... 3 lbs sugar at 8d a lb ... 2 lbs pepper 4s 4d ... 3 lbs almonds 12d ...' for a total expenditure of £46 6s 10.

These small humiliations were the first public sign that the three principal figures in the Pilgrimage were, in spite of the all-embracing pardon and the flatulent talk of clemency, marked men. But Norfolk came with his characteristic caution, based on a fine calculation of what was and was not profitable in a given situation. 'Force,' he said, 'must be meddled here with pleasant words as the case shall require.' And force, as he already knew by now, would have to be applied, if only to deal with events on the east coast that had occurred since his audience with the King. If there were to be other opportunities to follow the spirit of the sovereign's charge, rather than what the commission actually said, then a certain amount of guile might be necessary before force could be used to maximum effect.

Another indication of what might be in store for people who had been inclined to believe all the fair words that had lately been uttered, either by Norfolk or his master, took place as soon as Howard arrived in Yorkshire. Also waiting for him in Doncaster were the two younger Percy brothers, Sir Thomas and Sir Ingram. They had decided that they should at last make their obedience to the King and so they set off from Northumberland as January came to an end. Had they not made this move voluntarily, Sir Ralph Sadler was to have had them seized and brought south as prisoners, initially in a boat sailing from Berwick to Grimsby, to remove the risk of their being rescued as they were taken overland through many miles of country where the name of Percy rang as no other did, including the name of Henry VIII. They reached Doncaster on the very day that the Duke of Norfolk arrived from the opposite direction and there were given letters from the King, one addressed to each of them, which had arrived in Northumberland after they had left and which had been brought down post-haste to Yorkshire. These were a royal summons to travel to London without delay. To which Norfolk added his own encouragement and a letter which purported to ease their reception at court. So the Percy brothers, innocently – or maybe arrogantly, doing things the Percy way, in their own time – rode on to the South; and when they got there they were sent to the Tower, which only one of them would leave alive, and that briefly, to go to his execution on the other side of the city at Tyburn.

Norfolk was at York by the end of his first week in the North and there he swore to loyalty the city fathers and gentry assembled from each of the three Ridings, who were to take the oath home and administer it to all who were not included in the itinerary of those who were to receive it from the Duke in person. Robert Aske was among those who welcomed the Lieutenant and almost certainly continued in Thomas Howard's entourage to Carlisle and Durham. What his state of mind must have been by now can only be a matter of guesswork, for within the space of a few days he had received Babthorpe's enigmatically discouraging letter and, before it, one from the King himself, which referred to his help in controlling 'our subjects there who have been moved to a new commotion by that traitor Francis Bigod. We thank you, but would be glad to hear of some special deed in answer to our expectation.' The sole special deed Aske now had within his power in order to please his sovereign was to yield up another victim to Henry's appetite for revenge and he could do that only by betraying some old friend. Bad enough to sit through the trial of those indicted by Norfolk in York for their part in Bigod's uprising, as Aske could scarcely have avoided doing, given the sudden delicacy of his position and the overriding need to demonstrate his obedience in every possible way.

Already put to death in Hull were John Hallam, William Nicholson and Roger Kitchen, after being interrogated by John ap Rice, the commissioner who had been highly critical of Dr Legh's work the year before and who had been sent to the East

Riding by Henry specifically for this purpose. The three men had then been condemned on the orders of a royal commission, which consisted of the city's mayor, young Ellerker, Sir Robert Constable's brother Sir William, Sir John Constable and two of the local gentry who had originally been pressed into the Pilgrimage. Some members of Hallam's group still lingered in the city's gaol, but three canons of Watton Priory and three Watton labourers had been sent over to York and now faced justice from the Duke of Norfolk himself. Of these, only one of the canons (Harry Gyll, the sub-Prior) and one of the labourers were to die as a result of the first York trials, together with seven other men, including Ralph Fenton, who had been George Lumley's accomplice at Scarborough, and Anthony Peacock, the man who was abandoned by those who might have rescued him in Swaledale.

Norfolk's attention was then deflected from any other business in York by the sound of more thunder, this time in the North-west. It was preceded by heart-warming news for Thomas Howard about the capture of Sir Francis Bigod, who was found hiding with two servants in an unnamed Cumbrian chapel by men belonging to Sir John Lamplugh, another of the reluctant Pilgrim leaders who needed to earn some credit with the Crown. Bigod was hauled off to Carlisle Castle and from thence, eventually, he was sent down to London for trial. The day after Bigod was taken the Duke sent his serjeant-at-arms to seize Nicholas Musgrave and Thomas Tebay, who had once before defied an attempt to capture them by taking refuge in the Kirkby Stephen church tower. Since then, the town had become a headquarters for renewed rebel activity in Westmorland, sheltering, among others by this time, the fugitives from Lincolnshire and Richmondshire, William Leache and Ninian Staveley. Some of the disorders that began happening in the New Year were a result of Robert Pulleyn – joint leader with Musgrave in the local Pilgrimage – having changed sides, allying himself now with the Clifford family in the collection of taxes (thus breaking a specific promise he had made to the commons) and supposedly taking bribes from people who sought tenancies in the new Clifford enclosures along Mallerstang and upon Stainmore. As a result of this betrayal his home was raided and he would have been taken to Kirkby Stephen to face some very rough justice if friends had not intervened and guaranteed that he would stay put; yet another example of the commons submitting to the judgement of their betters.

On top of his instruction to the serjeant, the Duke of Norfolk also ordered another move by Sir Thomas Clifford, who had already failed once to secure Musgrave and Tebay. That had been no worse than a depressing setback to the Crown. This time there was to be something much worse than that: not quite a disaster, but certainly another humiliation for the Crown. Contrary to explicit instructions from the Duke, who ordered that none but highly disciplined troops must be used in this action, Clifford rode down to Kirkby Stephen with a rabble of Border reivers, who were always good for bloodshed so long as there was plenty to plunder at the end of it. They included the notorious Graemes of Esk, who subsequently had the impudence to claim a cessation of their rents in perpetuity, for services rendered on this and other occasions. At their coming, Musgrave and Tebay once more climbed up into the tower of St Stephen's and there, once again, put themselves out of reach; Leache and Staveley also appear to have made themselves scarce.

Down in the streets, however, things became desperate as Clifford's men cut loose and began to loot whatever they could reach. For once, though, they more than met their match, when the townsfolk rushed from their homes with all the dangerous implements they could lay their hands on. Frustrated by their inability to take their official quarry and by this unexpected hostility, the reivers rode a little way out of town, over its humpbacked bridge across the infant Eden, to try to snatch horses that might be found untended in the pastures towards Hartley and Winton. By the time they got back, the commons of Kirkby Stephen had already captured the Duke of Norfolk's serjeant-at-arms and one or two gentlemen travelling with Clifford. These the raiding party managed to retrieve after a tremendous struggle at the Low Mill bridge, which they then lost as the citizens gained the upper hand and not only chased them out of Kirkby Stephen, but as far along the road north as Brougham Castle, another Clifford stronghold, on the outskirts of Penrith. There, Sir Thomas's men had to take refuge and lick their wounds.

Blood had indeed been spilled that day, fatally in the case of two men from the little Westmorland town.

Much worse was to follow. Bills began to stir things up again after the action at Kirkby Stephen and it is believed that Musgrave, Leache, Staveley and the Dent leader John Atkinson were behind many of them. One which was composed only hours after the skirmish in the name of 'Captain of Poverty' exaggerated what had just occurred and demanded a reaction the next day. It said that the place had been attacked by 'our enemies the Captain of Carlisle and gentlemen of our Country of Westmorland, and hath destroyed and slain many our brethren and neighbours. Wherefore we desire you for aid and help according to your oaths and as ye will have help of us if your cause require, as God forbid. This Tuesday we command you every one to be at Kendal afore eight of the clock or else we are likely to be destroyed.'

Atkinson led a party to organise a muster there in the morning but he was rebuffed, perhaps because he was a Dent man and there had long been an enmity between the two towns; but the puzzling thing is that in October the Kendal commons had been willing to follow Atkinson's lead in marching upon Lancaster. Maybe the answer is simply that all Westmorland had become nervously and unpredictably aggressive, liable to snap at anybody who was not one of their own, as a result of what were seen as broken promises and commitments, and the tension that had been growing in the area ever since the Doncaster agreement and the consequent failure to take Carlisle.

In another example of the smouldering anger there the New Year had seen renewed pressure on priests in both Brough and Kendal to conduct services in the traditional Roman way: in the first instance Robert Thompson, who had been Captain Poverty's chaplain in October, prayed for the Pope and his cardinals, and this in due course sent him to the Tower of London. Of all the people in the North-west, the commons of Westmorland were readiest to make a second attempt on the Border city on 16 February. The impetus came from there and so did the majority of volunteers as well as the leaders now, who were Musgrave and Tebay. But these were joined by Cumbrians, by Yorkshiremen and by Lancastrians from the area round

Morecambe Bay. One company came up from Steeton in Craven, and another threw its weight behind a new assault in an overspill of hostility after the King's farmer Thomas Holcroft had antagonised the canons of Cartmel Priory, their servants and their tenants. We do not know for certain, but it is possible that, as well as demanding his dues, he had threatened to demolish the priory church, which was a focal point of life for all Cartmel parishioners. Holcroft was one of the rising gentry in Lancashire and – like Sir Arthur Darcy in Yorkshire – he had a good nose for the profit to be gained from religious houses. He eventually exchanged Cartmel in a commercial deal and bought all the Lancashire friaries for £126. He died in possession of seven manors and vast estates, after being appointed Knight Marshal of England.

That Friday, some 6000 rebels advanced to their old mustering place on the Broadfield outside Carlisle. They then closed up on the city walls, moving in formation behind a standard bearer who on this occasion was holding a cross. Their bowmen fired sheaves of arrows to reach the 500 troops, much better armed than the insurgents, who were waiting to withstand the attack. And, suddenly, all was chaos – but outside the walls, not within. Without any warning at all, 500 Border mercenaries led by Sir Christopher Dacre – the man who had persuaded the Pilgrims to turn back from their first sally against Carlisle – fell upon the rebels from behind. No sooner had these been thrown into confusion than the city gates opened and out poured the soldiers commanded by Sir Thomas Clifford, now returned to his official post after riding ahead of his Monday pursuers, who had seen him off as far as Brougham. Attacked from both sides, the rebels lost their nerve and fled, and what followed turned into a rout in which the humiliation of that ignominious flight four days earlier was fully avenged, with a great number of casualties of which only rumour exists. In London, the talk was of 700 killed, though how much of an exaggeration this was we shall never know. We are well aware of exactly what happened afterwards, though.

Dacre had been alerted by the Duke of Norfolk, who was at Fountains Abbey when he heard about the battle at Kirkby Stephen bridge and the failure of Sir Thomas. Clifford having proved himself useless, Norfolk sent an urgent despatch to Dacre, asking him to be ready for an attack on Carlisle and to conduct at least a holding operation there until the Duke could reach him with reinforcements; and while he was about it, Dacre was not to shrink from spilling rebel blood. The message ended with the persuasive words, 'Finally now, Sir Christopher, or never. Your loving cousin if ye do well now, or else enemy for ever.' Hastily, Norfolk gathered his own force together in the North Riding, with the ready co-operation of all the upper classes who desperately wished to find favour with the Crown. In the end, he had mustered no fewer than 4000 troops, 'well-willing nobles, gentlemen and serving men', many of them astride 'the best geldings he ever saw'.

His first instinct was to order that the torch should be put to the homes of the commons in Westmorland, in order to create a diversion which might relieve the pressure on Carlisle; then he would ride in to take overall command. But before he and his army could even leave Richmond, messengers had come through the night from Dacre to say that the rebels had been smashed, with 800 prisoners taken. From now on, Thomas Howard's expedition to the North was entirely punitive. It was also bent on exemplary punishments that would terrify the region and satiate the King, and this was because of what had – what hadn't, in truth – happened in Beverley. The sixty-two men who were taken prisoner there had been granted bail by the elder Ellerker on the application of Robert Aske's brother-in-law William Monckton, who was representing them, and their release effectively exonerated them of treason. This had produced one of Henry's most spectacular rages and Norfolk did not want to be on the receiving end of another such.

He reached Carlisle on Monday the 18th and there he quickly imposed martial law. This was signalled by flying the King's banner from the castle's keep, and it would not end until Norfolk decided that his business there was finished and the banner could be symbolically furled again. Henry's instructions on what must be done were perfectly explicit in a letter he wrote to Norfolk that week. After referring to the steps already taken he said that 'before you close it [the banner] up again you must cause such dreadful execution upon a good number of the inhabitants, hanging them on trees, quartering them, and setting their heads and quarters in every town, as shall be a fearful warning, whereby shall ensue the preservation of a great multitude'. Howard had already carried out the substance of these orders on his own initiative, because the communication didn't reach him until everything had been finished and the banner was furled, matters having been conducted with such haste that there was no time for dismemberment, the conventional refinement of punishment for treason. A speedy conclusion was necessary because, as Howard explained to the King's Council, he was obliged under martial law to be present at every execution and 'You will hardly believe the trouble I have to keep the prisoners, there are so many.' So he simply selected seventy-four of them for execution after what was effectively a very brief show trial. It was conducted without the assistance of a jury but with some sort of hearing, in which young Ellerker acted as the marshal who brought the men before the court, Robert Bowes appearing as the King's prosecutor. Howard actually admitted later that, if a jury had sat in Carlisle, no more than a fifth of the accused would have been found guilty as charged, because so many of them had pitiful stories to tell of taking part in the revolt only under extreme duress 'and a small excuse will be well believed here, where much affection and pity of neighbours doth reign'. How much of such affection there was he would shortly find out.

He was not without sympathy for some of the rebels himself. Of the ones who escaped these random executions, Howard wrote to Cromwell that 'The poor caitiffs who have returned home have departed without any promise of pardon but upon their good a-bearing. God knows they may well be called poor caitiffs; for at their fleeing they lost horse, harness, and all they had upon them, and what with the spoiling of them now and the gressing of them so marvellously sore in time past and with increasing of lords' rent by enclosings ... also that they have been so sore handled in times past which, as I and all here think, was the only cause of this rebellion.' For all that, he instructed the Earl of Derby, and Derby's cousin Lord Monteagle, to keep an eye open for any of these people who might try to take refuge in Lancashire. The hard side of him came out again in his report to the King two days later. Promising that the guilty would be put to death in every town where they dwelt, twelve to start with in Carlisle, he added that as many as possible would have their remains hanged in chains, which prolonged the spectacle, so long as the supply of iron kept up with the demand, and when that ran out, the rest would be treated likewise on the end of rope. Up in that part of the North, 'Iron is marvellous scarce', he said. One of Norfolk's victims was Thomas Tebay, captured and brought into Carlisle by the freebooting Graemes, who would have been especially glad to seize the man who had made such fools of them in Kirkby Stephen at the beginning of that week. His fellow steeplejack Nicholas Musgrave, however, managed to get away and was never heard of again, while William Leache and Ninian Staveley also escaped, though Staveley was subsequently caught and taken in for questioning.

The carnage of retribution for the events of 1537 in the North-west was spread across the whole of Cumberland and Westmorland and into Lancashire, where other executions took place. Four of the Cartmel canons (one of whom was sixty-eight years old) and ten of their parishioners – all described as 'husbandmen' – were hanged in Lancaster Castle for their part in the new rebellion, while the tanner who had led a company of men up to Carlisle from Craven was executed in Manchester. Westmorland suffered by far the greatest penalty, yielding fifty-three of the seventy-four victims, and they came from nineteen different towns and villages in the county. One of the places to suffer most was the parish of Lunds, which included the length of Mallerstang, where enclosures belonging to Henry Clifford and Sir Thomas Wharton had been pulled down in previous months, leading to the suspicion that these reprisals were not merely for offending the King. Ten men were put to death in that valley, nine of them coming from the grimly suggestive Hanging Lund, a hamlet in the shadow of Wild Boar Fell.[2]

There was a terrible and heartbreaking sequel to these and other deaths, in Cumberland as well as in Westmorland. By early April, after the bodies had been hanging for five weeks or more, they were in an advanced state of decomposition, a ghastly

2 The name, derived from Norse, means a hillside grove of trees.

warning to any who might be tempted to displease their sovereign again. The sight of them was eventually too much for the women whose husbands, sons, fathers and brothers they had been. At Eastertide, symbolically, they took what was left of their men down from the trees where the remains hung, though some by then lay on the ground because rotted flesh and disjointed bone had parted company from the ropes or the chains. The women took them away to give them decent Christian burial, but this was denied them at two places in Cumberland. The priest in charge at Brigham refused to have Richard Cragge's rebellious remains on consecrated ground and so he was buried in a ditch instead, his widow being helped by a cousin, who later died from a disease contracted by handling the putrefied corpse. Likewise, Percival Hudson's body was rejected at Torpenhow, though his widow outmanoeuvred the cleric there when 'three days after, she and a woman she hired buried him in Torpenhow churchyard at night'. John Bewley's wife wrapped what was left of him in a winding sheet, after it had fallen from the tree nine days previously and, with some help, she put him down when it was dark in Dereham churchyard; but his brother, like Richard Cragge's cousin, also died from an infection picked up from the corpse. Thomas Bell was properly buried at last in Cockermouth, after which his Bess contemplated a future without the bread-winner whose total wealth at the time of his death amounted to one shilling and one penny.

The ineffably priapic Henry was so astonished by these defiant acts of devotion and heroism that he assumed men must have been wholly responsible for them. Men did, indeed, sometimes help women to get the thing done, but it was wives and mothers, sisters and daughters who instigated it all. Such was Henry's wrath that Norfolk a month later claimed to have known nothing about the recovery of bodies until then. He nevertheless arraigned all the women involved, for examination in Cockermouth, Carlisle, Penrith and elsewhere, though nothing came of these actions and the women were allowed to return to what was left of their lives. The last that was heard of the matter was a communication on 22 May from Cromwell to Norfolk, deploring his slackness in obtaining crucial evidence. 'If those depositions had been earnestly taken,' he wrote, 'the truth might have been known.' Even at that late stage, six weeks or so after Easter, the Duke was told he 'must find out and punish the principal doers'. This instruction fell on deaf ears, for Thomas Howard had other work to do.

THE RECKONING

The Augustinian canons of Cartmel were not the only religious to be picked off that spring for, now that he had been given the pretext he needed, Henry was intent on a retribution against the monasteries that went far beyond beyond the destruction of their property and the acquisition of their wealth. He wanted blood above all things, and monastic blood would be an important and satisfying part of the ritual sacrifice he required. In his charge to Norfolk, which spoke savagely of the punishments that must follow the triumph at Carlisle, most of the King's anger was, in fact, directed against religious and the letter concluded with the following further injunction: 'Finally, as these troubles have been promoted by the monks and canons of those parts, at your repair to Sawley, Hexham, Newminster, Lanercost, St Agatha's [Easby] and such other places as have made resistance since the appointment at Doncaster, you shall without pity or circumstance, now that our banner is displayed, cause the monks to be tied up without further delay or ceremony.' Hanging, however, was only part of what was in store for such people if they were convicted of treason. But the thinness of Henry's self-justification is illustrated by his inclusion of Newminster in the list of prizes he had his eyes on. There is not the slightest evidence that the Cistercians of this abbey, situated near Morpeth in Northumberland, had anything at all to do with the Pilgrimage, let alone the post-pardon revolts, apart from accepting the rebel offer of restoration after being ejected by Cromwell's commissioners.

The Duke received Henry's communication when he was

about to set out for Hexham, by which time Sawley had already been taken care of. He had originally intended to go there himself if necessary, with a force of troops to back Sir Richard Tempest, whom he commissioned to oversee matters on his behalf. But when, on 13 February, Tempest arrived at the abbey, armed with nothing but a document from Norfolk which ordered the monks to leave forthwith unless they wished to be treated as rebels, Abbot Bolton and his brethren meekly complied, without this provoking the slightest reaction from the local Percy Fee commons, who had rushed to the abbey's assistance so ardently the previous October.

Some of these Cistercians were not to get off the hook as easily as that, however. The vastly incriminating letter which George Shuttleworth took to Sir Thomas Percy, pleading for his assistance and promising another rising on the Yorkshire–Lancashire border, had turned up among the papers which Percy's wife innocently handed over to the authorities when he was en route to London, and someone had to pay for that. Thomas Bolton himself was obviously the principal culprit, because the letter had been composed in the name of the abbot and the entire Sawley community. His chaplain, Richard Estgate, was also held particularly responsible, as were a couple of their brethren, Henry Bradford and Christopher Parish. The last two, in fact, getting wind of the very serious trouble they were in, escaped before they could be taken and never were brought to Henry's version of justice.

Bolton also made himself scarce after Tempest had closed Sawley down, but he was found later that week by Sir Arthur Darcy, who had gone to the monastery in order to take possession of it conclusively at last. 'No man knew where the abbot was,' Darcy told Cromwell, 'but I got secret information and twelve of my servants took him. He makes as though he could neither ride nor go, and lays all the blame on the commons that put him in against his will.' The sick Bolton was certainly captured, but what happened to him after that is something we shall never know for sure. Sir Stephen Hamerton would later report that he was sentenced to death, but no official record of his having been brought to trial exists, whereas the fate of other religious superiors is catalogued in some detail. It is perfectly possible that Thomas Bolton was despatched to the Tower of London, as a suspect who could be induced to yield much useful information before he was sent to the scaffold, and that illness finished him off either there or wherever else he was held. It is even conceivable that such sickness was brought on by his predicament and that he was literally frightened to death, having no doubt when Darcy showed up about what was ultimately in store for him. To the calculating Sir Arthur the Abbot of Sawley was nothing more than a mark of credit in the account he had opened with the King. When writing to Cromwell, he went out of his way to mention that servants of Tempest and one of his own tenants 'have wasted my goods and taken up my half-year's rents'. Also, that he had paid good money for the abbey's goods, which he never enjoyed.

We do know the fate of Richard Estgate. He, too, put some distance between himself and Sawley after 13 February, but in his case it was only a few miles downstream to Whalley Abbey, which stood beside a tributary of the Ribble. This was almost the wealthiest monastery in Lancashire, second only to Furness Abbey, as may be deduced from some of its expenditures. On provisions alone, the Whalley Cistercians (of whom there were never more than twenty-something in the 1530s) spent about £500 a year, more than half their annual income, though this outlay sustained not only the community itself and the abbey's frequent guests, but also twenty-four old and infirm people who were permanently housed on the premises. There was also one of the brethren to maintain as a scholar at Oxford, and the expenses incurred by Abbot John Paslew, who had a taste for travel that was exceptional in someone belonging to a closed order: a trip he made to London in 1520 had cost the community £26 5s. Some of his monks believed that their abbot made such journeys to trade in valuables belonging to the abbey including the sale, on one occasion, of 'about 165 lbs of silver to one Trappes and another goldsmith in London'.

With almost as many personal servants as he had monks under his obedience, Paslew lived very well indeed and did not stint himself in anything he did. His mitre was encrusted with jewels and silver-gilt attachments, and his two pastoral crooks were made of silver. He had a Lady Chapel built to remind posterity of his time as superior, and its architecture was so impressive that some people in Burnley hired Paslew's masons to repair their church, instructing them to add eighteen buttresses to the building, 'every buttress having a funnel upon the top according to the fashion of the funnels upon the new chapel of our Lady at Whalley'. But nothing in Burnley could hope to compete with Whalley's services, which were garnished with a richness of vestments, plate and jewellery that very few cathedrals in the land, and no other place of worship, could possibly have bettered. Of copes alone there were eighteen, all lavishly embroidered with vivid decorations, depicting in one case a portrait of Christ upon cloth of gold. There were no fewer than fifteen gilt chalices, and a silver-gilt cross embellished with figurines of Mary and St John.

This was the sister community which Richard Estgate joined, together with another Sawley monk, Henry Banaster, as they were entitled to under the provision that allowed the religious of suppressed houses to attach themselves to larger foundations of the same order which had not yet been dissolved; and the attraction for Estgate was the greater because his brother John was one of the Whalley Cistercians. But this could never have been a long-lasting refuge because Estgate would have been taken the moment his association with the Percy letter was deduced by the authorities. He then compounded his offence by trying to stir up rebellion again from the moment he settled down among his new brethren, composing and distributing, with the assistance of Banaster, seditious bills throughout Blackburnshire, where Whalley Abbey was a considerable landowner and dominating influence. Its great wealth of £900 per annum came from these holdings, and from others which yielded income in places as distant as the Wirral of Cheshire, the Lancashire coast and Pennine Rochdale.

Banaster evaded arrest for his activities, but Estgate was sent for trial at Lancaster early in March and there he was convicted of treason at the same hearing which resulted in the execution of the Cartmel canons and their parishioners. This was conducted not by Norfolk but by another member of the Privy Council, Robert Radcliffe, the Earl of Sussex, who had been commissioned to do in Lancashire what the Duke was doing elsewhere, a task which he was to share with the Earl of Derby. And Henry's charge to them was much the same as his order to

Thomas Howard, though it enlarged somewhat on his first ful-mination against all religious. The two Earls were to 'dilate' to the people of the North-west how monks, canons and nuns alike had been cushioned against the normal demands of life which were shared by the King and all English laypeople. They were told to explain that 'the prince must expend his treasure and risk his life in the defence of his poor subjects, while the monks and canons lie warm in their demesnes and cloisters; they may not fight for their prince and country, but have declared at this rebel-lion that they may fight against them. The husbandman and arti-ficer must labour in all weathers, and must go in person to defend his prince and country; the monk and the canon is sure at all times of a good house and good food...' and so on.

Sussex, Derby and the other members of their commission gathered in Warrington towards the end of February, and there they began collecting their evidence and administering the King's oath. The first three days of March they spent in Manchester, before moving on to Preston and then to Lancaster, after pausing to take stock of things at Whalley, whose fate they were about to decide. Richard Estgate went to the gallows as a result of their judgement and took with him two of the Whalley Cistercians, whose house in a sense had been polluted by its hapless association with Sawley. Far from having incited or par-ticipated in rebellious acts, as Thomas Bolton and his monks unquestionably had, the Whalley brethren had been most reluc-tant to become involved in the Pilgrimage of Grace and had sworn its oath only after Nicholas Tempest and his 400 commons threatened to burn down their monastery. Habitually they tried very hard to stay on the right side of the King's law and on at least two occasions they attempted to sweeten authori-ty with gifts of money: Cardinal Wolsey was presented with £22 in 1520, when he was nosing around religious houses in his capacity as Papal Legate, and Thomas Cromwell did even better, with an annual grant of £6 13s 4d from the abbey's funds. The only false move by the monks had been made in October, when a letter to Abbot Paslew from the Earl of Derby, which outlined his planned occupation of Whalley, was injudiciously passed on to the rebels; but that, of course, was before the pardon and should therefore have been excused.

Nothing of this counted on 9 March, however, when Paslew and Brother William Haydock were condemned to death in Lancaster. Haydock had pleaded guilty to only one of three treason charges brought against him, but the Abbot unfathomably pleaded guilty to all five listed in his indictment. At the same hearing John Estgate was acquitted after pleading not guilty to two charges, and when last heard of he had been allowed to join the Cistercians in faraway Neath. It was his brother Richard who was executed in Whalley, together with William Haydock. There has always been some confusion about where John Paslew met his end, but it seems likely that he was executed in Lancaster and that part of his dismembered body was then sent to Whalley to be exhibited as a warning and a lesson to all. Yet he might easily have saved himself had he not pleaded guilty as charged, for there was no evidence that he had ever uttered so much as a word against the King and not even the Earl of Sussex could have ignored that. As it was, because the law held that a monastery belonged to its superior and was therefore forfeited if he was convicted of treason, Whalley became a Crown property much sooner than would otherwise have been the case. Mercy was nevertheless shown to its Prior, Christopher Smith, who was allowed to stay on as priest to 3000 parishioners on the suggestion of Sussex, who advised Henry that 'it would be charitable to grant it, as he has been over 50 years a monk and is almost 80 years old, and is not likely long to continue'.

The Earl then turned his attention to Furness. Half hidden between the steep sides of an isolated valley, this was the richest Cistercian foundation in the country after Fountains, its income generated by tanning, quarrying, iron mines, salt pans, fishing, milling and other holdings as well as by its sheep-farming granges. Its up-to-date estates management had included the enclosure of land for pasture, which in recent times had produced friction with tenants whose common right to till the land if they wished had been lost as a result, most notably in Craven in 1535. The Abbot, Roger Pyle, had inherited a difficult situation from his predecessor, who had been responsible for the enclosures, and by temperament he was nervously aware of the need to placate those who might become hostile.

The most dramatic example of this was his decision to take

refuge with the Earl of Derby in October, while advising his monks to stay on good terms with the local commons. At one and the same time he was motivated by self-preservation and by a need, perhaps, to do what seemed best for the protection of the great asset which had been entrusted to his care. But in his absence at Lathom House, most of the Furness monks openly supported the Pilgrimage with the encouragement of the Prior, Brian Garner, who was in charge of things with Pyle no longer there. So Michael Hammerton, the cellarer, and others, with the support of their brethren, took £23 6s 8d as a donation to the cause and marched with the rebels to Dalton, where they called out the abbey's tenants and ordered them to muster fully harnessed on the morrow, or else risk having their homes burned down. A similar injunction was posted at Hawkshead. The threat was never carried out, even though some of the tenants did not respond, doubtless because they still felt sore about the enclosures. But before everything came to a standstill because of the agreement at Doncaster the Furness monks put more money in the rebel war chest and had a ready answer to any of their people who wondered what to do if the commons came knocking on their door. 'Agree with them, as we have done,' these were told. 'Now they must stick to it, or else never, for if they sit down both you and Holy Church is undone, and if they lack company we will go with them, and live and die to defend their most godly Pilgrimage.'

Roger Pyle returned to Furness in November and felt so intimidated by the atmosphere there that he said he was too frightened to go into the church alone at night. Two monks in particular, John Broughton and Henry Salley, were especially hostile to the King and what he had done, their talk so treasonable that Pyle would have done well to report them in order to save himself from an accusation of guilt by association; but he was too scared to do that. Instead, he instructed his community to obey the rules laid down by Drs Legh and Layton at their visitation early in 1536, which simply had the effect of dividing the community between those who were prepared to comply in the interests of security and those who would not compromise their beliefs for anything at all. By the time the Sussex commission got to work Pyle was worried that the rift developing among his brethren would endanger them all, and he was especially afraid that word would get out of talk by Broughton and Salley that was a blatant infringement of the pardon.

He had very good reason to be anxious, because denunciations had already begun, the bailiff of Dalton, Alexander Richardson, reporting to the commissioners that the monks had funded the rebellion and otherwise participated in it. Others, including Robert Legate, the Vicar of Dalton, who believed in Reform, also threw their weight into the balance against the monastery. But early in March, Sussex's investigators had concluded there was not enough solid evidence that the community as a whole had conspired to defy the pardon, and that therefore there were insufficient grounds for any action other than arresting the two obviously culpable monks. Messages went down to London asking for supplementary instructions and the reply came back that there must be further investigations, with the arrest of the Abbot and 'such of his monks as ye shall suspect' as a top priority. Sussex knew that there was no way within the law that Pyle could be taken, so he thought to devise another way to satisfy the King's lust for Furness to be brought down.

He had made his headquarters at Whalley after its abbey was confiscated and from there he played a master stroke. In early April, a couple of weeks after John Paslew's execution, he summoned Pyle to Whalley and the Abbot must have been thoroughly terrified by the time he came face to face with the Earl. He would have been well aware by now that Sussex was a much tougher customer than the Duke of Norfolk, much more inclined to execute than to play devious politics. And Pyle had, after all, just come through a gateway which may have been festooned with the remains of Richard Estgate and William Haydock, together with some part of Abbot Paslew's body; at any rate, these suggestive relics would have been highly visible somewhere nearby. If this was a calculated softening-up tactic it certainly worked. After further questioning, Sussex was more than ever convinced that Pyle could not be arraigned for treason, much less convicted, which would have given the Crown Furness Abbey in the same way that it had taken Whalley. He therefore made his visitor an offer. Why not, he suggested, simply surrender the abbey to the Crown as a token of goodwill and as a settling of all scores.

Roger Pyle probably didn't think twice about his answer but, yes, of course he was prepared to do that; he would have been willing to do anything that would remove this perpetual pressure once and for all. So documents were drawn up – more than once they were drawn up, so careful was Sussex not to leave any opportunities for legal challenges later on – and on 9 April Abbot Pyle and twenty-eight monks of Furness conclusively signed away their abbey and all its possessions to the King. Pyle then accepted the offer of a living in Dalton and quickly faded from the Crown's memory. The only monks to suffer the penalties of the law were Broughton and Salley, who were sent to Lancaster Castle and, though they never appeared at any trial, vanished and may well have died in captivity.

Sussex had created a new piece of case law in obtaining the forfeiture of a monastery by voluntary conveyance instead of by attainder. The Duke of Norfolk, meanwhile, was steadily making his way round the other side of the Pennines and closing down religious houses according to the older methods. By the last week in February he had suppressed Hexham in the same way that Tempest had disposed of Sawley, by simply ordering the community to leave; and the religious at Easby, Coverham and Newminster likewise did his bidding without making any fuss. More drastic measures were taken at Jervaulx and Bridlington, however, both having been implicated in the disturbances that had occurred since the pardon was announced. The Wensleydale abbey had been deeply involved in rebellion from the moment Leonard Burgh and his gang came knocking on its door in October, and in the New Year it had become tainted again, though Adam Sedbar had tried to put some distance between himself and the local commons this time. He had, however, despatched that compromising letter to Sir Thomas Percy with the support of his friend William Thirsk, the former Abbot of Fountains; and this act alone was enough to have them arrested on charges of treason, with Sedbar having much more to answer for on top of it. They were taken by Norfolk's men on 17 March, and were sent down to London for interrogation and trial before their executions in June at Tyburn.

By then the dissolution of Jervaulx had already taken place, precisely a week after its Abbot was found guilty and sentenced to death. As for Bridlington, it was secured for the Crown because its Prior, William Wood, had unforgivably sheltered the rebel songwriter Dr Pickering, though he was also charged with treason on the specious grounds that he had worked in collusion with Sir Robert Constable and had helped to incite the Bigod and Hallam risings; in fact, like many who would finish up on the gallows, he had done his best to prevent them. Wood might have saved himself had he been prepared to shop Constable, but this he refused to do. So he, too, was sent to London at the end of March and put to death alongside Adam Sedbar.

Even before Wood mounted the scaffold, Bridlington Priory, too, had become a Crown property. It was a prize that had Thomas Howard fairly drooling with anticipation of the profit to be made out of it. He was there for a couple of days in mid-May, having staked a claim to both it and Jervaulx in a letter to the King. 'I think I should be at the suppressing,' he wrote, 'because the neighbouring country is populous and the houses greatly beloved by the people, and also well stored with cattle and other things that will not come to light so well if I be absent.' The roof of Bridlington's barn particularly impressed him, 'all covered with lead the largest, widest and deepest roofed that I ever saw', worth something between £3000 and £4000, he thought, and conveniently near the sea so that it could easily be shipped out. As for the priory's jewellery and plate, Norfolk was allowed to have first pick before sending everything else to London. That amounted to three chests full of precious metal and stones, including three finely wrought pieces which inspired him to remark that 'if I durst … be a thief I would have stolen them to have sent them to the Queen's Grace, but now your Highness having them may give them unto her without offence'. He was no less enthusiastic about the spoils of Jervaulx (also 'well covered with lead'), from which he took a ring, a silver cross and some censers; and his appreciation of it was echoed by Sir Arthur Darcy, who believed it to be 'one of the fairest churches I have seen, fair meadows and the river running by it and a great demesne'. Darcy also reckoned that the King should shift his royal stud to the banks of the Ure, instead of breeding his horses at Thornbury in Gloucestershire.

Such were the processes and prizes of Henry's justice, in

which only the penalties were absolutely certain. How a man fared after being thrown into prison on suspicion of treason depended to some extent on his social standing and his wealth, or that of friends who might be prepared to buy him some relief. Nobles were sometimes placed in chambers with more than one room, with windows and very often with fires. Some degree of creature comforts such as these, and a better quality of food, could often be obtained if a prisoner had the means to buy them from his gaoler; otherwise he was in for a wretched time before his trial. Many cells, in the Tower of London, at Lancaster and elsewhere, were underground and so lacked light and fresh air; one particularly appalling dungeon in the Tower was known as 'little ease', so small that it was impossible to stand, lie or sit in it, and could only be endured in a prehensile crouch. Presumably in there it was not thought necessary to shackle the prisoner, though this was done often enough in more spacious surroundings, again with certain variations; and, again, with the possibility of obtaining relief if enough money changed hands. Leg irons were the most common form of restriction, though the Carthusian monks who faced execution in 1535 were chained standing by the neck, arms and legs to a post for thirteen days before going to their deaths.

The prisoner was held in such conditions for two purposes: one, obviously, was to ensure that he came to judgement at the appointed time, but the other was simply to break down his resistance to the interrogation which he always faced before his trial, answering questions which had usually been composed by Cromwell himself. Again, the questioning was conducted with two aims in mind: incriminating evidence of his own activities and the extraction of as much information as possible that would eventually incriminate others. To this end, the interrogation usually went on for at least days and often weeks, with repeated appearances before the examiners, but some people were held for much longer; like Sir Thomas More, who was arrested in the middle of April 1534 and not put on trial until July 1535. Torture was not unknown in Tudor England, often by depriving victims of food until they came up with the right answers, sometimes by racking them, but Henry VIII appears to have authorised it only once for anyone implicated in the Pilgrimage of Grace, and that was in the case of John Hallam and his accomplices – an indication, perhaps, of the extreme alarm that overcame the King when he was told that a second episode of the northern rebellion had just broken out. Young Ellerker, ap Rice and the others pursuing the enquiry in Hull were told that they were to use 'all the means you can devise by all kinds of tortures and otherwise to enforce them to declare the whole and plain truth of all things whereof they shall be examined...'

Substantially, a treason trial was conducted in much the same way as any other proceedings against criminal activity, unless martial law had been declared, when both sentence and execution were administered without the normal juridical processes. Invariably, however, the accused had to defend himself without any legal assistance, whereas the Crown had prosecutors to make its case – generally speaking, the attorney-general, the solicitor-general and the King's serjeant – but the hearing was before a jury which determined the outcome and a bench of justices who were principally there to uphold the law and to provide a summing-up before the jury retired; the death sentence, of course, was automatic if the jury turned its thumbs down. Whenever possible, the jurymen were from the same social level as the accused, though the minimum qualification was ownership of land worth forty shillings. They could be challenged by the defendant before his trial began, however, and in one recorded instance the challenge was made and allowed ten times.

If found guilty, the prisoner was permitted to make a speech and there was some provision for him to have his case reviewed in King's Bench, though this was not at all comparable to the modern system of appeals. The general rule was that the trial should be conducted in the county where the treason had been committed, but in exceptional circumstances ordered by the King events took their course in London instead. All the most prominent rebels of 1536–7, in fact, were interrogated in the Tower and their sentences were passed down after trial either in Westminster Hall (in Darcy's case) or in the Guildhall, though not all of them were executed in the capital. There was one other thing that the landed classes especially feared almost as much as the death penalty itself, and that was the forfeiture of their land and all their property to the Crown, to make what profit from these things that it could, leaving the family of anyone condemned for this crime without any inheritance and effectively destitute.

As for the ways in which a man found guilty of treason might meet his end, these varied from the merely barbaric to the hideously obscene, and the variation depended once more on social circumstances. Nobles were allowed the privilege of straightforward decapitation, and knights were first hanged till they were almost dead before being finished off with the axe. For everyone of lowlier rank the full penalty for treason meant hanging, drawing and quartering, one of the most disgusting ways of killing someone that mankind has ever devised. The victim was hauled through the streets from his prison to the scaffold fastened to a wicker hurdle, which was drawn like a dray by a horse, and at the end of this journey he was stripped before the noose was put round his neck. He was stood on a ladder, or something else that could swiftly be taken from under him, and when this had been removed, he was left hanging for a minute or two while the crowd looked on and applauded or jeered; and there were always big crowds for an execution, because it was regarded as one of the great English spectator events, an exciting way to start the day, with the business generally conducted no later than nine o'clock. With the rope tight round the victim's neck, an erection sometimes followed and even ejaculation could occur; and that was always good for a great roar of approval from the mob. But before the man was quite strangled to death he was cut down, because his executioners wished him to be conscious of what happened to him next.

First his genitals were cut off, then his belly was slit open and his intestines were dragged out, before the heart itself was finally cut away, all these parts being thrown into a fire that had been specially started nearby. Occasionally this butchery was horribly botched, as in the case of Thomas Prichard, priest, during Queen Elizabeth's reign. His executioner was so clumsy after making the incision that 'the Priest raised himself and putting out his hands, cast forward his own bowels, crying out "Miserere mei"'. The removal of the heart at least was a mercy, ensuring that the accused could not be aware of the final stage of his execution, which was the amputation of his limbs and the severing of his head; trophies which, like the trunk itself, would be put on display in places which were judged to attract the greatest publicity.

Whenever possible, most of the body was hung in chains rather than ropes, because that way the display lasted much longer, until nothing was left but the skeleton; the head, meanwhile, was impaled in some prominent place. It was, in fact, a custom that the Crown could minimise the suffering and humiliation of the extreme penalty by telling the hangman to make sure the victim was dead before being cut down, by waiving the drawing and quartering, or by allowing the body to be buried instead of being displayed. But custom said that this would only be done if the victim pleaded guilty to his crime, and sometimes not even then. The only alternative to this ghastly process occurred in the case of poisoners, whose crime was made treasonable after someone tried to kill the Bishop of Rochester. The guilty man, a cook, was boiled to death; and so was anyone else who used poison, until the act was repealed in 1547.

Otherwise, butchery was the fate which awaited all those whom the Duke of Norfolk and the Earl of Sussex hunted down at their sovereign's pleasure in the spring of 1537. Occasionally, one or other of these two was inclined to show compassion or insist on working within the strict limits of the law, but Henry invariably overruled them in order to secure his prey. Sussex, who had put in a good word for the old Prior of Whalley, also did his best to save the life of William Lancaster, who had been involved in sending inflammatory letters from Westmorland into North Lancashire. The Earl argued that this was an old man who had fought well for his king against the Scots and that he might therefore be spared in acknowledgement, but Henry would have none of it, insisted on an execution and so the veteran was sent to his death. An even greater example of the King's determination to draw blood was his response to the escape from his vengeance of the sixty-two men who had been released on bail by old Sir Ralph Ellerker after Sir Francis Bigod's escapade in Beverley. Even Ellerker's son had not escaped the King's anger at this failure to nail his quarry. 'And we require you to write,' young Sir Ralph was told, 'what moved you to condescend to the bailing of the persons of Bigod's conspiracy...' Not open to persuasion from any quarter, the King simply reversed the decision and so the sixty-two were rounded up again and sent for trial in York before a jury on 24 March. Crafty as ever, Norfolk decided to try just two men first, fully confident that they would be convicted, which would have implicated the rest of the Beverley prisoners with little more effort by the prosecutors. To this end, he placed a couple of known royalists on the panel, where they were expected to put pressure on the other jurymen and to report on their deliberations. The two accused had both been with Bigod at Beverley, but whereas Thomas Lutton was one of the sixty-two who were captured, the other, William Levening, had escaped and gone straight to Templehirst, later to Aughton, to seek the counsel of Lord Darcy, Sir Robert Constable and Robert Aske, who had advised that if he surrendered himself they would do what they could to plead with the Duke on his behalf.

Levening was the first of the two to be put up and, against all Norfolk's expectations, the jury acquitted him on the grounds that he had been forced to join Bigod's company; from which it followed that the cases against Lutton and the others likewise collapsed. One of the Duke's men on the jury, Thomas Delariver, revealed that the voting had been seven to five in Levening's favour, and that he had squeezed through because too many of the jurymen believed that the case against him was not unconnected with the fact that some of his land had already been granted to young Ellerker, who appeared as the principal witness for the prosecution. Delariver also revealed the pressure that Norfolk had put them under to speed deliberations that lasted a good thirty-six hours, a matter of sending two of his servants, 'who took away from them all that might keep them warm'.

Once more, the King exploded at a verdict going the wrong way and demanded that the names of the jurors be made known to him. This was a boundary which Thomas Howard would not cross, though his reasons were not wholly principled, for he recalled a York jury once before being summoned to Westminster and fined for failing to produce the verdict that Thomas Cromwell sought. Norfolk was canny enough to understand that if that – or worse – happened again, the consequences in the North might be more than Henry was prepared for. So he dodged the issue in a letter he wrote to Cromwell on the last day of March, pleading that he could not send up the names 'as the clerks who have the records dwell far from hence; but will send for them'. He added that if the Crown insisted on the jurymen being sent south, it would leave an impression that the King and his Council were trying to manipulate the English justice system by forcing people to act against their consciences. Back came the reply that the King thought Levening's treason manifest and that 'the matter must be bolted out, as it may reveal other important matters. You shall therefore send the names as before written, and do all that you can to beat out the mystery.' The names referred to were those of sixteen suspects which Cromwell called for, to which the King almost at once added five more of his own; and Henry's spite towards the jurymen was eventually forgotten in another welter of events.

For that very week saw the last attempt to revive the Pilgrimage of Grace. Throughout February, Sir John Bulmer and his consort Margaret Cheyney had been living quietly at Lastingham, watching Thomas Howard's progress round the North and wondering whether Sir John had been wise to tell his brother to set a watch for the arrival of Henry's ships and to prepare beacons in case it became necessary to raise an alarm. Halfway through March the King summoned them to London, which they took to be an ominous sign. A worried Bulmer at once asked for and received Norfolk's permission to delay their journey until Easter, which was less than three weeks away; and at the same time he wrote to his son Sir Ralph, who was still in the capital, asking him whether it was safe to go down to court. The reply was discouraging, Sir Ralph telling his father that he 'should look well after himself for, as far as he could perceive, all was falsehood that they were dealt withal'.

Something like panic then seized the couple, whose affection for each other at this time was well noted by others. A parish priest subsequently testified that 'she is feared that she should be parted from him forever...she peradventure will say "Mr Bulmer, for my sake break a spear" and then he like a dove will say "Pretty Peg, I will never forsake thee"'. Others heard Bulmer say that he would rather be put on the rack than be parted from his wife. For her part, she vowed that she would rather be torn to pieces than go to London, and she begged him to get a ship that would take them and their three-month-old son to the safety of Scotland. Exile, however, was more than Bulmer could face, which left them with only one alternative if Henry's summons was also to be ignored. They must start another rising and take their chance on its outcome. It was said that 'she enticed Sir John Bulmer to raise the commons again' and that 'Margaret counselled him to flee the realm (if the commons would not rise) than that he and she should be parted'.

Whichever of them it was who took the lead, both were equally involved in what happened afterwards. On 29 March, two days before Norfolk's permission expired, Bulmer's chaplain William Staynhus was told to find out from the neighbouring clergy whether or not the commons were likely to rise at a word of command, and he was to elicit this information by urging the priests in that part of the North Riding to divulge what was being told them in the confessional. Margaret certainly suggested the names of two or three that he should canvass in this way. Other soundings were taken and one of the people approached by Bulmer's envoys was the old Pilgrim leader Lord Lumley, whose son George was already held in the Tower of London for his part in the action at Scarborough and subsequent attempts to raise troops in support of Sir Francis Bigod. Old Lumley gave Bulmer the impression that he could raise 10,000 men in Cleveland and Durham, which caused Sir John to ride over to see him at Kilton Castle between Guisborough and the coast, and suggest that they 'could live strongly together till they might provide someway for themselves'. He also had it in mind 'suddenly to go and take the Duke's grace, and then all is our own...' Perhaps it was this hairbrained proposal to capture Norfolk that made Lumley realise the sheer impracticality of Bulmer's plan, for he suddenly changed tack, made his excuses and cleared off to another domicile of his at Sedgefield in Durham. Incoming messages from others who had been approached were also discouraging, especially the advice of the Rosedale parish priest, who dropped a heavy hint that the local commons were unlikely to trust themselves to Sir John or any other of the gentry, because they believed as strongly as anyone that such people had betrayed them to the government.

There was one last possibility that Bulmer decided to try and it was to make for his brother's home at Wilton Castle and there do what Lumley had declined to do: raise a new Cleveland host and with it strike at the Duke of Norfolk. Quite what he expected Sir William Bulmer to make of this we cannot tell, but he was certainly taking advantage of the fact that Sir William, having attached himself to Norfolk's entourage the moment the Duke arrived in Yorkshire, was not at home just then. Before Sir John could set off on this improbable adventure, however, the final setback to his hopes of fighting his way out of trouble occurred in the shape of a message from the parish priest of Loftus, which was next door to Kilton Castle. This Thomas Francke had been one of Robert Aske's first captains in the October rising in Howdenshire, but had soon returned to his own patch to raise more men and eventually turned up in York with the host led by Sir Thomas Percy, whose principal adviser he had become. Bulmer evidently expected support from him in view of this record, but it was the very reason why Francke now wished to have nothing more to do with potential trouble; if he confined himself to parochial duties he had a good chance that his past would not come back to haunt him in 1537. So his message to Sir John by way of William Staynhus was, 'If thy master be sent for to London let him go as he is commanded. I can give him no other counsel.'

What Sir John Bulmer's state of mind was, or Margaret Cheyney's, after receiving this rebuff we can only imagine, but they were not left much longer in suspense. Francke, in fact, went on to denounce them to Norfolk, as did Sir Francis Bigod's old adversary Gregory Conyers, who had got wind of what was afoot and had his own reasons for ingratiating himself with the authorities. The Duke had Bulmer and his Peg arrested in Easter week and they were sent down to London; for some reason, a day or two apart. She went first and was imprisoned we know not where, but he was put into the Tower. We have no record of Margaret's confession, either, though it was doubtless extracted, but Bulmer refused to say anything in his that would implicate her and he pleaded guilty to the treason charge, possibly in the forlorn hope that this would exonerate her. Both of them, in fact, originally pleaded not guilty before changing their minds while the jury was actually considering its verdict and one view is that they did so because they had been promised the King's mercy if they admitted their guilt. Bulmer referred to Cheyney as his wife and nothing else right up to the end, much to the irritation of his accusers and the judge. After the legal system had exhausted itself on them in the middle of May, both were sent for execution on the 25th of that month, Margaret to be burned at the Smithfield stake, Sir John to face the gallows at Tyburn. There seems to be no record of what became of their tiny son.

Others who were sent south with Bulmer, apart from Adam Sedbar, William Wood and possibly Thomas Bolton, were James Cockerell, former Prior of Guisborough, whom Bigod had tried to reinstate in defiance of Cromwell; William Todde, Prior of Malton, who was also tainted by an association with Bigod; and Edward Kirkby, who had offered to join the rebels in October after being deposed by the Crown as Prior of Rievaulx and whom Norfolk believed to have 'as false and traitorous heart as any in these quarters'. They had been preceded by Bigod himself, who was sent down from Carlisle; by George Lumley, Bigod's man at Scarborough; by George Shuttleworth, the Sawley messenger to Sir Thomas Percy; by Robert Thompson, Vicar of Brough and chaplain to the Host of the Four Captains; by Barnard Townley, another priest implicated in the same rebellion; by Dr John Pickering, sometime Prior of the York Blackfriars but lately rebel songwriter in Bridlington; by another John Pickering, who was merely Bigod's chaplain; by Dr John Dakyn, the Vicar-general of Richmond, who had at different times had connections with Jervaulx Abbey, Cartmel and Conishead Priories; by Sir Richard Tempest who, in spite of evicting the Sawley monks and performing other services for the Crown, was suspected of double-dealing by the Earls of Cumberland and Sussex alike and was indubitably brother to one of the first rebel leaders; and by Richard Bowyer, one of the burgesses who had yielded York to Aske's rebels and had acted as a messenger for Lord Darcy.

Then there were those who were dealt with in the North in addition to those whose trials and/or executions took place in Hull, Carlisle, Richmond, Lancaster, Manchester and Whalley. Many of them had the most tenuous connection with the rebellions, but they also included John Atkinson, one of the first captains in the Pilgrimage and prominent in the post-pardon rising in Westmorland, who was tried, found guilty and presumably executed, in Newcastle. Others were dealt with in York and Durham.

The fate of people who were arrested for their part in the insurrection was not always predictable, though the outcome for some was much more likely than for others. Sir Francis Bigod less than anyone, perhaps, could have expected to survive his actions at the turn of the year, long after Henry's pardon had been announced. Erratic until the end, he babbled his way to the gallows. His deposition to his examiners was a highly confused statement, in which he reckoned that it would be worth the authorities' while to search the homes of the Dean of York and his canons, where 'great provisions of new harness' might be found, but said he had nothing against the clerics personally. He also swore that his younger brother Ralph had nothing at all to do with his own activities, but begged his captors not to tell Ralph anything he said lest it was assumed that he, Francis, had accused the young man of something. In contrast to Bigod, Lord John Hussey may be counted one of the more unfortunate people to receive the death penalty, for he had been held in suspense ever since the collapse of the Lincolnshire rising, in which he had played almost no part at all, and that obviously under duress and in fear, and since when his behaviour had been immaculate. Above all the victim of Henry's vicious nature, his last weeks were unsuspectingly spent fussing about inconsequential things – the prospective marriage of Mrs Ashley and Peter Mewtas, Lady Lisle's ermine bonnets, which were not yet ready, the barrel of puffins for Mr Marshall, which George Rolles had delivered – with nothing at all to suggest that he expected to be arrested, sent for trial and finish up at the block. When darkness fell he bore his fate stoically, without even a whimper of a plea for mercy.

Sir Stephen Hamerton and Nicholas Tempest, who had jointly led the Craven rebels in October but had kept out of trouble since, were two others who clearly had no premonition of disaster when told that they were required in London, for they went up as free men, only to be arrested on their arrival and put into the Tower. It has been suggested that, because of his passivity since Doncaster, Hamerton may have found himself in this predicament because of a long-standing feud with the Earl of Derby's family, the Stanleys; and, certainly, there is sufficient evidence that a number of old scores were settled with the collusion of the Crown, under the guise of punishment for treason, to warrant such a supposition. It was enough to finish off Hamerton, if this was the case, after he had reversed his original plea of not guilty, as did Sir Thomas Percy; presumably, in each instance, to avoid the worst that the executioner could do to them. The fate of Nicholas Tempest, like Hamerton's, was inextricably tangled with that of the Sawley monks in the autumn, though the indictment against him attached as much weight to some letters he had exchanged with Darcy in January, none of which spoke ill of the King or proposed breaking his law. He was condemned to death, above all, because of his leadership in October, even though he joined the Pilgrimage only after the local commons had threatened to kill his son John.

Nicholas's brother Sir Richard Tempest, however, never came to trial on what, again, would have been trumped-up charges: he died of the plague in prison that August, and two others who never emerged from the Tower were Sir Ingram Percy and Robert Thompson, the Vicar of Brough who had acted as chaplain to the Host of the Four Captains. As for the four captains themselves, we can only be sure of Thomas Burbeck's fate, which was execution after the failed siege of Carlisle; the other three disappeared at about that time and may have been killed in the subsequent rout of the Cumbrian rebels, or possibly they escaped, as many people with their record did. William Leache was the most remarkable survivor of the lot: having evaded Henry's justice after the Lincolnshire rising, he did so a second time in the North and was never heard of again after the skirmish at Kirkby Stephen. Nor was Nicholas Musgrave, who had been a leader of the local Pilgrims in October and twice defied Thomas Clifford by taking refuge in the church tower. Robert Esch, the Friar of Knaresborough and self-appointed propagandist, whose misinformation raised false hopes in Sir Francis Bigod, was another who got away scot-free.

Ninian Staveley probably saved his life by incriminating Adam Sedbar and the Jervaulx community; otherwise the failure to send him for trial is inexplicable, when his deposition on St George's Day made perfectly clear his own central involvement in the Wensleydale rising, as did Sedbar's own testimony. There were a number of other anomalies. Sir John Bulmer's son Ralph, whose letters from London were clearly treasonable, was first of all condemned and then pardoned; and Bigod's chaplain John Pickering, just as culpable, was also allowed to live. The other Pickering, who had done nothing more than write songs, finished on the Tyburn gallows, as did John Cockerell, whose life in and out of Guisborough Priory had merely been one of inactive complaint. Young George Lumley paid for his escapade at Scarborough with his life, but his father and Lord Latimer, old Pilgrims both, saved themselves by bribing Cromwell to look the other way, even though Lord Lumley might have been thought tainted by his association with Bigod. Dakyn and Shuttleworth, Todde and Kirkby, Townley and Bowyer all came through their imprisonment unscathed; and it would have been particularly monstrous if Shuttleworth had not been spared, when all he had done was to run a message for the Abbot of Sawley to Sir Thomas Percy.

Like Percy, the three leading figures in the Pilgrimage of Grace also went to London of their own volition after being summoned by the King. This was a circumspect move by Henry, who had the sense to understand that the violent seizure of Aske, Darcy and Constable might provoke yet another rising, when everyone knew that each of them had worked very hard to prevent the post-pardon revolts, had done nothing at all to infringe the terms settled at Doncaster. The chief reason he was so outraged by the collapse of the second York trials is that William Levening was supposed to have been the sprat that caught the bigger fish, simply because he had gone to Templehirst and Aughton to seek advice after Beverley, in which case the failure of the three to report him to the authorities could justify charges against them of misprision, that is, of deliberately concealing a treason. Sir Robert Constable was the first to receive the instruction, on 19 February, but he delayed his departure so long that in the first week of March the Duke of Norfolk was commanded to arrest him if need be and to set coastal watches lest he try to escape by sea. Shortly after this,

Constable appears to have started the journey without an escort and he was certainly in the Tower by Easter week. So was Lord Darcy, who set off on 1 April, apparently believing that he was to receive the King's commendation for obeying Henry's instruction to refortify and victual Pontefract Castle in the third week of January. And so was Robert Aske, who left Aughton on 24 March under a similar misconception, encouraged by Norfolk to understand that he would be received warmly for his efforts since Doncaster and since his surprisingly agreeable meeting with the King over Christmas and the New Year; indeed, he carried with him a letter of recommendation from the Duke. He was uneasy enough, however, to leave a gelding at Buntingford in case he needed to get a message back to Yorkshire. His servant Robert Wall, who had been brought up with him from childhood, accompanied him on the journey and might well have been the one to ride back home with the terrible news that his master had been arrested the moment he reached London, but 'Wall died six or seven days after Aske was in the Tower, for sorrow, saying the commissioners would hang him, draw him and quarter him'.

Before any other action was taken against the three Pilgrim leaders in the capital, an indictment had to be made out against them and the other captives in London, and had to be heard by a jury in the North according to the legal requirement in cases of treason before a trial could be held anywhere. To make assurance double sure, the Duke empanelled in York two juries of twenty-one and twenty of the county gentlemen respectively, and the first of these very carefully included many kinsmen of the accused, including two sons-in-law of Constable, five men who had close ties with Darcy and Aske's own eldest brother John. The object was not principally to put these relatives through an extreme form of mental torment, but to ensure the indictment of the accused and possibly add to the haul. For John Aske and his colleagues were in a predicament that a much later century would memorably identify as a Catch 22 situation whereby, if they didn't convict, they themselves might be charged with something nasty and the convictions would be obtained anyway from the second jury, which would replace the first; and Norfolk had many more of the Yorkshire gentry held in reserve in case anyone else was inclined to resist the intimidation that he had so cunningly contrived. It was said that the city had not seen so many gentlemen gathered together in forty years.

When he arrived in London, Constable found that charges had been laid against him by three men. One of these was John Folbery, the former Pilgrim who had betrayed John Hallam in Hull and who now deposed that Constable had been against the second appointment with Norfolk in Doncaster. And so he had, during the York council, though this was reported by Folbery to imply that Sir Robert was opposed to the agreement later reached at Doncaster, which was false. The turncoat further alleged that Constable had written a letter to Bigod, which encouraged Sir Francis to delay the start of his rising until the weather was better when, in fact, its purpose was to stop him rising at all. Nicholas Rudston was another whose evidence was used against Constable, this time about the injudicious letter which Sir Robert had tried to conceal after realising that it might incriminate him. The third of the witnesses for the prosecution was young Sir Ralph Ellerker, who quoted the letter Constable had written to him in an attempt to secure the release of the two messengers Bigod had sent to Hull; and this, again, was distorted into an allegation that Constable was implicated in the events which took place there and in Beverley.

The case against him was, in almost every way, a put-up job if it was supposed to refer to nothing but the post-pardon events. Both Ellerker and Rudston, of course, had been part of the original Pilgrimage as well as Folbery and there is little doubt that the three of them were prepared to misrepresent Constable in order to improve their own standing in the eyes of the Crown. Ellerker almost certainly was also motivated by the old animosity he and Sir Robert had shared before October 1536 brought them together in the same cause. Constable must have realised, the moment the charges were laid, what was in store for him. He was a strong-minded man, but a letter he wrote to his son just after his conviction shows that his nerve had at last started to go. He asked Marmaduke 'to entreat my lord of Rutland to get the Queen to sue to the King for my life, that I may all my life lament my offences and serve God...Make quick suit either now or never.' He suggested that if money changed hands it might help matters and reminded his son that he owed a Mr Lambert £125 8s 3d. 'I charge you see them discharged if I die.' In fact, his death was certain and he would have known it, even as he was writing that.

Thomas Lord Darcy went very bravely to his end. At his examination he was sheer defiance and he even challenged the Lord Privy Seal to his face. 'Cromwell,' he said, 'it is thou that art the very original and chief causer of this rebellion and mischief, and art likewise causer of the apprehension of us that be noble men and dost daily earnestly travail to bring us to our end and to strike off our heads, and I trust that or thou die, though thou wouldst procure all the noblemen's head within the realm to be stricken off, yet shall there one head remain that shall strike off thy head.' Alas, there is no record of Cromwell's response; only that he, who drew up the indictment against Darcy, was also one of those who adjudicated at his trial. According to custom, as a member of the nobility, Darcy was allowed to be tried by his peers, and so the hearing in Westminster Hall was before the Marquis of Dorset, the Earls of Oxford, Shrewsbury, Essex, Cumberland, Wiltshire and Sussex, Viscount Beauchamp and the Lords de la Warre, Cobham, Matravers, Powes, Morley, Clynton, Dacre of the South, Mountjoy, Windsor, Bray, Mordaunt, Burgh and Cromwell, with the Marquis of Exeter presiding as Lord High Steward of the court.

Part of the evidence they heard was extracted from Darcy's papers, which had been seized the moment he left Yorkshire. He was a considerable correspondent who had kept a copy of everything he had ever written, and many of these documents, together with incoming letters, were selected to support the charge of treason, their import generally being distorted in order to make the point. A memorandum attached to one that he had sent to Sir Oswald Wilstrop on 21 January observed that 'he trusted to hear, at Norfolk's coming, of a free parliament and liberty to declare learning and grievances. Whereby appears he continues in his traitor's heart, trusting to have reformation according to his untrue and wilful mind.' It was noted that a letter to Aske had been signed 'yours faithfully, Thomas Darcy', from which it was concluded that 'there is a great fidelity betwixt the lord Darcy and Robert Aske, being but a mean person'. A letter had been written to Darcy after Christmas by his servant Parker 'signifying the state of the lord of Derby and the country about him' and from this 'it appears all the North is ready to rise if anyone puts out the monks of Sawley. Writes also of the state of Kendal and thereabouts (Parker would not have written this if it was not Lord Darcy's pleasure, and Darcy never disclosed it. Whereby his traitorous heart appeareth.)' At his examination, Darcy was interrogated at some length about the Badge of the Five Wounds, which seemed to obsess his questioners, who put no fewer than fifteen questions to him about it ('If they were new, who made them and where? ... Was it not for setting forth the insurrection in Yorkshire, encouraging the soldiers to believe their rebellion was for the Defence of the Faith? ...'). So the often loaded questions were remorselessly added to the documentary haul. And from a farrago of misrepresentation, wishful thinking, nit-picking and downright perjury a case was constructed to suggest that Darcy had encouraged the activities of Hallam and Bigod, and that his every act of loyalty to the Crown both before and since the pardon was, in fact, the opposite and treasonable.

A medley of nine knights and three gentlemen served as the jury in the trial of Robert Aske, the same men who convicted Constable, Bigod, Sir Thomas Percy, Bulmer, Cheyney and Hamerton. They sat almost five weeks after Aske's examination began on 11 April, his final interrogation taking place on 11 May. In this time he was required not only to give an account of himself and his activities but also to answer no fewer than 107 formal questions, many of which were also put to Darcy, Constable and Hussey at their examinations, a number of them composed by Cromwell himself. Some of Aske's replies were recorded in his own hand, the rest reported by the clerks acting for his examiners, who included the notorious Drs Legh and Layton, another commissioner, Dr Petre, and the Lieutenant of the Tower, Sir Edward Walsingham, with Legh's critical colleague John ap Rice also sometimes present. The first question was 'How long after the insurrection in Lincolnshire, and also that of Yorkshire, bruits [rumours] were stirred abroad in these countries that church goods should be taken away, and that there should stand but one parish church within ... miles?' The last one wanted to know: 'Whether ye had any communication with

Robt. Bowes, Chaloner and Babthorpe, and what each of them said?' In between, there were questions about his correspondence, what he said to people who objected to certain Acts of Parliament, whether he himself objected to the King being known as the Church's Supreme Head, who had decided to canvass the clergy before and at the Pontefract conference, whether he or someone else had invited them to say whether the rebellion was lawful or not; and many other topics.

His answers were often lengthy, his reply to the first question rambling through a description of his encounter with George Hudswell. Longest of all was his reply to Question 23, which wanted to know why he objected to certain of the King's Acts. It took a short essay for him to get the answer to that one off his chest, for it reviewed his feelings about everything from the suppression of the religious houses to the declared illegitimacy of Henry's daughter Mary, from the legislation affecting inheritance to that which proclaimed Henry's Supremacy. But he was capable of one-liners, too. Question 34 wanted to know whether he condemned the clerics of the New Learning 'because they spake against the Bishop of Rome?' He replied, 'Amongst other things, that was one of the causes then.' The most striking thing about all of Robert Aske's testimony is how very straightforward he was, especially for one in such a predicament as his. It was as though he was not only incapable of telling a lie but even of obfuscating the truth. Asked to recall where he had been in the company of Darcy and Constable in 1536, you can almost see him scratching his head in recollection before telling his examiners, 'They were all together as beforesaid at Pomfret, and not after that all three together till Mr Bowes' coming home or else till he sent his first letter down, and my lord of Norfolk's letter also. Also at the last council at Pomfret. These three times were together, and no oftener.' When he was asked about the Badge of the Five Wounds, his response was 'Lord Darcy gave him a cross with the Five Wounds on it, but who first invented that badge he cannot say ...'

They gradually wore him down with the interrogations and with other indications that things were going against him. These included a deposition by Christopher Aske, which came in just after all the questioning was done and referred to his 'ungracious brother Robert Aske, after many defiances', whom he had tried to persuade to seek the King's pardon, but who preferred to discuss a different agenda with Lord Darcy. After a month in the Tower, Robert's spirit began to break, as a pathetic letter which he wrote to his captors indicates. It besought the King and Cromwell to be merciful and gracious unto him and went on, 'I am not able to live for none of my friends will not do nothing for me, and I have need to have a pair of hose, a doublet of fustian, a shirt for I have but one shirt here and a pair of shoes. I beseech you heartily that I may know your mind herein ... for the love of God.' The request was ignored so that, after his last examination by Legh and ap Rice, he tried again: 'Good Mr Doctor I beseech you to send me money and my stuff ... for neither have I money nor gear to wear, as ye saw for yourself. For the reverence of God send me the same or else I know not how to do nor live, and that Mr Pollard be remembered for the same.' Richard Pollard was the examiners' principal clerk.

Aske then had just over seven more weeks to live, but there is no evidence that he ever received any of the things he wanted. The Crown was never generous to people in the Tower, carefully noting how much it cost to keep them alive there, which was money that they or their estates would have to find in the end. Aske was down for 6s 8d a week, as was the Vicar of Louth and George Lumley, but the tariff was variable, so that Lord Darcy's time cost twenty shillings a week, Sir Stephen Hamerton's ten shillings, while the Lincolnshire commons who were to be tried in London were expected to survive on 40d a week.

The trials often lasted no more than a day, even when the prisoner pleaded not guilty, as each of the three principal Pilgrims did; and execution usually followed very soon afterwards. Having been tried and sentenced on Tuesday, 15 May, Darcy should have been beheaded on the Saturday but his execution was delayed because Henry was unsure whether he should be put to death in front of his own people or down in the capital. The King's first thought was that all three principals should be executed in Doncaster 'or thereabouts', which would be a fitting way 'to knit up this tragedy'. It was Norfolk who persuaded him that the risks of another rising were too great if Darcy were sent to the North; and so the thing was done at Tower Hill on the last day of June, after Darcy had spent time with his confessor, Henry Aglionby, Prior of Beverley, and heard a mass. That was one of the two personal requests he made; the other was his begging to be buried beside his wife at Greenwich. He also asked that his debts might be paid and caustically forgave the King the £4400 which, he said, the Treasury owed him. Henry himself was unwilling to forgive anything and Darcy was not buried beside his wife but close to the Tower, his head being displayed on London Bridge, which not infrequently exhibited any number of impaled and rotting remains for the attention of citizens sailing underneath it or crossing the Thames. The shabbiness of the King was repeated some weeks after Old Tom's execution, when he was posthumously stripped of his Order of the Garter, his stall in St George's chapel at Windsor being given to, of all people, Thomas Cromwell, after Darcy's gilded nameplate had been removed from its back.

Constable and Aske were tried the day after Darcy, and Sir Robert was the first of them to face the executioner, but not until 6 July. The King was adamant that both men should be finished off in the North, at places particularly associated with their activities, and this time Norfolk did not attempt to dissuade him. They travelled together from London in the same train that took Lord Hussey to his death at Charles Brandon's hands in Lincoln; and from there they both continued to Hull, where Constable had briefly been in command of its rebel garrison. He was still worrying about the debt to Mr Lambert, so much so that he asked Cromwell to see that it was discharged, just in case his son overlooked the matter. There were also, he pointed out, servants' wages to be taken care of, including Matthew Pool's annual forty shillings, which would be due at Lammas.

There was a pause when the prisoner reached Hull because his captors wanted to execute him on a market day, so that the maximum number of people would be able to watch and draw their conclusions from his death. In the waiting time, Constable was asked if he had anything to add to his written account of the rebellion and he said that there had been the odd remark by Darcy that he had deliberately forgotten because Old Tom at that stage was still alive; but now it didn't matter any more. On the Friday of that week, Constable was taken to the scaffold which was pointedly set up at the Beverley Gate, where Hallam had been lost. He was asked by the priest officially attending the execution to confess the treason he had committed after the pardon was announced, but this Constable refused to do. And so he met his end steadfastly, at the hands of those who bore him great malice. Norfolk, who was in charge of the arrangements for both Constable and Aske, gloated that Sir Robert 'doth hang above the highest gate in the town, so trimmed with chains...that I think his bones will hang there this hundred year'.

From Hull, Robert Aske was taken on to York, in whose Minster he had once been received as an anointed chief; or, as the government saw it, 'where he was in his greatest and most frantic glory'. He, too, had made his last petitions before leaving the Tower of London, one of them asking Henry's forgiveness for his offences and that 'the King will be gracious to his brother and name who never offended'; and he, too, was worried about leaving debts behind. He begged his Grace to see to it that these should be met 'as far as his goods will stretch', remembering twenty shillings owed to 'Brown's wife of Watling Street' and twice as much to Mr Shakerley of London. He then besought Cromwell to do what he could to hold the King to the payment of such debts, part of which could be offset by the sale of 'stuff of mine at the Cardinal's Hat, London, etc; a gown of tawny silk faced with velvet, a jacket of crimson silk that the King's Grace gave me, a crimson satin doublet and a pair of scarlet hose and other trifles', plus four geldings which he owned and 'divers stuff' that would be found in his rooms at Gray's Inn and at his house in Hampshire, where he owned a little land. Oh, and there was a Mr Richardson who was owed 6s 8d for land at Bubwith, near Aughton, which Aske had bought without knowing Richardson's title. Almost as an afterthought he requested one thing for himself – 'let me be full dead ere I be dismembered'. And, for once in his life, Henry showed mercy to someone helplessly in his power. The executioner was told to make sure that Aske was dead before he was cut down from the gallows.

Market day had been chosen for this execution, too, high upon the mound on which Clifford's Tower stood and within sight of York Minster. The same chaplain who had attended Sir Robert

Constable in Hull the week before was with Aske as well and this Richard Coren also was reminded of certain debts to be repaid, including £4 10s owed to Mr Crake, whose sheep Aske had bought. Coren again tried to extract a confession from his prisoner, but was only told a couple of things that Aske revealed – like Constable – because no one involved could any longer be hurt by what he said. They were that Darcy had spoken to Chapuys, the imperial ambassador, about obtaining assistance from the Continent, and that he, Darcy and Constable had planned to send Dr Waldby to Flanders 'for aid and ordnance'. He also took a final swipe at Cromwell, claiming that the Lord Privy Seal 'did not bear so great a favour to my lord of Norfolk as he thought he did; which thing I have kept secret from my said lord of Norfolk'. Thomas Howard, of course, had long since worked that out for himself. In reporting this conversation, Coren nevertheless peevishly noted that both Aske and Constable 'thought a religion to keep secret between God and them rather than open their whole stomach; from which opinion I could not abduce them'. But, then, he had been instructed to obtain much more useful information than he had been given, something that might incriminate the still living.

When Aske was brought out of his cell that Thursday morning at York, before he was tied to the hurdle that would take him to the scaffold, he confessed that he had offended God, the King and the world. He was then dragged through the centre of the city, 'desiring the people ever as he passed by to pray for him'. When he was taken from the hurdle he was led up the mound and into Clifford's Tower for a little while, until the Duke of Norfolk arrived. On being brought out again he was given the opportunity, like all condemned men, to make a final statement to the watching crowd. And in this he said that there were two things which had aggrieved him. One was that Cromwell had sworn that all northern men were traitors, 'wherewithal he was somewhat offended'. The other was that the Lord Privy Seal 'sundry times promised him a pardon of his life, and at one time he had a token from the King's Majesty of pardon for confessing the truth'. In reporting this, Coren added, 'These two things he showed to no man in these North parts, as he said, but to me only; which I have and will ever keep secret.'

As soon as Norfolk was ready for the spectacle, Aske climbed to the gallows on top of the tower, asked for forgiveness again 'and after orisons made on the ladder, commended his soul to God'. When they had finished butchering his body, it was hung there in chains; and John Aske, summoned with others of the Yorkshire gentry to be present, was one of those who watched all the things they did to his youngest brother. Soon afterwards he became seriously ill.

THE AFTERMATH

The bloodshed did not end there and protest went on even after Sir John Bulmer's frantic last attempt to rekindle rebellion. In July, a week before Aske's execution, a seditious bill appeared on the door of the Premonstratensian Shap Abbey, in Westmorland, which some thought might have been the work of still dissident Cistercians from Furness, embittered by the recent loss of their own house. It exhorted people to 'rise again and come into Lancashire', in which case they 'should find a captain and money ready to receive them'. Faced with this, Cromwell's commissioners 'used circumspection and wrote to the men of worship in the parts to which the monks went, to watch them'. Several weeks after Bulmer and Margaret Cheyney were arrested, a thirty-two-year-old Holderness widow named Mabel Brigge started a black fast, an art of witchcraft in which she was said to be well-practised, one of her reputed successes being a man whose neck was broken as a result of her maledictions. A black fast lasted for one consecutive day in each of six consecutive weeks, and the object of Brigge's efforts in May 1537 was to damage both the King and 'this false Duke' for what they had done to the North of England. The matter didn't, in fact, come to light until eight months after the event and only then because malicious gossip had reached the ears of the authorities. But that was enough to settle Brigge's fate: after examination and sentence in April 1538, she was duly sent, as Margaret Cheyney had been, to the stake, probably as much for her witchcraft as for her treason.

Executed on the same day was John Dobson, Vicar of

Muston, near Filey, who was the victim of three spiteful parish-ioners. He himself was strong in his attachment to Rome while most of his congregation appear to have been in favour of Reform – he had stopped praying for the King during the Pilgrimage but preached on the Royal Supremacy in November 1537 because his people insisted that he must. His churchman-ship alone would have been enough to get him into some sort of trouble, but what cost him his life was his habit of making sub-versive predictions, including a version of that old standby the Mouldwarp prophecy, and one in which he foretold that the Lumleys would unseat Henry from his throne. For these senti-ments, which he was peddling throughout the summer of 1537, he was sentenced to death, after being denounced simply because he was unpopular.

Robert Metcalfe, Augustinian Prior of Newburgh, close to the North Riding village of Coxwold, was taken by the authori-ties in December 1537 for uttering treasonable sentiments, one of which was his opinion that the King and the Duke should have been hanged back to back. He was another denounced mali-ciously, this time by a servant of his who felt that he had not been adequately esteemed. Under examination, this Brian Boye was instructed to repeat his allegations directly to Metcalfe, 'who denied it with many oaths and defiances'. The Prior was impris-oned in York for a start, while the authorities weighed up the evidence. At one stage they were in favour of letting him go because Boye seemed a thoroughly unreliable witness; but Henry's vindictiveness settled a man's fate once again. He told his Council in the North that if this business was handled 'with dexterity, it will appear that the prior has a cankered heart'. The Council was in charge of affairs up there by then, Norfolk having at last been allowed to return to the South in the autumn, after repeated requests to be released from what he regarded as an extended form of penal servitude. As a result of the royal dictum, Metcalfe was transferred to Pontefract Castle without trial and in captivity there he died in April 1538. But he was not the most unfortunate or the last of the King's victims in the sovereign's great appetite for punishment after the Pilgrimage of Grace.

That wretched distinction goes to Thomas Miller, Lancaster Herald, who had served his master obediently and well throughout the troubled times of 1536 and 1537 – sixteen men, in fact, had been executed in Durham because they attacked him there at the end of December. His greatest fault was a degree of self-importance, which was swollen by his involvement in some weighty matters of state, though he never had nearly as much influence over the rebels as he probably imagined. But he had made a mistake in treating with them while the battle lines were being drawn up before Doncaster and in the message he took back to the royal commanders afterwards. He had encouraged the Pilgrim leaders to believe that if they desisted from fighting, good things would result from their patience. According to Henry's warped reasoning, this meant he had told them that Cromwell would be handed over to them and all their other demands would be met. On going back to Doncaster, the zealously efficient Miller had given the commanders his estimate of the rebel force's strength; and this was interpreted as deliberately discouraging the King's army from facing up to the rebels. In all, Lancaster Herald faced five charges of treason, the first being that 'he encouraged the rebels at Pontefract by kneeling before Robert Aske'. Some of the charges were evidently inspired by Thomas Hawley, Clarencieux Herald, who held a number of grudges against Miller, one of which was to do with a customary order of seniority and precedence which had been reversed when it was decided that Miller should announce the King's pardon in the North-east – which was regarded as potentially the most difficult territory – while Hawley was effectively demoted to the north-western beat. As a result, Miller was tried and executed in York on 1 August 1538, having, after he was condemned, 'used himself like a good Christian'. Reporting this final act of vindictiveness to Cromwell, Serjeant Jenney seemed proud that 'I devised that Lancaster's head should be set up by the body of Aske', who had been dead for more than a year by then. We shall never know why it had taken Henry so long.

Also by then, if we include the Lincolnshire executions, approximately 200 people had been judicially put to death for their activities in those five tumultuous months of his reign. Assessments have varied over the years, largely because no conclusive information exists on some who simply ceased to be mentioned in the Crown records after their arrest and who may have ended on the scaffold, died in captivity, been acquitted or simply have been released after preliminary questioning; but the most recent tally has suggested that 153 at most were executed after the post-pardon revolts in the North of England, with forty-six accounted for in Lincolnshire. On top of those figures, of course, we should bear in mind that an unrecorded number of rebels were killed in the rout that followed the failed siege of Carlisle. Some commentators have pointed out that this death toll was trifling compared with the bloodletting that followed the German Peasants' War in the previous decade; and the numbers involved were indeed massively different. But the tens of thousands killed in Germany died because bloodthirsty armies were let loose on them; they were not put to death by a lawful judicial process sanctioned by a parliament.

A potentially dangerous threat to the stability of the realm after the post-pardon revolts occurred the day Lord Darcy was sentenced to death. At the back end of 1536 Henry's nephew, James V of Scotland, went to France to prepare for his wedding to Francis I's daughter Madeleine. This duly went ahead as planned on New Year's Day, though the groom was not in the best possible shape for the ceremony, having received a nasty bang on his head while jousting the day before, 'being a sore blemish in his face all this triumphing time'. But it was the indisposition of his new wife, who was consumptive, and the winter weather, as bad at sea as it was on land, which caused their departure from Rouen to Scotland to be postponed until the first week in May. James had wished to travel home across England, to make things easier for his bride, but his uncle had refused his request, understandably enough: at the height of his unpopularity, the last thing Henry needed was a possible contender for his throne canvassing the English from one end of the country to the other. This was another reason for the delay.

In the better weather of spring, however, the couple set sail in a convoy of ten French and four Scottish vessels, which dropped anchor off Scarborough on the evening of 15 May, the intention being to obtain some victuals for the rest of the voyage. But before anyone could go ashore a boat came out with a dozen fishermen aboard, who said that they wished to speak to King James, who was taken aback when they fell to their knees, 'imploring him to come in as they were oppressed and slain'. Not at all happy with the role that they were wishing on to him,

James decided to sail further up the coast for the provisions, heaving to a second time off Whitburn, a few miles south of the Tyne. There, ten more men came out to his vessel and said much the same thing as the Scarborough fishermen. A party of French and Scots then went ashore, but they also included an Englishman in the French service, James Crane, who was, in fact, one of Cromwell's spies. Once ashore, Crane found the parish priest, Robert Hodge, and coaxed him to answer a number of leading questions. The unsuspecting Hodge said quite a lot of treasonable things, including his desire to see Cromwell and Norfolk hanged from the same tree and his wish that James had come five months earlier, in which case he would have been carried in triumph to London. He even went so far as to indicate the best place for such an invading force to come ashore. 'Lo,' he said, gesturing to the sandy beaches nearby, 'here is as good and ready a landing for men as any place in England.' The Scottish King's ship and her consorts weighed anchor and sailed on to the Forth. But Crane later reported what had happened and what had been said to his real master. In September, Robert Hodge, the leader of the fishermen and one of the party who put out from Whitburn were tried and executed in Newcastle.

Some people of consequence who had served the King steadfastly throughout the great rebellion also became victims of Henry's paranoia. First to go was Henry Courtenay, Marquis of Exeter, who had been variously an envoy to Spain, Constable of Windsor Castle, a member of the King's Council and his devoted supporter in the divorce proceedings against Catherine, before being appointed one of the royal commanders in October 1536. He was a cousin of Cardinal Pole, also a grandson of Edward IV, and he was a member of the so-called White Rose party, a collection of courtiers who had little time for the new doctrines of the English Church and hoped that somehow or other the Emperor would intervene to restore the old ways. They did nothing but talk about such dreams, however, finding it much more expedient to enjoy their privileges than to risk losing them through action; not one of them apart from Lord Darcy raised a finger to assist the Pilgrimage.

Because of his associations and his birth, Courtenay was always a potential threat to the sovereign: a man of the blood royal who might first covet the throne and then be tempted to do something about it if enough popular and influential support came his way. He had, in fact, been banished from court for a while in 1531 because his servants had been heard gossiping tendentiously. Forgiven their indiscretions, Courtenay returned to the royal favour but by then he had developed an unremitting dislike of Cromwell, which was heartily reciprocated by the Lord Privy Seal. Nevertheless, Henry commissioned him as a subordinate to Norfolk in October 1536 but, after battle had been averted at Doncaster, his troops were disbanded and he went home to his estates in Devon, never to return to the North. Courtenay was a powerful figure in the West Country and there is no doubt that in the restlessness of 1537, which occurred in Cornwall and elsewhere, many looked to him for a lead in challenging the Crown about their grievances which, as in the North, were partly religious and partly economic. Cromwell represented this to Henry as a serious conspiracy with Courtenay at its head and, as the King's suspicions were being aroused, they were fuelled by a groundless belief that the Marquis of Exeter had been plotting with Reginald Pole, obviously to arrange continental assistance in another rebellion. In November 1538 Courtenay was sent to the Tower, tried by his peers at the beginning of the following month and beheaded on Tower Hill six days later, on 9 December.

Thomas Cromwell himself was the next to fall. His disgrace was largely engineered by his enemies at court, of whom there were many, but the chief and the most dangerous ones were the Duke of Norfolk, who regarded him as an upstart, and the Bishop of Winchester, Stephen Gardiner, who had hoped to succeed Wolsey in high government office, but was beaten to it by the jack of all trades from Putney. These two finally cornered him on the religious issues that by then had bedevilled the land for a decade.

Cromwell had been instrumental in advancing the cause of Reform in collaboration with Thomas Cranmer, by trundling through Parliament a set of new Injunctions in 1538, which, among other things, stipulated that every church 'shall provide on this side the first Easter next coming one book of the whole Bible of the largest volume, in English ... whereas your parishioners may most commodiously resort to the same and read it...'¹ What offended Norfolk, Gardiner and anyone else who cherished such old ways as Henry had allowed to continue in his new Church, however, was Item 10, which specified that 'if you have heretofore declared to your parishioners anything to the extolling or setting forth of pilgrimages, feigned relics or images, or any such superstition, you shall now openly, afore the same, recant and reprove the same...' Henry was persuaded that the author of those strictures was nothing less than a heretic who must be removed. His Lord Privy Seal might still have survived – he was made Earl of Essex only weeks before his end – had it not been for one other, and almost ludicrous, circumstance. In an effort to strengthen England's position in Europe, Cromwell had worked hard to marry Henry off to Anne of Cleves, who was not quite the comely proposition in the flesh that the King had been led to expect from Holbein's portrait of her, painted specifically to give his Grace an impression of what was on offer from the Rhineland. The marriage was an unconsummated disaster, in which Henry was looking for a way out from the moment he entered it. Never one to pass up a golden opportunity, the Duke made sure that his attractive and flirtatious niece, Catherine Howard, was introduced to the King's circle at Greenwich and the inevitable quickly followed.

Henry was induced to blame Cromwell for everything that seemed to be getting out of control in his realm; represented by fresh growls of discontent in the country, increasing factionalism in his Church, and a serious embarrassment to a man who did not like being made to look a fool in front of his subjects. His foreign policy was struggling, too, and to improve matters Norfolk was sent across the Channel to detach Francis from his alliance with the Emperor, a fruitless exercise in the end. When the Duke came home he was ready to make a move in domestic affairs. No sooner had Cromwell been given his new title, in the spring of 1540, than his enemies closed in, while he did his best to hit back, sending an episcopal ally of Gardiner, and others, to prison. But Norfolk and everyone else who held him in contempt were too

1 Another important step forward was the injunction that every church must henceforth maintain a register of all baptisms, marriages and burials in its parish, which gave the English one of their most reliable records of local history.

much for him and persuaded Henry that what the Pilgrim leaders had always said of Cromwell was perfectly true: that he was a low usurper of power who had assiduously feathered his own nest by accepting bribes as well as by plundering the monasteries. They added a list of charges which were often fabricated: that he had freed people suspected of treason, for instance, and that he himself had indulged in treasonable talk. And on top of that, sire, he was clearly a heretic, who had engaged in an incriminating correspondence with Lutherans and had tolerated heresies which he knew were being widely aired in Calais; had, indeed, sent Reforming preachers from England to spread the heresies even further.

On such grounds was Thomas Cromwell sent to the Tower in the second week of June, after Norfolk had personally arrested him in the King's Council. And though it is hard not to feel that a kind of justice was done to a man who had been responsible for so much misery, coldly and ruthlessly imposed, there was something truly tragic in his end which went beyond the classical humiliation of the mighty figure brought low. He lay in the Tower for seven weeks after being refused a trial, his guilt established by a bill of attainder. Only Cranmer spoke up for him while this procedure was being carried through both Houses of Parliament, the Archbishop generously and bravely writing to the King that Cromwell 'was such a servant, in my judgement, in wisdom, diligence, faithfulness, and experience, as no prince in this realm ever had ... I pray God continually night and day, to send such a counsellor in his place whom your Grace may trust, and who for all his qualities can and will serve your Grace like to him.' To no avail. From his cell, a broken Cromwell pleaded for the King's mercy, but received no reply. On 28 July he went to the block on Tower Hill and in an address to the crowd he said, 'I intend this day to die God's servant, and believe in the holy Catholic faith.' A few hours later Henry married Catherine Howard, who received Cromwell's lands as a wedding present.

Norfolk was the one who got away, the victim who was reprieved by a last-minute fluke. He prospered for some time after the Lord Privy Seal's death, though perhaps not in the way that he might have wished; for no one man would step into Cromwell's shoes in Henry's declining years, the King's Privy Council at last coming fully into its own as the collective supervisor of government affairs. Norfolk was therefore but one of a number holding the reins of power though, increasingly, Henry made it plain to all of them that he would always have the last say on policy; he did not intend for a third time to allow this to be made elsewhere behind his back. In this new order Thomas Howard found himself doing again in 1542 what he had always done best, fighting the Scots and creating terror along the Borders. Two years later Henry went to war with France once more and the Duke was part of a victorious English army there as well. Meanwhile, a balance of power in the Council changed, and in the conflict of ambitions there the fortunes of two men in particular had risen above the rest. One was Edward Seymour, Earl of Hertford, the other John Dudley, Viscount Lisle. Both belonged to the more Protestant wing of the English Church and both had long harboured animosity towards Thomas Howard, not so much because in religion he was one of the old guard, as because he had for so long enjoyed a special entrée at court, partly because he was the King's most highly regarded soldier and suppressor of rebellion, partly because he was head of a dynasty which had supplied two queens of England in recent years and had an insatiable appetite for power.

In 1546, when the monarch's health had begun very seriously to decline, Seymour and Dudley attacked Howard by initially getting at his son Henry, the Earl of Surrey, who was out of favour with the King for having failed to live up to expectations in the campaign that took Boulogne; he also stood accused of various religious offences, including eating meat in Lent. But what put him in the Tower on the authority of the two councillors was supposedly treasonable talk in the past against both Wolsey and Cromwell, and a hint he had given somebody that, when Henry VIII died, the Duke of Norfolk would be the best candidate for the throne. There was one other thing: Surrey had been insanely arrogant enough to include in his coat of arms Edward the Confessor's own achievements, which was held to be as high a form of treason as anyone could commit. Under interrogation he appears to have said things which incriminated his father, including information about secret visits to the French ambassador and Howard's attitude to the Royal Supremacy.

The Duke was therefore, with Henry's approval, taken to the

Tower, too, where his questioning dwelt largely on religious matters, which were deemed serious enough to warrant his being charged with treason as well. The son was beheaded for his role as the bait in this business and the father was also destined for the block. And Norfolk, like Cromwell, asked the King for a mercy that again was withheld, from a victim whose ambitions had always been suspect. Instead, the dying Henry gave his assent to a bill of attainder during the last week in January 1547. The morning after this was passed on the 27th of the month, Thomas Howard was due to mount the scaffold on Tower Hill. But in the small hours of that day Henry himself died, attended by Catherine Parr, his sixth wife. It has never been clear why Norfolk's execution was not subsequently carried out, though it was obviously connected in some way with the sovereign's death. One speculation is that a majority of the Council, while happy enough to see the end of the Duke, were fastidiously inclined to postpone the event until at least a decent period of national mourning had passed. But the postponement lasted a long time, as did Thomas Howard's sojourn in the Tower. He remained there throughout the six years of Edward VI's reign, but was released when Henry's daughter Mary at last came into her own. Not only that, but his title was restored to him, he rejoined the Privy Council and was instituted into the Order of the Garter. Not much loved, but laden with honours, he died as Duke of Norfolk in his own bed at Kenninghall in 1554, when he was eighty-one years old. He was the greatest survivor of them all.

Many people prospered after the Pilgrimage of Grace and some of them had been Pilgrim leaders up to December 1536. Within twelve months, 'the King's Council in the northern parts' was reconstituted to succeed the northern council lately answerable to the Duke of Norfolk, which was itself the successor of earlier councils that had been formed up there, had functioned and then been dissolved almost sporadically. The new body had jurisdiction over the five northernmost English counties (thereby excluding Lancashire), which gave it the authority to dispense justice on behalf of the Crown in almost every area of life, from breaches of the peace to the settlement of debts, from the apprehension of heretics to the protection of morals, from agricultural practices to the plight of the poor. About the only thing the Council could not do was sentence someone to death, which remained a function of long-established practices of the law including martial law, as imposed by the Duke of Norfolk. It was also responsible for raising troops to defend the Border, which at last took that service away from powerful nobles like the Percies and therefore made such magnates less of a threat to the King's majesty.

The same end was achieved by the stipulation that a position on the Council could in no circumstances become hereditary. The Bishop of Durham, Cuthbert Tunstall, was made its first president, a position he accepted most unwillingly, because he wished to spend what was left of his life – which had lately been far too eventful for his taste – quietly preaching and teaching theology. Nor was he happy to discover that one of his new colleagues was none other than Robert Bowes, who had led the rebel party which ransacked Tunstall's palace at Bishop Auckland and caused him to flee to the safety of Norham in the early days of the Pilgrimage. Also among the first councillors were William Babthorpe and Robert Chaloner, who had both been part of the inner council of the Pilgrimage before Doncaster, Sir Thomas Tempest, who had hazarded his life by writing his opinions down for the weekend conclave in Pontefract, and Sir Ralph Ellerker, who had gone with Bowes to place the Pilgrim grievances before the King after the truce at Doncaster.

Those two had come back to tell Aske, Darcy, Constable and the other Pilgrim principals that they were convinced of the King's good intentions, and their behaviour was certainly changed by their protracted stay at court; but one senses a fundamental difference between the two men. Ellerker comes across as a cold opportunist, who backed whichever horse was likely to be the winner but never had his heart in the rebellion. He had a hand in the deaths of both Hallam and Constable, and was one of the first Pilgrims to become an active royalist, unlike Bowes, whose first instinct was not to switch sides, but to prevent further rebellion by calming things down while also prudently watching his back. Nor did Bowes, as Ellerker did, accept a role in the government's post-pardon military dispositions, though Bowes too had been a fighting soldier some years before the Pilgrimage of Grace. But from the moment he joined the Duke of Norfolk's progress round the North in February 1537 his allegiance was firmly with the Crown and it is possible that this was as much as anything an act of resignation to what by then seemed inevitable. It was also his prize opportunity to revive a career in the royal service that had come to nothing with the end of Cardinal Wolsey's patronage. He prospered exceedingly in the following years, fighting the Scots again alongside Norfolk, becoming a notable administrator of the Borders and a Member of Parliament, rising to the Privy Council in 1551 and becoming Master of the Rolls twelve months later. By then he was Sir Robert Bowes, having been knighted two years after the Pilgrimage was put down.

Ellerker did not do nearly so well for himself in the end. He, too, became an MP, which turned out to be the summit of his career, though he also headed a commission which reviewed the Border defences and did some fighting across the Channel, where he died, in Boulogne, in 1546.

Only one man who attended the first meeting of the Council in the North would enjoy a more spectacular rise than Robert Bowes, and he was Robert Holgate, who had been Prior of Watton when he antagonised John Hallam, but was already Bishop of Llandaff in 1537, succeeded Tunstall as President of the Council the following year (on a salary of £1000), and would be Archbishop of York after Edward Lee died in 1544.

One other old rebel, who was not on the Council, lived to enjoy an office which had seemed most unlikely in the hectic days of October 1536. He was Sir Edward Dymmoke, who had led the bloodthirsty men of Horncastle after being press-ganged into the Lincolnshire rising by William Leache and his crew, and eventually became the King's treasurer in Boulogne during the six years of English sovereignty there.

Sir Thomas Wharton did rather well for himself, too. Having managed to avoid any implication in the events of 1536, he soon became trusted as one of the Crown's most effective invigilators over Westmorland in the New Year. His reward was to be made ruler of the West March at the expense of Henry Clifford – the new man brought in specifically to reduce the risk of yet another powerful northern magnate ever threatening the Crown. As such, Wharton was also raised to the baronage. He died a considerable landowner and a very wealthy man. And he founded, in Kirkby Stephen, a grammar school.

The biggest winner of all, of course, was Henry VIII, whose image was only slightly improved by holding, 'in the King's most benign remembrance', the wives and children of Hussey, Bulmer, Bigod, Percy, Hamerton, Nicholas Tempest and Lumley, together with the sons of Sir Robert Constable and Lord Darcy, which may be thought an hypocrisy. Though he suffered humiliation in his dealings with the Pilgrims when they were in a position of strength, Henry's terrifying viciousness, his duplicity, his overwhelming self-confidence and his sharp eye for opportunity, when geared to the power he had at his disposal, were enough to see him through a difficult time, which could conceivably have cost him his throne. He won in ways that enriched him as well, not only acquiring much new wealth from a dissolution of religious houses that did not end until Waltham Abbey in Essex fell in March 1540, but at last coming into his takings from the Percy estates. For, the day before Old Tom Darcy went to the block as a criminal, the sickly and unbalanced Earl of Northumberland at last gave up the ghost, 'all his body the colour of saffron', and his funeral was the mournful spectacular that Darcy would have been treated to had he not died in disgrace.

First came twenty men in black gowns bearing torches in single file, with any number of standard and banner bearers, pursuivants, heralds, coats of arms belonging both to the King and to 'the defunct', principal mourners (one of whom was Richard Cromwell) and scores of tenants, menservants, grooms and other retainers in solemn procession behind the corpse, which was escorted by eight yeomen and eight gentlemen, who were themselves surrounded by twelve torchbearers to illuminate the banners posted at each corner of the hearse. And this funereal event was spread over some forty-eight hours, with several masses to be said before a large congregation and with banqueting still to be enjoyed the day after the interment was carried out. Having just disposed of Sir Thomas Percy and put his younger brother Sir Ingram out of reach in the Tower, the King was now not only able to enjoy Henry Percy's inheritance, which had long been promised him; he was also, for the first time in his life, able to contemplate a future in which a considerable threat to his power in the North was nullified. Sir Thomas Percy had left two young sons, as well as a wife distraught by her innocent contribution to his fate, but Norfolk arranged for Sir Thomas Tempest to be custodian of the boys until they reached maturity. That way, the tenacious and mythical Percy grip on the imagination of the North might be loosened indefinitely.

There are two very obvious questions to be asked about the Pilgrimage of Grace and its preliminary south of the Humber, and one of them concerns the participation of gentlemen and others of the upper class. It would take a cynic to deny that, for whatever reasons, Lord Darcy and Sir Robert Constable gave themselves wholeheartedly to the rebellion, even though both of them were brought into it reluctantly. The same applies to Robert Aske and, although some have seen him as an opportunist, almost a creature of the King after he was first summoned to court, it seems reasonable to reply that, if that was indeed so, he was a different sort of opportunist from young Sir Ralph Ellerker: he did not put the boot into anyone in order to serve his own purposes. One does not have to accept the implicit judgement of the Dodds sisters and Dom David Knowles that Aske was immaculate, that he 'not Henry was the true representative of all that was most characteristic and most sincere in England', to conclude that the charge of venality is unwarrantedly harsh. It may well be thought, in truth, that his greatest fault – certainly as the leader of a rebellion which sought to change the sovereign's mind by force of arms if need be – was his *naïveté* in taking the cunning and mendacious Thomas Howard and his sovereign at their word. That and his susceptibility to the flattering attentions of his king, which stopped his lawyer's head working as efficiently as it had been trained to do. What he did not do was to abandon those whom he had led to Doncaster; instead, when he thought he saw the chance of a just solution to all their problems, he tirelessly went from one place to another, begging his old comrades not to upset the applecart. But what was Robert Aske thinking when he accepted the Duke of Norfolk's invitation to be present at the post-pardon trials in

York, Carlisle and Durham? That is the great imponderable about his behaviour because, manifestly, he turned some sort of corner there. Perhaps, for the first time, he was afraid.

Aske had a vision of something that had nothing to do with ambition or even self-preservation, but we are left wondering how many of the Pilgrim leaders really shared this. Even Darcy and Constable did not show the passion that Aske revealed when he set down his view of the monasteries for consideration at the Pontefract conference. Perhaps it was this characteristic which persuaded the commons that Aske was the right man to lead them, when they might have done better to choose someone whose name had a ring to it and who had proven military experience. Constable is an obvious candidate and so is Sir Thomas Percy, as would Lord Darcy have been had he not been so unwell. But it is possible that no one else at that level communicated such a zeal as Robert Aske clearly did; it is also conceivable that no one at that level really wanted the job, for reasons to do with self-preservation, and that the others could spot a willing horse when they saw one. Almost every one of the sixty-odd nobles, knights and gentlemen who were active in the Pilgrimage (or whatever the true figure is), like their counterparts in Lincolnshire, were, after all, coerced into joining by one means or the other; a number almost certainly did so because they could not be sure that their servants would protect them if they refused. Very few seem to have volunteered entirely of their own free will, not even Robert Aske, who was on his way to a new law term in London when he was intercepted by George Hudswell and his men. He was only subjected to comparatively mild intimidation, and he could have disengaged himself from the affair the moment he crossed the river and went home, yet chose not to; but others must have been scared out of their wits when angry revolutionaries came knocking at their door. Many were threatened with decapitation on the spot, others with having their families harmed or their property razed; Nicholas Tempest was not the only one to be told that his son would be killed unless he joined up. And it is all very well for the Doddses to remark that the commons were very big on threats they never actually carried out, which is true enough, but that probably didn't occur to Tempest or to anyone else in his position.

The generating force in the Pilgrimage of Grace was that of a menacing commons, producing a movement which, stimulated by the priesthood, began at the bottom and worked its way upwards. It needed to enrol the gentry, the knights and the lords in order to seem more credible and significant, and perhaps because of a deep psychological need formed across the centuries, to obey other men who were born to the habit of command. And though the grievances and the hardships which created the rebellion of 1536 were genuine enough in people who were poor and exploited and victimised by their betters, and who deserve our sympathy even at this distance, it is a depressing fact that the momentum of the Lincolnshire rising and of its sequel north of the Humber depended almost wholly on the ugly power of the mob. The only more depressing thing is the number of people who were prepared to betray old comrades *in extremis*, even within the same family. According to Norfolk, the Dent leader John Atkinson was shopped 'by his own sister's son'; and, though Christopher Aske did not do anything quite as low as that, he certainly didn't improve his brother's chances of survival by his deposition to the authorities. These were not isolated examples of treachery.

We must not be shocked that the gentry started looking for a way out as soon as a hint of one appeared. This understandable reaction by originally unwilling participants makes it all the more remarkable that while they were active in the Pilgrimage they appeared to give it all they had got, risking execution and all the other nasty things that might befall them if things went wrong. Sir Robert Constable, whose first reaction was to make for the sanctuary of Pontefract Castle, became the Pilgrimage's principal firebrand, the one above all others who wanted to press on towards London after Doncaster. Robert Bowes led his rebels as skilfully and belligerently (as Cuthbert Tunstall could testify) and with as much commitment as any captain in the rebellion, but he was only incorporated into it when several hundred men caused him and his two brothers to surrender Barnard Castle to them. William Stapleton was press-ganged into service (with some encouragement for the commons from his sister-in-law) after his brother had made it plain he was not interested, yet he became one of the most effective commanders, who captured Hull and was, almost literally, champing at the bit to get at Doncaster. After peace had been made with Norfolk there, Stapleton was one of those who slipped away from the Pilgrimage into anonymity. The former leader in Westmorland, Robert Pulleyn, clearly wished to do the same, though his attempt to resume life as a tax-paying and law-abiding citizen was upset by the resentment of his old comrades, who regarded him as a traitor to their cause even though, unlike some of the Pilgrim gentry, he did not try to persuade them to pin their hopes to the King's integrity. It is difficult to believe that such men shared Aske's passionate desire to be the true defender of the faith in England.

The other question that has to be asked about the Pilgrimage of Grace is whether it could possibly have achieved its several aims if, instead of accepting the Duke of Norfolk's assurances and holding its fire indefinitely, it had pressed on as intended before the truce at Doncaster. There can be little doubt that if those 30,000 rebels had crossed the River Don to take on what there was of a royal army on the southern bank, especially if they had done so before Peter Mewtas brought the guns up to Doncaster bridge, they would have smashed their way through the King's men without much trouble. For Henry's troops were not only outnumbered by more than three to one at least, but they were facing a foe which was fired up in a cause that mattered to them, a cohesive force which was skilfully led; whereas the poor footsloggers in the royal companies were demoralised before they even started fighting, hungry, hard-up, soaked to the skin and entirely lacking in any motivation to serve a cheeseparing master who didn't seem to know what he was doing and had never bothered to sustain them in any particular. The cavalry were not in a much better state. The likelihood is that either just before, during or immediately after an engagement with the Pilgrims, large numbers of the royal rank and file would have walked away or changed sides; and after that, anything might have been possible as a roll-on effect gathered pace. The level of dissidence waiting to be tapped across the rest of England was an unknown quantity, but widespread dissidence there certainly was. Faced with a triumphant army that had just swept aside the King's own soldiers, had humbled such celebrated commanders as the Duke of Norfolk and the Earl of Shrewsbury, an incalculable number of

Henry's subjects would have decided to sign up, too, either out of principle or because it seemed the better and safer bet in the circumstances.

If that had happened in December 1536, if Henry had been confronted with his own subjects bearing down on him in alarming numbers and with unprecedented hostility, he would have had only two choices. He could have done the brave thing and tried to fight them off, or he could have sued for peace on the Pilgrims' terms. A third alternative – to take himself elsewhere in order to fight another day – is hardly a realistic proposition because it is difficult to think of anyone who would have been willing to have him. He had become the great European maverick and, unlike the unadulterated Protestants of northern Europe who had also cut themselves off from the old faith, he had spat upon everybody's beliefs, including theirs. If he had opted for battling things out, his chances of survival would most likely have been slim, when monarchs could be put to death like anyone else if they failed to win in peace or war.

If he had sued for peace, he would have accepted a humiliation so unbearable to his overweening nature that he might no longer have had the strength of purpose to devise some cunning new strategy that would in the end restore his authority. Nor, in such a scenario, is it likely that he would have found many who were resolute and loyal and convinced enough to stand with him, waiting for better times to return; Cromwell, Cranmer and others he had been able to rely on throughout the transforming years would, one way or another, no longer have been available. And if the Pilgrims had succeeded in their enterprise, to the extent of toppling Henry VIII or obtaining his lasting compliance, the course of English religious history would certainly have been changed, whatever other grievances were or were not relieved. Without a wholly amenable Henry, his daughter Mary would have been placed on the throne and the land would have been restored to the Roman obedience for the foreseeable future, as it was for five years after she succeeded her half-brother in 1553. There would have been no more Thomas Cranmer and probably no Richard Hooker in the next generation, no anyone who impressed upon the English Church its most characteristically Anglican caste marks; no Authorised Version of the Bible, no Book of Common Prayer, no sense of direction depending equally on Scripture, tradition and reason.

Always there will be speculation about what would have followed if the rebels of 1536 had reached London and cornered the King at Greenwich or in the Tower, or had watched him flee before the menace of their approach. And there will never be an end to asking ourselves why the Pilgrims decided not to press on from Doncaster. Was it because the upper classes cynically seized the first opportunity that had presented itself to detach themselves from the commons and recover their own place in the sun? Or because they really did trust Norfolk and Henry as much as appearances suggest? Or was it a simple failure of nerve when the most important decision of their lives had to be made instantly, a retreat from the awful possibility of failure itself and its consequences? An unwillingness to plunge the country into a civil war which, theoretically at least, might have ensued? Did the fact that plague was rampant in the South of England in 1536 (it spread to the North the following year) enter the calculations of the Pilgrim inner council at all? There is no evidence that it did. But, then, there is no evidence for anything but an assumption by Aske, Darcy and others (always excepting Sir Robert Constable) that Norfolk would deliver on Henry's promises; only supposition exists for the other possibilities, yet all the alternatives are plausible.

As it was, the property speculators who might have been stopped in their tracks had the great rebellion succeeded made fortunes out of the dissolution of the monasteries: men like Alderman Sir Richard Gresham, a Londoner and the purchaser of Fountains Abbey and most of its estates, who, in 1539, descended on York, where he bought up more than 400 dwellings that had belonged to the city's religious houses, which he then milked for their rents in a cash flow that went down to the capital instead of circulating round York. This draining of northern wealth was one of the complaints that Robert Aske, in particular, had made. On top of that was what the Crown creamed off from the dissolution, which doubled its income at the start of Henry's reign to £200,000 a year by 1540. Taxation was undiminished while Henry was alive, with the same purposes as before: to maintain the King in all his expenditures and not simply for the defence of the realm.

As for the wider social and economic difficulties that had so concerned a large proportion of the commons in the Pilgrimage, far from being relieved by a monarch who might have learned several lessons from his rebellious subjects, fresh grievances concerning the plight of the peasant in particular surfaced again a couple of years after Henry's death, this time in the West Country and East Anglia. In the first of these outbursts, religious dissent caused rebellion in Cornwall and Devon as much as economic grievances, the first rumbles of discontent clearly audible in 1547 before bursting into organised resistance at Bodmin and in the adjacent county at Sampford Courtenay in 1549. This culminated in a siege of Exeter, which cost several hundred lives before the city was relieved and the rebels were defeated in a fight at Clyst St Mary. A manifesto which they drew up indicated that, as well as complaints about the new Prayer Book, about the abandonment of Latin in the liturgy, about the substitution of bread for wafers at the communion, they were also much exercised about new taxes on sheep and woollen cloth, which were causing steady inflation, with rumour reckoning that they would soon be paying a poll tax on their geese, their pigs and their other stock. There was trouble, too, over enclosures further afield, in Somerset and Wiltshire.

And then, towards the end of June 1549, an even greater rebellion broke out at Wymondham in Norfolk, which quickly spread into Suffolk. It began on a feast day associated with Thomas Becket, with local enclosures a particular target of peasant anger, but by no means the only one. People were also aggrieved by rack-renting, by the rise in food prices, by a steady erosion of tenant rights. The rising found a leader in Robert Kett, a Wymondham tanner, who led a march on Norwich and set up camp outside the city, with maybe 16,000 men at his back; one of them lowered his hose and tauntingly bared his backside at the defenders, among whom was an archer who, with commendable accuracy, shot an arrow into his rump. Soon, East Anglia was dotted with such ingatherings, each of them determined to obtain relief from traditional exploitation, whether by the Crown or by local landowners, including the Howards at Kenninghall; the rebels must have gained some satisfaction from the fact that, just then, the Duke himself was shut away in the

Tower. But Kett's Rebellion ended tragically after he and his people took the city, with a counter-attack by 12,000 troops, many of them foreign mercenaries, which some believe cost 3000 rebels their lives. Kett himself was hanged at Norwich Castle and maybe fifty of his supporters were also executed.

As significant as anything about the risings in the West Country and East Anglia, which were also echoed along the Thames Valley and, a few years later, in Kent, is that they suggest a very substantial degree of support that would have been ready and waiting for action if the Pilgrimage of Grace had carried out its original plan and marched south from Doncaster.

Meanwhile, the birth pains of Henry's new Church continued for many years after he had gone and even while he was still on the throne, one spasm was followed by another. The Bishops' Book (*The Institution of a Christian Man*) of 1537, a collection of sermons designed to steer the nation into the new ways of thinking, and Cromwell's Injunctions of 1538 were succeeded by Cranmer's Thirteen Articles; and all these documents were in greater or lesser degree influenced by the Lutheran doctrines embodied in the Wittenberg Articles of 1536 and the Augsburg Confession of six years earlier, Cranmer's text most of all, though he retained a characteristic independence of thought while embracing Lutheran principles.

Henry had evidently given scant attention to the Bishops' Book when it appeared, having too many other things on his mind that year, including the birth of his son and the death of his wife. When he did take a proper look at it he decided that it had gone too far, was much too Protestant for his taste. So, much to Cranmer's chagrin, he pressed for a revision, which duly appeared in 1543 as *Necessary Doctrine and Erudition for any Christian Man*, though it became more widely known as the King's Book. Much more conservative than its predecessor, it extolled the installation of images in churches, both of Christ and of the saints, and encouraged the use of incense at such memorials, thus extending the King's sympathy for such practices far beyond the position he had taken in the Ten Articles of 1536. It drew the line at pilgrimages to particular shrines, however, the cult of Thomas Becket being particularly reviled – and Henry still didn't have any time for Purgatory. In this fashion his

English Church struggled towards an enduring identity, which would also be shaped by its experience under the cradle Protestant Edward, the intensely Catholic Mary and Elizabeth, who had no great religious convictions but whose reign in the end took the English even further from obedience to Rome. At least her people were spared the terror of unmitigated religious warfare, which would ravage continental Europe in the seventeenth century. And they had to wait 105 years after the Pilgrimage of Grace for their civil war which, although terrible enough, was never principally about religion at all.

POSTSCRIPT

Remembrancers of the Pilgrimage are spread across the land. The most conspicuous are the northern religious buildings, too often ruined, whose last incumbents were implicated in the rising or cited by rebels as victims of the policies which largely brought it about. What's left of Whalley Abbey is within a stone's throw of a busy highway, but its gateway is largely the same as it was on the day when the butchered remains of three monks may have been hung from it. Others are more isolated in greater tranquillity, in landscapes that have changed little since they were the scene of so much turmoil. The Ure still flows broadly through sheep pastures and, on its western bank, the great grey stones that once were Jervaulx stand reproachfully gaunt and tumbled, almost within sight of Bolton Castle, which Lord Scrope abandoned rapidly, leaving his wife and infant son to face the advancing rebels alone. Tucked into its secluded valley so that it is quite hidden from the busyness of nearby Barrow, the red sandstone remains of Furness rear high above the watercourse which the monks diverted from a natural stream to run behind their dormitory, so that it would serve as a cleansing Cistercian sewer. Sawley, the source of so much trouble, has been greatly battered by the centuries but is still majestically overlooked by the whaleback of Pendle Hill and nestles unobtrusively below the thickly wooded ridge from which a Pilgrim host might have fallen upon the Earl of Derby; but now it has saxifrage, toadflax and speedwell growing on its crumbled surfaces, and it is disturbed by nothing much more than the sound of a passing tractor. The principal building at Cartmel still flourishes, as it was allowed to even after its canons had been executed, because it functioned as a parish church as well as a priory; and so it does still, so mindful of its past responsibilities that a fresh loaf of bread is placed daily upon a shelf, lest any of the parish poor are in need of it.

Other churches, in Lincolnshire as well as in the North, still stir the memory of 1536–7. At Horncastle their keepsake is an embellishment of thirteen scythe blades above an arch of the south chapel, which were very probably carried by companions of the men who did Dr Rayne to death and after him a hapless servant; almost the only blood that was deliberately shed by insurgents from October right up to the end of the Pilgrimage. At Louth, the pulpit from which Thomas Kendall preached the sermon which sparked the rising has not survived to this day; but the church which he would still otherwise recognise is so utterly beautiful inside, as well as so captivating without, that only an insensate clod could fail to understand why such passions were raised when it appeared to be threatened by the Crown.

There are other ruins and one of them gives an idea of the state in which the dithering Edward Lee lived at his archiepiscopal palace of Cawood. Most of it has been reduced, but still intact is a wing of red brick alongside a crenellated stone gatehouse which boasts an exceedingly handsome bay window, complete with glass. Nothing is left of Lord Darcy's home at Templehirst, but there are enough remaining clues to the castle which he surrendered to Robert Aske, and which subsequently became a Pilgrim base, for us to appreciate what a mighty fortress Pontefract was in the sixteenth century. Built of masonry that is generally two feet thick and sometimes more, portions of the outer walls still stand some distance above the ground, as does a bit of the Great Hall, parts of some defensive towers, the bakehouse, the brewhouse and the kitchen, all scattered around what was once the inner bailey, but is now a well-kept lawn. Much more miserable than this wreckage is the landscape which these bygones overlook from their challenging position upon a small hill: the loud-mouthed commerce of Petworld and £-Stretcher, rows of municipal housing and a distant view of a power station's cooling towers. Other castles have fared better: the one at

Lancaster, where, rising powerfully over the quays and old ware-houses beside the Lune and its fishing smacks, it is still, as then, a place of captivity; and at Skipton, where the fortification crouches above the parish church and the market place, with 'Desormais' still in fretstone above the gate and with the Clifford banner flying from its battlements, though Cliffords have not lived there since the seventeenth century.

The only inhabited place associated with the Pilgrimage which has been even more violated than Pontefract is Doncaster. The bridge, which was the key to so much that happened there in 1536, has long since been replaced, or reinforced, or otherwise changed out of all recognition, putting it far beyond imagination, so that even a fantasist would have difficulty in envisaging what this crossing must have looked like when Peter Mewtas brought up the artillery, and when negotiating teams clattered back and forth over it between the Pilgrim army and the Duke of Norfolk's headquarters in what turned out to be the crucial moment of the entire rebellion. Instead, the bridge at Doncaster today is a perpetual bedlam of heavy traffic, night and day, inching its way in great gusts of diesel fumes, or rushing head-long up and down the Great North Road that took Robert Aske and others to their various destinies. It is not even possible to stand at water level within sight of the crossing, because the River Don's banks here have been transmogrified into an industrial estate with prohibiting notices everywhere. Yet other bridges that played their part in the Pilgrimage have been almost untouched by the long centuries since; at Kirkby Stephen, where the Westmorland rebels saw off Thomas Clifford and his men, still hump-backed and so narrow that only one vehicle can cross it at a time; at Kexby and Sutton, which were secured by a scouting party before Aske's cautious advance on York.

Inevitably, the rural parts of Lincolnshire and the North have come off best. Even York – still recognisably a great medieval city which is glorified by its Minster – can sometimes make you wish the tourist industry had never been invented, though it helps if you remember that its winding sixteenth-century streets would generally have been crammed with people, too; but in the shadow of Clifford's Tower, where Robert Aske was executed, there is now an expensive and very short-term parking lot, which says as much as anything about the passage of time. At Hull it is still possible at the waterfront (much reduced for reasons to do with very recent maritime history) to enjoy a whiff of the days when this was a leading Tudor port, with goods coming along waterways from distant Halifax into the Humber before being shipped up and down and across the North Sea; but not a trace remains of the Beverley Gate, where John Hallam was betrayed and where Sir Robert Constable was executed and left hanging in chains.

Far better to potter around the northern countryside, for there it takes little imagination to sense a roll-back of the years to the time when English history might have been changed for better or worse. Where a host of rebels first mustered at Neals Ing, on the flank of Fountains Fell, the bleakness is exactly the same that they knew, relieved only by a solitary and more recent farm building, together with some drystone walls. The same goes for Mallerstang, where ten Westmorlanders were executed and where, along the long length of that valley, only the odd farmhouse or cottage has been built since then. The massively sweeping curve of Dentdale would likewise still be perfectly recognisable by John Atkinson and the host he first marched to Kendal and then to Lancaster. On Derwentwater, the island on which the rack-renter Peter Middleton was besieged for months is empty of everything but trees and the ruins of his house, almost invisible in the undergrowth. Nowhere else in the Pilgrim countryside has come off as badly as Moota Hill, on which Cumbrians mustered more than once, and which has been defaced by the excavation of a quarry and then by the imposition of a television mast.

There are portraits and memorials galore associated with the Pilgrimage but, with very few exceptions, they celebrate those who were obedient to the Crown. Most painted of all, of course, was Henry himself, but we also know what Cromwell looked like, and Thomas Howard, Charles Brandon, Edward Stanley, Henry Clifford and Robert Holgate. There is even an engraving of Thomas Hawley, Clarencieux Herald, whose spitefulness helped to send his colleague Thomas Miller to his death. There is an effigy of George Talbot and his two wives in the Shrewsbury Chapel of Sheffield Cathedral, and Henry Clifford's tomb stands beside the altar in Skipton parish church. Edward Lee, who almost made a vocation of being betwixt and between the Pilgrims and the Crown, is commemorated by a window in Magdalen College, Oxford and his remains are probably somewhere beneath York Minster; at any rate, they were buried there, under a large blue marble stone in the choir, which was 'removed and cut up to form the dark pattern of the new pavement then being laid' in 1736.

There is scarcely anything to jog the memory about people who were arraigned for their association with the Pilgrimage. No portraits (unless something has remained undetected for four centuries) and only two or three other mementoes. A memorial tablet to Old Tom Darcy is in the porch of St Botolph Without Aldgate in the City of London, and in the North Riding church at Kirby Hill there is a monument to Dr John Dakyn, who tried to calm the religious of Conishead and Cartmel, told the parishioners of Romaldkirk to return certain things stolen from the Bishop of Durham, and then had to put up with examination in the Tower. A few days later Adam Sedbar was consigned much more ominously to the same place and on the wall of his cell in the Beauchamp Tower his name was chiselled in high relief – 'Adam Sedbar Abbas Iorevall. 1537' – obviously with the collusion of the royal gaolers, who could be very obliging in providing the wherewithal for such vanities so long as money was not overlooked. Sedbar's initials had already been carved on a sumptuous wooden screen which belonged to his Jervaulx Abbey but which, since the Dissolution, has enriched the choir of the church at Aysgarth, a few miles away. Another abbot, John Paslew of Whalley, has been pictured on his way to execution in a Victorian lithograph doubtless created to fortify nineteenth-century North Lancashire Catholic piety.

No such things are left to connect us to the chief captain of the Pilgrimage, though a dwelling in Hawes, at the top of Wensleydale, is named Aske House, which is a reminder of sorts; and above the doorway of St Agatha's church, adjacent to the ruins of Easby Abbey, are carved the arms of Scrope, Conyers and Aske, the last referring to the parent family which was rooted in Swaledale, not the branch that moved to the East Riding before Robert Aske was born there. Robert's home is the best place to contemplate his memory, not in the glory of York Minster, where he was received as a conqueror, or at the Tower of London, where he was held for interrogation by Cromwell's examiners, or at the mound of the castle where he was put to death. Here, amidst the flatlands of the East Riding, whose twisty-twirly lanes seem to take ages to get you anywhere through fields that are sometimes fragrant with lavender, are the most natural memories of him. Aughton has changed only a little since the sixteenth century, mostly because half a dozen council houses have been added to the village's one street, and because the manor in which John, Christopher and Robert Aske were born does not exist any more apart from the earthworks of its foundations, together with the ditch that was its moat, which marks the boundary of the nearby 'big house'.

Neither of the two surviving brothers lived much beyond Robert's death in 1537. Christopher was the first of them to go, in 1539, and John followed shortly after his own eldest son died in 1542. He left four other male descendants and three daughters but the last entry for any kin in the parish register was made in 1672, when Richard Aske, the parish clerk, was buried on 17 April. There were still Askes in the next village of Bubwith, however, as recently as 1892. But no one of that name is even in the district telephone directory today. People, as well as times, have moved on. This is the most significant change of all hereabouts.[1]

Before he died, Christopher Aske was responsible for rebuilding the Aughton church tower in the Perpendicular style, which was then on its way out, and into the masonry was worked, presumably on his authority, an inscription which has puzzled us ever since, not least because it combines English, French and Latin of the period. It reads 'Christofer le second fitz de Robart Aske ch'r oublier ne doy Ao Di 1536'. The Doddses suggested alternative translations for this, the first being 'I (the tower) ought not to forget Christopher, second son of Robert Aske, knight, AD 1536', the other one reading 'Christopher, the second

1 However, one of John Aske's descendants returned to Aughton in 2001, when his ashes were interred beside the church tower. He was Sir Conan Aske, who had been brought up in Scarborough, had been a soldier, schoolmaster and priest during a very long life, and had spent his later years in Worcestershire.

son of Robert Aske knight. I ought not to forget AD 1536'. Was it, then, the self-reproach of a guilty man? Or the self-satisfaction of one who was untroubled by his younger brother's fate? It is a strangely taunting enigma built into the place where Robert Aske had worshipped, where he became so attached to his faith that he was prepared to die in its defence. He knew well the stones of All Saints, and the dogtoothed Norman arch above its chancel step, and the brasses commemorating two fifteenth-century ancestors of his, and the brick wall surrounding the grassy churchyard, separating it from the Derwent ings, which flooded every winter when the river overflowed. As it still does, so that the floodwater continues to lap the churchyard wall in time of unusually heavy spate. The wildfowl still come to the flooded fields in great flocks then and make their winter home there, just as they did 450 years ago, since when so very little has changed. For this is a lonely village, set in a countryside which the modern world seems largely to have ignored, and the past feels very close at hand, with all its grief, its bitterness and its dreadful memories of that hazardous time. Aughton is a place for collecting such thoughts.

BIBLIOGRAPHY

ABBREVIATIONS

BP	Borthwick Papers
CWAAS	*Cumberland and Westmorland Antiquarian Society, Transactions*
CS	Chetham Society
ERA	*Transactions of the East Riding Antiquarian Society*
EHR	*English Historical Review*
HA	Historical Association
HJ	*Historical Journal*
HR	*Historical Research*
LCAS	*Transactions of the Lancashire and Cheshire Antiquarian Society*
LP	*Letters and Papers, Foreign and Domestic, of the Reign of Henry VIII, 1509–47*, edited by J. S. Brewer, James Gairdner and R. H. Brodie (21 volumes, London, 1862–1932)
NEEHI	North-East England History Institute
NH	*Northern History*
P & P	*Past and Present*
RHS	Royal Historical Society, *Studies in History* Series
SAHS	Scarborough Archaeological and History Society
SCH	*Studies in Church History*
SS	Surtees Society
WYAS	West Yorkshire Archaeology Service
YASRS	Yorkshire Archaeological Society, Record Series
YATJ	*Yorkshire Archaeological and Topographical Journal*
YPRS	Yorkshire Parish Registers Society

Astill, G. and Grant, A. (eds), *The Countryside of Medieval England* (Oxford, 1988)

Baker, J. H., *The Third University of England: the Inns of Court and the Common Law Tradition* (Selden Society, 1990)

Bateson, M., 'The Pilgrimage of Grace and Aske's Examination' (EHR 5, 1890)

Bax, E. Belfort, *The Peasants' War in Germany 1525–1526* (New York, 1968)

Bean, J. M. W., *The Estates of the Percy Family 1416–1537* (Oxford, 1958)

Beckingsale, B. W., *Thomas Cromwell, Tudor Minister* (London, 1978)

Bellamy, J., *The Tudor Law of Treason* (London, 1979)

Bernard, G. W., *The Tudor Nobility* (ed. Manchester, 1992)

————, *The Power of the Early Tudor Nobility: a study of the Fourth and Fifth Earls of Shrewsbury* (Brighton, 1985)

————, *War, Taxation and Rebellion in early Tudor England* (Brighton, 1986)

Berry, E. K. (ed.), *Swaledale Wills and Inventories 1522–1600* (YASRS, 1998)

Bettenson, H. (ed.), *Documents of the Christian Church* (Oxford, 1963)

Bindoff, S. (ed.), *The House of Commons 1509–1558* (3 vols, London, 1982)

Binns, J., *Scarborough and the Pilgrimage of Grace* (SAHS 33, 1997)

Blickle, P., *The Revolution of 1525: the German Peasants' War from a new perspective* (Baltimore and London, 1981)

Bowker, M., 'Lincolnshire 1536; heresy, schism or religious discontent' (SCH 9, 1972)

————, *The Henrician Reformation; the diocese of Lincoln under John Longland 1521–1547* (Cambridge, 1981)

Bownes, D. M., *The Post-pardon Revolts, December 1536–March 1537* (Manchester, 1995)

Bray, G. (ed.), *Documents of the English Reformation* (Cambridge, 1994)

Brigden, S., 'Thomas Cromwell and the "brethren"' in Festschrift for G. R. Elton, *Law and Government Under the Tudors* (Cambridge, 1988)

Broce, G. and Wunderli, R. M., 'The Funeral of Henry Percy, Sixth Earl of Northumberland' (Albion 22, 1990)

Browne, J., *The Fabric Rolls and Documents of York Minster* (York, 1862)

Burnet, G., *The History of the Reformation of the Church of England* (Oxford, 1829)

Bush, M. L., 'Capt Poverty and the Pilgrimage of Grace' (HR 65, 1992)

———, 'Enhancements and importunate charges: an analysis of the tax complaints of October 1536' (Albion 22, 1990)

———, '"Up for the commonweal": the significance of tax grievances in the English Rebellion of 1635' (EHR 106, 1991)

———, 'The problem of the far North: a study of the crisis of 1537 and its consequences' (NH 6, 1971)

———, *The Pilgrimage of Grace: a Study of the Rebel Armies of October 1536* (Manchester, 1996)

———, 'The Richmondshire Uprising of October 1536 and the Pilgrimage of Grace' (NH 29, 1993)

Bush, M. L. and Bownes, D., *The Defeat of the Pilgrimage of Grace: a Study of the Postpardon Revolts of December 1536 to March 1537 and their Effect* (Hull, 1999)

Chandler, J. (ed.), *John Leland's Itinerary: travels in Tudor England* (Stroud, 1993)

Charlesworth, J. (ed.), 'Aughton Parish Registers' (Vol. 86 of YPRS series, 1929)

Clay, C. G. A., *Economic Expansion and Social Change: England 1500–1700* (Cambridge, 1984)

Clay, J. W., 'Yorkshire Monasteries: Suppression Papers' (YAS, Vol. 48, 1912)

Cox, J. C. (ed.), 'William Stapleton and the Pilgrimage of Grace' (ERA 10, 1903)

Cross, C. and Vickers, N., 'Monks, Friars and Nuns in Sixteenth Century Yorkshire' (YASRS 150, 1995)

Daniell, C., *Death and Burial in Medieval England 1066–1550* (London, 1997)

Davies, C. S. L., 'The Pilgrimage of Grace reconsidered' (P & P 41, 1968)

———, 'Popular Religion and the Pilgrimage of Grace' in *Order and Disorder in Early Modern England*, edited by A. Fletcher and J. Stevenson (Cambridge, 1987)

Dickens, A. G., *The English Reformation* (London, 1964)

————, 'Secular and religious motivation in the Pilgrimage of Grace' (SCH 4, 1967)

————, 'The Clifford Letters of the Sixteenth Century' (SS 172, London, 1962)

————, *Lollards and Protestants in the Diocese of York 1509–1558* (London, 1982)

————, 'Royal pardons for the Pilgrimage of Grace' (YAJ 33, 1936–8)

————, 'New Records of the Pilgrimage of Grace' (YAJ 33, 1936–8)

————, 'Robert Holgate: Archbishop of York and President of the King's Council in the North' (BP 8, Borthwick Institute, York, 1955)

————, *Thomas Cromwell and the English Reformation* (London, 1959)

Dodds, M. H. and R., *The Pilgrimage of Grace 1536–1537 and the The Exeter Conspiracy 1538* (2 vols, Cambridge, 1915)

Dudding, R. C., *The First Churchwardens' Book of Louth 1500–1524* (Oxford, 1941)

Duffy, E., *The Stripping of the Altars* (London, 1992)

————, *Saints and Sinners: a History of the Popes* (Yale, 1997)

Dugdale, W., *Monasticon Anglicanum*, Vol. 5 (London, 1946)

Ellis, S. G., 'A border baron and the Tudor state: the rise and fall of Lord Dacre of the North' (HJ 35, 1992)

Elton, G. R., 'Politics and the Pilgrimage of Grace' in *After the Reformation* edited by B. Malament (Manchester, 1980)

————, *England Under the Tudors* (London, 1991)

————, *Reformation Europe 1517–1559* (2nd edn, Oxford, 1999)

————, *Policy and Police: The Enforcement of the Reformation in the Age of Thomas Cromwell* (Cambridge, 1972)

Emden, A. B., *A Biographical Register of the University of Oxford AD 1501 to 1540* (Oxford, 1974)

English, B., *The Great Landowners of East Yorkshire 1530–1910* (New York, 1990)

Fieldhouse, R. and Jennings, R., *A History of Richmond and Swaledale* (London, 1978)

Fletcher, A. and MacCulloch, D., *Tudor Rebellions* (4th edn, London, 1997)

Fletcher, A. and Stephenson, J., *Order and Disorder in Early Modern England* (Cambridge, 1985)

Froude, J. A., *History of England* (Vol. III, London, 1870)

Gairdner, J., *Letters & Papers, Foreign & Domestic, of the Reign of Henry VIII* (London, 1864–1932, Vols VI, VIII, IX, XI, XII, XIII and XIV)

Gunn, S. J., 'Peers, commons and gentry in the Lincolnshire revolt of 1536' (P & P 123, 1989)

———, *Charles Brandon, Duke of Suffolk c. 1484–1545* (Cambridge, 1988)

Guy, J., *Tudor England* (Oxford, 1988)

Haigh, C. A., *Reformation and Resistance in Tudor Lancashire* (Cambridge, 1975)

———, *English Reformations* (Oxford, 1993)

———, 'The last days of the Lancashire monasteries and the Pilgrimage of Grace' (CS, 3rd series, 17, 1969)

Haigh, C. A. (ed.), *The English Reformation Revised* (Cambridge, 1987)

Harrison, S. M., 'The Pilgrimage of Grace in the Lake Counties 1536–7' (RHS 27, 1981)

Head, David M., *The Ebbs and Flows of Fortune: the life of Thomas, 3rd Duke of Norfolk* (London, 1995)

Heal, F., and O'Day, R., *Church and Society in England: Henry VIII to James I* (London, 1977)

Heath, P., *The English Parish Clergy on the Eve of the Reformation* (London, 1969)

Hill, C., *Puritanism and Revolution* (London, 1958)

———, *Economic Problems of the Church* (Oxford, 1956)

Holdsworth, W. S., *A History of English Law* (17 vols, London, 1922–66)

Horrox, R. (ed.), *Beverley Minster: an illustrated history* (Beverley, 2000)

Hoskins, W. G., *The Making of the English Landscape* (London, 1965)

Houlbrouke, R., *Church Courts and the People during the English Reformation 1520–1579* (Oxford, 1979)

Hoyle, R. W., 'The first earl of Cumberland; a reputation reassessed' (NH 22, 1986)

———, 'Thomas Master's narrative of the Pilgrimage of Grace' (NH 21, 1985)

————, 'Early Tudor Craven' (YASRS 145, 1985)

————, *The Pilgrimage of Grace and the Politics of the 1530s* (Oxford, 2001)

Hume, M. A. S. (ed.), *The Spanish Chronicle of King Henry VIII* (London, 1889)

James, M. E., 'Obedience and dissent in Henrician England: the Lincolnshire Rebellion 1536' (P & P 48, 1970; and P & P 123, 1989)

————, 'The first earl of Cumberland and the decline of northern feudalism' (NH 1, 1966)

————, *Family, Lineage and Civil Society; a study of society, politics and mentality in the Durham region 1500–1640* (Oxford, 1974)

————, 'The Concept of Order and the Northern Rising' (P & P 60, 1973)

————, 'Two Tudor Funerals' (CWAAS, Vol. 66, 1966)

Kelly, J. N. D., *The Oxford Dictionary of the Popes* (Oxford, 1990)

Kermode, J., *Medieval Merchants: York, Beverley and Hull in the later Middle Ages* (Cambridge, 1998)

Knowles, D., *The Monastic Order in England* (Cambridge, 1940)

————, *The Religious Orders in England* (Vol. III, Cambridge, 1959)

Langland, W., *Piers Plowman*, edited by J. F. Goodrich (Harmondsworth, 1966)

Leach, R. F., 'Beverley Town Documents' (Selden Society 14, 1900)

MacCulloch, Diarmaid, *Thomas Cranmer* (New Haven and London, 1996)

————, *Tudor Church Militant: Edward VI and the Protestant Reformation* (London, 1999)

Mackie, J. D., *The Oxford History of England: the Earlier Tudors 1485–1558* (Oxford, 1992)

Manning, R. B., *Village Revolts: social protest and popular disturbances in England 1509–1640* (Oxford, 1988)

Megarry, R. E., *Inns Ancient and Modern; a topographical and historical introduction to the Inns of Court* (Selden Society, 1972)

Merriman, R. B., *Life and Letters of Thomas Cromwell* (2 vols, Oxford, 1968 edn)

Midmer, R., *English Medieval Monasteries 1066–1540: a summary* (London, 1979)

Miller, H., *Henry VIII and the English Nobility* (Oxford, 1986)

Newman, C. M., *Robert Bowes and the Pilgrimage of Grace* (NEEHI, Middlesbrough, 1997)

Palliser, D. M., 'The Reformation in York 1534–1553' (Borthwick Papers 40, York, 1971)

———, *Tudor York* (Oxford, 1979)

Pevsner, N. B. L., *The Buildings of England: Co. Durham* (Harmondsworth, 1953)

———, *The Buildings of England: Cumberland and Westmorland* (Harmondsworth, 1967)

———, *The Buildings of England: Lincolnshire* (Harmondsworth, 1967)

———, *The Buildings of England: North Lancashire* (Harmondsworth, 1969)

———, *The Buildings of England: Northumberland* (Harmondsworth, 1957)

———, *The Buildings of England: Yorkshire; York and the East Riding* (Harmondsworth, 1972)

———, *The Buildings of England: Yorkshire; The North Riding* (Harmondsworth, 1966)

———, *The Buildings of England: Yorkshire; The West Riding* (Harmondsworth, 1959)

Prescott, H. F. M., *The Man on a Donkey* (London, 1952)

Reid, R. R., *The King's Council in the North* (London, 1975)

———, 'The Office of Warden of the Marches: its Origin and Early History' (EHR, Vol. XXXII, 1917)

Rex, R., *Henry VIII and the English Reformation* (London, 1993)

Roberts, I., *Pontefract Castle* (WYAS, 1990)

Russell, J. C., *British Medieval Population* (Albuquerque, 1948)

Scarisbrick, J. J., *Henry VIII* (London, 1976)

———, *The Reformation and the English People* (Oxford, 1984)

Shuffrey, W. A., *Churches of the Deanery of North Craven* (Leeds, 1914)

Slavin, A. J., *Politics and Profit: a Study of Sir Ralph Sadler 1502–1547* (Cambridge, 1966)

Smith, L. T., *The Itinerary of John Leland in or about the Years 1535–1543* (London, 1964)

Smith, R. B., *Land and Politics in the England of Henry VIII: the West Riding of Yorkshire* (Oxford, 1970)

Stamp, D. and Hoskins, W. G., *The Common Lands of England and Wales* (London, 1963)

Sumption, J., *Pilgrimage, an Image of Medieval Religion* (New Jersey, 1975)

Swanson, R. N., *Church and Society in Late Medieval England* (Oxford, 1989)

Taylor, S., *Cartmel: People and Priory* (Kendal, 1955)

Tempest, A. C., 'Nicholas Tempest: a Sufferer in the Pilgrimage of Grace' (YATJ, Vol. 11, 1891)

Thirsk, J., *Tudor Enclosures* (HA Pamphlet 41, 1958)

Thomas, K., *Religion and the Decline of Magic* (London, 1971)

Toller, T. N., *Correspondence of Edward, Third Earl of Derby* (CS new series 19, 1890)

Tonge, T., *Heraldic Visitation of the North Counties in 1530* (SS 41, 1890)

Venn, J. and J. A., *Alumni Cantabrigienses* (4 vols, Cambridge, 1922–7)

Wagner, A., *Heralds of England* (London, 1967)

Ward, A., *The Lincolnshire Rising 1536* (Nottingham, 1986)

Watson, J. B., 'The Lancashire gentry and the public service 1529–58' (LCAS 73, 1963)

Weeks, W. S., 'Abbot Paslew and the Pilgrimage of Grace' (LCAS 47, 1930–1)

Whitaker, T. D., *A History of Richmondshire...* (London, 1823)

———, *History and Antiquities of the Deanery of Craven* (Leeds, 1878)

White, H. C., *Tudor Books of Saints and Martyrs* (Wisconsin, 1963)

Whiting, R., *The Blind Devotion of the People: Popular Religion and the English Reformation* (Cambridge, 1989)

Woodward, G. W. O., *The Dissolution of the Monasteries* (London, 1966)

Wriothesley, C., *A Chronicle of England* (Camden Society 53, 1852)

Youings, J., *The Dissolution of the Monasteries* (London, 1971)

SOURCE NOTES

(In quotations from *Letters & Papers*, the figures
refer to documents, not pages)

FOREWORD

p.xiv   'the comon voce and fame' LP XI, 534
p.xv   'Finally, as these troubles' LP XII (I), 479
        'that all Religious persons' Hoyle, Master, p.78
        'cause all the monks' J.W. Clay, p.34
        'if this project had started' Bush/Bownes, p.v
p.xvi   'Oh, Aske' *A Pilgrimage of Grace: the diaries of Ruth Dodds
        1905–1974*, edited by Maureen Callcott (Whitley Bay,
        1995) p.34
p.xvii 'What is badly needed' Bush, p.6

CHAPTER II **A Turning Point**

p.5   'a formidable, captivating' Scarisbrick, p.17
p.6   '20 masses of Jesus' quoted Haigh, *Reformation and
        Resistance*, p.68
p.7   'a delightful, well–illustrated' Duffy, *Altars*, p.50
p.9   '*Inter faeces*' quoted in *Francis of Assisi* by Adrian House
        (London, 2000) p.94
        'This holy Council' Bettenson, p.135
p.11   'The pope by his...' ibid., pp.185–91
p.13   'On this I take...' ibid., p.201
p.14   'Crush them...' quoted Belfort Bax, pp.277–8

CHAPTER III **Defender of the Faith**

p.20   'declare by your authority' quoted Scarisbrick, p.259
p.22   'the competence of' ibid., p.76
p.24   'be but half' quoted Mackie, p.355

p.25 'Where by divers sundry' Bray, pp.78–83

p.26 'The King our Sovereign' ibid., pp.113–14
'annates, first-fruits' ibid., pp.88–90
'this your grace's' ibid., p.95

p.27 'was always busy' Elton, *Policy and Police*, p.341
'full power and authority' Bray, p.114

p.30 'that he will not find' LP VIII, 822

p.31 'There can be not better' LP IX, 622

p.32 'The King sends a doctor' LP VI, 19

p.33 '*Haltemprice...* Rents' YASRS, Vol.18 (1912) pp.16–18

p.36 'especially that' LP XI, 1143

p.37 'had taken over' quoted Challis, p.82

p.38 'relatively poor' Hoyle, *Pilgrimage*, p.427
'the last place' quoted Dodds, Vol.II, p.145

p.39 'was a certain barbarous' quoted MacCulloch, *Cranmer*,
p.178
'a formidable' Haigh, *Reformation and Resistance*, p.46
'They were taught' Thomas, p.10

p.40 'Much ill cometh' LP XII (1), 318

p.42 'one of the most brute' quoted James, P & P, Vol.48
(1970), p.4

CHAPTER IV **The Lincolnshire Rising**

p.45 'one of the most majestic' Pevsner, *Lincolnshire*, p.300

p.46 'thousands of ounces' Dudding, p.xviii
'next day they should have' LP XII (1), 481
'Masters, step forth' ibid.
'a silver dish' LP XI, 828

p.48 'Let your frugal' quoted Bowker, *Henrician Reformation*,
p.17

p.49 'and in doing this' quoted Davies, P & P, Vol.41 (1968),
p.68
'Ye shall swear' quoted Dodds, Vol.I, p.109

p.53 'the common voice' LP XI, 534

p.60 'Masters, there is' quoted Dodds, Vol.I, pp.102–3

p.67 'on my troth' LP XI, 589

p.69 'the Traitors and Rebels' LP XI, 780

CHAPTER V **The Man with One Eye**

p.72   'we two have but' LP XI, 1103
        'Foorth shall come' quoted Dickens, *Lollards*, p.128

p.75   'dancing and other Noblemen's' quoted Holdsworth,
        Vol.II, p.484

p.78   'as an ornament' quoted Horrox, p.53
        'so cruel and fierce' LP XII (1), 201

p.79   'it was wont' quoted Duffy, *Altars*, p.395

p.81   'and lame both' LP XII (1), 392
        'God's blessing' ibid.
        'Master William' quoted Cox, p.86

p.82   'moved them to proceed' LP XII (1), 392
        'to God and our' quoted Bush, p.32
        'which was like to come' LP XII (1), 392

p.84   'make your proclamation' LP XI, 622

p.85   'He must be brought' LP XII (1), 919
        'the Earl of Cumberland' LP VIII, 991

p.86   'as an incompetent' Bush, p.304

p.87   'afore any either' LP XI, 841
        'to certain unlawful' ibid., 564
        'Thy master is' ibid., 841

p.89   'Down with the' LP XII (1), 1035
        'there was an abbot' ibid., 369

p.91   'say they have licence' quoted Duffy, *Altars*, p.388
        'wise men that know' quoted Dodds, Vol.I, p.193

p.92   'the pretended King's' LP XI, 841

CHAPTER VI **The Rebel Armies**

p.94   'O Pomfret, Pomfret!' Earl Rivers in *King Richard III*,
        Act III Scene III

p.97   'oaths to suffer' LP XI, 563
        'not one gun' ibid., 692

p.99   'bade God be with' ibid., 828

p.103   'enemies to' quoted Bush, p.297

p.105   'the breaking of all these' ibid., p.333

p.107   'strongly built' Chandler, p.267

p.108   'by the good and loving' LP XI, 872

p.110   'Archers horsed and harnessed' ibid., 652
        'These were all' LP XIV (1), 940

p.115 'put religious persons' LP XII (1), 29
'the alteration' ibid., 786
'One summer season' Langland, p.25
p.117 'to be true' LP XII (1), 687
p.118 'spread abroad' ibid., 1019
'the cruel Haman' ibid., 1021
'Christ crucified' Bateson, EHR, Vol.5 (1890) pp.344–5

CHAPTER VII **Victories and Surrenders**

p.121 'attended to the church' quoted Palliser, *Reformation*, p.2
p.122 'coverings of beds' quoted Duffy, *Altars*, p.44
p.123 'at the acting of' quoted Palliser, *Reformation*, p.7
'false both to' ibid.
'they would keep' LP XII (1), 392
p.124 'vital gun powder' LP XI, 789
p.128 'Ye shall not' LP XI, 705
'Lords, knights, masters' ibid.
p.129 'disdaining that' LP XII (1), 392
p.131 'Never sheep ran' LP XI, 774
'if the articles' LP XII (1), 852
'By the suppression' LP XI, 705
p.132 'to overawe their' ibid., 646
'Go bid your father' LP XII (1), 783
p.133 'we in the castle' LP XI, 60
p.134 'that if we refused' LP XII (1), 1022
p.135 'considering the danger' ibid.
p.136 'The Five Wounds' Dodds, Vol.I, p.129
p.137 'a man of parts' ibid., p.228
'Aske, the captain' quoted Hoyle, NH, Vol.11 (1985),
p.70
p.138 'keeping his port' LP XI, 826
'The poor man' quoted Dodds, Vol.I, p.240

CHAPTER VIII **To March on London**

p.141 'In one sense' Bush, p.153
p.143 'I defy you' quoted Dodds, Vol.I, p.210
p.145 'which were so strong' LP XI, 927
p.147 'they might lay' LP XII (1), 369
p.149 'false flattering boy' ibid., 578

'Having since heard' ibid., 1034
'the ways and passages' quoted Toller, p.42

p.150 'If on your coming' LP XI, 894
'stick together' LP XII (1),849

p.151 'to be of good cheer' ibid., 652
'would be a means' quoted Toller, p.44

p.154 'Son Thomas' LP XII (1), 852

CHAPTER IX **A Battle Waiting to be Won**

p.158 'of persons who are to supply' LP XI, 580

p.159 'two or three carts' ibid., 625
'at least 400 bows' ibid., 726

p.161 'the chief and best captain' LP XIII (2), 732

p.162 'neither I nor' LP XI, 800
'Great murmur' ibid., 831

p.163 'to give them' ibid., 716
'politic device' ibid., 816

p.164 'I think it unwise' ibid., 625
'effusion of blood' Bateson, EHR, Vol.5 (1890), p.337

p.165 'betwixt the hosts' ibid.

p.167 'then do your worst' LP XI, 625
'Sir, most humbly' ibid., 864

p.168 'all other their demands' quoted Bush, p.389
'garrison war' LP XII (1), 900

p.169 'villein blood' ibid., 1022

p.170 'what to do with Aske' Hoyle, *Pilgrimage*, p.299

p.172 'God of his infinite' Hoyle, Master, NH 21 (1985), p.71
'Hold up thy long claw' LP XI, 1086

p.173 'The pestilence' Hoyle, Master, NH 21 (1985), p.71.

p.174 'They wished the King' LP XI, 1319
'the fury of the commons' ibid., 1225
'wild people' ibid., 1045

p.175 'as weary a man' ibid., 909

CHAPTER X **Back from the Brink**

p.177 'kept every man' quoted Tempest, p.260
'in divers places' Hoyle, Master, p.72

p.179 'when the thieves' quoted Bush, p.335

p.180 'dragons and mermaids' Pevsner, *Cumberland*, p.99

p.182 'but craft and falsehood' quoted Bush, p.352
p.183 'most of the tenants' quoted Harrison, p.111
p.185 'weeping, ever wishing' LP XII (1), 698
'three or four' quoted Dodds, Vol.I, p.285
p.186 'the Cross and Wounds' ibid., p.274
p.187 'your shameful insurrection' LP XI, 957
p.193 'have most credit' ibid., 1120
'principal beginners' ibid.
p.194 'God save the King' LP XII (1), 1013
'dead or alive' LP I, 995
'quick or dead' ibid., 1007
p.195 'I cannot do it in no wise' quoted Dodds, Vol.I, p.291
'alas my good lord' LP I, 1045

CHAPTER XI **The King's Great Bluff**

p.198 'after three long' LP XII (1), 1186
p.200 'been accustomed' LP I, 1067
p.201 'light him with a candle' ibid., 1059
p.202 'a fell cruel man' quoted Dodds, Vol.I, p.211
p.204 'the goodness of' ibid., p.313
'their example shall' LP XI, 1032
'as he had broken' LP XII (1), 466
p.206 'Look you well' LP XI, 1170
'or else we are fully' Hoyle, Master, p.73
p.209 'trussed up and' LP XII (1), 865
p.213 'the great slackness' LP XI, 1175

CHAPTER XII **To Doncaster Bridge...**

p.215 'one Diamond' LP XII (1), 946
'using himself tenderly' LP XI, 1128
p.217 'so that the said' LP XII (1), 901
p.219 'to have the heretics' ibid.
p.221 'the common laws' LP XI, 1182
p.223 'a remedy against' LP XII (1), 901
'to have the law' LP XI, 1244
'the lands in' LP XII (1), 901
p.224 'Richard Cromwell' ibid., 1175
'Pardon by Act' LP XI, 1246
p.226 'up a height' LP XII (1), 1021

p.229 'we be not' quoted Dodds, Vol.I, p.383
p.230 'as though you should send' LP XI, 1227
p.231 'There remains' ibid., 1237
p.232 'but you must do so' ibid., 1225
'You said you would' LP XII (1), 901
p.233 'we thought the' LP I, 1236
p.235 'three low obeisances' Bateson, EHR, Vol.5 (1890), p.341
'all true Catholics' LP XI, 1336
p.236 'the said commons' Bateson, p.341
p.237 'so persuaded' ibid.
p.239 'saying all these words' ibid., p.342

CHAPTER XIII A Smouldering Fire

p.240 'In that point' LP XI, 1271
p.241 'his grace shall' ibid., 1410
p.242 'whereby was like' ibid., 1276
p.245 'There is now some hope' Hoyle, Master, p.75
'I trust you have' LP XI, 1410
p.246 'conceived a great' ibid., 1306
p.247 'Such a sight' ibid., 1369
p.248 'Be ye welcome' Hume, p.264
p.249 'a jacket of crimson' LP XII (1), 1224
'the first and best' Dodds, Vol.II, p.37
'First, the same' Bateson, EHR, Vol.5 (1890), pp.331 *et seq*
p.252 'to get the favour' LP XI, 1284
p.253 'right joyous' LP XI, 1371
p.254 'ungodly handled' LP XII (1), 50
p.255 'to take all malefactors' quoted Bush/Bownes, p.171
'certain gentlemen' LP XI, 1299
'the special brethren' ibid., 1218
p.256 'to consider their present' ibid., 785
'ye may do' LP XII (1), 1034
p.257 'like to have been' ibid., 914
p.259 'he came along' LP XII (1), 201
p.260 'Because ye are' ibid., 298
'if the northern men' ibid.
'they would have first' ibid., 1001
p.262 'Hull was false' ibid., 201

CHAPTER XIV **The Fatal Division**

p.266 'the gentlemen will' LP XII (1), 201
'the King's Highness' ibid.
'Mr Hallam. I pray you' ibid.

p.268 'utterly bent' ibid., 1012

p.270 'had it not been bruited' ibid., 70
'to destroy the Duke' ibid., 1012

p.271 'was at London' ibid., 81

p.272 'Master Dean' LP XI, 655
'throughout all these' LP XII (1), 71

p.273 'Commons keep well' ibid., 201
'reckoning them' ibid., 1175

p.276 'my heart doth even' quoted Dickens, *Lollards*, p.65

p.278 'because of my learning' LP XII (1), 145

p.280 'For my own part' ibid., 143

p.281 'he thought' ibid., 201

p.283 'Francis Bigod, Knight' ibid., 369

p.284 'there was no talk' ibid., 578
'which shall be' ibid., 369

p.286 'Come hither' quoted Dodds, Vol.II, p.63

p.287 'exhorted Hallam' LP XII (1), 202
'torn with wild' ibid., 141

p.288 'Many men and children' ibid., 338
'Fie!... will ye' ibid., 202

CHAPTER XV **The Return of the Duke**

p.291 'He will not rise' LP XII (1), 393

p.292 'none of the prisoners' ibid., 174

p.293 'a very fair creature' Wriothesley, Vol.I, p.64

p.294 'laid wait for him' LP XII (1), 1083
'Marry, very well' ibid.

p.295 'I fear it is high' LP I, 1408

p.296 'diligent service' LP XII (1), 66
'And if so' ibid., 1130

p.297 'heard no more' ibid., 259

p.300 'captains of Westmorland' ibid., 914

p.301 'Is your hearts' quoted Dodds, Vol.II, p.111
'he shall assemble' LP XII (1), 98

p.304 'six stall-fed' ibid., 350

'Force ... must be' ibid., 362
p.305 'our subjects there' ibid., 209
p.308 'our enemies' ibid., 411
p.310 'Finally now, Sir' ibid., 439
'well-willing nobles' ibid., 448
'before you close it' ibid., 479
p.311 'You will hardly believe' ibid., 468
'and a small excuse' ibid., 498
'The poor caitiffs' ibid., 478
p.312 'Iron is marvellous' ibid., 498
p.313 'three days after' ibid., 1214
'If those depositions' ibid., 1257

CHAPTER XVI **The Reckoning**

p.315 'Finally, as these troubles' LP XII (1), 479
p.316 'No man knew' ibid., 506
p.317 'about 165 lbs' ibid., 621
p.318 'every buttress' quoted Haigh, *Last Days*, p.56
p.319 'the prince must expend' LP XII (1), 302
p.320 'it would be charitable' ibid., 840
p.321 'Agree with them' ibid., 841
p.322 'such of his monks' ibid., 706
p.324 'I think I should be' ibid., 1172
'one of the fairest' ibid., 59
p.326 'all the means you can' quoted Dickens, YAJ, Vol.33
(1936–7), p.302
p.327 'the Priest raised' quoted Bellamy, p.204
p.328 'And we require you' LP XII (1), 228
p.329 'who took away' ibid., 731
p.330 'as the clerks' ibid., 777
'the matter must be bolted' ibid., 864
'should look well' ibid., 1087
'she is feared' ibid., 1084
p.331 'she enticed' ibid., 1087
'could live strongly' ibid.
p.332 'If thy master' LP XII (2), 12
p.333 'as false and traitorous' quoted Bush/Bownes, p.138
p.334 'great provisions' LP XII (1), 532
p.337 'Wall died' ibid., 1082

p.338 'to entreat my lord' ibid., 1225
p.339 'Cromwell ... it is thou' ibid., 976
       'he trusted to hear' ibid., 848
p.340 'If they were new' ibid., 900
       'How long after' ibid., 900
p.341 'because they spake' ibid.
       'Amongst other things' ibid., 901
       'They were all together' ibid.
       'ungracious brother' ibid., 1186
p.342 'I am not able' ibid., 946
       'Good Mr Doctor' ibid., 1175
       'to knit up this' LP XII (2), 77
p.344 'doth hang above' ibid., 229
       'where he was in his greatest' ibid., 133
       'the King will be' LP XII (1), 1223
p.345 'for aid and ordnance' LP XII (2), 205

CHAPTER XVII **The Aftermath**

p.347 'rise again and come' LP XII (2), 205
       'this false Duke' LP XIII (1), 487
p.348 'who denied it' LP XII (2), 1231
       'with dexterity' ibid.
p.349 'he encouraged the rebels' LP XIII (1), 1311
       'used himself like' LP XIII (2), 20
p.350 'being a sore blemish' LP XII (1), 53
       'imploring him to come in' ibid., 1286
p.351 'Lo ... here is as good' LP XII (2), 422
p.352 'shall provide' quoted Bray, p.179
p.354 'was such a servant' quoted MacCulloch, *Cranmer*, p.270
       'I intend this day' quoted Brigden, p.48
p.359 'in the King's most benign' LP XIII (1), 1
       'all his body the colour' quoted Broce/Wunderli, p.202
p.360 'not Henry was the true' Knowles, *Religious Orders*,
       Vol.III, p.335
p.362 'by his own sister's' LP XII (1), 825

CHAPTER XVIII **Postscript**

p.373 'removed and cut up ...' Browne, p.128
p.374 'I (the tower)' Dodds, Vol.I, p.61

INDEX

THE PILGRIMAGE OF GRACE

Ellerker, Sir Ralph (young Sir Ralph)
  (cont.)
  at court, 186, 187
  departure delayed, 190
  Henry's letter handed to, 190
  Darcy writes to, 195
  Darcy's letter to Talbot about
    detention of, 199
  returns to rebel leaders with message
    from Henry, 200–201
  at York conference, 204
  Henry writes to, 213–14
  and meeting with Howard at
    Doncaster, 234
  and garrison at Hull, 241
  makes peace with Henry, 244
  mentioned in Aske's account of
    Pilgrimage, 249
  and Bigod, 290
  arrives in Beverley, 292
  Rudston passes letter to, 296
  as mayor of Hull, 306
  as marshal at court in Carlisle, 311
  instructed to use torture, 326
  Henry angry with, 328
  and Levening's trial, 329
  as prosecution witness at Constable's
    trial, 338
  on King's Council in the north, 357
  subsequent career, 358
  brief mentions, 193, 198, 296, 360
Ellerker, Thomas, 75, 124
Ellerker, William, 249
Ellerker family, 80–1, 139; *see also*
  individual family members
Ellerton, Prior of (James Lawrence),
  192
Ely, 45
  Bishop of (Thomas Goodrich), 53
Elyson, Christopher, Vicar of
  Arncliffe, 272
Endmoor, 106
Erasmus, Desiderius, 4, 10, 23, 90
  *Enchiridion Militis Christiani
  (Handbook of the Christian Soldier),*
  10
Esch, Robert, The Friar of
  Knaresborough xxii, 80, 82, 267,
  282, 283, 284, 291, 335

Esk, 307
Essex, Sir William, 212
Estgate, John, 318, 320, 322
Estgate, Richard, 203, 256–7, 316,
  317, 318, 319
Everingham, 191, 264
Evers, Sir Ralph (elder), 285
Evers, Sir Ralph, 202, 204, 213, 241,
  274, 279, 280, 285, 296
Ewcross, 106
Exeter, 39, 123, 366
Exeter, Henry Courtenay, Marquis of
  see Courtenay, Henry, Marquis of
  Exeter

Faith, Captain (John Beck), 104
Fawcett, Richard, 108, 143, 271–2
Faxfleet Ness, 75
Fayrfax, Thomas, 8
Fenton, Ralph, 282, 285–6, 306
Ferdinand of Aragon, 12, 95
Ferrybridge, 130
Field of the Cloth of Gold, 21, 36, 48,
  65
Fisher, John, Bishop of Rochester, 34
Fitzwilliam, Sir William, 201, 240,
  241, 245
Five Wounds of Christ
  badge, 136, 171, 239, 340, 341
  banner, 2, 136, 155, 171
Flamborough, 123
Flanders, 211, 345
Flodden Field, 62, 84, 139, 158, 271,
  281
Florens, William, 182
Folbery, John, 287, 288, 338
Foster, Thomas, 46
Fountains Abbey, 29, 270, 271, 309,
  320, 365, 788
Fountains Fell, 372
France, 15, 355
Francis I, King of France, 13, 21, 210,
  211, 350, 353
Francis of Assisi, 10
Franciscans, 28, 81, 234, 236
Francke, Thomas, 332
Frankishe, John, 50, 55
Frederick, Elector of Saxony, 14